SOLARO
STUDY GUIDE

English Language Arts 4

SOLARO Study Guide is designed to help students achieve success in school. The content in each study guide is 100% curriculum aligned and serves as an excellent source of material for review and practice. To create this book, teachers, curriculum specialists, and assessment experts have worked closely to develop the instructional pieces that explain each of the key concepts for the course. The practice questions and sample tests have detailed solutions that show problem-solving methods, highlight concepts that are likely to be tested, and point out potential sources of errors. **SOLARO Study Guide** is a complete guide to be used by students throughout the school year for reviewing and understanding course content, and to prepare for assessments.

Rao,Gautam,1961 –
SOLARO STUDY GUIDE – English Language Arts 4 (2013 Edition) Common Core State Standards

1. Mathematics – Juvenile Literature. I. Title

Publisher
Gautam Rao

Castle Rock Research Corporation
2410 Manulife Place
10180 – 101 Street
Edmonton, AB T5J 3S4

1 2 3 MP 15 14 13

Printed in the United States of America

CASTLE ROCK
RESEARCH CORP

Dedicated to the memory of Dr. V. S. Rao

THE *SOLARO STUDY GUIDE*

The *SOLARO Study Guide* is designed to help students achieve success in school and to provide teachers with a road map to understanding the concepts of the Common Core State Standards. The content in each study guide is 100% curriculum aligned and serves as an excellent source of material for review and practice. The *SOLARO Study Guide* introduces students to a process that incorporates the building blocks upon which strong academic performance is based. To create this resource, teachers, curriculum specialists, and assessment experts have worked closely to develop instructional pieces that explain key concepts. Every exercise question comes with a detailed solution that offers problem-solving methods, highlights concepts that are likely to be tested, and points out potential sources of errors.

The *SOLARO Study Guide* is intended to be used for reviewing and understanding course content, to prepare for assessments, and to assist each student in achieving their best performance in school.

The *SOLARO Study Guide* consists of the following sections:

TABLE OF CORRELATIONS

The Table of Correlations is a critical component of the *SOLARO Study Guide*.

Castle Rock Research has designed the *SOLARO Study Guide* by correlating each question and its solution to Common Core State Standards. Each unit begins with a Table of Correlations, which lists the standards and questions that correspond to those standards.

For students, the Table of Correlations provides information about how each question fits into a particular course and the standards to which each question is tied. Students can quickly access all relevant content associated with a particular standard.

For teachers, the Table of Correlations provides a road map for each standard, outlining the most granular and measurable concepts that are included in each standard. It assists teachers in understanding all the components involved in each standard and where students are excelling or require improvement. The Table of Correlations indicates the instructional focus for each content strand, serves as a standards checklist, and focuses on the standards and concepts that are most important in the unit and the particular course of study.

Some concepts may have a complete lesson aligned to them but cannot be assessed using a paper-and-pencil format. These concepts typically require ongoing classroom assessment through various other methods.

LESSONS

Following the Table of Correlations for each unit are lessons aligned to each concept within a standard. The lessons explain key concepts that students are expected to learn according to Common Core State Standards. As each lesson is tied to state standards, students and teachers are assured that the information will be relevant to what is being covered in class.

EXERCISE QUESTIONS

Each set of lessons is followed by two sets of exercise questions that assess students on their understanding of the content. These exercise questions can be used by students to give them an idea of the type of questions they are likely to face in the future in terms of format, difficulty, and content coverage.

DETAILED SOLUTIONS

Some study guides only provide an answer key, which will identify the correct response but may not be helpful in determining what led to the incorrect answer. Every exercise question in the *SOLARO Study Guide* is accompanied by a detailed solution. Access to complete solutions greatly enhances a student's ability to work independently, and these solutions also serve as useful instructional tools for teachers. The level of information in each detailed solution is intended to help students better prepare for the future by learning from their mistakes and to help teachers discern individual areas of strengths and weaknesses.

For the complete curriculum document, visit www.corestandards.org/the-standards.

*SOLARO Study Guide*s are available for many courses. Check www.solaro.com/orders for a complete listing of books available for your area.

For more enhanced online resources, please visit www.SOLARO.com.

Student-Oriented Learning, Assessment, and Reporting Online

solaro

SOLARO is an online resource that provides students with regionally and age-appropriate lessons and practice questions. Students can be confident that SOLARO has the right materials to help them when they are having difficulties in class. SOLARO is 100% compliant with each region's core standards. Teachers can use SOLARO in the classroom as a supplemental resource to provide remediation and enrichment. Student performance is reported to the teacher through various reports, which provide insight into strengths and weaknesses.

TABLE OF CONTENTS

Key Tips for Being Successful at School

KEY TIPS FOR BEING SUCCESSFUL AT SCHOOL

KEY FACTORS CONTRIBUTING TO SCHOOL SUCCESS

In addition to learning the content of your courses, there are some other things that you can do to help you do your best at school. You can try some of the following strategies:

- **Keep a positive attitude:** Always reflect on what you can already do and what you already know.

- **Be prepared to learn:** Have the necessary pencils, pens, notebooks, and other required materials for participating in class ready.

- **Complete all of your assignments:** Do your best to finish all of your assignments. Even if you know the material well, practice will reinforce your knowledge. If an assignment or question is difficult for you, work through it as far as you can so that your teacher can see exactly where you are having difficulty.

- **Set small goals for yourself when you are learning new material:** For example, when learning the parts of speech, do not try to learn everything in one night. Work on only one part or section each study session. When you have memorized one particular part of speech and understand it, move on to another one. Continue this process until you have memorized and learned all the parts of speech.

- **Review your classroom work regularly at home:** Review to make sure you understand the material you learned in class.

- **Ask your teacher for help:** Your teacher will help you if you do not understand something or if you are having a difficult time completing your assignments.

- **Get plenty of rest and exercise:** Concentrating in class is hard work. It is important to be well-rested and have time to relax and socialize with your friends. This helps you keep a positive attitude about your schoolwork.

- **Eat healthy meals:** A balanced diet keeps you healthy and gives you the energy you need for studying at school and at home.

HOW TO FIND YOUR LEARNING STYLE

Every student learns differently. The manner in which you learn best is called your learning style. By knowing your learning style, you can increase your success at school. Most students use a combination of learning styles. Do you know what type of learner you are? Read the following descriptions. Which of these common learning styles do you use most often?

- **Linguistic Learner:** You may learn best by saying, hearing, and seeing words. You are probably really good at memorizing things such as dates, places, names, and facts. You may need to write down the steps in a process, a formula, or the actions that lead up to a significant event, and then say them out loud.

- **Spatial Learner:** You may learn best by looking at and working with pictures. You are probably really good at puzzles, imagining things, and reading maps and charts. You may need to use strategies like mind mapping and webbing to organize your information and study notes.

- **Kinesthetic Learner:** You may learn best by touching, moving, and figuring things out using manipulatives. You are probably really good at physical activities and learning through movement. You may need to draw your finger over a diagram to remember it, tap out the steps needed to solve a problem, or feel yourself writing or typing a formula.

SCHEDULING STUDY TIME

You should review your class notes regularly to ensure that you have a clear understanding of all the new material you learned. Reviewing your lessons on a regular basis helps you to learn and remember ideas and concepts. It also reduces the quantity of material that you need to study prior to a test. Establishing a study schedule will help you to make the best use of your time.

Regardless of the type of study schedule you use, you may want to consider the following suggestions to maximize your study time and effort:

• Organize your work so that you begin with the most challenging material first.

• Divide the subject's content into small, manageable chunks.

• Alternate regularly between your different subjects and types of study activities in order to maintain your interest and motivation.

• Make a daily list with headings like "Must Do," "Should Do," and "Could Do."

• Begin each study session by quickly reviewing what you studied the day before.

• Maintain your usual routine of eating, sleeping, and exercising to help you concentrate better for extended periods of time.

CREATING STUDY NOTES

MIND-MAPPING OR WEBBING

Use the key words, ideas, or concepts from your class notes to create a mind map or web, which is a diagram or visual representation of the given information. A mind map or web is sometimes referred to as a knowledge map. Use the following steps to create a mind map or web:

1. Write the key word, concept, theory, or formula in the centre of your page.

2. Write down related facts, ideas, events, and information, and link them to the central concept with lines.

3. Use coloured markers, underlining, or symbols to emphasize things such as relationships, timelines, and important information.

The following mind map is an example of one that could help you develop an essay:

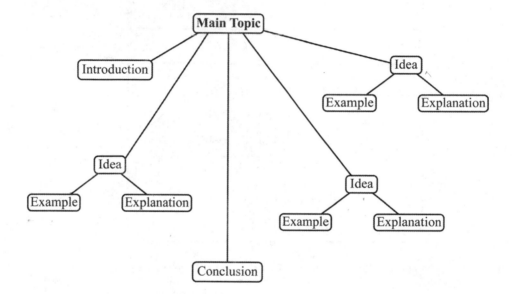

INDEX CARDS

To use index cards while studying, follow these steps:

1. Write a key word or question on one side of an index card.

2. On the reverse side, write the definition of the word, answer to the question, or any other important information that you want to remember.

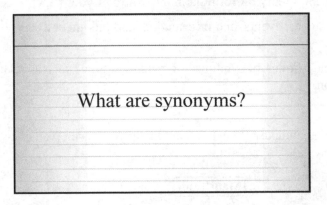

SYMBOLS AND STICKY NOTES—IDENTIFYING IMPORTANT INFORMATION

Use symbols to mark your class notes. The following are some examples:

*   An exclamation mark (!) might be used to point out something that must be learned well because it is a very important idea.

*   A question mark (?) may highlight something you are not certain about

*   A diamond (◊) or asterisk (*) could highlight interesting information that you want to remember.

Sticky notes are useful in the following situations:

*   Use sticky notes when you are not allowed to put marks in books.

*   Use sticky notes to mark a page in a book that contains an important diagram, formula, explanation, or other information.

*   Use sticky notes to mark important facts in research books.

Castle Rock Research

MEMORIZATION TECHNIQUES

- **Association** relates new learning to something you already know. For example, to remember the spelling difference between dessert and desert, recall that the word *sand* has only one *s*. So, because there is sand in a desert, the word *desert* has only one *s*.

- **Mnemonic** devices are sentences that you create to remember a list or group of items. For example, the first letter of each word in the phrase "Every Good Boy Deserves Fudge" helps you to remember the names of the lines on the treble-clef staff (E, G, B, D, and F) in music.

- **Acronyms** are words that are formed from the first letters or parts of the words in a group. For example, RADAR is actually an acronym for Radio Detecting and Ranging, and MASH is an acronym for Mobile Army Surgical Hospital. HOMES helps you to remember the names of the five Great Lakes (Huron, Ontario, Michigan, Erie, and Superior).

- **Visualizing** requires you to use your mind's eye to "see" a chart, list, map, diagram, or sentence as it is in your textbook or notes, on the chalkboard or computer screen, or in a display.

- **Initialisms** are abbreviations that are formed from the first letters or parts of the words in a group. Unlike acronyms, an initialism cannot be pronounced as a word itself. For example, GCF is an initialism for **G**reatest **C**ommon **F**actor.

KEY STRATEGIES FOR REVIEWING

Reviewing textbook material, class notes, and handouts should be an ongoing activity. Spending time reviewing becomes more critical when you are preparing for a test. You may find some of the following review strategies useful when studying during your scheduled study time:

- Before reading a selection, preview it by noting the headings, charts, graphs, and chapter questions.

- Before reviewing a unit, note the headings, charts, graphs, and chapter questions.

- Highlight key concepts, vocabulary, definitions, and formulas.

- Skim the paragraph, and note the key words, phrases, and information.

- Carefully read over each step in a procedure.

- Draw a picture or diagram to help make the concept clearer.

KEY STRATEGIES FOR SUCCESS: A CHECKLIST

Reviewing is a huge part of doing well at school and preparing for tests. Here is a checklist for you to keep track of how many suggested strategies for success you are using. Read each question, and put a check mark (✓) in the correct column. Look at the questions where you have checked the "No" column. Think about how you might try using some of these strategies to help you do your best at school.

Key Strategies for Success	Yes	No
Do you attend school regularly?	✓	
Do you know your personal learning style—how you learn best?	✓	
Do you spend 15 to 30 minutes a day reviewing your notes?	✓	
Do you study in a quiet place at home?	✓	
Do you clearly mark the most important ideas in your study notes?		✗
Do you use sticky notes to mark texts and research books?		✗
Do you practise answering multiple-choice and written-response questions?	✓	
Do you ask your teacher for help when you need it?	✓	
Are you maintaining a healthy diet and sleep routine?	✓	
Are you participating in regular physical activity?	✓	

Castle Rock Research

Class Focus

CLASS FOCUS

Table of Correlations

Standard		Concepts	Page
4RL	Reading Standards for Literature		
4RL.1	*Refer to details and examples in a text when explaining what the text says explicitly and when drawing inferences from the text.*	Supporting Generalizations about Text with Textual Evidence	22
		Supporting Conclusions about Text with Textual Evidence	23
4RL.2	*Determine a theme of a story, drama, or poem from details in the text; summarize the text.*	Summarizing Text after Reading	25
		Recognize a Theme within a Text	27
		Demonstrate an Understanding of the Main Idea within a Text	86
		Identifying the Main Idea and Supporting Details	87
4RL.3	*Describe in depth a character, setting, or event in a story or drama, drawing on specific details in the text.*	Determining What Characters are Like by Looking at What They Say	31
		Determining What Characters Are Like by Looking at What They Do	32
		Identify the Main Events of the Plot	35
		Understand How A Situation Causes Character's Actions	41
		How Setting Causes a Character's Actions	42
		Understand How Traits Cause Character's Actions	42
		How Motivations Cause a Character's Actions	43
		Identify the Setting Within a Text	44
		Distinguishing Supported Inferences in Text	90
4RL.4	*Determine the meaning of words and phrases as they are used in a text, including those that allude to significant characters found in mythology.*	Using Context to Understand Unfamiliar Words	45
		Understand Content-Specific Vocabulary	91
4RL.5	*Explain major differences between poems, drama, and prose, and refer to the structural elements of poems and drama when writing or speaking about a text.*	What Is A Play?	48
		What Is Non-Fiction?	50
		What Is Poetry?	52
		What Is Fiction?	54

		What Is a Concrete Poem?	55
		What Is a Rhyming Pattern?	55
		Proposition and Support	93
4RL.6	*Compare and contrast the point of view from which different stories are narrated, including the difference between first- and third-person narrations.*	Identify a First Person Point of View	57
		Identify a Second Person Point of View	59
		Identify a Third Person Point of View	61
		Compare and Contrast Information	62
4RL.7	*Make connections between the text of a story or drama and a visual or oral presentation of the text, identifying where each version reflects specific descriptions and directions in the text.*	The Function and Effect of Imagery	64
		Metaphors—Their Functions and Their Effect	65
		Symbolism - Its Functions and Its Effects	66
		The Purpose of Visual and Graphic Materials	67
		Use Retelling as a Reading Strategy	68
		How Point of View Affects Format and Presentation	70
		How Format Makes Information Accessible	96
		How Graphics Make Information Accessible	99
		How Diagrams Make Information Accessible	100
		How Illustrations Make Information Accessible	101
		Charts Make Information Accessible	103
		Understand How Maps Make Information Accessible	104
4RL.9	*Compare and contrast the treatment of similar themes and topics and patterns of events in stories, myths, and traditional literature from different cultures.*	Recognize a Theme within a Text	27
		Compare and Contrast Information	62
		Evaluate Archetypal Patterns in Myths	71
		Evaluate Archetypal Patterns through History	72

		Evaluating Archetype Patterns across Cultures	73
4RL.10	By the end of the year, read and comprehend literature, including stories, dramas, and poetry, in the grades 4–5 text complexity band proficiently, with scaffolding as needed at the high end of the range.	What Is A Play?	48
		What Is Fiction?	54
		What Is A Short Story?	75
		What Is a Fable?	76
		What Is a Novel?	76
		What Is a Folktale?	77
		What Is an Adventure Story?	81
		What Is A Mystery Story?	84
		What is a Fantasy?	85
4RI	**Reading Standards for Informational Text**		
4RI.1	Refer to details and examples in a text when explaining what the text says explicitly and when drawing inferences from the text.	Supporting Generalizations about Text with Textual Evidence	22
		Supporting Conclusions about Text with Textual Evidence	23
4RI.2	Determine the main idea of a text and explain how it is supported by key details; summarize the text.	Summarizing Text after Reading	25
		Recognize a Theme within a Text	27
		Demonstrate an Understanding of the Main Idea within a Text	86
		Identifying the Main Idea and Supporting Details	87
4RI.3	Explain events, procedures, ideas, or concepts in a historical, scientific, or technical text, including what happened and why, based on specific information in the text.	Determining What Characters are Like by Looking at What They Say	31
		Determining What Characters Are Like by Looking at What They Do	32
		Identify the Main Events of the Plot	35
		Understand How A Situation Causes Character's Actions	41
		How Setting Causes a Character's Actions	42
		Understand How Traits Cause Character's Actions	42
		How Motivations Cause a Character's Actions	43
		Identify the Setting Within a Text	44
		Distinguishing Supported Inferences in Text	90

4RI.4	Determine the meaning of general academic and domain-specific words or phrases in a text relevant to a grade 4 topic or subject area.	Using Context to Understand Unfamiliar Words	45
		Understand Content-Specific Vocabulary	91
4RI.5	Describe the overall structure of events, ideas, concepts, or information in a text or part of a text.	What Is Non-Fiction?	50
		Identify a Compare/Contrast Pattern in Informational Text	92
		Identify Sequential/Chronological Pattern in Text	92
		Proposition and Support	93
		Identifying Cause-and-Effect Patterns in Informational Text	96
4RI.6	Compare and contrast a firsthand and secondhand account of the same event or topic; describe the differences in focus and the information provided.	Identify a First Person Point of View	57
		Identify a Second Person Point of View	59
		Identify a Third Person Point of View	61
		Compare and Contrast Information	62
		Compare Information on One Topic from Many Sources	94
		Contrast Information on One Topic From Many Sources	95
4RI.7	Interpret information presented visually, orally, or quantitatively and explain how the information contributes to an understanding of the text in which it appears.	The Function and Effect of Imagery	64
		Metaphors—Their Functions and Their Effect	65
		Symbolism - Its Functions and Its Effects	66
		The Purpose of Visual and Graphic Materials	67
		Use Retelling as a Reading Strategy	68
		How Point of View Affects Format and Presentation	70
		How Format Makes Information Accessible	96
		How Graphics Make Information Accessible	99
		How Diagrams Make Information Accessible	100

		How Illustrations Make Information Accessible	101
		Charts Make Information Accessible	103
		Understand How Maps Make Information Accessible	104
		Understanding How Graphic Organizers Make Information Accessible	104
4RI.8	*Explain how an author uses reasons and evidence to support particular points in a text.*	Identify Evidence that Supports the Main Ideas in a Text	105
4RI.9	*Integrate information from two texts on the same topic in order to write or speak about the subject knowledgeably.*	Recognize a Theme within a Text	27
		Compare and Contrast Information	62
		Evaluate Archetypal Patterns in Myths	71
		Evaluate Archetypal Patterns through History	72
		Evaluating Archetype Patterns across Cultures	73
		Combine Information from More than One Source	107
4RF	Reading Standards: Foundational Skills		
4.RF. 3a	*Know and apply grade-level phonics and word analysis skills in decoding words. Use combined knowledge of all letter-sound correspondences, syllabication patterns, and morphology to read accurately unfamiliar multi-syllabic words in context...*	Using Context to Understand Unfamiliar Words	45
		Using Inferencing to Understand Unfamiliar Words	109
		Understanding Words by Finding Familiar Words Within Unknown Words	111
		Using Prefixes and Suffixes to Understand New Words	113
		Using the "Does it Make Sense" Strategy to Understand Text	116
		Use Phonetic Knowledge to Figure Out Words	117
		Choose Precise Words for Writing Tasks	119
		Using the "Sound-Out" Strategy for Unfamiliar Words	120
4.RF. 4a	*Read with sufficient accuracy and fluency to support comprehension. Read on-level text with purpose and understanding.*	Using Appropriate Strategies for Full Comprehension	122
		Read Aloud Fluently	123

		Read Aloud Accurately	124
4.RF. 4b	*Read with sufficient accuracy and fluency to support comprehension. Read on-level prose and poetry orally with accuracy, appropriate rate, and expression on successive readings.*	Read Aloud Fluently	123
		Read Aloud Accurately	124
		Read Aloud with Appropriate Pacing	126
		Read Aloud with Appropriate Intonation	127
		Read Aloud With Appropriate Expression	129
4.RF. 4c	*Read with sufficient accuracy and fluency to support comprehension. Use context to confirm or self-correct word recognition and understanding, rereading as necessary.*	Using Context to Understand Unfamiliar Words	45
		Using the "Does it Make Sense" Strategy to Understand Text	116
		Using the Re-Read Strategy to Determine Unfamiliar Words	131
4.W	**Writing Standards**		
4W.1a	*Write opinion pieces on topics or texts, supporting a point of view with reasons and information. Introduce a topic or text clearly, state an opinion, and create an organizational structure in which related ideas are grouped to support the...*	Create a Written Piece to Convince	132
		Create an Introductory Paragraph	133
		Use Similarities and Differences to Convey Information	134
		Use Chronological Order for Conveying Information	156
		Use Cause and Effect for Conveying Information	158
4W.1b	*Write opinion pieces on topics or texts, supporting a point of view with reasons and information. Provide reasons that are supported by facts and details.*	Create a Written Piece to Convince	132
		Create Support Paragraphs with Facts, Details, and Explanations	135
4W.1c	*Write opinion pieces on topics or texts, supporting a point of view with reasons and information. Link opinion and reasons using words and phrases.*	Use Connecting Words to Link Ideas in Sentences	136
		Demonstrate Knowledge of Word Origins	137
4W.1d	*Write opinion pieces on topics or texts, supporting a point of view with reasons and information. Provide a concluding statement or section related to the opinion presented.*	Create a Written Piece to Convince	132
		Create a Concluding Paragraph That Summarizes Main Points	139
4W.2a	*Write informative/explanatory texts to examine a topic and convey ideas and information clearly. Introduce a topic clearly and group related information in paragraphs and sections; include formatting, illustrations, and multimedia when...*	How Illustrations Make Information Accessible	101
		Create a Written Piece to Inform	140
		Create a Written Piece to Explain	141

		Construct Meaning Using Headings	142
4W.2b	Write informative/explanatory texts to examine a topic and convey ideas and information clearly. Develop the topic with facts, definitions, concrete details, quotations, or other information and examples related to the topic.	Create Support Paragraphs with Facts, Details, and Explanations	135
		Create a Written Piece to Inform	140
		Create a Written Piece to Explain	141
		Create Narratives that Use Concrete Sensory Details	143
4W.2c	Write informative/explanatory texts to examine a topic and convey ideas and information clearly. Link ideas within categories of information using words and phrases.	Use Connecting Words to Link Ideas in Sentences	136
4W.2d	Write informative/explanatory texts to examine a topic and convey ideas and information clearly. Use precise language and domain-specific vocabulary to inform about or explain the topic.	Choose Precise Words for Writing Tasks	119
		Use Content-Specific Vocabulary in your Writing	144
4W.2e	Write informative/explanatory texts to examine a topic and convey ideas and information clearly. Provide a concluding statement or section related to the information or explanation presented.	Create a Concluding Paragraph That Summarizes Main Points	139
4W.3a	Write narratives to develop real or imagined experiences or events using effective technique, descriptive details, and clear event sequences. Orient the reader by establishing a situationand introducing a narrator and/or characters; organize...	Create a Story with a Logical Sequence	146
		Create a Story with Relationships between Characters and Plot	148
		Narrative-Descriptive Writing	151
		Identifying the Speaker or Narrator in a Text	151
4W.3b	Write narratives to develop real or imagined experiences or events using effective technique, descriptive details, and clear event sequences. Use dialogue and description to develop experiences and events or show the responses of characters...	Understand How A Situation Causes Character's Actions	41
		Narrative-Descriptive Writing	151
		Write a Story Beginning that has Action	153
		Create a Story Beginning Using Dialogue	154
4W.3d	Write narratives to develop real or imagined experiences or events using effective technique, descriptive details, and clear event sequences. Use concrete words and phrases and sensory details to convey experiences and events precisely.	Create Narratives that Use Concrete Sensory Details	143
		Narrative-Descriptive Writing	151
4W.3e	Write narratives to develop real or imagined experiences or events using effective technique, descriptive details, and clear event sequences. Provide a conclusion that follows from the narrated experiences or events.	Create a Concluding Paragraph That Summarizes Main Points	139

4W.4	Produce clear and coherent writing in which the development and organization are appropriate to task, purpose, and audience.	Set a Purpose for Writing	159
		Use Knowledge of a Rubric to Enhance Writing	160
4W.5	With guidance and support from peers and adults, develop and strengthen writing as needed by planning, revising, and editing.	Thinking of a Story Topic	162
		Using a Checklist to Edit your Story	164
		Revising Your Written Work To Provide Focus	166
		Revising Your Work to Expand Relevant Ideas	168
		Generating Ideas For A Non-Fiction Topic Using A Word Web	171
		Generating Ideas for a Non-Fiction Topic Using the KWL Chart	174
		Generating Ideas for a Non-Fiction Topic Using Mind Mapping	175
		Using A Checklist to Edit your Non-Fiction Writing	178
		Revising Your Non-Fiction Writing Piece to Provide Focus	181
		Revise Your Non-Fiction Writing to Expand on Relevant Ideas	182
		Use the Appropriate Graphic Organizer to Sort Information	184
4W.6	With some guidance and support from adults, use technology, including the Internet, to produce and publish writing as well as to interact and collaborate with others; demonstrate sufficient command of keyboarding skills to type a minimum of...	Use Electronic Dictionaries and Thesauruses	185
4W.7	Conduct short research projects that build knowledge through investigation of different aspects of a topic.	Use Criteria to Assess the Research Process	186
4W.8	Recall relevant information from experiences or ather relevant information from print and digital sources; take notes and categorize information, and provide a list of sources.	Use the Appropriate Graphic Organizer to Sort Information	184
		What is a Bibliography?	188
		Create a Bibliography	188
		Gather Facts using Primary Resources	189
		Gather Facts Using Secondary Resources	190

		Analyze Details and Information from Reference Material	190
4W.9a	*Draw evidence from literary or informational texts to support analysis, reflection, and research. Apply grade 4 Reading standards to literature.*	Supporting Generalizations about Text with Textual Evidence	22
		Supporting Conclusions about Text with Textual Evidence	23
		Making Inferences While Reading	192
		Making Inferences About Characters	193
4W.9b	*Draw evidence from literary or informational texts to support analysis, reflection, and research. Apply grade 4 Reading standards to informational texts.*	Supporting Generalizations about Text with Textual Evidence	22
		Supporting Conclusions about Text with Textual Evidence	23
		Identify Evidence that Supports the Main Ideas in a Text	105
4W.10	*Write routinely over extended time frames (time for research, reflection, and revision) and shorter time frames (a single sitting or a day or two) for a range of discipline-specific tasks, purposes, and audiences.*	Set a Purpose for Writing	159
		Select a Paragraph Focus Based on Purpose	194
		Select a Paragraph Focus Based on Audience	195
4SL	**Speaking and Listening Standards**		
4SL.1a	*Engage effectively in a range of collaborative discussions (one-on-one, in groups, and teacherled) with diverse partners on grade 4 topics and texts, building on others' ideas and expressing their own clearly. Come to discussions...*	Working in a Group: Adding Your Part to a Discussion	196
4SL.1b	*Engage effectively in a range of collaborative discussions (one-on-one, in groups, and teacherled) with diverse partners on grade 4 topics and texts, building on others' ideas and expressing their own clearly. Follow agreed-upon rules...*	Working in a Group: Adding Your Part to a Discussion	196
		Working in a Group: Being a Good Listener	197
		Working in a Group: The Presenter Role	197
4SL.1c	*Engage effectively in a range of collaborative discussions (one-on-one, in groups, and teacherled) with diverse partners on grade 4 topics and texts, building on others' ideas and expressing their own clearly. Pose and respond to...*	Working in a Group: Adding Your Part to a Discussion	196
		Use Questioning for Communicating	199
		Clarifying Meaning in a Group Discussion	200
		Make and Share Connections when Interacting with Others	202
		Asking and Answering Questions to Convey Information	202

4SL.1d	Engage effectively in a range of collaborative discussions (one-on-one, in groups, and teacherled) with diverse partners on grade 4 topics and texts, building on others' ideas and expressing their own clearly. Review the key ideas...	Working in a Group: Reflecting	204
4SL.2	Paraphrase portions of a text read aloud or information presented in diverse media and formats, including visually, quantitatively, and orally.	Paraphrase Information Sources	205
4SL.3	Identify the reasons and evidence a speaker provides to support particular points.	Identify Evidence that Supports the Main Ideas in a Text	105
4SL.4	Report on a topic or text, tell a story, or recount an experience in an organized manner, using appropriate facts and relevant, descriptive details to support main ideas or themes; speak clearly at an understandable pace.	Read Aloud with Appropriate Pacing	126
		Create Support Paragraphs with Facts, Details, and Explanations	135
		Determine Relevance and Adequacy of Information	206
		Set a Purpose for Presenting	208
4SL.5	Add audio recordings and visual displays to presentations when appropriate to enhance the development of main ideas or themes.	Use Visuals to Engage an Audience	209
		Use Visuals to Sustain an Audience Throughout a Presentation	210
		Use Visuals to Engage an Audience at the End of a Presentation	211
		Use Audio to Engage an Audience	211
4SL.6	Differentiate between contexts that call for formal English and situations where informal discourse is appropriate; use formal English when appropriate to task and situation.	Demonstrate Voice Through Word Choice	245
4L	Language Standards		
4L.1a	Demonstrate command of the conventions of standard English grammar and usage when writing or speaking. Use relative pronouns (who, whose, whom, which, that) and relative adverbs (where, when, why).	Using Adverbs in your Writing	213
		Using Pronouns Correctly in Writing and Speaking	214
4L.1b	Demonstrate command of the conventions of standard English grammar and usage when writing or speaking. Form and use the progressive verb tenses.	Using Appropriate Verb Tenses in your Writing	215
4L.1d	Demonstrate command of the conventions of standard English grammar and usage when writing or speaking. Order adjectives within sentences according to conventional patterns.	What is an Adjective?	217
		How to Use Adjectives in your Writing	218
4L.1e	Demonstrate command of the conventions of standard English grammar and usage when writing or speaking. Form and use prepositional phrases.	Combining Sentences with Prepositional Phrases	219

		Using Prepositions In Your Writing	221
4L.1f	Demonstrate command of the conventions of standard English grammar and usage when writing or speaking. Produce complete sentences, recognizing and correcting inappropriate fragments and run-ons.	What is a Complete Sentence?	223
		What Is a Sentence Fragment?	224
		Run-On Sentences	224
4L.1g	Demonstrate command of the conventions of standard English grammar and usage when writing or speaking. Correctly use frequently confused words.	Spell Correctly One-Syllable words that are Common Homophones	226
		Correctly Use Verbs (lie/lay;sit/set)	226
4L.2a	Demonstrate command of the conventions of standard English capitalization, punctuation, and spelling when writing. Use correct capitalization.	Capitalizing Proper Nouns	229
		Starting a Sentence with a Capital	230
		Using Capitals in Titles	230
		Apply Appropriate Capitalization with Holidays	231
		Apply Appropriate Capitalization with Special Events	232
		Capitalize the Names of Newspapers	233
		Capitalize the Names of Magazines Correctly	234
4L.2b	Demonstrate command of the conventions of standard English capitalization, punctuation, and spelling when writing. Use commas and quotation marks to mark direct speech and quotations from a text.	Use Quotation Marks for Spoken Words	235
		Using Commas in Direct Quotations	236
4L.2c	Demonstrate command of the conventions of standard English capitalization, punctuation, and spelling when writing. Use a comma before a coordinating conjunction in a compound sentence.	Use Compound Sentences in Writing and Speaking	238
		What is an Independent Clause?	239
4L.2d	Demonstrate command of the conventions of standard English capitalization, punctuation, and spelling when writing. Spell grade-appropriate words correctly, consulting references as needed.	How to Use a Dictionary	240
		How to Use a Thesaurus	242
4L.3a	Use knowledge of language and its conventions when writing, speaking, reading, or listening. Choose words and phrases to convey ideas precisely.	Choose Precise Words for Writing Tasks	119
4L.3b	Use knowledge of language and its conventions when writing, speaking, reading, or listening. Choose punctuation for effect.	Use Periods	243
		Use Question Marks	243
		Use Exclamation Marks	244
4L.3c	Use knowledge of language and its conventions when writing, speaking, reading, or listening. Differentiate between contexts that call for formal English and situations where informal discourse is appropriate.	Demonstrate Voice Through Word Choice	245

4L.4a	Determine or clarify the meaning of unknown and multiple-meaning words and phrases based on grade 4 reading and content, choosing flexibly from a range of strategies. Use context as a clue to the meaning of a word or phrase.	Using Context to Understand Unfamiliar Words	45
		Using the "Does it Make Sense" Strategy to Understand Text	116
4L.4b	Determine or clarify the meaning of unknown and multiple-meaning words and phrases based on grade 4 reading and content, choosing flexibly from a range of strategies. Use common, grade-appropriate Greek and Latin affixes and roots as clues to...	What are Word Origins?	246
		Define Unfamiliar Words Using Word Origins	246
4L.4c	Determine or clarify the meaning of unknown and multiple-meaning words and phrases based on grade 4 reading and content, choosing flexibly from a range of strategies. Consult reference materials, both print and digital, to find the...	Using a Thesaurus to Determine the Meaning of an Unfamiliar Word	247
		Using a Dictionary to Determine Unfamiliar Words	249
		Using a Picture Dictionary to Determine an Unfamiliar Word	250
		Using a Glossary to Determine an Unfamiliar Word	250
4L.5a	Demonstrate understanding of figurative language, word relationships, and nuances in word meanings. Explain the meaning of simple similes and metaphors in context.	What is a Metaphor?	251
		What is a Simile?	252
4L.5b	Demonstrate understanding of figurative language, word relationships, and nuances in word meanings. Recognize and explain the meaning of common idioms, adages, and proverbs.	What Are Idioms?	253
4L.5c	Demonstrate understanding of figurative language, word relationships, and nuances in word meanings. Demonstrate understanding of words by relating them to their opposites (antonyms) and to words with similar but not identical meanings (synonyms).	What are Synonym Words?	254
		Demonstrate Knowledge of Synonym Words	255
		What are Antonym Words?	256
		Demonstrate Knowledge of Antonym Words	257
4L.6	Acquire and use accurately grade-appropriate general academic and domain-specific words and phrases, including those that signal precise actions, emotions, or states of being and that are basic to a particular topic.	Understand Content-Specific Vocabulary	91
		Choose Precise Words for Writing Tasks	119
		Use Content-Specific Vocabulary in your Writing	144
		Understand Language Appropriate for Variety of Contexts	259

4RL.1   Refer to details and examples in a text when explaining what the text says explicitly and when drawing inferences from the text.

SUPPORTING GENERALIZATIONS ABOUT TEXT WITH TEXTUAL EVIDENCE

Generalizations occur when the author makes a statement that goes beyond what the evidence supports. Generalizations usually contain words like *always*, *never*, *all*, *must*, *everyone*, and *nobody*. An example of a generalization would be to write the statement "All soccer players will tell you that their shoes are their most important equipment." The word *all* makes this a generalization because there are probably players for whom different pieces of equipment are more important. You cannot ask every single soccer player in the world what they think the most important piece of equipment is, so a more fair statement to make would be "Shoes are a very important piece of equipment for soccer players."

When you read a text, you can generalize or draw broader conclusions. Just make sure that you can support your conclusions or generalizations with evidence from the text.

Example

Tsunamis are caused by underwater earthquakes and volcanic eruptions, and they are the largest waves of all (**main idea**). Earthquakes occur when two **tectonic plates** collide or slide past each other. When an earthquake occurs under the ocean, the ocean bottom shakes. This movement causes the water above to become **displaced**. Waves of energy spread out in all directions from the source of the vibrations in ever-widening circles. As the tsunami approaches shore, the waves rub against the sea floor. **Friction** causes the waves to slow down and build from behind, creating huge piles of water that crash onto the shore.

All the other sentences support the main idea that tsunamis are caused by underwater earthquakes and volcano eruptions. The main idea is kind of a generalization in that it states a fairly broad main idea for the paragraph. You could support a few other generalizations, as well:

• Tsunamis will not occur in a land-locked area.
• Waves of energy spread in all directions from the source.
• Water only builds up as it slows down.
• People in coastal areas where tectonic plates meet could be in danger from tsunami activity.

4W.9a Draw evidence from literary or informational texts to support analysis, reflection, and research. Apply grade 4 Reading standards to literature.

4W.9b Draw evidence from literary or informational texts to support analysis, reflection, and research. Apply grade 4 Reading standards to informational texts.

4RI.1 Refer to details and examples in a text when explaining what the text says explicitly and when drawing inferences from the text.

Supporting Conclusions about Text with Textual Evidence

After reading a piece of writing you should think about the text and come to a conclusion on what you have read. A conclusion is the main idea of the text.

Support your conclusion about a story using the following three steps:

1. Read the story
2. Think about what you have read and what the story means to you and form a conclusion.
3. Reread the story, and support your ideas with evidence from the story.

Reading the Piece of Writing

Read "The Clever Turtle", and try to come to a conclusion about what you have read.

The Clever Turtle

Come south of the equator, to the western coast of Africa, to where lies the land of Angola. Come to the village and sit around the evening fire and hear the old-time tales. Come help the storyteller weave a spell as he tells of the clever turtle.

One day, so goes the tale, a man left his village to tend to his field of maize. But he found only an open, empty place where before the young corn had stood straight and tall.

The man looked down at the poor broken stalks and saw a large turtle dozing in the sun. He caught the turtle and carried it back to the village.

The man said: "What can we do to this turtle? It has crushed my corn."

The people said: "We should punish it. That is what we should do."

The man said: "How can we punish it?"

The people said: "Cook him for stew!"

The turtle said: "That's exactly what to do! I'd make a tasty turtle stew. But please, don't throw me into the river!"

The man said: "This turtle is not afraid of fire. What else can we do?"

The people said: "Tie him to a tree!"

The turtle said: "Do anything you like with me. Tie me to the strongest tree. But please, *please*, don't throw me into the river!"

The man said: "This turtle is not afraid of fire. This turtle is not afraid of rope. What else can we do?"

The people said: "Place him in a hole in the ground!"

The turtle said: "What is all this talk about? Dig the hole deep so I can't climb out. But please, *please*, PLEASE, don't throw me into the river!"

The man said: "This turtle is not afraid of fire. This turtle is not afraid of rope. This turtleis not afraid of earth. Now, what can we do?"

The people said: "Throw him into the river!"

The turtle said: "NO! Not the river! Can't you see? That river will be the end of me!"

The people said: "We have found a way. We will throw him into the river!"

So the people carried the turtle to the river bank.

They threw him far out to where the water was the deepest. But suddenly the river water whirled and swirled and splattered and splashed, and up paddled the turtle as pleased as could be.

The man said: "I think that turtle has tricked us."

The people said: "Indeed! That turtle has been more clever than we!"

The turtle said: "Born and bred in a river bed! Born and bred in a river bed! You just could not get the best of me!"

Then the clever turtle swam away and was never ever seen near the village again.

—retold by A.K. Roche

WHAT THE STORY MEANS TO YOU

Think about the clues in the story, your own background knowledge, and form a conclusion.

Example
I think that this story is trying to teach us not to give up even in tough situations.

REREADING THE STORY AND LISTING THE INFORMATION THAT SUPPORTS YOUR CONCLUSION

Example
The turtle gets captured and does not stop trying to get free until he does.

You can support your conclusion by the information in the following list:

- Every time the people suggest a way to punish the turtle, he shows no fear of what they suggest and tells them not to throw him in the river. The people say: "Cook him for stew!" The turtle says: "That's exactly what to do! I'd make a tasty turtle stew. But please, don't throw me into the river!"
- The turtle is being tricky by suggesting to the people not to throw him into the river, because that is what he really wants them to do. In reality, the turtle wants them to throw him into the river because that is where he was "Born and bred" (line 35).
- The people continue suggesting different ways to punish the turtle, but he continues to show no fear of what they suggest.
- Finally, the people believe that the turtle is really afraid of the river so they decide to punish him by throwing him into the river. The people say: Throw him into the river!" The turtle says: "NO! Not the river! Can't you see? That river will be the end of me!"
- The turtle gets away from the people. He never gives up until he is free.

4RL.2   Determine a theme of a story, drama, or poem from details in the text; summarize the text.

4RI.2   Determine the main idea of a text and explain how it is supported by key details; summarize the text.

SUMMARIZING TEXT AFTER READING

When you summarize a text, you give a shortened version of it in your own words. You need to be sure that you have the main idea and the important supporting details so that you can recall (remember) the information. There are many ways to organize ideas from a text.

You can use:

- Classification—grouping the same ideas together
- Sequencing—arranging ideas in order (e.g., first, second, third)
- Illustrations—pictures, graphs, diagrams, lists

Whatever you find that helps you the most is the method that you should use. Read the following passage about whales carefully, taking note of the main ideas.

Example

Diving to the Depths

Northern bottle-nosed whales are wonderful divers, as are sperm whales. They can stay submerged for up to 70 min at a time and can dive as deep as 800 m. Cetaceans are mammals, so they have lungs. Proportionally, their lungs are smaller than those of humans. So, how do they manage to set those diving records?

When a northern bottle-nosed whale comes to the surface to breathe, it exhales and then inhales 90% of all the air its lungs can contain, compared with the 75% that a human does. It has more available oxygen than a human does because it is better at emptying and refilling its lungs, not because its lungs contain proportionally more air.

The oxygen captured during inhalation is then stored in its blood in a protein called hemoglobin. Cetaceans have a higher volume of blood than humans, so they have more hemoglobin in their blood vessels and muscles. This means they can accumulate more oxygen reserves and stay underwater longer.

A summary of this passage might read something like this:

Northern bottle-nose whales are such wonderful divers that they can dive to a depth of almost half a mile and can stay underwater for as long as 70 minutes. They are such great divers because they can almost completely empty and then refill their lungs with air and they can store large amounts of oxygen in their blood.

You can also summarize a text in chart form.

In a summary chart, you can organize your thoughts to help you stay focused and on topic. Here is an example of a summary chart.

TOPIC:_____

What I Know	What I Want to Know	What I Learned

4RL.9   Compare and contrast the treatment of similar themes and topics and patterns of events in stories, myths, and traditional literature from different cultures.

Recognize a Theme within a Text

The theme is what an author wants his or her readers to remember the most. It is the underlying message or idea of the work.

Identifying the theme is not always easy, so some detective work may be necessary.

Example

For instance, the theme of lost friendship and how it can be like losing a part of yourself in the story "A Secret for Two" may be more difficult to identify than the clear theme in O. Henry's "The Gift of the Magi", which is that the thought behind a gift is more important than the gift itself.

A Secret for Two

Montreal is a very large city, but, like all large cities, it has some very small streets. Streets, for instance, like Prince Edward Street, which is only four blocks long, ending in a cul-de-sac. No one knew Prince Edward Street as well as did Pierre Dupin, for Pierre had delivered milk to the families on the street for thirty years now.

During the past fifteen years the horse which drew the milk wagon used by Pierre was a large white horse named Joseph. In Montreal, especially in that part of Montreal which is very French, the animals, like children, are often given the names of saints. When the big white horse first came to the Provincale Milk Company he didn't have a name. They told Pierre that he could use the white horse henceforth. Pierre stroked the softness of the horse's neck; he stroked the sheen of its splendid belly and he looked into the eyes of the horse.

"This is a kind horse, a gentle and a faithful horse," Pierre said, "and I can see a beautiful spirit shining out of the eyes of the horse. I will name him after good St. Joseph, who was also kind and gentle and faithful and a beautiful spirit."

Within a year Joseph knew the milk route as well as Pierre. Pierre used to boast that he didn't need reins —he never touched them. Each morning Pierre arrived at the stables of the Provincale Milk Company at five o'clock. The wagon would be loaded and Joseph hitched to it. Pierre would call "Bon jour, vieille ami," as he climbed into his seat and Joseph would turn his head and the other drivers would smile and say that the horse would smile at Pierre. Then Jacques, the foreman, would say, "All right, Pierre, go on," and Pierre would call softly to Joseph, "Avance, mon ami," and this splendid combination would stalk proudly down the street.

The wagon, without any direction from Pierre, would roll three blocks down St. Catherine Street, then turn right two blocks along Roslyn Avenue; then left, for that was Prince Edward Street. The horse would stop at the first house, allow Pierre perhaps thirty seconds to get down from his seat and put a bottle of milk at the front door and would then go on, skipping two houses and stopping at the third. So down the length of the street. Then Joseph, still without any direction from Pierre, would turn around and come back along the other side. Yes, Joseph was a smart horse.

Pierre would boast at the stable of Joseph's skill. "I never touch the reins. He knows just where to stop. Why, a blind man could handle my route with Joseph pulling the wagon."

So it went on for years—always the same. Pierre and Joseph both grew old together, but gradually, not suddenly, Pierre's huge walrus mustache was pure white now and Joseph didn't lift his knees so high or raise his head as much. Jacques, the foreman of the stables, never noticed that they were both getting old until Pierre appeared one morning carrying a heavy walking stick.

"Hey, Pierre," Jacques laughed. "Maybe you got the gout, hey?"

"Mais oui, Jacques," Pierre said a bit uncertainly. "One grows old. One's legs get tired."

"You should teach that horse to carry the milk to the front door for you," Jacques told him. "He does everything else."

He knew every one of the forty families he served on Prince Edward Street. The cooks knew that Pierre could neither read nor write, so instead of following the usual custom of leaving a note in an empty bottle if an additional quart of milk was needed they would sing out when they heard the rumble of his wagon wheels over the cobbled street, "Bring an extra quart this morning, Pierre."

"So you have company for dinner tonight," he would call back gaily.

Pierre had a remarkable memory. When he arrived at the stable he'd always remember to tell Jacques, "The Paquins took an extra quart this morning; the Lemoines bought a pint of cream."

Jacques would note these things in a little book he always carried. Most of the drivers had to make out the weekly bills and collect the money, but Jacques, liking Pierre, had always excused him from this task. All Pierre had to do was to arrive at five in the morning, walk to his wagon, which was always in the same spot at the curb, and deliver his milk. He returned some two hours later, got stiffly from his seat, called a cheery "Au 'voir" to Jacques, and then limped slowly down the street.

One morning the president of the Provincale Milk Company came to inspect the early morning deliveries. Jacques pointed Pierre out to him and said: "Watch how he talks to that horse. See how the horse listens and how he turns his head toward Pierre? See the look in that horse's eyes? You know, I think those two share a secret. I have often noticed it. It is as though they both sometimes chuckle at us as they go off on their route. Pierre is a good man, Monsieur President, but he gets old. Would it be too bold of me to suggest that he be retired and be given perhaps a small pension?" he added anxiously.

"But of course," the president laughed. "I know his record. He has been on this route now for thirty years and never once has there been a complaint. Tell him it is time he rested. His salary will go on just the same."

But Pierre refused to retire. He was panic-stricken at the thought of not driving Joseph every day. "We are two old men," he said to Jacques. "Let us wear out together. When Joseph is ready to retire—then I, too, will quit." Jacques, who was a kind man, understood.

There was something about Pierre and Joseph which made a man smile tenderly. It was as though each drew some hidden strength from the other. When Pierre was sitting in his seat, and when Joseph was hitched to the wagon, neither seemed old. But when they finished their work, then Pierre would limp down the street slowly, seemingly very old indeed, and the horse's head would drop and he would walk very wearily to his stall.

Then one morning Jacques had dreadful news for Pierre when he arrived. It was a cold morning and still pitch-dark. The air was like iced wine that morning and the snow which had fallen during the night glistened like a million diamonds piled together.

Jacques said, "Pierre, your horse, Joseph, did not wake up this morning. He was very old, Pierre, he was twenty-five and that is like being seventy-five for a man."

"Yes," Pierre said slowly. "Yes. I am seventy-five. And I cannot see Joseph again."

"Of course you can," Jacques soothed. "He is over in his stall, looking very peaceful. Go over and see him."

Pierre took one step forward, then turned. "No… no… you don't understand, Jacques."

Jacques clapped him on the shoulder. "We'll find another horse just as good as Joseph. Why, in a month you'll teach him to know your route as well as Joseph did. We'll…" The look in Pierre's eyes stopped him. For years Pierre had worn a heavy cap, the peak of which came low over his eyes, keeping the bitter morning wind out of them. Now Jacques looked into Pierre's eyes and saw something which startled him. He saw a dead, lifeless look in them. The eyes were mirroring the grief that was in Pierre's heart and his soul. It was as though his heart and soul had died.

"Take today off, Pierre," Jacques said, but already Pierre was hobbling off down the street, and had one been near one would have seen tears streaming down his cheeks and have heard half-smothered sobs. Pierre walked to the corner and stepped into the street. There was a warning yell from the driver of a huge truck that was coming fast and there was the scream of brakes, but Pierre apparently heard neither.

Five minutes later an ambulance driver said, "He's dead. Was killed instantly."

Jacques and several of the milk-wagon drivers had arrived and they looked down at the still figure.

"I couldn't help it," the driver of the truck protested, "he walked right into my truck. He never saw it, I guess. Why, he walked into it as though he were blind."

The ambulance doctor bent down. "Blind? Of course the man was blind. See those cataracts? This man has been blind for five years." He turned to Jacques, "You say he worked for you? Didn't you know he was blind?"

"No….no…." Jacques said, softly. "None of us knew. Only one knew—a friend of his named Joseph…. It was a secret, I think, just between those two."

—*by* Quentin Reynolds

Try not to confuse theme with topic or subject. These are what a work is about, while theme is the author's underlying message about a topic or subject. Here is an example from "The Gift of the Magi".

Example

Topic: When you love someone, you are willing to give up prized possessions.

Theme: The thought behind the gift is more important than the gift itself.

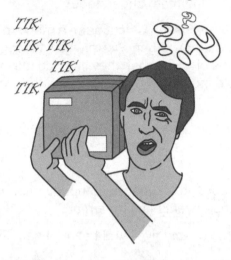

Find theme in three steps:

1. Find the BIG IDEA
   The "Big Idea" of a passage is the same as the main topics of the passage. Ask yourself, what are the common ideas that appear throughout a passage? One helpful hint would be to list the topics that reoccur in a passage. This will help you focus on the theme of the passage.
2. Listen to what the characters do and say.
   Know that you have determined a main topic focus on how the characters' react to the idea. This step will give you good insight to help you understand the theme.
3. Write a statement.
   A theme statement should be a complete sentence that defines the passage's main idea.
   The statement should be general and should relate to the entire passage. Remember that the theme statement should not summarize the passage.

4RL.3   Describe in depth a character, setting, or event in a story or drama, drawing on specific details in the text.

4RI.3   Explain events, procedures, ideas, or concepts in a historical, scientific, or technical text, including what happened and why, based on specific information in the text.

DETERMINING WHAT CHARACTERS ARE LIKE BY LOOKING AT WHAT THEY SAY

There are many ways to tell things about a character in a text you are reading.

Sometimes the way you know some of these characteristics, are simple. Sometimes the author tells you about these characteristics directly, like what color of hair they have, what they are wearing, what jobs they have or what kind of personality thay have.

But sometimes an author is not that direct. They have the reader, determine what the characters are like in indirect ways, and the reader is left to infer what the character is like.

The author may do this through may different ways. The way you will focus on in this lesson is inferring what a character is like through the things that they say.

By really focusing on the things a character says can give you a lot of insight and details to the character's profile.

Example

"Mary!" Amy screamed, "You are the most selfish, annoying, ugly girl I have ever met!"

By hearing the character, Amy say something like this, you could infer that she may have these characteristics:

- She is unfriendly.
- She is over dramatic.
- She is upset.
- She is frustrated.
- She is mean.
- She is a bully.
- She might be young and somewhat immature to say those things.

Do you see how many conclusions you can infer about Amy's character?

Let's try another one together.

Example

Miss Miller bent down to the hurt little boy who was whimpering and she said, "O honey, please let me help you. Let me clean that scrap up and get you out on that playground again. Everything will be ok, my friend. You will be ok."

By hearing the character, Miss Miller, speak to the little boy, you could infer that Miss Miller may have these characteristics:

- She is kind.
- She is gentle.
- She is caring.
- She is warm-hearted.
- She is a helper.
- She is friendly.
- She is supportive.
- She is comforting.

Example

Now it's your turn.

Can you determine some of the characteristics of Misty by looking at the words she says? Once you think you've got some ideas about Misty's character, then check your answers below.

"Mom! It's just not fair! I only got 12 presents for Christmas and Julie got 13!" Misty whined. "I only got the SuperAmazing Doll, instead of the SuperStellar Doll I really wanted!"

How do you think you did?

Were you able to figure out some things about Misty's character, based on what she has said above? If you think you have, check out some possible answers below.

- She is spoiled.
- She is selfish.
- She is greedy.
- She is ungrateful.
- She likes to compare.
- She is a whiner.

Can you now see how an author can give the readers ideas of what the character is like through their speech? By looking at the character's speech, the reader can inference what the character is like in some ways.

DETERMINING WHAT CHARACTERS ARE LIKE BY LOOKING AT WHAT THEY DO

There are many ways to tell things about a character in a text you are reading.

Sometimes, the way you know some of these characteristics is simple. Sometimes, the author tells you directly about these characteristics, like their hair color, what they are wearing, their jobs, or what kind of personality they have.

Sometimes, an author is not that direct. They have the reader determine what the characters are like in indirect ways, and the reader is left to infer what the character is like.

The reader can infer what a character is like in many different ways. One way of inferring what a character is like is by the things that they do.

By focusing on the things a character does can give you a lot of insight and details to the character's profile.

Example

Andy dribbled down the court, sweat dripping from his forehead. He looked up towards the basket and saw an wide opening straight through two of the opposing players. He dribbled as fast as could towards the hoop and threw up a shot. Swish! Andy beamed with pride as his teammates gave him high-fives and slaps on the back. That was his fiftieth basket that game. He was proud of his success and knew it was the result of the hours and hours of practice each night he had spent with his dad and brother in the driveway growing up.

By reading the passage, you can infer the following things about Andy's character:

- He is a basketball player.
- He is talented.
- He is nice to his team mates.
- His team members like him
- He is dedicated and/or driven.
- He practices a lot.

Example

James brought his vehicle to a stop and jumped out. He went to the back of his red-and-blue vehicle and opened up the back doors. Inside, he was overwhelmed with packages and packages and letters and more letters. He knew that today was an especially busy day at work, as it was nearing the Christmas season. He grabbed one medium-sized package and walked up the walkway to the front door of this broken down, ratty home. He knocked on the door three times, not knowing what to expect or who would be answering the door. Suddenly, a little blond girl with pigtails opened the door. She had an adorable smile and she looked up to James and his large, bulky form. He gave a warm, gentle smile to the little girl, and suddenly, her mother game to the door. "I have a package for you ma'am, if you will please just sign here." James said, as he motioned a clipboard toward her with a pen, pointing to the area she needed to sign. "Thank you." The women said softly and handed the clipboard and pen back to James. "Have a wonderful day and an even better Christmas," James said as he shot another friendly smile to the little girl and turned to head back to his truck. He knew he had a lot of deliveries to still do if he was going to get home in time to see his own little girl get home from school.

By reading the actions that the character, James, the reader could infer that he may have these characteristics:

- James is a delivery man.
- He is a large man.
- He is friendly.
- He has a daughter.
- He was cheerful.
- He was kind and nice.

Example

Try to determine some of the characteristics of Michael from reading about his actions in the following paragraph.

Michael sat silently on the sofa in front of the television with his remote near his side. He had chip crumbs scattered all over himself. He reached into the large bag of chips and shoved another handful into his mouth. Then, he reached for the package of chocolate and ate six pieces in a row. He squirmed a bit in his seat, as he had not moved from that spot in over two days. Suddenly, the phone rang and he could barely get up out of his spot on his sofa because he was so full and lacked so much energy.

You might have been able to infer the following characteristics about Michael by reading about his actions:

- Michael is lazy.
- Michael is a couch potato.
- Michael is an overeater.
- Michael likes junk food.
- Michael likes food.

Can you now see how an author can give the readers ideas of what the character is like through their actions? By looking at the character's actions, the reader can infer what the the character is like in some ways.

IDENTIFY THE MAIN EVENTS OF THE PLOT

The plot is the series of events that happen throughout the story. The plot is the story line.

It is important to recognize the main events in a story to help you fully understand what the story is about.

The plot of a story may have many little events happening, but it is important to pick out the main events in order to comprehend the main ideas of the story. When you are trying to restate the main ideas of the plot, try to think of the most important points of the story. If you retold the story and left out one of the plot points, would it make a difference or change the story? If the answer is is NO, then it is probably not a main event in the plot. If the answer is YES, it is probably one of the main events in the plot.

HOW DOES THIS WORK?

As you read the story below, see if you can remember the main events in the plot, so that you could retell them to someone else.

Example

A Secret Lost in the Water

After I started going to school my father scarcely talked any more. I was very intoxicated by the new game of spelling; my father had little skill for it (it was my mother who wrote our letters) and was convinced I was no longer interested in hearing him tell of his adventures during the long weeks when he was far away from the house.

One day, however, he said to me:

'The time's come to show you something.'

He asked me to follow him. I walked behind him, not talking, as we had got in the habit of doing. He stopped in the field before a clump of leafy bushes.

'Those are called alders,' he said.

'I know.'

'You have to learn how to choose,' my father pointed out.

I didn't understand. He touched each branch of the bush, one at a time, with religious care.

'You have to choose one that's very fine, a perfect one, like this.'

I looked; it seemed exactly like the others.

My father opened his pocket knife and cut the branch he'd selected with pious care. He stripped off the leaves and showed me the branch, which formed a perfect Y.

'You see,' he said, 'the branch has two arms. Now take one in each hand. And squeeze them.'

I did as he asked and took in each hand one fork of the Y, which was thinner than a pencil.

'Close your eyes,' my father ordered, 'and squeeze a little harder … Don't open your eyes! Do you feel anything?'

'The branch is moving!' I exclaimed, astonished.

Beneath my clenched fingers the alder was wriggling like a small, frightened snake. My father saw that I was about to drop it.

'Hang on to it!'

'The branch is squirming,' I repeated. 'And I hear something that sounds like a river!'

'Open your eyes,' my father ordered.

I was stunned, as though he'd awakened me while I was dreaming.

'What does it mean?' I asked my father.

'It means that underneath us, right here, there's a little fresh-water spring. If we dig, we could drink from it. I've just taught you how to find a spring. It's something my own father taught me. It isn't something you learn in school. And it isn't useless: a man can get along without writing and arithmetic, but he can never get along without water.'

Much later, I discovered that my father was famous in the region because of what the people called his 'gift:' before digging a well they always consulted him; they would watch him prospecting the fields or the hills, eyes closed, hands clenched on the fork of an alder bough. Wherever my father stopped, they marked the ground; there they would dig; and from there water would gush forth.

Years passed; I went to other schools, saw other countries, I had children, I wrote some books and my poor father is lying in the earth where so many times he had found fresh water.

One day someone began to make a film about my village and its inhabitants, from whom I've stolen so many of the stories that I tell. With the film crew we went to see a farmer to capture the image of a sad man: his children didn't want to receive the inheritance he'd spent his whole life preparing for them—the finest farm in the area. While the technicians were getting cameras and microphones ready the farmer put his arm around my shoulders saying:

'I knew your father well.'

'Ah! I know. Everybody in the village knows each other… No one feels like an outsider.'

'You know what's under your feet?'

'Hell?' I asked, laughing.

'Under your feet there's a well. Before I dug I called in specialists from the Department of Agriculture; they did research, they analyzed shovelfuls of dirt; and they made a report where they said there wasn't any water on my land. With the family, the animals, the crops, I need water. When I saw that those specialists hadn't found any I thought of your father and I asked him to come over. He didn't want to; I think he was pretty fed up with me because I'd asked those specialists instead of him. But finally he came; he went and cut off a little branch, then he walked around for a while with his eyes shut; he stopped, he listened to something we couldn't hear and then he said to me: 'Dig right here, there's enough water to get your whole flock drunk and drown your specialists besides.' We dug and found water. Fine water that's never heard of pollution.'

The film people were ready; they called to me to take my place.

'I'm gonna show you something,' said the farmer, keeping me back, 'You wait right here.'

He disappeared into a shack which he must have used to store things, then came back with a branch which he held out to me.

'I never throw nothing away. I kept the alder branch your father cut to find my water. I don't understand, it hasn't dried out.'

Moved as I touched the branch, kept out of I don't know what sense of piety—and which really wasn't dry—I had the feeling that my father was watching me over my shoulder; I closed my eyes and, standing above the spring my father had discovered, I waited for the branch to writhe, I hoped the sound of gushing water would rise to my ears.

The alder stayed motionless in my hands and the water beneath the earth refused to sing.

Somewhere along the roads I'd taken since the village of my childhood I had forgotten my father's knowledge.

'Don't feel sorry,' said the man, thinking no doubt of his farm and his childhood; 'nowadays fathers can't pass on anything to the next generation.'

And he took the alder branch from my hands.

—by Roch Carrier

Below are the main events from the plot of the story that were important to the purpose of the text.

1. The father teaches his child (the narrator) about alders and says, "You have to learn how to choose one."
2. They find a perfect Y-shaped one; the narrator and the father hold onto each end of the branch; the branch begins to shake and the narrator hears the sounds of a river. The father tells him there is a spring below where they are standing.
3. The narrator hears that his father was known for his special gift to find water underground.
4. The narrator goes to see the village of his childhood which is being filmed, and meets an old farmer who says he knew the narrator's father and how the narrator's father had found water for him.
5. The farmer brings a branch over to the narrator that his father had used to find water for him many years before.
6. The narrator holds onto it, and tries to discover water, but does not feel anything.
7. The farmer takes the branch away from the narrator and says, "Don't feel sorry, nowadays fathers can't pass on anything to the next generation."

Try This!

Can you identify the main events that happen in the plot of the following passage? Once you think you have identified them all, check out your answers below.

The Clever Turtle

Come south of the equator, to the western coast of Africa, to where lies the land of Angola. Come to the village and sit around the evening fire and hear the old-time tales. Come help the storyteller weave a spell as he tells of the clever turtle.

One day, so goes the tale, a man left his village to tend to his field of maize. But he found only an open, empty place where before the young corn had stood straight and tall.

The man looked down at the poor broken stalks and saw a large turtle dozing in the sun. He caught the turtle and carried it back to the village.

The man said: "What can we do to this turtle? It has crushed my corn."

The people said: "We should punish it. That is what we should do."

The man said: "How can we punish it?"

The people said: "Cook him for stew!"

The turtle said: "That's exactly what to do! I'd make a tasty turtle stew. But please, don't throw me into the river!"

The man said: "This turtle is not afraid of fire. What else can we do?"

The people said: "Tie him to a tree!"

The turtle said: "Do anything you like with me. Tie me to the strongest tree. But please, *please*, don't throw me into the river!"

The man said: "This turtle is not afraid of fire. This turtle is not afraid of rope. What else can we do?"

The people said: "Place him in a hole in the ground!"

The turtle said: "What is all this talk about? Dig the hole deep so I can't climb out. But please, *please*, PLEASE, don't throw me into the river!"

The man said: "This turtle is not afraid of fire. This turtle is not afraid of rope. This turtleis not afraid of earth. Now, what can we do?"

The people said: "Throw him into the river!"

The turtle said: "NO! Not the river! Can't you see? That river will be the end of me!"

The people said: "We have found a way. We will throw him into the river!"

So the people carried the turtle to the river bank.

They threw him far out to where the water was the deepest. But suddenly the river water whirled and swirled and splattered and splashed, and up paddled the turtle as pleased as could be.

The man said: "I think that turtle has tricked us."

The people said: "Indeed! That turtle has been more clever than we!"

The turtle said: "Born and bred in a river bed! Born and bred in a river bed! You just could not get the best of me!"

Then the clever turtle swam away and was never ever seen near the village again.

—*retold by* A.K. Roche

HOW DID YOU DO?

If you were able to identify all the important main events from the plot in the story above, check out the answers below.

1. A man leaves his village to go tend to his maize.
2. He finds all the corn stalks wrecked and broken, and a turtle nearby sleeping.
3. The man takes the turtle back to the village and asks the people what they should do to punish the turtle for wrecking his maize.
4. The people come up with different ideas and each time the turtle just replies with, "Do anything you like to me, just don't throw me in the river."
5. The people decide to throw the turtle in the river.
6. The turtle swims easily and plays in the river, so the people realize they have been tricked by the turtle.
7. The turtle swims away, never to be seen by the village again.

4W.3b *Write narratives to develop real or imagined experiences or events using effective technique, descriptive details, and clear event sequences. Use dialogue and description to develop experiences and events or show the responses of characters...*

UNDERSTAND HOW A SITUATION CAUSES CHARACTER'S ACTIONS

An author needs to create a situation for the characters in his story, a situation that causes the story to unfold. If the situation or problem is easily resolved, then the story is over.

The following story is a great example of how a situation caused a character's actions.

Example

We all know the story of Cinderella. The story begins with Cinderella being placed in a bad situation when her father dies and she's left to live with her mean stepmother and terrible stepsisters. A ball is being held at the palace so that the prince can find a bride, and Cinderella wants to attend but has nothing to wear. Suddenly, her Fairy Godmother appears and turns her rags into a beautiful dress and a pumpkin into a carriage. She arrives at the ball, dances with the Prince and has to quickly leave before the magic wears off. As she runs away from the palace, she loses one of her glass slippers. The Prince searches far and wide until he finds the girl who wore the slipper. Cinderella and the Prince live happily ever after.

The situations which led to Cinderella's happily ever after are shown in chart form below.

Situation	Character's Actions
Her father died.	She became a servant girl.
A visit by her Fairy Godmother.	She goes to the Palace Ball.
She meets the Prince.	She falls in love.
The clock strikes midnight.	She runs out but drops her slipper.
The Prince finds the slipper and begins to search for Cinderella.	She is unhappy until he finds her and she fits the shoe.

Each situation caused the characters to react to what was happening. The more situations that arise, the longer your story will be.

No matter what kind of situation a character is put in, they will react in a certain way. If a character is put in a scary situation, they will probably act scared and their reaction might be to run or scream.

How Setting Causes a Character's Actions

The setting of a story can strongly influence the character's choices. Sometimes, it limits what a character can and cannot do.

For example, consider the setting suggested by the following phrase:

"It was a dark and stormy night…"

This type of setting shows the reader that the characters are probably not out for a stroll in the park. Setting affects what a character is doing and ultimately begins that character's journey.

A person is shaped by where the person comes from. For example, living in the 1920s versus the 1990s makes a profound difference to the lives of the characters. In the 1920s, the characters might more polite, and discrimination was common at that time:

Think about the story "Little Red Riding Hood". The setting is in a village near the forest. Little Red Riding Hood must go through the woods to get to her grandmother's house, and it is in the woods that she encounters a big, bad wolf.

If Little Red Riding Hood lived in a city, that setting would change the story line because big, bad wolves do not usually live in the city!

Understand How Traits Cause Character's Actions

Traits are the qualities that a character possesses like being happy, lovestruck, or embarrassed. These traits are revealed through the character's actions.

Example

Character's Action	Traits Revealed
The Big Bad Wolf blew down the First Piggy's house.	The Big Bad Wolf is mean, nasty, and heartless.
The witch gave Snow White a poison apple.	The witch is wicked, jealous, and evil.
The Beast saved Belle when the wolves began attacking her.	The Beast was courageous, helpful, and fierce.

The Gingerbread man was driven by fear but his courage enabled him to jump up from the pan and run away instead of being eaten. However, another of his traits was foolishness. He was too foolish to see through the fox's tricks enough to run away again at the river, and this caused him to be eaten later. This is one of many examples showing how a character's traits cause a character's actions.

How Motivations Cause a Character's Actions

A character needs motivation to take action. Motivation is what drives the character to act the way he or she does. Characters can be motivated by all sorts of different things. Consider the following examples.

Example

In *Romeo and Juliet*, Juliet was motivated by her love for Romeo. Her motivation was so strong that she chose to go against her parents' wishes and marry him anyway.

Example

In *The Wizard of Oz*, Dorothy was motivated by her desire to be reunited with her family in Kansas. Throughout the story, she stayed strong.

Example

In "Three Billy Goats Gruff", the billy goats were motivated to cross the bridge by their hunger for fresh, green pastures.

In each of the given stories, characters were motivated by a strong desire that led them to act in a certain way throughout the story.

IDENTIFY THE SETTING WITHIN A TEXT

The *setting* is where the story takes place. It may include the time and location.

Example

Read the passage below and identify the setting.

Campers and Aliens

One day, my family went camping. My brothers and I decided to stay by the campfire while my parents went for a walk. That was when the aliens came. We didn't see them coming out of the spaceship toward us until suddenly my brother Tyler shouted, "Wow, look at those creatures!" They walked across the river and said they wanted to be our friends because they were new to Earth and very hungry. Tyler went inside the tent and grabbed some hot dogs and marshmallows. The aliens really liked our food. They each ate four hot dogs! That surprised me because I never thought aliens would like human food. Then the aliens told me that they had to go back to their planet. They walked to their spaceship and vanished. When Mom and Dad came back, I told them how exciting it was to finally meet aliens. Then we all went to bed.

Answer: The story takes place in the campground.

Evidence: "my family went camping", "My brothers and I decided to stay by the campfire", "walked across the river"

4RL.4   *Determine the meaning of words and phrases as they are used in a text, including those that allude to significant characters found in mythology.*

4RI.4   *Determine the meaning of general academic and domain-specific words or phrases in a text relevant to a grade 4 topic or subject area.*

USING CONTEXT TO UNDERSTAND UNFAMILIAR WORDS

Sometimes, when you are reading, you will come across a word that you do not understand or know. Often, you will not have a dictionary on hand when you are reading, but the you will want to know what a word means. When this happens, it is important that you stop and try a few different strategies to figure it out. If you do not, it could affect your comprehension of the whole text.

One strategy is to see the word in its context. This means you may need to reread the sentence or even the paragraph that contains the word. You also may need to read ahead a bit, to try figuring out what is being talked about in the passage. When you have a solid understanding of the context, you will be more likely to figure out what the unfamiliar word might mean. When you are rereading or reading ahead, it is important that you look for familiar words or ideas that may give you a hint as to what the unfamiliar word means. These hints are called *context clues*.

If this still has not helped, you could try asking yourself, "What word do I know that would make sense in the place of the new word in this sentence?" Then try substituting the familiar word in the sentence and read the passage to see if the word makes sense in the text.

Example

Using the nonsense word TALIBUSIXA, see if you can give a logical meaning to it by using the context clues in the following paragraph.

What kinds of things were in this paragraph that help give clues to the context of the word TALIBUSIXA?

Jacob traveled for a long time to get to his friend's home in Toronto. The TALIBUSIXA took four days on the bus. He was so tired when he arrived in Toronto. He was so happy that the bus ride had come to an end. Jake was so relieved to find his friend waiting for him at the bus station.

Some of the context clues in the passage might be the words *traveled*, *bus*, *distance*, and *Toronto*.

You could come to a conclusion that the word might mean trip or journey just by looking at the context clues.

When you read the sentence over using your inferred words or ideas, the paragraph still makes sense, and it has not changed the meaning of what is being relayed to the reader. It fits!

Example

Try to figure out the following highlighted word's meaning without using a dictionary. See if there are any context clues that can help you figure out what the word might mean.

Marla was good at many sports. She excelled in fencing, target shooting, swimming, running, and horsemanship. She decided to compete in the PENTATHLON rather than having to choose one of the events.

Some of the words that might give context clues in this paragraph are: *excelled*, the list of the five sports (*fencing*, *target shooting*, *swimming*, *running*, and *horsemanship*) *compete*, and *events*.

Do you think you figured out the meaning of the word PENTATHLON by using the context clues in the paragraph?

You can infer, by looking at the context clues, that the word PENTATHLON has something to do with a sporting event. You can infer that Marla was going to be involved in all five of the listed sports she excelled in because she did not want to have to choose only one of the events.

The meaning of the word PENTATHLON actually means a contest featuring five different events. It is usually a track and field event, and incorporates the skills of shooting, swimming, fencing, equestrian (horsemanship) and running.

4RL.5   Explain major differences between poems, drama, and prose, and refer to the structural elements of poems and drama when writing or speaking about a text.

WHAT IS A PLAY?

A play is a type of drama, or literary form used in theater. It is usually written in a "script", where the characters speak dialogue back and forth to each other. Plays are usually written for performing, rather than for reading. Plays are stories that we see and hear, rather than read.

Example

---

from Pygmalion, Act I

The Daughter: *(in the space between the central pillars, close to the one on her left)* I'm getting chilled to the bone. What can Freddy be doing all this time? Hes been gone twenty minutes.

The Mother: *(on her daughter's right)* Not so long. But he ought to have got us a cab by this.

A Bystander: *(on the lady's right)* He wont get no cab not until half-past eleven, missus, when they come back after dropping their theater fares.

The Mother: But we must have a cab. We cant stand here until half-past eleven. It's too bad.

The Bystander: Well, it aint my fault, missus.

The Daughter: If Freddy had a bit of gumption, he would have got one at the theater door.

The Mother: What could he have done, poor boy?

The Daughter: Other people got cabs. Why couldnt he?

Freddy rushes in out of the rain from the Southampton Street side, and comes between them closing a dripping umbrella. He is a young man of twenty, in evening dress, very wet around the ankles.

The Daughter: Well, havnt you got a cab?

Freddy: Theres not one to be had for love or money.

The Mother: Oh, Freddy, there must be one. You cant have tried.

The Daughter: It's too tiresome. Do you expect us to go and get one ourselves?

Freddy: I tell you theyre all engaged. The rain was so sudden: nobody was prepared; and everybody had to take a cab. Ive been to Charing Cross one way and nearly to Ludgate Circus the other; and they were all engaged.

The Mother: Did you try Trafalgar Square?

Freddy: There wasnt one at Trafalgar Square.

The Daughter: Did you try?

Freddy: I tried as far as Charing Cross Station. Did you expect me to walk to Hammersmith?

The Daughter: You havnt tried at all.

The Mother: You really are very helpless, Freddy. Go again; and dont come back until you have found a cab.

Freddy: I shall simply get soaked for nothing.

The Daughter: And what about us? Are we to stay here all night in this draught, with next to nothing on. You selfish pig—

Freddy: Oh, very well: I'll go, I'll go.

He opens his umbrella and dashes off Strandwards, but comes into collision with a flower girl, who is hurrying in for shelter, knocking her basket out of her hands. A blinding flash of lightning, followed instantly by a rattling peal of thunder, orchestrates the incident.

The Flower Girl: Nah then, Freddy: look wh' y' gowin, deah.

Freddy: Sorry. *(he rushes off)*

The Flower Girl: *(picking up her scattered flowers and replacing them in the basket)*Theres menners f' yer! Te-oo banches o voylets trod into the mad.

—*by* George Bernard Shaw

4RI.5   Describe the overall structure of events, ideas, concepts, or information in a text or part of a text.

WHAT IS NON-FICTION?

Non-Fiction is meant to be factual information. Non-fiction is true.

TYPES OF NON-FICTION TEXTS

There are many types of non-fiction texts. Some of these are listed below:

- Essays
- Recipes
- Diagrams
- Journals
- Biographies
- Autobiographies
- Travel books
- Scientific papers
- User manuals
- Blueprints
- Histories
- Documentaries
- Text books
- Memoirs
- Book reports

Example

Below is a non-fiction piece about weather forecasting:

Weather Lore

Weather forecasting is a modern science. Years ago (before 1930), predicting tomorrow's weather was little more than a guessing game. From experience, farmers and fishermen learned what to watch for. They made up easy-to-remember rhymes and sayings about ways to predict weather. Some of their notions are still with us today. A few of them are based on scientifically valid concepts. But most are wrong as often as they are right.

Each February 2, we are reminded faithfully about the story of the groundhog and his shadow. If the groundhog comes out of his burrow at noon on that day and sees his shadow, we are in for six more weeks of winter. If not, according to the legend, mild weather can be expected. Weather records have proved the groundhog wrong many, many times.

However, some animal behavior is a good predictor for the weather, at least during the next few hours. Some farm animals know when a storm is coming and will seek shelter; others become agitated and restless. Ants and spiders scurry at top speed to complete their tasks. Bees return to the hive.

Today, most weather lore is simply quaint—not very useful in modern life, but fun.

"Squirrel's tail fluffy, winter will be blustery" is one of hundreds of weather rhymes about animals, birds and insects. Another supposed predictor is the wooly caterpillar: if the black band on the caterpillar's back is wide in autumn, the winter will be severe. Scientists say, however, that neither squirrels' tails nor caterpillars' backs predict winter weather.

"A coming storm your shooting corns will presage" is one of many old sayings suggesting that aches and pains are worse when a storm is approaching. This may be true. Some aches could be aggravated because humidity is maximum and atmospheric pressure minimum just before and during a storm.

"If the sun red should set, the next day surely will be wet." Well, it depends on where you live because the following rhyme says the opposite: "Red sky in the morning, sailors take warning; red sky at night, sailors' delight."

"If wooly fleeces spread the heavenly way, be sure no rain disturbs the day." This rhyme refers to a sky of small puffy cumulus clouds. It tells us that no rain will fall that day. This would be true most of the time, but a cumulonimbus cloud can develop, bringing thunderstorms.

Another legend states that rain will arrive soon if frogs creak louder than usual. This is probably true, because frogs are most active in damp weather.

"It's raining cats and dogs" is a very old expression. In mythology, cats were associated with rain and dogs with wind. So a windy rainstorm was called a cat-and-dog storm.

—from *Exploring the Sky by Day: The Equinox Guide to Weather and the Atmosphere* by Terence Dickinson

Non-fiction is meant to be true information which can be presented in many different forms.

WHAT IS POETRY?

Poetry refers to poems. Poems often have rhythm, and they sometimes rhyme, especially those that are written for children. They often use very colorful and expressive language to explain an idea or event. Songs are examples of poetry, as are nursery rhymes, limericks, and many picture books. Poetry can often be recognized by the way that it looks on the page. Writers often choose to either group the text in verses or shape the printed words in interesting patterns.

These two verses are from a traditional folksong and use both rhythmic words and rhymes.

Example

from The Fox

The fox went out on a chase one night,

He prayed to the moon to give him light,

For he had many a mile to go that night

Before he reached the town-o, town-o, town-o

He had many a mile to go that night

Before he reached the town-o.

He ran 'til he came to a great big pen,

Where the ducks and the geese were kept therein.

He said "A couple of you are gonna grease my chin

before I leave this town-o, town-o, town-o!

A couple of you are gonna grease my chin,

before I leave this town-o!"

CONCRETE POEMS

A poem about the sun might be written with the words forming the circular shape of the sun. A poem that visually represents its topic is called a **concrete poem**.

Example

burns!
hot so hot
bright so bright
sun sun sun sun
warms all it touches
eye in the sky
watching plants grow
life!

LIMERICKS

A five line poem (in which lines 1, 2, and 5 rhyme and lines 3 and 4 rhyme, following an *aabba* rhyme pattern) is called a **limerick**.

Example

There was a young lady from Niger,
Who smiled as she rode on a tiger!
They came back from the ride
With the lady inside
And the smile on the face of the tiger!

HAIKUS

A non-rhyming, three line poem with a total of 17 syllables is a called a **haiku**.

Example

A red ladybug
Lands on my jelly sandwich
Catcher in the rye!

Here is another haiku. The Japanese are known for creating hundreds of these simple but elegant poems.

Example

The first snow this year
Dusted the forest with white
World of cool beauty.

4RL.10   By the end of the year, read and comprehend literature, including stories, dramas, and poetry, in the grades 4–5 text complexity band proficiently, with scaffolding as needed at the high end of the range.

WHAT IS FICTION?

Fiction is a story that is not true. The author uses his or her imagination to tell a story that is not based on facts. You do not read fiction to gain information but rather to enjoy a story. *Pinocchio* and *Tom Sawyer* are examples of popular fictional stories.

WHAT IS A CONCRETE POEM?

In a **concrete poem**, the words or lines have been arranged to look like the subject of the poem or some of the main ideas in the poem.

When you write a concrete poem, you can be creative with the shape of the poem as well as its wording.

For example, the following concrete poem has an unusual shape.

burns!
hot so hot
bright so bright
sun sun sun sun
warms all it touches
eye in the sky
watching plants grow
life!

The different line lengths in this concrete poem look like a tree. The tree shape represents growing plants.

Another idea would be to place the poem inside a sun shape.

In this example, the words are still arranged in the tree shape to represent growing plants, but the tree is now inside the sun. That shows the sun surrounding or embracing the plants with the warmth and light that they need for life and food production.

WHAT IS A RHYMING PATTERN?

The rhyming pattern of a poem is shown by a letter at the end of each line. For example, if the first and third lines rhyme and the second and fourth lines rhyme in one stanza, the rhyming pattern would be written out as *abab*, as in this poem by Lewis Carroll.

How Doth the Little Crocodile

How doth the little crocodile	*a*
Improve his shining tail,	*b*
And pour the waters of the Nile	*a*
On every golden scale!	*b*

How cheerfully he seems to grin,
How neatly spreads his claws,
And welcomes little fishes in
With gently smiling jaws!

—by Lewis Carroll

Ballads and folksongs have definite rhyming patterns and are divided into verses or stanzas.

The following two verses are from a traditional folksong.

Example

from **The Fox**

The fox went out on a chilly night,	*a*
He prayed for the moon to give him light,	*a*
For he'd many a mile to go that night,	*a*
Before he reached the town-o, town-o, town-o	*b*
He'd many a mile to go that night,	*a*
Before he reached the town-o.	*b*

He ran til he came to a great big pen,
Where the ducks and the geese were put therein,
"A couple of you will grease my chin,
Before I leave this town-o, town-o, town-o,
A couple of you will grease my chin,
Before I leave this town-o."

—by Burl Ives

The rhyming pattern in the first stanza would be written out as *aaabab*.

4RL.6 *Compare and contrast the point of view from which different stories are narrated, including the difference between first- and third-person narrations.*

4RI.6 *Compare and contrast a firsthand and secondhand account of the same event or topic; describe the differences in focus and the information provided.*

IDENTIFY A FIRST PERSON POINT OF VIEW

First person point of view is when the author is speaking from his/her own perspective. This means they are telling the story from their own view using words like "I, me, my, mine".

Example

Look at the passages below and identify which one is speaking from the the first person point of view.

Passage A

On the May long weekend, Erin went camping with her parents to Banff National Park. She wasn't very happy because all of her friends were getting together and she wasn't able to go. When Erin and her parents got to the camp site, she decided to take a walk in the forest. She could feel the long green grass tickle her legs. As Erin walked along the forest trail, she looked up the hill and saw an opening. Erin was very curious to see what was in the cave so she made her way up the hill. When she reached the cave, she was a little bit scared. Erin's heart started to race and her hands began to sweat. As she walked down the dark creepy cave, her eyes started adjusting to the dim light. She could feel the cool damp air reach her nose. It smelled very musty. When her eyes finally adjusted fully to the light, she looked up and saw big black hairy bats hanging from the roof of the cave. Erin stopped dead in her tracks. Her heart was ready to jump out of her chest when she saw a bat flap its wings. She screamed out loud and ran out as fast as she could.

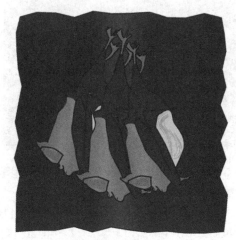

Passage B

On the May long weekend, I went camping with my parents to Banff National Park. I wasn't very happy because all of my friends were getting together and I wasn't able to go. When we got to the camp site, I decided to take a walk in the forest. I could feel the long green grass tickle my legs. As I walked along the forest trail, I looked up the hill and saw an opening. I was very curious to see what was in the cave so I made my way up the hill. When I reached the cave, I was a little bit scared. My heart started to race and my hands began to sweat. As I walked down the dark creepy cave, my eyes started adjusting to the dim light. I could feel the cool damp air reach my nose. It smelled very musty. When my eyes finally adjusted fully to the light, I looked up and saw big black hairy bats hanging from the roof of the cave. I stopped dead in my tracks. My heart was ready to jump out of my chest when I saw one flap its wings. I screamed out loud and ran out as fast as I could.

Passage C

On the May long weekend, you went camping with your parents to Banff National Park. You were not very happy because all of your friends were getting together and you weren't able to go. When you and your parents got to the camp site, you decided to take a walk in the forest. You could feel the long green grass tickle your legs. As you walked along the forest trail, you looked up the hill and saw an opening. You were very curious to see what was in the cave so you made your way up the hill. When you reached the cave, you were a little bit scared. Your heart started to race and your hands began to sweat. As you walked down the dark creepy cave, your eyes started adjusting to the dim light. You could feel the cool damp air reach your nose. It smelled very musty. When your eyes finally adjusted fully to the light, you looked up and saw big black hairy bats hanging from the roof of the cave. You stopped dead in your tracks. Your heart was ready to jump out of your chest when you saw a bat flap its wings. You screamed out loud and ran out as fast as you could.

Answer: Passage B is speaking in the first person's point of view because it uses the words "I and my" throughout the passage.

On the May long weekend, I went camping with **my** parents to Banff National Park. I wasn't very happy because all of **my** friends were getting together and I wasn't able to go. When we got to the camp site, I decided to take a walk in the forest. I could feel the long green grass tickle **my** legs. As I walked along the forest trail, I looked up the hill and saw an opening. I was very curious to see what was in the cave so I made **my** way up the hill. When I reached the cave, I was a little bit scared. **My** heart started to race and **my** hands began to sweat. As I walked down the dark creepy cave, **my** eyes started adjusting to the dim light. I could feel the cool damp air reach **my** nose. It smelled very musty. When **my** eyes finally adjusted fully to the light, I looked up and saw big black hairy bats hanging from the roof of the cave. I stopped dead in **my** tracks. **My** heart was ready to jump out of **my** chest when I saw one flap its wings. I screamed out loud and ran out as fast as I could.

Identify a Second Person Point of View
Second Person Point of View

Second person point of view is when the author is telling the story directly to the reader using words like "you, your". This makes the reader the main character of the story.

Look at the paragraphs below and identify which one is speaking in the the second person point of view.

Paragraph A

On the May long weekend, you went camping with your parents to Banff National Park. You were not very happy because all of your friends were getting together and you weren't able to go. When you and your parents got to the camp site, you decided to take a walk in the forest. You could feel the long green grass tickle your legs. As you walked along the forest trail, you looked up the hill and saw an opening. You were very curious to see what was in the cave so you made your way up the hill. When you reached the cave, you were a little bit scared. Your heart started to race and your hands began to sweat. As you walked down the dark creepy cave, your eyes started adjusting to the dim light. You could feel the cool damp air reach your nose. It smelled very musty. When your eyes finally adjusted fully to the light, you looked up and saw big black hairy bats hanging from the roof of the cave. You stopped dead in your tracks. Your heart was ready to jump out of your chest when you saw a bat flap its wings. You screamed out loud and ran out as fast as you could.

Paragraph B

On the May long weekend, I went camping with my parents to Banff National Park. I wasn't very happy because all of my friends were getting together and I wasn't able to go. When we got to the camp site, I decided to take a walk in the forest. I could feel the long green grass tickle my legs. As I walked along the forest trail, I looked up the hill and saw an opening. I was very curious to see what was in the cave so I made my way up the hill. When I reached the cave, I was a little bit scared. My heart started to race and my hands began to sweat. As I walked down the dark creepy cave, my eyes started adjusting to the dim light. I could feel the cool damp air reach my nose. It smelled very musty. When my eyes finally adjusted fully to the light, I looked up and saw big black hairy bats hanging from the roof of the cave. I stopped dead in my tracks. My heart was ready to jump out of my chest when I saw one flap its wings. I screamed out loud and ran out as fast as I could.

Paragraph C

On the May long weekend, Erin went camping with her parents to Banff National Park. She wasn't very happy because all of her friends were getting together and she wasn't able to go. When Erin and her parents got to the camp site, she decided to take a walk in the forest. She could feel the long green grass tickle her legs. As Erin walked along the forest trail, she looked up the hill and saw an opening. Erin was very curious to see what was in the cave so she made her way up the hill. When she reached the cave, she was a little bit scared. Erin's heart started to race and her hands began to sweat. As she walked down the dark creepy cave, her eyes started adjusting to the dim light. She could feel the cool damp air reach her nose. It smelled very musty. When her eyes finally adjusted fully to the light, she looked up and saw big black hairy bats hanging from the roof of the cave. Erin stopped dead in her tracks. Her heart was ready to jump out of her chest when she saw a bat flap its wings. She screamed out loud and ran out as fast as she could.

Answer: Paragraph A is speaking in the second person point of view because it uses the words "you and your" throughout the Paragraph.

On the May long weekend, **you** went camping with **your** parents to Banff National Park. **You** were not very happy because all of **your** friends were getting together and **you** weren't able to go. When **you** and **your** parents got to the camp site, **you** decided to take a walk in the forest. **You** could feel the long green grass tickle **your** legs. As **you** walked along the forest trail, **you** looked up the hill and saw an opening. **You** were very curious to see what was in the cave so **you** made **your** way up the hill. When**you** reached the cave, **you** were a little bit scared. **Your** heart started to race and **your** hands began to sweat. As**you** walked down the dark creepy cave, **your** eyes started adjusting to the dim light. **You** could feel the cool damp air reach **your** nose. It smelled very musty. When **your** eyes finally adjusted fully to the light, **you** looked up and saw big black hairy bats hanging from the roof of the cave. **You** stopped dead in **your** tracks. **Your** heart was ready to jump out of **your** chest when **you** saw a bat flap its wings. **You** screamed out loud and ran out as fast as **you** could.

IDENTIFY A THIRD PERSON POINT OF VIEW
THIRD PERSON POINT OF VIEW

Third person point of view is when the author refers to his/her characters as "he, she, him, her, it, they".

Example

Look at the paragraphs below and identify which one is speaking in the the third person point of view.

Paragraph A

On the May long weekend, you went camping with your parents to Banff National Park. You were not very happy because all of your friends were getting together and you weren't able to go. When you and your parents got to the camp site, you decided to take a walk in the forest. You could feel the long green grass tickle your legs. As you walked along the forest trail, you looked up the hill and saw an opening. You were very curious to see what was in the cave so you made your way up the hill. When you reached the cave, you were a little bit scared. Your heart started to race and your hands began to sweat. As you walked down the dark creepy cave, your eyes started adjusting to the dim light. You could feel the cool damp air reach your nose. It smelled very musty. When your eyes finally adjusted fully to the light, you looked up and saw big black hairy bats hanging from the roof of the cave. You stopped dead in your tracks. Your heart was ready to jump out of your chest when you saw a bat flap its wings. You screamed out loud and ran out as fast as you could.

Paragraph B

On the May long weekend, Erin went camping with her parents to Banff National Park. She wasn't very happy because all of her friends were getting together and she wasn't able to go. When Erin and her parents got to the camp site, she decided to take a walk in the forest. She could feel the long green grass tickle her legs. As Erin walked along the forest trail, she looked up the hill and saw an opening. Erin was very curious to see what was in the cave so she made her way up the hill. When she reached the cave, she was a little bit scared. Erin's heart started to race and her hands began to sweat. As she walked down the dark creepy cave, her eyes started adjusting to the dim light. She could feel the cool damp air reach her nose. It smelled very musty. When her eyes finally adjusted fully to the light, she looked up and saw big black hairy bats hanging from the roof of the cave. Erin stopped dead in her tracks. Her heart was ready to jump out of her chest when she saw a bat flap its wings. She screamed out loud and ran out as fast as she could.

Paragraph C

On the May long weekend, I went camping with my parents to Banff National Park. I wasn't very happy because all of my friends were getting together and I wasn't able to go. When we got to the camp site, I decided to take a walk in the forest. I could feel the long green grass tickle my legs. As I walked along the forest trail, I looked up the hill and saw an opening. I was very curious to see what was in the cave so I made my way up the hill. When I reached the cave, I was a little bit scared. My heart started to race and my hands began to sweat. As I walked down the dark creepy cave, my eyes started adjusting to the dim light. I could feel the cool damp air reach my nose. It smelled very musty. When my eyes finally adjusted fully to the light, I looked up and saw big black hairy bats hanging from the roof of the cave. I stopped dead in my tracks. My heart was ready to jump out of my chest when I saw one flap its wings. I screamed out loud and ran out as fast as I could.

Answer: Paragraph B is speaking in the third person point of view because it uses the words "she and her" throughout the paragraph

On the May long weekend, Erin went camping with **her** parents to Banff National Park. **She** wasn't very happy because all of **her** friends were getting together and **she** wasn't able to go. When Erin and **her** parents got to the camp site, **she** decided to take a walk in the forest. **She** could feel the long green grass tickle her legs. As Erin walked along the forest trail, she looked up the hill and saw an opening. Erin was very curious to see what was in the cave so **she** made **her** way up the hill. When **she** reached the cave, **she** was a little bit scared. Erin's heart started to race and **her** hands began to sweat. As **she** walked down the dark creepy cave, **her** eyes started adjusting to the dim light. **She** could feel the cool damp air reach **her** nose. It smelled very musty. When **her** eyes finally adjusted fully to the light, **she** looked up and saw big black hairy bats hanging from the roof of the cave. Erin stopped dead in **her** tracks. **Her** heart was ready to jump out of **her** chest when **she** saw a bat flap it's wings. **She** screamed out loud and ran out as fast as **she** could.

4RI.9   Integrate information from two texts on the same topic in order to write or speak about the subject knowledgeably.

COMPARE AND CONTRAST INFORMATION

When you *compare* two things, you look at the ways in which two or more things are alike. When you *contrast* two things, you look at the ways in which they are different. The overlapping circles below form a Venn diagram. This kind of diagram is used to compare and contrast two things—in this case, fiction and non-fiction. The space where the circles overlap contains similarities, or things that are common to both fiction and non-fiction. The separate parts contain the things that are different.

COMPARING AND CONTRASTING WOLVES AND DOGS

Another way of comparing and contrasting is to list the similarities and differences.

COMPARING WOLVES AND DOGS

- similar appearance
- can interbreed
- carnivorous (meat eaters)
- give birth to pups
- four-footed mammals
- have coats of fur that thicken in winter

CONTRASTING WOLVES AND DOGS

- wolves are wild; dogs are domestic
- wolves are unpredictable, would not make good pets
- wolves are hunters and scavengers; dogs depend on humans to feed them
- dogs can be trained to work for humans: guide dogs, sled dogs, sheep dogs, retrievers, etc.

4RL.7   Make connections between the text of a story or drama and a visual or oral presentation of the text, identifying where each version reflects specific descriptions and directions in the text.

4RI.7   Interpret information presented visually, orally, or quantitatively and explain how the information contributes to an understanding of the text in which it appears.

THE FUNCTION AND EFFECT OF IMAGERY

Imagery in writing is the use of figurative language like metaphors, similes and personifications.

Imagery is a way authors create vivid descriptions in their written pieces. They use imagery as a way to appeal to their audiences' five sense (taste, touch, hearing, smell and sight) and from there they paint a clear picture of the scene, the character and/or the ideas in the readers' minds.

A writer will use words or phrases that can help the reader relate, by triggering the memory of a personal experience. When an author uses imagery correctly in their writing, it can make the reader truly experience what the author is trying to say, in the way that the author wants their ideas to be understood.

Authors will use imagery in their writing to make it more visually effective or meaningful, depending on the purpose for their writing. When an author uses imagery, he/she is trying to make you see something through new eyes. The author wants you to understand more than the literal meaning of the object/idea he/she is speaking about.

SOME EXAMPLES OF IMAGERY

Example

The wind whispered softly in her ear to calm her down.

(The wind is being compared to the human action "whispering" in a way to have the reader visualize the calming affect it had on the girl.)

Example

I felt as light as a cloud on warm summer day.

(The author is saying that the narrator felt very light and free as a cloud might be in the sky. Do you see how instead of just telling you "I felt light." The author has given another way for you to understand how light, with a visual image, "as a cloud.")

Example

The cat was a streak of lightning across the floor chasing the mouse.

(The image that the author is trying to get you to visualize, is the cat being fast, like a bolt of lightning in the sky. The cat was quick.)

METAPHORS—THEIR FUNCTIONS AND THEIR EFFECT

A metaphor is a comparison of two things to help better describe one of the two things, without using the words "like" or "as."

Some examples of a metaphor are as follows:

Example

The stars were diamonds in the sky.

To little Bobby, the tub was a giant sea.

He is a mountain of a man.

He had the eye of a tiger.

Authors will use a metaphor in their writing to make it more visually effective or meaningful, depending on the purpose for their writing. When an author uses a metaphor, he/she is trying to extend beyond the literal meaning of the object/idea he/she is speaking about.

Some of the major functions and effects a metaphor can serve in one's writing are as follows:

- Metaphors can add to the poetic language of a text.
- Metaphors can give other mental images to help aid in the memory of certain concepts or ideas.
- Through rich language, a metaphor can impact a readers emotional side more vividly.
- Metaphors can help resolve any confusion and help aid in the perception of an idea or concept.
- Metaphors can help aid in the understanding of a concept or idea.
- Metaphors can help spark more creativity.
- Metaphors can help influence the mind set of a reader/listener on a particular concept or issue.
- Metaphors can give new meaning to a word or group of words.

SYMBOLISM - ITS FUNCTIONS AND ITS EFFECTS

Writers will use tools called literary devices to add meaning to their stories and to make them interesting to read. There are many literary devices but in this lesson we are going to focus on symbolism, the functions and effects it has in written pieces.

Symbolism, in general terms, is using one thing to stand for something else.

It can be a representation of something beyond what is actually being described. Symbolism is usually used to give a deeper meaning or significance to another idea, object, event or relationship.

The writer uses the object, situation or action within a story to indirectly suggest another meaning.

It is usually used to expand and intensify the meaning being portrayed within the written piece.

Example
An American flag might help symbolize the United States.

Using a tiger in a written piece might help symbolize the idea of strength or fierceness.

Using a dove in a written piece might help symbolize the idea of peace.

Using a white lamb in a written piece might help symbolize the idea of peace, gentleness or innocence.

The use of different colors can also help symbolize different things. Purple may symbolize royalty and green may symbolize money or envy.

A story may be at a dramatic part or climax, where the conflict between the characters is at it's peak, or the emotions of the characters are very high, an author may then have a storm happening. The storm may help symbolize the feelings or emotions of the characters at that moment in the story.

Symbolism can have many different function and effects on a reader, depending on the purpose of the author.

Some of these functions and effects are as follows:

- Symbolism can help communicate to people beyond the use of words.
- "A picture is worth a thousand words" is a great concept to describe symbolism in some cases. A picture can trigger or inspire meaning to something that might not have been as effective through words.
- Each symbol can bring personal significance to each person depending on their relationship, background knowledge or personal experiences with a particular symbol. Sometimes it is impossible to know what one's reaction might be to symbolism for these very reasons.
- Differing personal and cultural backgrounds may influence the way one interprets a symbol.
- Symbolism can be difficult or easy to interpret, depending on the authors purpose for writing.

THE PURPOSE OF VISUAL AND GRAPHIC MATERIALS

Have you ever heard the saying, "A picture is worth 1,000 words"? Well, many authors have thought of that very saying. Many people are visual learners, and sometimes need a picture or a graphic to help them understand a topic a little better. For example, if you were learning about an eclipse of the moon, you might want some graphics to help show you where the moon, earth and sun are positioned, instead of just reading about it, and trying to create your own mental picture in your mind.

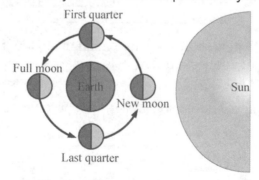

Sometimes authors will use illustrations in their story books to help the reader have a clearer idea of what the characters and setting actually look like.

Graphics in a text are usually used to add important information or enhance the learning or enjoyment of the text.

Graphics will be used to add to the information or to enhance the message in a particular text. Depending on the purpose for the graphic, there are many different types of graphics that can be used. A graphic may come in the form of a:

- picture
- photograph
- diagram
- table
- chart
- graph
- time line
- flow chart
- web diagram
- Venn diagram

Suppose you were trying to describe to your mother how you want to rearrange your room after she paints the walls. Would it be easier to just show her what you mean with a diagram?

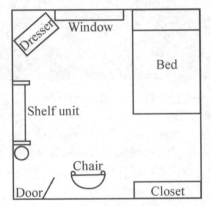

A graphic in a text may be used to help relay the information being taught using one particular image, or by using meaningful patterns or sequences. For example, a diagram may use one particular image, while a flow chart may arrange its information in a sequential order using a few different images.

Some graphics may be used to purely add enjoyment or humor to the text.

USE RETELLING AS A READING STRATEGY

To help yourself understand a story better, it is a good idea to retell, in your own words, the important events that happened in the story. Try to keep the retelling simple and in the order in which the events happened. Read the following excerpt from "The Watcher"

from The Watcher

George was a watcher. He watched TV. He watched cars, trucks and big machines. George watched clouds in summer…and snow falling in winter. George loved to watch shoppers at the mall and birds at the bird feeder….

One Monday at noon, …George sat quietly eating his lunch, watching the helpers dish out macaroni and hot dogs, watching orange juice rising up through drinking straws, watching the kids trade their desserts and watching the rain stream down the windows.

Suddenly, from across the room, George noticed Sarah, a girl from his class. She was clutching her throat and staring wildly at the kids around her.

"Sarah!" yelled George….

George saw the school nurse walking in the hall. George sprang out of his seat, jumped over two tables and shouted, in his loudest voice, "Miss Clayton!"

The nurse stopped and looked at George.

"Sarah's choking!" yelled George. He pointed at her.

Miss Clayton ran to Sarah. She knew just what to do.

When Sarah was breathing again, Miss Clayton led her away.

Everyone looked at George.

"It's a good thing you were here, George," said Dan.

"I saw a safety show on TV," said George. "It said to stay calm and take charge. So I did."

The kids all slapped George on the back and said, "Great!" and "Excellent!"…

—*by* Brenda Silsbe

Here is one example of how you could retell the passage:
As George ate his lunch, he was watching everyone around him. Suddenly he saw Sarah choking. He jumped up and shouted at the school nurse whom he saw walking by. The nurse quickly helped Sarah breathe again and took her away. All the other children told George what a great job he had done.

As you can see, the retelling is much shorter than the original story. However, it contains the key things that happened. It is like a summary of the story, that helps you remember what the story is about.

How Point of View Affects Format and Presentation

Point of view is defined as the angle of vision (like a camera) from which the story is told. There are three main points of view.

1. First person point of view is when the story is told from a personal perspective. You can recognize these stories because of the use of the pronouns *I*, *me*, *my*, *we*, and *us*.
2. Second person point of view is when the author uses the pronouns *you* and *your*. Second person point of view is most often used in choose-your-own adventure stories and when an author wants to give directions.
3. Third person point of view is when the story is told from the perspective of a narrator. You can recognize third person point of view by the author's use of the pronouns *he*, *she*, *his*, *they*, and *their*.

Format refers to the way that ideas and information are organized to make them easier to understand. Just like the alphabetical format of a dictionary makes words easier to locate, using the appropriate format in your writing, and understanding different formats in written materials, allow you to find and use information in ways that help you succeed in school and in life.

Format also refers to the way a book is put together to make it easier to use or more appealing to readers. For instance, picture books with single lines of the story at the bottom of each page are a familiar format in children's literature. Format includes such things as the following:

- Frequency and type of illustrations
- Type and size of font in printed text
- Use of color
- Inclusion of graphs, charts, maps, etc.
- How information is presented
- How information is ordered
- Inclusion of information "helps" like glossaries, indexes, appendixes, etc.

Some examples of information books that are recognizable by their formats are as follows:

- Encyclopedias
- Dictionaries
- Thesauruses
- Atlases
- Almanacs
- Textbooks
- Manuals

Point of View for Dictionary

The point of view is impersonal (third person). The purpose of the format is to communicate information about words in a clear manner. The numbers show the list of meanings from most common to least common. Italics are used to set examples apart from definitions.

> **cool** (kōōl), adj. –er, -est, *n., v. –adj.* 1. moderately cold. 2. permitting relief from heat; *a cool dress.* 3. not excited; calm. 4. lacking in cordiality. 5. calmly audacious. 6. unresponsive; indifferent. 7. *Slang.* a. great; excellent. b. socially adept. –n. 8. a cool part, place, or time: *the cool of the evening.* 9. calmness; composure. *–v.i., v.t.* 10. to become or make cool

POINT OF VIEW FOR SPECIAL NEEDS TEXT

The point of view is impersonal (third person) but intended to help a person with limited vision in a very personal way. The format of a Braille text has raised points in word patterns, so that a blind person can read the same words as a sighted person by using their fingertips against the raised patterns.

POINT OF VIEW FOR BUSINESS LETTER ENVELOPE

The point of view is implied to be second person, because the envelope is addressed to the intended receiver. The format is neat and tidy for clarity. The capital letters make the addresses look formal, because this is for a business letter.

EVALUATE ARCHETYPAL PATTERNS IN MYTHS

Myths are stories that are told about certain cultures and traditions. A myth seeks to explain why things are as they are, such as why rain falls. Some are based on truth but may have some fictional parts added.

Archetypal patterns occur again and again in myths.

WHAT IS AN ARCHETYPAL PATTERN?

An **archetype** is an image, symbol, or a specific character type, that is used repeatedly in a piece of literature. This repeated use us known as a pattern.

An archetype can be any type of typical person or personality in any culture; for example, a mother type, a father type, or a hero type.

Example

A mother type can be different from one person to the next, but when you look at history and mythological stories you can get a clear picture of the archetypal mother type. These mothers can be elevated into something more, like a queen or a goddess.

In Greek mythology, the symbol of goodness in motherhood is the Greek Goddess, Ceres (Earth Mother).

Example

Myths usually have some sort of hero in them. The hero in a myth is also an archetype. The typical hero usually changes the world through invention or discovery of things in such areas as agriculture, songs, fires, traditions or religions.

Following is a summary of the Greek myth explaining how the seasons came to be. Can you determine what the archetypes are?

Example

In the myth, Demeter, goddess of agriculture, has a beloved daughter, Persephone. Persephone disappears one day while taking a walk. It turns out that the Earth has opened and swallowed the girl. Down, down into the Underworld she has fallen, captive of Hades, god of the Underworld. Her mother is crazy with grief. Zeus, king of the gods, sends his messenger to fetch her back. Before letting Persephone go, Hades tricks her into swallowing six pomegranate seeds. Forever, she will have to return to him for six months out of each year. When Persephone returns to the Underworld, the chill winds of autumn and winter cover the earth. Six months later, the first blossoms of spring announce her arrival back to the welcoming arms of her mother, Demeter. That is how we have spring and summer.

Were you able to identify the archetypes in the above passage? If so, check out your answers below.

Hades - the god of the underworld - "The Bad Guy" archetype
Persephone - "Beloved Daughter" archetype
Zeus - King of the Gods - "The Good Guy" archetype
Demeter - "Welcoming Mother" archetype

EVALUATE ARCHETYPAL PATTERNS THROUGH HISTORY

WHAT IS AN ARCHETYPAL PATTERN?

An **archetype** is an image or symbol or a specific character type, that is used repeatedly in a piece of literature.

An archetype can be any type of typical person or personality in any culture; for example, a mother type, a father type, or a hero type.

Archetypal patterns occur again and again in history.

People who become well known in a certain area and then become a symbol for their area of expertise, actions or ideas can become archetypes in history.

Example

Mother Teresa is an archetype in history as a saintly woman.

Leonardo Divinci is an archetype in history for a talented artist.

Michael Jordan is an archetype in history for a superstar basketball player.

The archetypal reference to someone from history might sound something like this:

"That kid is going to be a Wayne Gretzky by the time he's eighteen."

EVALUATING ARCHETYPE PATTERNS ACROSS CULTURES

What is an archetypal pattern?

An **archetype** is an image or symbol or a specific character type, that is used repeatedly in stories, plays, and poetry.

An archetype can be any type of typical person, personality, or symbol in any culture; for example: a mother type, a father type, or a hero type.

Archetypal patterns can occur across cultures.

In many cultures, hope and good are usually associated with light, while evil is usually associated with dark.

ARCHETYPAL PATTERNS IN GREEK CULTURE

Example

If you look at the Greek gods, Ares is the god of war who is known for hatred and angry characteristics.

Ares is relative to the evil or dark side of human nature, and therefore can be associated with a dark archetype.

Example

The Greek goddess, Demeter, is the goddess of fertility and rebirth. The hope for rebirth can also represent a light archetype.

ARCHETYPES ACROSS CULTURES

Below are some commonly used archetypes that can carry across cultures. That means you will see them in stories from many different cultures.

Common archetypes that relate to the family are:

- Father—powerful, strong, stern, provider
- Mother—nurturing, soothing
- Child—beginning, birth

Common archetypes that are found in stories are:

- Hero—champion, achiever, savior/rescuer
- Old, wise man—guidance and knowledge
- Witch or sorcerer—danger, evil

Common archetypes that relate to animals are:

- Cat—crafty, self serving
- Dog—faithful, loyal
- Horse—enduring, persistent

WHAT IS A SHORT STORY?

In general, a *short story* is a fictional story that is usually written in a narrative format.

The length, form, and style can vary, depending on the preference of each individual author.

A short story is not as detailed or as complex as a novel. It will usually follow a simple beginning, middle and end format. A short story will usually have a single plot line, with a narrow focus, usually one simple setting, a few characters and a simple problem to solve. A short story will usually only cover a short time span.

Example

The Dinner Party

The country is India. A colonial official and his wife are giving a large dinner party. They are seated with their guests—army officers and government attachés and their wives, and a visiting American naturalist—in their spacious dining room, which has a bare marble floor, open rafters, and wide glass doors opening onto a veranda.

A spirited discussion springs up between a young girl who insists that women have outgrown the jumping-on-the-chair-at-the-sight-of-a-mouse era and a colonel who says that they haven't.

"A woman's unfailing reaction in any crisis," the colonel says, "is to scream. And while a man may feel like it, he has that ounce more of nerve control than a woman has. And that last ounce is what counts."

The American does not join in the argument but watches the other guests. As he looks, he sees a strange expression come over the face of the hostess. She is staring straight ahead, her muscles contracting slightly. With a slight gesture she summons the servant standing behind her chair and whispers to him. The servant's eyes widen: he quickly leaves the room.

Of the guests, none except the American notices this or sees the servant place a bowl of milk on the veranda just outside the open doors.

The American comes to with a start. In India, milk in a bowl means only one thing—bait for a snake. He realizes there must be a cobra in the room. He looks up at the rafters—the likeliest place—but they are bare. Three corners of the room are empty, and in the fourth the servants are waiting to serve the next course. There is only one place left—under the table.

His first impulse is to jump back and warn the others, but he knows the commotion would frighten the cobra into striking. He speaks quickly, the tone of his voice so arresting that it sobers everyone.

"I want to know just what control everyone at this table has. I will count to three hundred—that's five minutes—and not one of you is to move a muscle. Those who move will forfeit fifty rupees. Ready!"

The twenty people sit like stone images while he counts. He is saying "…two hundred and eighty…" when, out of the corner of his eye, he sees the cobra emerge and make for the bowl of milk. Screams ring out as he jumps to slam the veranda doors safely shut.

"You were right, Colonel!" the host exclaims. "A man has just shown us an example of perfect control."

"Just a minute," the American says, turning to his hostess. "Mrs. Wynnes, how did you know that cobra was in the room?"

A faint smile lights up the woman's face as she replies: "Because it was crawling across my foot."

—by Mona Gardner

WHAT IS A FABLE?

A fable is a short fictional tale. It usually has characters which are animals, and a moral lesson to be learned through its story.

Well-known fables are stories from Aesops´ Fables, such as "The Tortoise and The Hare" (where the moral of the lesson is "Slow and steady wins the race") or "The Lion and The Mouse" (where the moral of the story is that even little friends may prove to be big friends in the end.)

Example
Below is an example of a fable:

Snakes Eat Frogs

"Hi, Momma!" Snake-boy hissed as he hopped up for a kiss. "What's for dinner? I'm starved!"

His mother took one look at Snake-boy bouncing around on the floor and screamed, "Land sakes, boy! What in the world are you doing? You're going to break every bone in your body!"

"I'm hopping, Momma. My friend, Frog-child, taught me how to do it. We had so much fun playing in the meadow! What's for dinner?"

His mother nearly swallowed her tongue. "Did you say you were playing with a frog?"

"Yeah, Momma. We had a great time. What's for dinner?"

"Snake-boy," his mother cried. "Come here, and stop that ridiculous hopping."

The little snake slithered quickly onto her lap.

"Snake-boy, snakes EAT frogs. You may have played with him all day, but snakes eat frogs: when you get hungry, you eat him!"

Snake-boy was both horrified and bewildered.

"But Momma, Frog-child is my friend. We played together and told stories—and he taught me how to hop. I couldn't eat him!"

"Snake-boy," sighed his mother, "snakes eat frogs. Don't come home asking for dinner when you've been playing with a frog all day!"

Snake-boy slithered to the entrance of the burrow and thought about what his mother had told him.

—from *In the Great Meadow* by Skid Crease

WHAT IS A NOVEL?

A novel is a fictional piece of writing that tells a story. It is greater in length than a short story, so the story has more twists and turns in the plot, and usually has a larger number of characters.

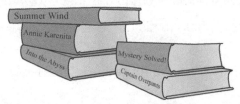

Most of the time, a novel will tell a story through character development and a series of events that allow the reader to understand the message or theme through a story line structure.

Novels are read by people of all ages, especially for their entertainment value. There are all types of genres of novels and graphic novels (a novel with pictures) to be read by all types of readers. Examples of these genres include the following:

- Mystery
- Adventure
- Fantasy
- Science fiction
- Historical

WHAT IS A FOLKTALE?

Folk tales are traditional stories that are usually passed down through word of mouth from generation to generation. Legends are also considered to be folktales according to this definition.

- Folktales will usually teach you a lesson about a culture's beliefs or practices.
- Folktales usually deal with good versus evil.
- The characters who do the good deeds always win in the end, and the evil characters are usually defeated or suffer suitable punishment for their wrongdoings.

The following stories are two examples of folktales.

Example

The Night Troll and Her Boat at Mývatn

It is the general consensus that Lake Mývatn and the area around it, with its splendor and variety of landscape and its abundance of natural resources, are one of the Creator's masterpieces. The lake and its environs are also one of Iceland's major tourist attractions, often called by such names as the "jewel of the north".

Lake Mývatn (Midge Lake) derives its name from the clouds of midges that may be seen there on fine days. When the vast numbers of midges fly up in a dark mass, it sometimes seems as if the sun is covered by cloud. Lake Mývatn is 36.5 km^2 in area, and hence Iceland's fourth-largest lake. It is relatively shallow, no more than 4.5 m at its deepest point. The shore of the lake is heavily indented, and there are about 40 islands and islets of different sizes. One of the best known of these is Slútnes, famed for its luxuriant vegetation. Mývatn boasts abundant bird life, including a larger number of duck species than anywhere else on earth. The ducks' nesting colonies were an important resource in times past and duck eggs are still gathered today. The lake also offers better trout fishing than any Icelandic lake, and the Mývatn trout is reputed to be better and tastier too. The trout in the lake have always been a valued resource; in former times it was said that there was never famine at Mývatn, even though people might be dying of hunger in other regions.

The people of the Mývatn area have fished the lake since time immemorial, and a tale is told of successful fishing there in the 13th century, when Bishop Guðmundur the Good was traveling about the country. Once the bishop arrived at Mývatn, accompanied as usual by a great number of followers. He stayed overnight with all his company at Reykjahlíð, which has long been a calling-place for visitors to the lake, and still is. The farmer was not prepared for such a large number of guests and he ran out of food. Then he resorted to slaughtering three of his cows to feed all the visitors. Bishop Guðmundur was most grateful to the farmer for his hospitality and generosity, and he blessed all the resources of the Reykjahlíð estate. After this the farmer caught so much fish that summer that the catches more than compensated for the value of the three cows. Such good fortune was attendant on playing host to Guðmundur the Good and his followers.

Lake Mývatn and its surroundings are well worth additional consideration: south of the lake rise two great table mountains, Bláfjall and Sellandafjall, and to the southeast is Búrfell. In the east are the mountains Hverfjall and Námafjall, and to the north Krafla, Hlíðarfjall, and Vindbelgjarfjall. Large lava fields may be seen east of Lake Mývatn, and bizarre lava formations are found at Dimmuborgir (Dark Fortresses), along the lake at Kálfastrandarvogar and elsewhere. A huge explosion crater on the northwest side of Mt. Krafla, Víti (Hell), formed in an explosive eruption in 1724—the start of the "Mývatn Fires" which continued for five years. Recent lava fields may be seen around Leirhnjúkur and northwest of Mt. Krafla; these date from the "Krafla Fires" of 1975–84. Hverfjall, like Víti, is an explosion crater, formed about 2,500 years ago. Other important landmarks around the lake include the pseudo-craters at Skútustaðir, the geothermal area at Námaskarð with its sulphur and mud springs, and a delightful garden of trees and flowers that has been cultivated on Höfði, a small headland projecting out into the lake.

East of Lake Mývatn are Lúdentsborgir, a row of craters that derive their name from Lúdent, an explosion crater a little farther east. South of Lúdent is a slope known as Nökkvabrekka (nökkvi is a kind of boat, brekka = slope). A solitary rock on the slope resembles a boat in shape. The story of this boat or nökkvi is recounted in a folk tale:

Long, long ago, a troll-wife lived in the highland above Mývatn, which has been known ever since as Skessuhali (Troll-wife's Ridge). She was a night troll, and they are of such a nature that they must not see the sun, so they do their work by night. The troll-wife did the Mývatn folk great harm, for instance by stealing fish from the lake during the night. She is said to have had a small boat, which she rowed out on the lake, then carried home on her back before dawn.

One summer there were good catches in Strandarvogur bay. This was the best fishing-place in Lake Mývatn, and it has generally been so. The troll-wife made a habit of stealing the fish from the bay every night and the farmer at Strandarvogur was most discontented with this. One night in late summer, the troll-wife made for the bay to go fishing but when she arrived the farmer was there, fishing in her place. She did not feel able to tackle the farmer, for he had another three men with him. So she decided to wait until he had finished fishing.

But the farmer took his time, because he knew what the troll-wife planned to do and so he went on till near morning. The troll-wife was growing impatient but she did not want to give up and leave. When the farmer finally stopped his fishing, the troll-wife went and laid her nets in the bay. When she had finished fishing, she set off for home. But when she was a little more than halfway home to Skessuhali, the sun came up. Then the troll-wife is said to have put down the boat and climbed into it. And both boat and troll-wife turned to stone.

Evidence of the troll-wife's sad demise may still be seen. The boat still stands on Nökkvabrekka, about halfway between Mývatn and Skessuhali. The boat is similar in shape to those that are generally used for fishing on the lake, but larger. Signs of oars and rowlocks are even visible. And a pile of rock in the stern of the boat is believed to be the troll-wife, in her last resting place.

—*by* Jón R. Hjálmarsson, *translated by* Anna Yates

Example

Folktales usually take place in a faraway land and will usually have talking animals, royalty, peasants, or mythical creatures as characters. The shepherdess and her sisters in this next story were most likely peasants.

The Legend of the Panda

Long years ago, Dolma, a young shepherdess, lived with her sisters in the Wolong Valley, deep in the mountains of Sichuan province.

Each day, Dolma led her small flock of sheep up the steep slopes of the nearby mountain. The rat-a-tat of woodpeckers echoed as Dolma and her companions traveled past frosty waterfalls and over moss-covered rocky paths to the fragrant meadows.

While the sheep grazed, Dolma collected herbs to make medicines for the villagers. She also gathered mountain blossoms—red and gold poppies, gentians as blue as the mists that veiled the mountaintops, and purple violets that lifted their tiny faces to the sunlight.

On a morning when the air was sweet with spring, a young animal crept from the nearby evergreen forest. "Will you join our flock, little Beishung?" laughed Dolma.

By the trickling stream, the white cub nibbled tender shoots. His hunger satisfied, he frolicked among the sheep and lambs like a furry acrobat celebrating the end of the bitter winter. And each day thereafter, the white cub joined Dolma's flock to feed and play.

As she had so often, one day Dolma left her flock to gather herbs. Among the dewy grasses, she filled her basket and returned to the meadow. Dolma smiled to see her peaceful flock.

Suddenly, a snow leopard pounced from a tree. With teeth bared, he attacked the white cub. "Beishung!" cried Dolma, as the sheep fearfully bleated.

The leopard's sharp claws tore at the helpless little Beishung. Yet Dolma, without a thought for her own safety, grabbed a stout branch and rushed forward to beat the leopard mightily.

The wounded cub withdrew weakly into the flock. The angry leopard, eager to claim a life, turned upon Dolma. Moments later, the shepherdess lay lifeless upon the trampled grass, the basket's blossoms and herbs strewn about her.

Great were the lamentations in the Wolong Valley when the people learned of Dolma's death. Heavy was the grief of all the Beishung. They knew of Dolma's kindness to the cub, and of the brave act that had saved him from the leopard's claws.

On the appointed day, the sorrowful villagers gathered with Dolma's heartbroken sisters to bury the shepherdess. Gray clouds hung heavily over the mountains as the white cub led the Beishung to join the funeral procession.

As the bamboo grasses rustled in damp winds, the mourners smeared themselves with ashes. The Beishung wiped their tear-filled eyes with sooty paws and hugged themselves as they wept. They covered their ears against the loud lamentations and, wherever the animals touched their snowy bodies with ash, the black soot stained forever the thick white fur.

Dolma's sisters [were] convinced they could not live without her … As the sisters' cries reached the snow-capped mountaintops, the earth beneath their feet spoke to them with fierce rumblings, as if it, too, were mourning. The villagers fell back in awe as the earth suddenly split wide and received the four loving sisters. Where the meadow once lay rose a mountain of four peaks that reached beyond the clouds.

And this is exactly why to this day, the giant panda, the "bamboo-eater," wears the black marks of mourning in memory of the brave shepherdess, Dolma. His home and refuge is in the protective forests of Siguniang, the "Mountain of the Four Sisters."

Author's Note

Giant panda fossils found in Asia reveal that the mammal appeared nearly two million years ago....

Pandas belong to their own subfamily within the bear family.... In China, the panda is called *daxiong mao*, meaning "large bear cat."

The panda has the digestive system of a carnivore, or meat-eater; however, through the centuries, it has adapted to a vegetarian diet and feeds mainly on the leaves and stems of bamboo. In fact, the panda spends most of its waking hours eating up to forty pounds of bamboo each day. Its flexible forepaws allow the panda to hold onto its food. Strong flattened molars and powerful jaw muscles enable the panda to crush tough bamboo stalks, and a thick lining protects the panda's esophagus from bamboo splinters.

The giant panda has thick, coarse fur that protects it from the cool, damp climate of the Chinese forests. Some scientists believe that the panda's black markings provide camouflage in the shadows of the forests; others think the coloring warns other animals to keep away from the panda's territory.

The panda leads a solitary life of eating and sleeping, except in the spring when mating may occur. One or two tiny cubs, covered in fine white fur, are born in August or September. After one month, they develop their black panda markings. The young live with their mother until they're about eighteen months old. Then the pandas are on their own as the mother leaves to breed once again.

Scientists estimate that fewer than one thousand pandas remain living in the wild in China today. As people develop more land, the bamboo groves are destroyed and the panda has less to eat, and a smaller area to inhabit. Climate changes and the natural life cycle of the bamboo in some areas have left the panda with little to eat. Despite strict laws, hunters continue to trap and kill the panda as its pelt becomes increasingly valuable.

Efforts to save the endangered panda—the international symbol for the World Wildlife Fund—have been well-documented. The WWF is an agency that has been working on panda conservation in China since 1980. A captive breeding program at Wolong, China's largest panda reserve, has been successful in recent years: thirty-six cubs have been born since 1987, and twenty-one have survived past six months.

There are plans to create new reserves in China, and to establish links between isolated panda populations. Special programs continue to alert the world of the decreasing number of pandas, and recent technology provides more options in the fight to save the endangered panda.

—by Linda Granfield

What Is an Adventure Story?

An adventure story is a fictional written genre or type of story that usually involves action-filled and thrilling experiences for the characters. Adventure stories usually have engaging plot lines and daring heroes who manage to come through victorious when faced with trials and dangers.

An adventure story has these characteristics:

- Can vary in length, depending on the author's purpose and his/her intended audience.
- Still needs to follow the basic story line structure to be complete.

The following passage could be a great beginning to an adventure story.

Example

from Hoot

Roy would not have noticed the strange boy if it weren't for Dana Matherson, because Roy ordinarily didn't look out the window of the school bus. He preferred to read comics and mystery books on the morning ride to Trace Middle.

But on this day, a Monday (Roy would never forget), Dana Matherson grabbed Roy's head from behind and pressed his thumbs into Roy's temple, as if he were squeezing a soccer ball. The older kids were supposed to stay in the back of the bus, but Dana had snuck up behind Roy's seat and ambushed him. When Roy tried to wriggle free, Dana mushed his face against the window.

It was then, squinting through the smudged glass, that Roy spotted the strange boy running along the sidewalk. It appeared as if he was hurrying to catch the school bus, which had stopped at a corner to pick up more kids.

The boy was straw-blond and wiry, and his skin was nut-brown from the sun. The expression on his face was intent and serious. He wore a faded Miami Heat basketball jersey and dirty khaki shorts, and here was the odd part: no shoes. The soles of his bare feet looked as black as barbecue coals.

Trace Middle School didn't have the world's strictest dress code, but Roy was pretty sure that some sort of footwear was required. The boy might have been carrying sneakers in his backpack, if only he'd been wearing a backpack. No shoes, no backpack, no books—strange, indeed, on a school day.

Roy was sure that the barefoot boy would catch all kinds of grief from Dana and the other big kids once he boarded the bus, but that didn't happen....

Because the boy kept running—past the corner, past the line of students waiting to get on the bus; past the bus itself. Roy wanted to shout, "Hey, look at that guy!" but his mouth wasn't working so well. Dana Matherson still had him from behind, pushing his face against the window.

As the bus pulled away from the intersection, Roy hoped to catch another glimpse of the boy farther up the street. However, he had turned off the sidewalk and was now cutting across a private yard—running very fast, much faster than Roy could run and maybe even faster than Richard, Roy's best friend back in Montana. Richard was so fast that he got to work out with the high school track squad when he was only in seventh grade.

Dana Matherson was digging his fingernails into Roy's scalp, trying to make him squeal, but Roy barely felt a thing. He was gripped with curiosity as the running boy dashed through one neat green yard after another, getting smaller in Roy's vision as he put a wider distance between himself and the school bus.

Roy saw a big pointy-eared dog, probably a German shepherd, bound off somebody's porch and go for the boy. Incredibly, the boy didn't change his course. He vaulted over the dog, crashed through a cherry hedge, and then disappeared from view.

Roy gasped.

"Whassamatter, cowgirl? Had enough?"

This was Dana, hissing in Roy's right ear. Being the new kid on the bus, Roy didn't expect any help from the others. The "cowgirl" remark was so lame, it wasn't worth getting mad about. Dana was a well-known idiot, on top of which he outweighed Roy by at least fifty pounds. Fighting back would have been a complete waste of energy.

"Had enough yet? We can't hear you, Tex." Dana's breath smelled like stale cigarettes. Smoking and beating up smaller kids were his two main hobbies.

"Yeah, okay," Roy said impatiently. "I've had enough."

As soon as he was freed, Roy lowered the window and stuck out his head. The strange boy was gone.

Who was he? What was he running from?

Roy wondered if any of the other kids on the bus had seen what he'd seen. For a moment he wondered if he'd really seen it himself.

—by Carl Hiaasen

What Is A Mystery Story?

A mystery story is usually about a crime that is central to the plot where the main character or characters need to solve a problem surrounding the crime. A mystery story tends to have several unexpected twists and turns, with a high energy story line to keep the audience engaged and interested.

Example

---

from "The Outlaw Who Wouldn't Give Up"

LAUGH IN THE DARK FUN HOUSE, 1976. A television crew is filming an episode for the *Six Million Dollar Man* inside a fun house in Long Beach, California. When they set up the cameras in a dark corner, the director doesn't like the looks of the dummy dangling from the ceiling. It is sprayed with glow-in-the-dark paint and doesn't fit the scene.

A technician reaches up to remove the dummy. Plunk! The arm falls off. Everyone is shocked to see that this arm has a real bone. The dummy is a mummy, and no one knows who it is or how it got there. They call a medical examiner, and another mummy mystery begins.

As usual the mummy has clues. A look at the bones and tissues reveals a man about thirty years old with unhealthy lungs, probably from pneumonia. But he died from a gunshot wound in his chest. A copper bullet jacket still in the body turns out to be .32 caliber made between the 1830s and World War I.

Those are interesting clues but only the beginning. The examiner looks into the mummy's mouth. Inside is a 1924 penny and a ticket stub from "Louis Sonney's Museum of Crime, So. Main St., L.A." A check of driver's license records turns up Dan Sonney, who says that his father bought the mummy (they thought it was a dummy too) in the 1920s from an unknown source. Louis had a traveling road show called "The March of Crime" and charged people twenty-five cents to see the "outlaw who would never be captured live." When Louis died in 1949, the road show was put into storage until 1971. Then these items were bought by Spoony Singh, owner of the Hollywood Wax Museum.

Spoony thought the mummy was made from papier-mâché and sent it off to Mount Rushmore to be part of a haunted house. It was returned as "not being lifelike enough." Eventually the body lost its identity and ended up dangling at the fun house in front of the TV crew.

It takes only a few days to get this much information, but questions still remain. Who was this man? The police want to identify the body. They keep looking and find an old partner of Louis Sonney's who remembers buying the mummy from a retired coroner in Tulsa, Oklahoma. The partner thinks the mummy had been a robber.

Then people in Oklahoma get involved in this mummy mystery. The history buffs search through libraries and state records and come up with a prime suspect: Elmer McCurdy, alias Elmer McCuardy, Elmer McAudry, Frank Curtis, and Frank Davidson. Profession? Outlaw. They find one final clue that only a mummy could solve. Elmer had a scar two inches long on the back of his right wrist.

Elmer's age and height match up with the mummy. And then, even though his skin is now hard and cracked, the two-inch scar can still be seen on the wrist just as described in the prison records.

Now that Elmer McCurdy is identified, the police manage to gather some details about how he died. As the story goes, he joined a gang that robbed a train in Kansas. The gang hoped to get several thousand dollars being sent as a payment to Indian tribes, but they picked the wrong train. Instead they got forty-six dollars and some whiskey. Elmer drank some of the whiskey and slept in a hayloft until the posse found him early the next morning. There was a gun battle, and three times Elmer was asked to give up. He refused every time and was eventually killed on October 7, 1911. Since no one claimed the body, the coroner preserved him in arsenic and for a nickel allowed the curious to take a peek at Elmer, who became known as the "Bandit Who Wouldn't Give Up." After five years carnival owners posing as "relatives" claimed him and got him started in sideshows and circuses. Eventually he became an attraction without a name.

After he was identified in 1977, Elmer was given a eulogy on television and flown back to Oklahoma on a jet never seen in his lifetime. He is buried there under two cubic yards of concrete just in case anyone might think about digging him up and looking at him one more time.

—from *Mummy Mysteries: Tales from North America* by Brenda Z. Guiberson

WHAT IS A FANTASY?

A fantasy is a type of genre. It is a fictional story that usually takes place in strange, imaginary worlds. The writer uses their creative imagination to tell the story. Unicorns, mythical creatures, mermaids, heroes, and magic are some of the elements found in a fantasy.

Example
- The Harry Potter Series
- The Chronicles of Narnia (including *The Lion, the Witch, and the Wardrobe*) by C.S. Lewis
- *Alice in Wonderland* by Lewis Carroll
- *The Secret World of Og* by Pierre Berton
- *Lord of the Rings* by J.R.R. Tolkien

DEMONSTRATE AN UNDERSTANDING OF THE MAIN IDEA WITHIN A TEXT

If you were asked to explain in one sentence what a reading passage was about, this would be the main idea. Very often the title gives the reader the main idea, but not always. Sometimes the title is to short to give enough information.

Example
For example, if you were given a passage with the title "Dolphins Are Our Friends," the main idea might well be something like "Dolphins are our friends and it is important to protect them." If the same passage were just called "Dolphins," you would definitely have to read further to figure out what the author's main point about dolphins would be.

If the passage does not have a title, thinking about what title you would give it may help you to come up with the main idea.

Very often the main idea is given in one strong sentence either near the beginning or at the end of the passage. In the dolphin passage we just imagined, the last sentence of the passage might be something like "You can see how important it is to protect these wonderful creatures from fishermen and from pollution of their ocean homes." This probably sums up the whole passage.

You can also think about why you think the author wrote the text to help give you the main idea.

IDENTIFYING THE MAIN IDEA AND SUPPORTING DETAILS

Can you pick out the main ideas and the supporting details in the following article?

When you read each paragraph, ask yourself these questions:

- What is the topic or central idea in this paragraph?
- Which sentence expresses the central idea? (Hint: often the first sentence, but not always)
- What are the details that explain, support, or expand that main idea?

FROM "MONSTER WAVES, TSUNAMIS"

Tsunamis

Tsunamis are caused by underwater earthquakes and volcanic eruptions, and they are the largest waves of all. Earthquakes occur when two **tectonic plates** collide or slide past each other. When an earthquake occurs under the ocean, the ocean bottom shakes. This movement causes the water above to become **displaced**. Waves of energy spread out in all directions from the source of the vibrations in ever-widening circles. As the tsunami approaches shore, the waves rub against the sea floor. **Friction** causes the waves to slow down and build from behind, creating huge piles of water that crash onto the shore.

Rogue Waves

Sometimes, groups of large ocean waves caused by a storm slam into a powerful ocean current passing in the opposite direction. When this happens, several storm waves pile up to form gigantic waves called rogue, or freak, waves. These waves can be more than 100 feet (30 meters) tall and can bury cargo ships beneath the sea. Rogue waves are most common off the coasts of Japan, Florida, and Alaska. Currently, a project known as WaveAtlas monitors the oceans with satellites. Over the next few years, oceanographers hope to analyze these satellite images to help them better understand why freak waves occur.

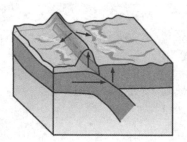

In the open ocean, tsunamis can be 100 miles (161 km) long and travel up to 500 miles per hour (805 km/h). Tsunamis pass under ships easily because the waves do not build until they approach land.

Whirlpools

Whirlpools are revolving currents formed by the meeting of opposite-moving ocean currents, the collision between currents and tides, or tides moving along uneven coasts. When churning, whirlpools make a loud sucking noise. Small ships may become trapped and wrecked by the force of the revolving water. Larger ships find steering difficult. The best-known whirlpool is the Maelstrom, off the coast of Norway. Here, currents flowing through **fjords** around islands create the whirlpool. Another well-known whirlpool is named the Old Sow and is formed between New Brunswick and Maine.

Physical barriers in the water can create whirlpools because they disrupt the regular flow of water.

Krakatoa

On August 27, 1883, an undersea volcano called Krakatoa erupted in the Indian Ocean. The force of the explosion caused a tsunami with waves more than twelve stories high. The waves were so powerful that small islands were washed away and thousands of boats were sunk. As the waves circled the southern tip of Africa, they entered the Atlantic ocean, traveling at 400 miles per hour (640 km/h). The tsunami destroyed more than 300 communities and killed over 36,000 people.

Scientists believe that the waves from Krakatoa circled the globe two or three times before running out of energy.

An Example to Use as a Model

The paragraph below is about tsunamis, one of the main topics in the article. The main idea of the paragraph is underlined. The numbered sentences contain supporting details about the main idea.

Sometimes, groups of large ocean waves caused by a storm slam into a powerful ocean current passing in the opposite direction.(1) When this happens, <u>several storm waves pile up to form gigantic waves called rogue or freak waves</u>.(2) These waves can be more than 100 feet (30 meters) tall and can bury cargo ships beneath the sea.(3) Rogue waves are most common off the coasts of Japan, Florida, and Alaska. (4) Currently, a project known as WaveAtlas monitors the oceans with satellites.(5) Over the next few years, oceanographers hope to analyze these satellite images to help them better understand why freak waves occur.(6)

TRY IT YOURSELF

You could try to make brief notes for each paragraph. Put the main idea at the top of the list of supporting details as a heading. Under that heading, list the supporting details. The notes on the first main paragraph might look something like the example below.

Example

Main Idea:Tsunamis are largest the waves:

• Caused by underwater earthquakes and volcanoes
• Tectonic plates move and displace water
• Wave energy meets friction from sea floor
• Friction causes waves to pile up as they near land
• Piled up waves crash over the land

ANOTHER WAY TO LOOK AT MAIN IDEAS AND SUPPORTING DETAILS

If you do not want to put the ideas in lists, you could try a method that is more like a diagram. Below you can see the main ideas and supporting details from an article about poisonous spiders. Even though you have not read the article, you can clearly see the important information arranged in a detail map. The main ideas are on the left. The supporting details are to the right in boxes. For example, the first main idea is that there are several types of poisonous spiders. The supporting details are a naming of the main types of poisonous spiders: black widows, brown recluse, hobo spiders, and yellow sac spiders.

In a main idea or detail map, you list the main ideas on the left, with the details going across the page. Here is an example of a detail map made from an article about poisonous spiders:

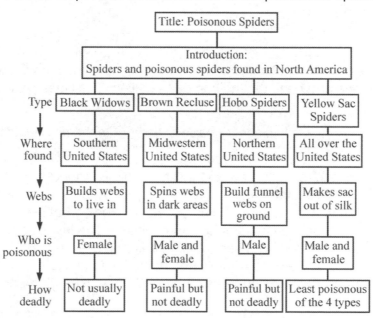

If you are able to pick out the main ideas and supporting details from what you read, you have mastered one of the most important skills in good reading comprehension. Remember, good readers make great students, because they feel successful in school.

DISTINGUISHING SUPPORTED INFERENCES IN TEXT

Do you remember what an inference is? An inference is an idea that is suggested or implied by the text, but not something that you are told directly. For example, if your brother slams the front door and comes stomping toward you with a scowling face, you can be pretty sure that he is not too happy that you borrowed his video game without asking. You do not have to be directly informed that he is angry. That is inference.

Supported inferences are different from inferences made by making predictions or using your prior knowledge. Supported inferences can be backed up with evidence from a passage. You can support an inference by using the following aspects of a passage:

- Significant quotes from the text, especially statements by respected experts on the topic or issue
- Well-known or proven facts
- Statistics
- Examples from the text that support your point. You should always use specific examples from a story, for instance, to support your conclusions about a character. When you write about a poem, you should quote phrases or words that illustrate the poet's use of imagery to achieve a special mood or particular effect.

To practice inferring while reading, ask yourself the following questions:

1. What do I think this story/text is about?
2. How did I know that?
3. How do I think the character feels?
4. Why did I think that would happen?
5. How did I know that?
6. What is the author actually saying?
7. What is the author leading me to believe? How?

Example

In this paragraph from *Magyk*, the highlighted sentences give you the clues you need to know that Boy 412 had been unhappy in the army and that he had been bullied. The clues provide the support for the inference that he is unhappy.

"Good morning, everyone!" Aunt Zelda's cheery voice called out to the pile of quilts and their inhabitants by the fire.

Boy 412 woke up in a panic, expecting to have to tumble out of his Young Army bed and line up outside in thirty seconds flat for roll call. **He stared uncomprehendingly at Aunt Zelda, who looked nothing like his usual morning tormentor, the shaven-headed Chief Cadet, who took great pleasure in chucking buckets of icy water over anyone who didn't jump out of bed immediately. The last time that had happened to Boy 412, he had had to sleep in a cold, wet bed for days before it dried out.** Boy 412 leaped to his feet with a terrified look on his face but relaxed a little when he noticed that Aunt Zelda did not actually have a bucket of icy water in her hand. Rather, she was carrying a tray laden with mugs of hot milk and a huge pile of hot buttered toast.

UNDERSTAND CONTENT-SPECIFIC VOCABULARY

Often, you can understand the meaning of a word by reading it in context. The word context refers to the words in the sentence around a word. The *context* of a word will help you to understand the word.

This means you may need to **re-read the sentence or even the paragraph that contains the word**. You also may need to **read ahead** a bit, to try figuring out what is being talked about in the passage. When you understand the context, you will be more likely to figure out what the unknown word might mean. When you reread or read ahead, look for familiar words or ideas that may give you a hint about the unfamiliar word.

Example
The lady was always very *generous*. She gave the children toys to play with and homemade cookies to eat.

If you did not understand the meaning of the word generous when you read that the woman gave toys and cookies to the children, you could probably guess that *generous* means almost the same as *kind* or *giving*.

As a student, you have to read all the time in most of your subjects. Most of these subjects are presented in units or chapters. Most units, no matter what the subject is, will have some terms you will have to learn. Before you can understand the unit, you must understand central vocabulary terms. Often, subject-specific terminology is introduced at the beginning of a new unit or chapter. For instance, before beginning a poetry unit, most English teachers will review terms such as *simile*, *lyric*, *metaphor*, and so on, because these terms are often used with poetry.

VOCABULARY SIGNALS

- **bolded** in math, social studies, and science textbooks
- defined at the beginning of a new chapter
- defined at the bottom of the page or at the back of the textbook
- used by the teacher on the board, overhead, or for assignments

Learning new words helps you better understand and remember information, ideas, and concepts.

TRICKS FOR LEARNING TERMS

Some strategies for adopting new words are to

- add them to your personal vocabulary list
- learn the meaning of the words in the content area
- practice spelling them correctly, even if you have to check back in the textbook
- use them in answers and assignments
- give them a permanent home in your "mental computer" (brain) so you can retrieve them as needed

IDENTIFY A COMPARE/CONTRAST PATTERN IN INFORMATIONAL TEXT

It is important to be able to recognize a compare/contrast pattern in information passages and articles. This is a way of organizing information and facts in a way that shows similarities and differences between two things, groups, animals, places, etc.

Read the passages below to see if you can identify which one contains the **compare/contrast pattern**.

Example

Jaguars and Leopards

Jaguars and leopards are close cousins that are very similar in appearance. The jaguar has a thicker body than the leopard, with shorter legs and a shorter tail. The spots on a leopard are smaller and closer together than on a jaguar. The spots on a jaguar are larger and uneven. One of the most significant differences between the two animals is that the jaguar lives primarily in North and South America, whereas the leopard lives in Africa and Asia. Both animals have cat-like qualities and are excellent predators that can run at tremendous speeds.

The Cheetah

The cheetah is a member of the cat family. It is well known for its tremendous speed, reaching up to 65 mph. A cheetah has a tan-colored coat with small black spots; however, a cheetah does not have spots on its belly. The cheetah only lives to be about 12 years old in the wild. Its favorite foods include gazelles and hares. The cheetah can be found in Africa, Asia, and the Middle East.

IDENTIFY SEQUENTIAL/CHRONOLOGICAL PATTERN IN TEXT

A sequential/chronological pattern in text is important because it helps the reader make sense of what's happening. A story that follows a fixed order of events is more likely to be understood and remembered by the reader.

Can you identify which of the following paragraphs has a sequential/chronological pattern?

Paragraph #1

As I was packing my suitcase, I wondered how long I would be gone. Suddenly, I heard the taxi pull up in my driveway. I grabbed my luggage, purse and tickets and hurried out the door. It took about 15 minutes to get to the airport. I unloaded my luggage, checked-in, and headed to the terminal to await my flight. It was finally time to board the flight. I was excited and scared all at the same time. Hours passed and I was about to arrive in a different land. I never thought I'd have the courage to put my life on hold and help re-build a town that had been so badly damaged by an earthquake. They needed me and I was finally here to help.

Paragraph #2

I was excited and scared all at the same time. I grabbed my luggage, purse and tickets and hurried out the door. As I was packing my suitcase, I wondered how long I would be gone. Hours passed and I was about to arrive in a different land. Suddenly, I heard the taxi pulled up in my driveway. They needed me and I was finally here to help. I unloaded my luggage, checked-in, and headed to the terminal to await my flight. It took about 15 minutes to get to the airport. I never thought I'd have the courage to put my life on hold and help re-build a town that had been so badly damaged by an earthquake. It was finally time to board the flight.

If you chose paragraph #1, then you are correct. If a story has clearly organized ideas that follow a consistent pattern, then the reader will be able to easily follow and understand the story.

PROPOSITION AND SUPPORT

Most of the time, writers organize their information to best persuade readers to agree with their ideas or opinions. Their opinions are supported by several reasons or arguments. Read the paragraph below to see how persuasive information can be organized.

Logging companies should choose selective logging over clear-cut logging in order to benefit the environment. In selective logging, only certain trees are cut, but clear-cut logging is easier, cheaper and knocks down every single tree. Just one tree is probably home to hundreds of insects, and there are birds and mammals who live at different levels in the forest. Many wildlife species, such as lynxes and snowshoe hares, need an old growth forest with a mixture of live, dead, and rotting trees. People, however, need forest wood for houses and furniture. Selective logging not only provides wood for people, it also protects the forest habitat by leaving some trees standing.

You could summarize the proposition and support like this:

Proposition: Selective logging is better for the environment than clear-cut logging.

Support (arguments or reasons):

1. Selective logging leaves some trees standing
2. Insects, animals, and birds need live, dead, and rotting trees in their habitat
3. Clear-cut logging removes all live trees
4. With selective logging, people can still have lumber and wildlife can still have some trees
5. Both groups benefit, making the extra expense worthwhile

COMPARE INFORMATION ON ONE TOPIC FROM MANY SOURCES

If you are assigned a research project on endangered animals, you are going to review many resources such as books and videos before deciding what information to use. One book might list the White Rhino as the most critically endangered animal on earth, while other sources might state it as number two on the list of most endangered animals.

Your job is to compare the information in each of the sources, and decide which source is more credible and reliable. Determine which information is conflicting and which is consistent. Also, if 10 resources state the White Rhino as the second most endangered animal, and only 2 resources state it as the most endangered, then you can choose to go with the majority.

If you are researching information on the Giant Panda from three different sources, it is important to compare the information from all three sources before using it. This will help you determine accurate and reliable information.

CONTRAST INFORMATION ON ONE TOPIC FROM MANY SOURCES

Contrasting information on one topic from many sources allows you to develop a broad view of the topic, and also helps you to eliminate inaccurate or questionable information and facts from your notes.

If you are assigned a research project on endangered animals, you are going to review many resources such as books and videos before deciding what information to use. One book might list the Bengal tiger as the fastest animal on earth, while other sources might state it as number two on the list of the world's fastest animals.

Your job is to compare the information in each of the sources and decide which is more credible and reliable. Decide which information is conflicting and which is consistent. Also, if 10 resources state the Bengal tiger as the fastest animal and only 2 resources state it as the second fastest, then you should choose to go with the most consistent resources. In this case, it would be the 10 resources that state the Bengal tiger is the fastest animal on earth.

Example

Let's say you are researching information on African elephants and you use several resources for your research. You will notice that many of the resources will repeat the same information. However, some resources may show contrasting information. It is during this time that you will need to determine which information is more credible. You may choose to search out other resources to continue to compare with the one containing the contrasting information.

Once you have collected multiple resources with enough information, you must determine which information is the most relevant to your research topic and/or assignment given.

IDENTIFYING CAUSE-AND-EFFECT PATTERNS IN INFORMATIONAL TEXT

Writers use cause and effect to develop paragraphs. These paragraphs tell why events happened and why things are as they are. A cause-and-effect pattern is often used in writing that informs, explains, or persuades.

Some cause-and-effect words and phrases are *because*, *as a result*, *why*, *when*, *therefore*, *so*, *for this reason*, and *if… then*.

Example
It was Games Day at school, and the children were looking forward to a day of playing games outside.

However, at 11:30 A.M., a thunderstorm with lightning, strong winds, and heavy rains began, which resulted in all the children having to go indoors. Because the afternoon activities were canceled, the children had to stay in their classroom.

You can put the examples you have found into a table.

Cause	Effect
Thunderstorm	Children went inside.
Activities canceled	Children stayed in the classroom.

HOW FORMAT MAKES INFORMATION ACCESSIBLE

The way that a passage is organized is called *format*. The format of a research paper is different from the format of poem. The format of your writing should make it easier for readers to follow and understand what you have written.

Following are some examples of information books that are recognizable by their formats.

- Dictionary
- Encyclopedia
- Thesaurus
- Atlas
- Manual

Illustrated below are some examples of formats that make the type of information being presented very accessible.

BUSINESS LETTER FORMAT

The format of the letter is set up to clearly show dates, addresses, the sender and receiver of the letter, and its purpose.

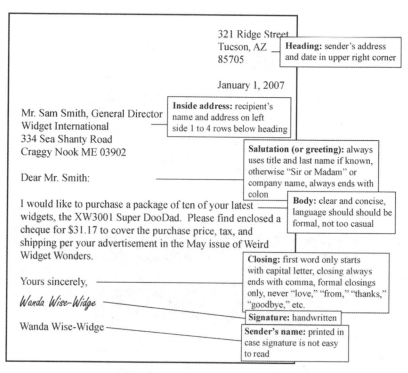

DIAGRAM FORMAT

When diagrams are formatted clearly in your science text, with arrows and labels, it is easy for you to learn the information. You can see at a glance that this diagram demonstrates the water cycle.

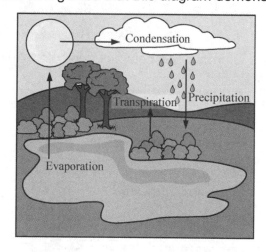

NEWSPAPER FORMAT

Headlines, subheads, and photographs help readers to locate information quickly in a newspaper. Those items help to make up the format of a newspaper.

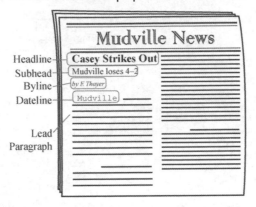

CALENDAR FORMAT

When you check the calendar, you want to be able to quickly spot the day and date of your next baseball game, or whether your birthday falls on a weekend. The format of a calendar is clear and easy to use for daily events and special occasions.

July 2013						
S	M	T	W	T	F	S
1	2	3	4	5	6	7
8	9	10	11	12	13	14
15	16	17	18	19	20	21
22	23	24	25	26	27	28
29	30	31				

BROCHURE FORMAT

The format of a brochure presents information in columns and colorful pictures to help readers scan the information quickly and efficiently.

How Graphics Make Information Accessible

Graphics are visual additions to a story, article or book, like photographs, illustrations, charts, or graphs. When you are reading a fiction or non-fiction book that has graphics to accompany the text, it is important to recognize that the graphics are there to add to your understanding.

If the graphics are in a story book, they may have more details then the text mentions. These graphics can help in your understanding of the story line or the characters within the story.

Example

A picture book story says: Mary received the important letter from her mother and as she read it, she cried and cried.

This story may have a graphic that has picture of the letter her mother wrote, or other pictures that help you as a reader to understand the effect of the letter on Mary.

Example

If a short story or chapter book has a story about a group of friends who were fund raising for their club, a graphic in this fictional story may be a chart of their total earnings, as the book continues, and as they raise more and more money.

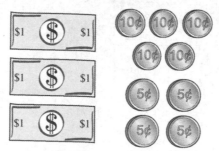

This graphic can give you more information and further support the text. It can also give more of a visual understanding to those who need it. Some students learn more from pictures than they do from the printed text.

These are just a few examples of how graphics can make information accessible in a fictional story.

If there are graphics in a non-fiction text, these graphics can be informative about the topic being discussed or explained.

Example

If a text book you are reading is talking about the provinces of Canada, a graphic that might accompany the text could be a map of Canada with the provinces outlined.

This graphic can be beneficial to you the reader, as it shows a visual of where the provinces are located within Canada and what they may look like in comparison to one another.

How Diagrams Make Information Accessible

A **diagram** is a simple drawing of an object or a process. It can be used to explain what happened in an experiment. It can be used to explain how something works. A diagram is sometimes easier to understand than words. All parts of the diagram should be labeled.

This student-drawn diagram shows how water goes through different states in the water cycle. Sometimes it might be necessary to draw a diagram to show how you arrived at an answer or conclusion.

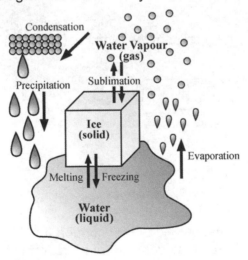

You can make a map diagram to show where something is. For example, a student drew a map to show the location of a pond. This is the pond that the student used to perform a nature study for her science project.

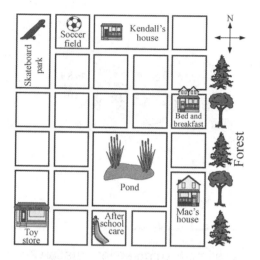

4W.2a   Write informative/explanatory texts to examine a topic and convey ideas and information clearly. Introduce a topic clearly and group related information in paragraphs and sections; include formatting, illustrations, and multimedia when...

HOW ILLUSTRATIONS MAKE INFORMATION ACCESSIBLE

When you are reading a fiction or non-fiction book that has illustrations to accompany the text, it is important to recognize that the illustrations are there to add to your understanding.

If the illustrations are in a story book, they may have more details then the text mentions. These illustrations can help in your understanding of the story line or the characters within the story.

Example

A picture book story says, "Jack was always getting into trouble."

What might come to your mind as a visual in your head?

Without looking at the illustration in the book, you may think this story was talking about a young, mischievous boy.

To your surprise, the illustration has a picture of a little puppy dog eating a child's shoe.

Jack is not a boy, he is a puppy!

This is just one example of how illustrations can make information accessible in a fictional story.

If there are illustrations in a non-fiction text, these illustrations can be informative about the topic being discussed or explained.

Example

In a book all about kangaroos, one page may be talking about how mother kangaroos carry their babies in their pouch.

If you have never heard of, or seen a kangaroo pouch, you may not be able to understand what a pouch is.

In the illustration that accompanies this page there is a picture of a mother kangaroo carrying the baby kangaroo in her pouch.

This illustration would be very helpful to understand what a kangaroo's pouch looks like.

CHARTS MAKE INFORMATION ACCESSIBLE

Charts can help you organize your information so that it is easier to understand.

KINDS OF CHARTS

For example, a **sequence chart** might look like this.

Topic

First
↓
| Then |
↓
| Then |
↓
| Then |
↓
| Last |

On a **similar/different chart**, you can list things that are the same and things that are different.

Topic

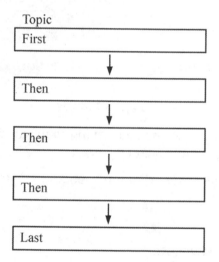

On a **summary chart**, you can organize your thoughts to help you stay focused and on topic. The chart below is a special kind of summary chart called a KWL chart.

Topic

What I Know	What I Want to Know	What I Learned

UNDERSTAND HOW MAPS MAKE INFORMATION ACCESSIBLE

Maps are pictures or drawings of places. Maps can show the way to places like bird's nests, which may be through paths in the forest. Maps are also used to find out about the locations of places and about the roads that go to those locations. For example, if you wanted to know where Jacksonville was located in Florida, you could look at the map shown here:

A map of Florida

Maps are drawn to scale. This means that one inch on the map stands for a set distance in real life. You can find out how far away a location is using this scale.

Maps also have legends. Legends describe what the lines and markers on the map mean. A map might show the following features:

- Bodies of water
- Landforms, such as mountains and valleys
- Heights of mountains and depths of valleys
- Parks and wildlife areas
- Number of people in an area
- Transportation information, such as railways and airports

UNDERSTANDING HOW GRAPHIC ORGANIZERS MAKE INFORMATION ACCESSIBLE

Graphic organizers are tools that you can use to group and organize text information. The following graphic organizers can help you make information more accessible:

- Lists
- Outlines
- Story maps
- Information webs
- Sequencing charts

Example

Information webs can be used to organize descriptive or informative passages. Suppose you read a passage that describes different games that are played with balls. You could organize the information in the passage into an information web. Here is a simple information web for ball games. It could be part of a larger web for sports.

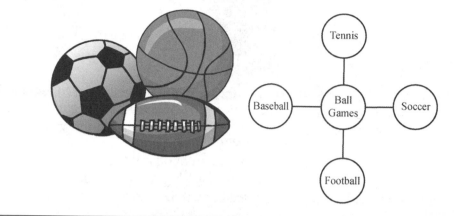

Example

Another example of a graphic organizer is a **story map**. A story map can help you understand or remember the different parts of a story.

If you fill out the given chart with information from a story, you might understand the story better and be able to remember it more clearly later on.

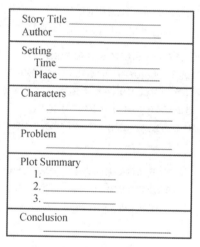

4RI.8   Explain how an author uses reasons and evidence to support particular points in a text.

IDENTIFY EVIDENCE THAT SUPPORTS THE MAIN IDEAS IN A TEXT

Authors must have a logical story line, that usually has events which build upon one another to make an engaging plot. There are key events or ideas within the text that are used to help support the main ideas. Authors may use specific details in the descriptions of the characters, the setting, the plot line, etc., that give evidence about the main ideas of the entire text.

In the following passage, the author, Aaron Taouma, provides evidence throughout about the main idea of the story.

As you read the passage, try to pick out details in the story which help support the main idea.

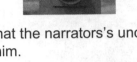

The main idea is based around the fact that the narrators's uncle is a crazy cab driver who never fails to entertain the people who get a ride with him.

An Invite from Uncle

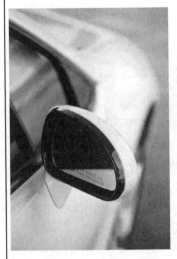

Driving in Uncle's taxi was like entering another world, a crazy, mixed-up world where anything could and did happen. This world is my Uncle's home, not a taxi but a rolling chariot of dreams and tales and you as his special guest.

Just getting into Uncle's taxi, you knew this was something different. He would decorate the inside of his taxi with all kinds of frilly bits, a mix between kitsch and FOB, Christmas lights, pictures of Jesus, hanging tennis balls and even a disco ball.

Uncle also played a mix of Island and rock and roll music on his tape deck and you could be forgiven for thinking that you were riding in a rolling disco or even an evangelist tour bus. But this simply was Uncle, a part of him.

Uncle loved telling stories. He especially loved the one about the Elvis impersonator who jumped into his taxi and instead of paying for his fare plugged a microphone into Uncle's sound system and sang for the entire ride. Apparently, things got so carried away that when they stopped at the lights the impersonator jumped out and danced and sang on the street. Uncle turned up the sound and the whole street stopped to look and listen. It was a real traffic-stopper, Uncle would say.

Yep, Uncle had all the celebs in his taxi and it was funny how whoever was in the news at the time, Uncle just happened to have picked them up the night before: Mini-Me from *Austin Powers*, Mr. T from *The A-Team*, even Michael Jackson and his monkey. My Uncle had them all and with each there was a story, a fantastic story to be told.

Uncle's driving was a whole other experience too, a scary and nerve-racking one. He wouldn't drive as such but let his taxi drive while he sat and talked. Uncle would turn and look you straight in the eyes and have whole conversations, including hand gestures and self-applause, while the taxi swerved from side to side, over the median strip, towards parked and oncoming cars and back again. The whole time you would sit holding on for dear life, with a look of horror on your face as you screamed, "Look at the road!"

Then Uncle would drop you off, shaken and yet exhilarated. He would smile and say, "See you soon," and you would stand on the street dumbfounded at the very thought.

But you know what? Uncle never ever had an accident and driving with him was cheaper and more exciting than an amusement park or a show. So, if you're looking for an experience in the city, look for a taxi, the one with the flashing lights and a disco ball. There you'll find my Uncle. He'll invite you into his world, his home and an experience you won't soon forget.

—by Aaron Taouma

Some of the evidence in the text that helps support the main idea from the story, "An Invite From Uncle" is as follows:

- "Driving in Uncle's taxi was like entering another world, a crazy mixed up world, where anything could happen."
- "You as his special guest."
- "Just getting into Uncle's taxi, you knew this was something different."
- "Uncle loved telling stories."
- "… the whole street stopped to look and listen."
- "My uncle had them all and with each there was a story, a fantastic story to be told."
- "Uncle's driving was a whole other experience too, a scary nerve wracking one."
- "Then Uncle would drop you off, shaken and yet exhilarated."
- "Driving with him was cheaper and more exciting than an amusement park or a show."
- "He'll invite you into his world, his home and an experience you won't soon forget."

Do you see how these specific lines in the passage really help give evidence that supports the main idea of the text? Do you see that the narrator's uncle was an entertaining cab driver who made a difference in the many people's lives he met?

These sentences directly affect the ideas presented in the story. They help build and support the main idea, and the text would not be the same without them.

COMBINE INFORMATION FROM MORE THAN ONE SOURCE

When you are learning about a topic, it is a good idea to read several articles. What information gets repeated? What information is different or new? After you read, you can write down some of the comparisons (similarities) and contrasts (differences) that you find. As you see what facts get repeated, it becomes easier to combine the information from different sources.

Imagine that you have a research topic: "The California Gold Rush." You have found the following three articles:

- "The California Gold Rush"
- "California Gold Rush"
- "The Rush for Gold"

As you read each article, you could underline interesting or important facts or ideas.

You can then compare the articles by creating a chart with the information that you have read. On the chart, use only words that you understand. This will make it easier for you to combine and present your research.

Article 1: The California Gold Rush	Jan 24, 1848, James Marshall finds nuggets near building site for John Sutter's mill
	Half a million people came
	1849: found gold in quartz, led to underground mine lasting 100 years
	1852: gold production reached $81 million
	Lasted from 1848 to 1864
Article 2: California Gold Rush	Jan 1848 gold discovered at Sutter's mill
	Lasted from (1848 to 1855)
	300,000 people came
	Gold seekers called "forty-niners"
	Faced many hardships
	Simple panning led to more complicated methods
	Great wealth for a few
	Good Effects: San Francisco, roads, churches, schools, towns, laws, new state (1850), railroads
	Bad Effects: Native Americans attacked, environment
Article 3: The Rush for Gold	Many did not find expected gold
	Started businesses they had been in before
	Lasted 1849 to mid-1850s
	Ended in 1859 when silver was discovered in Nevada
Same in All 3 Articles	Started in 1848 (Article 3 says "By 1849 the rush was on.")
	Started in California
	People came from all over the U.S.

Here are some ways that you can think critically about this information:

1. Notice the information that differs in the three articles, like the actual dates of the gold rush. You could conclude that dates are rough estimates, especially when different observers attach them to different important research questions, like "What event started the California Gold Rush?"
2. Notice the different information from each article that you could include in a report under your own headings.
3. Notice that you have many facts about the Gold Rush. These often include names of people and places, and dates of specific events like discoveries.
4. Notice that the articles contain opinions of the writer, like "a half million people from around the world descended upon California" and "some 300,000 people came to California." Opinions of the writer may or may not be true.
5. Come up with a main topic for your research, for example: "The Gold Rush helped create the state of California." Pick a topic that you can support with facts, evidence, or knowledge from the ideas and information in the articles.

As you think about the information you have collected, using guidelines similar to those above, you will be able to combine your information in a report or writing piece, using your own subtopics and without repeating information.

4.RF.3a Know and apply grade-level phonics and word analysis skills in decoding words. Use combined knowledge of all letter-sound correspondences, syllabication patterns, and morphology to read accurately unfamiliar multi-syllabic words in context...

USING INFERENCING TO UNDERSTAND UNFAMILIAR WORDS

Sometimes when you are reading, you will come across a word that you do not understand or do not know. When this happens, it is important that you stop and try a few different strategies to figure it out. If you don't, your comprehension of the story or passage could be affected.

One strategy is to use **inferencing** skills to figure out what an unfamiliar word might mean, by seeing it in its context. **Inferencing** means making your best educated guess about a word by using your background knowledge and ideas to help figure out an answer. You will need to figure out what a word might mean from the clues the author gives you, as well as using your own knowledge and experience.

You may need to **reread the sentence or even the paragraph that the word falls in**, or **read ahead** a bit to try figuring out what is being talked about in the passage. When you have a solid understanding of the context, you will be more likely to figure out what the unfamiliar word might mean, and begin thinking of different similar words that could fit in its place.

If this still has not helped, you could try asking yourself, "What word do I know that would make sense in the place of the new word in this sentence?" Then try substituting the familiar word in the sentence and read the passage to see if the word makes sense in the text.

TRYING OUT THE STRATEGY

Using a nonsense word, **MAXORIUM**, let's see if we can give a logical meaning to it, by using it in the context of the paragraph.

Jacob could hardly wait for the **MAXORIUM**. Five more days! Feverishly, he worked every waking minute to complete his model rocket. Last year, he had placed 2nd. Jacob was sure that this Saturday, he would be taking home the winner's trophy!

What word could you put in the place of the nonsense word, **MAXORIUM** in this sentence, based on the clues in the paragraph?

Some of the clues in the passage might be: **worked**, **complete**, **model rocket**, **winner's trophy**.

We could conclude that the word might mean a science fair or contest.

Now, read the sentence using our predicted word meaning and see if it makes sense. It fits!

NOW IT'S YOUR TURN

Read the following passage and see if you can infer a meaning for the unfamiliar highlighted word. Remember to see what other words in the passage may be giving you clues as to what the word might mean.

Sally woke up from her deep sleep. She could not believe she had slept for so long. She got out of her bed, got dressed and headed down to the kitchen. "Man, I am thirsty," she thought to herself. She reached up into the cupboard, grabbed a **BRIDA** and then poured herself some orange juice. "Delicious!" she thought.

Do you think you have any guesses as to what the nonsense word **BRIDA** might mean?

Here are some clues if you need some help: She's in the **kitchen**. She's **thirsty**. She went into the **cupboard**, grabbed a **BRIDA**. She **poured** herself some **orange juice**.

We could probably come to the conclusion that the word **BRIDA** might mean, **cup** or **mug**.

Replace our mystery word **BRIDA** with the word **cup**.

Sally woke up from her deep sleep. She could not believe she had slept for so long. She got out of her bed, got dressed and headed down to the kitchen. "Man, I am thirsty," she thought to herself. She reached up into the cupboard, grabbed a **CUP** and then poured herself some orange juice. "Delicious!" she thought.

The word **cup** would easily fit in place of **BRIDA**. It would make sense in the context and does not change the meaning of the passage.

UNDERSTANDING WORDS BY FINDING FAMILIAR WORDS WITHIN UNKNOWN WORDS

Sometimes when you are reading, you will come across a word that you do not understand. Often we do not have a dictionary on hand when we are reading, and we want to know what a word means. When this happens, try a few different strategies to figure it out. It could affect your comprehension of the text.

One strategy is to break the unfamiliar word down into smaller more familiar parts, because the word itself can give you clues about its meaning.

You are a detective trying to decode smaller words in the big, unfamiliar word! Figuring out each part of the word can help you determine its meaning. Breaking the word into separate parts, like its root word, the prefix and the suffix, can help unlock the actual meaning of the word.

Example

1. Look for familiar root words in a word. (For example: *Unfamiliar* - the root word is *familiar*)
2. Look at the the prefixes or suffixes of a word. (For example: *Unfamiliar* - the **un** is the prefix of the word)

In the word *unfamiliar* - we can determine the root word is *familiar*, meaning common or well known, and the prefix is UN - which usually means "not" or "opposite". Therefore, we can determine that the word *unfamiliar* means "not common".

TRY THIS STRATEGY

In the sentence below, TRIPOD is the word we are trying to figure out.

Example

Sophie took her camera out of its case and put it on the her TRIPOD to get ready to take a picture of herself and her friends.

When you look at the word *tripod*, you can see the prefix of the word is "TRI". Where else have you seen the prefix "TRI" in other words? Have you seen *triangle, tricycle, triceratops*? What would you guess TRI might indicate?

A triangle has three sides

A tricycle has three wheels

A triceratops dinosaur has three large horns

We can assume "TRI" means three. Now seeing the word TRIPOD in its sentence, we might assume it was a stand with three legs to hold the camera.

Once you have broken the word into smaller parts or words, see if it would make sense in its context. Our guess of a TRIPOD being a stand with three legs would make sense in the context of the sentence.

Now It's Your Turn

Can you figure out the meaning of the unfamiliar word, *rearrange*, in the following sentence? First, remember to find the root word, then see if you can find a familiar prefix or suffix.

My mom was upset with the renovations in our living room. She said she was going to have to REARRANGE all the new furniture so it would all fit inside.

Can you identify the root word? How about the prefix in the word? What other words have you heard of that have the same prefixes?

Think you have it? Check your answer below.

The root word of *rearrange* is "ARRANGE" and the prefix is "RE" Have you heard of the word of *arrange* before? It means to organize.

Have you ever heard of any other words that have the prefix "re" in them? How about these words: *rebuild, replay, rewrite, remake*? They all mean to do something over again; therefore, we can assume that the prefix "RE" means to do again or do over.

USING PREFIXES AND SUFFIXES TO UNDERSTAND NEW WORDS

Sometimes when you are reading, you will come across a word that you do not understand. Often you do not have a dictionary on hand when you are reading, and you want to know what a word means. When this happens, it is important that you stop and try a few different strategies to figure it out. It could affect your comprehension of the text.

One strategy is to break the unfamiliar word down into smaller, more familiar parts, because the word itself can give you clues about its meaning.

You are a detective trying to decode smaller words within a bigger, unfamiliar word. Figuring out each part of the word can help you determine its meaning. Breaking the word into separate parts, and looking at the prefix and the suffix, can help unlock the actual meaning of the word. The root word is the core of the word, the prefix is at the beginning of a word and a suffix is at the end of a word.

First, you want to look for familiar root words in a word. (For example: unfamiliar - the root word is familiar) Then you will also want to look at the the prefixes or suffixes of a word. (For example: unfamiliar - the 'un' is the prefix of the word)

In the word *unfamiliar* - we can determine the root word is *familiar*, meaning common or well known, and the prefix is UN - which usually means "not" or "opposite" So therefore we can determine that the word *unfamiliar* means "not familiar."

Below is a table of commonly used suffixes and prefixes. It would be useful for you to get to know these prefixes and suffixes, as that will help you with your word comprehension for years to come.

Common Suffixes	Common Suffix Word Meaning	Suffix Word Example
able	tells what kind	suitable, lovable
al	having to do with something	magical, national
ance	act, process of, state of	disappearance
ant	having the quality, manner or condition of a person, "one who..."	assistant, observant
ary	belonging to, connected with	legendary, momentarily
en	made of	wooden
ful	full of, or characterized by	hopeful, sorrowful
hood	the state of being	manhood, falsehood
ion	the act of	expression, perfection
less	unable, without	needless, regardless
ly	in what way or manner	lovely, gladly

Common Prefixes	Common Prefix Word Meaning	Prefix Word Example
ab	from	abnormal
ad	to	admit, adhere
be	by	before
com	with, together	compact
de	from	deduct
dis	apart	disappear, disengage
en	in	enjoy
ex	out	exhale
in	in	inhabit
in	not	incorrect
pre	before	preview, prediction
pro	for, forward	propel, pronoun
re	back	renovate, reconsider
sub	under	submarine
un	not	unhappy, uncommon

TRY THIS STRATEGY

In the passage below, *abolishable* is the word we will try to figure out.

The undercover cop told his partner that once he read the police report, it would be ABOLISHABLE. No one could ever see what he was about to read, and therefore he knew it had to be destroyed and never found again.

When you look at the word *abolishable*, you can see the root word is *abolish*? The suffix is ABLE. Where else have you seen words with the suffix "ABLE"? *Lovable, huggable, avoidable, comfortable*. What might ABLE indicate? *Lovable* means "able to love", *Huggable* means "able to hug", *avoidable* means "able to avoid", and *comfortable* is "able to have comfort". Therefore we might assume *abolishable* might mean "able to abolish". Abolish means to destroy.

Seeing the word *abolishable* in its sentence above, we might assume it means to destroy or get rid of.

It is safe to say that that meaning would make sense in the context of the paragraph.

NOW IT'S YOUR TURN

Can you determine the meaning of the word, *recover*, in the following sentence? First remember to find the root word, then look for a familiar prefix or suffix.

My mom was upset with the pop stains on the easy chair in our family room. She said she was going to have to RECOVER it before Grandma arrived for her visit.

Need a hint?

Can you identify the root word? How about the prefix in the word? What other words have you heard of that have the same prefixes?

Think you have it? Check your answer below.

The root word of *recover* is "COVER" and the prefix is "RE". Have you heard of the word of "COVER" before? It means to hide something from view.

Have you ever heard of any other words that have the prefix "re" in them? How about these words: *restore, refocus, restate, return*? They all mean to do something over again; therefore, we can conclude that the prefix "RE" means to do again or do over.

4L.4a   Determine or clarify the meaning of unknown and multiple-meaning words and phrases based on grade 4 reading and content, choosing flexibly from a range of strategies. Use context as a clue to the meaning of a word or phrase.

4.RF.4c   Read with sufficient accuracy and fluency to support comprehension. Use context to confirm or self-correct word recognition and understanding, rereading as necessary.

USING THE "DOES IT MAKE SENSE" STRATEGY TO UNDERSTAND TEXT

Sometimes when you are reading, you may come across words that you are unfamiliar with. There are many great strategies you can use to try figuring out these unknown words. One strategy is called the "Does it make sense?" strategy. What this strategy involves, is stopping your reading when you come to a part that is unfamiliar to you. It is at this time that you must ask yourself, "Does this make sense?"

If your answer is "no," you must go back and read over the text again.

Example

Read the following passage carefully. Ask yourself, "Does it make sense?"

Suzie gazed at the fridge for a long moment. "I wonder if it's done yet," she muttered.

Finally, she could wait no longer. She was so hungry! Suzie opened the fridge door, and there sat the huge piece of chocolate cake that she had been thinking about. "Aww…," whispered Suzie. "It needs to cook a little longer." Disappointed, she closed the fridge door and went back outside to play.

At first, the story may seem normal - a small girl opens the fridge because she is hungry, finds a piece of cake…. But, wait! Why would she say that the cake needs to cook longer, if it is in the fridge? Maybe if she was looking in the oven, it would make sense, but the cake is already cooked. The only food that might need more time in the fridge would be something like jello, or pudding, or perhaps some popsicles that her mother was freezing for a snack later. In other words, the story so far does not make sense.

Although the example above is quite silly, it shows the importance of text "making sense" to the reader. If what you are reading does not make sense to you, always reread that part. Sometimes you have:

- misunderstood a word
- misread a word that has a similar spelling
- read something into the sentence that wasn't there
- skipped over a few words or even a whole line

This strategy also works to help you understand strange new words that you encounter in text.

Example

"Tim's mother said he would have to visit an ophthalmologist before school started in September."

If you came across the word *ophthalmologist* in your novel, it might not make sense at first, because it is a strange word. However, if an earlier chapter mentioned that the main character, Tim, was looking at TV and complaining to his mother that the picture was "fuzzy", you could think of a phrase like "eye doctor", and try substituting it for the unfamiliar word. Would the sentence make sense now?

USE PHONETIC KNOWLEDGE TO FIGURE OUT WORDS

Phonetic knowledge refers to your knowledge of word and letter sounds. As a beginning reader, you learned the sound of long and short vowels, all the consonants, plus blends of many letters such as *oo*, *ea*, *ck*, *cl*, *fr*, and so on. You learned about syllables, which contain one vowel sound each. Sounding out each letter or letter chunk in a word is a very common strategy to figure out an unfamiliar word.

When sounding out a word you should first look to see if there are smaller words inside the word that you recognize. Letter chunks like the "ch" sound or the "sh" sound are usually easy to recognize.

When you sound out a word, you should start with the first letter, and say each letter sound out loud. Then, blend the sounds together. Try to say the word to see if you can recognize it.

Example

"It rained so hard that I got on my rain boots, ran outside and splashed in the puddles."

If you were unfamiliar with the word *splashed*, you would start by sounding out the first letter and continue to sound out each of the letters in the word.

Note: If you recognize a blend such as "sh", you know that those two letters, when placed together, make a different sound than if they were apart.

YOUR TURN

Look closely at the words below. Which words do you think are real words and which are alien words (meaning not real words)? You will need to use the "sounding out" strategy to help you decide.

- swamp
- kinter
- spectacular
- wunto
- karmpooa
- zebra
- terprimjo
- windy
- chocolate
- raggit

ANSWERS

Check your answers below. The words listed are <u>real words.</u>

- swamp
- spectacular
- windy
- chocolate
- zebra

<u>Alien words</u> are listed below:

- kinter
- wunto
- karmpooa
- terprimjo
- raggit

4L.6   Acquire and use accurately grade-appropriate general academic and domain-specific words and phrases, including those that signal precise actions, emotions, or states of being and that are basic to a particular topic.

CHOOSE PRECISE WORDS FOR WRITING TASKS

Precise means exact. Choosing precise words means that you are trying to choose the words that most exactly fit the:

- situation
- person who will be reading your assignment
- form you are using (letter, journal, story, note, etc.)
- idea or event you are trying to describe
- personality of the character who is speaking

The word **diction** refers specifically to word choice. You do not want to use words that will make understanding your ideas harder than is necessary. Instead, you should aim for accuracy and precision in your word choice. Only turn to special terms when more common words are not available to describe what you need to describe. Since diction is closely related to voice, the words you choose also give readers an impression of where you are placing yourself in relation to them. If your writing contains many unusual or long words, some readers may feel put off by your diction, and your time spent writing will be wasted. It is best to select common words so the reader's attention is not distracted from the ideas you are discussing.

Most of the time, identifying appropriate language becomes almost an automatic skill. Identifying and using appropriate language tends to be a matter of courtesy, necessity, or straightforward common sense. It is wise to adapt as the situation requires.

Sometimes, identifying appropriate language is as simple as being sensitive to situations. For example, when you leave your locker and walk through the doorway of your classroom, you will probably temporarily quit using the casual and slangy language you were enjoying with your friends before class. You will instead use more formal language, especially when the teacher is nearby! If you are asked to write something, you will try to use words that you are sure the teacher will like to read. However, even "appropriate" language can be exact and precise. Try to say exactly what you mean, even if you have to pause before you begin to write.

Writers choose their words carefully to fit the audience, text form, and purpose of their writing. For example, when writing a business letter, a writer should use a simple and more formal style than when writing a diary or blog entry. In the same way, a poet must choose his words very carefully to fit the form of the poem and capture the image or feeling he wants to express as precisely as possible. When writing a haiku, for example, a poet will choose very different words than when writing a limerick or a rhyming ballad on the same subject.

USING THE "SOUND-OUT" STRATEGY FOR UNFAMILIAR WORDS

Sometimes when you are reading, you will come across a word that you do not know. There are several strategies you can use to figure out the unknown word. One of these is called the **"sounding it out"** strategy.

Taking words apart, breaking them into chunks or syllables may be helpful in sounding out the unknown word.

Example
When sounding out the word "butter", breaking it into syllables would sound like "but - ter"

CONSONANT BLENDS

You can also look for familiar consonant blends. For example, try sounding out words that have "th" as a blend, such as thirty, three, think. Can you hear the consonant blend?

Other consonant blends you should be familiar with are in the table below:

Consonant Blends	Word Blend Examples
bl	blend, black, blue
br	break, brand, bring
ch	chapter, cheese, chain
cl	climb, clean, clock

Consonant Blends	Word Blend Examples
cr	cross, crow, crop
dr	drag, draw, dream
fl	flag, fly, flower
fr	friend, frog, free
gl	glad, glass, glue
gr	grass, green, grow
pl	plan, play, plus
pr	pray, press, predict
sh	shape, shade, sheep
sl	slam, sleep, slow
sm	small, smile, smoke
st	stand, steep, stop
th	that, there, think
wh	while, white, when

VOWEL SOUNDS

It is also important that you understand letter sounds as well as your long and short vowel sounds. Correctly determining the proper vowel sounds can really help you sound out your unknown words.

A, E, I, O, U are vowels. Each vowel can make two sounds; a long sound and a short sound. If there is only one vowel in a word, it will usually make a short sound. If there are two vowels in a word, then the first vowel will make a long sound and the second vowel will either stay silent or make a short sound.

Below are some long and short vowels that you should know:

Vowel Sound	Word Example
Short A sound	cap - the word "cap" only has one vowel "a" Hence, it has a short "a" sound.
Long A sound	cape - the word "cape" has two vowels. The vowel is an "a" and makes a long sound. The second vowel "e" sounds silent.
Short E sound	get - the word "get" only has one vowel "e" Hence, it has a short "e" sound.
Long E sound	read - the word "read" has two vowels. The vowel is an "e" and makes a long sound. The second vowel "a" sounds silent.
Short I sound	rid - the word "rid" only has one vowel "i" Hence, it has a short "i" sound.
Long I sound	ride - the word "ride" has two vowels. The vowel is an "i" and makes a long sound. The second vowel "e" sounds silent.
Short O sound	rod - the word "rod" only has one vowel "o" Hence, it has a short "o" sound.

Vowel Sound	Word Example
Long O sound	road -the word "road" has two vowels. The vowel is an "o" and makes a long sound. The second vowel "a" sounds silent.
Short U sound	tub - the word "tub" only has one vowel "u" Hence, it has a short "u" sound.
Long U sound	tube - the word "tube" has two vowels. The vowel is a "u" and makes a long sound. The second vowel "e" sounds silent.

4.RF.4a Read with sufficient accuracy and fluency to support comprehension. Read on-level text with purpose and understanding.

USING APPROPRIATE STRATEGIES FOR FULL COMPREHENSION

A good reader knows that when they read something, it is supposed to make sense. When you lose meaning of what you are reading, you need to choose a strategy that will help you make better sense of the text.

Strategies are ways to make learning easier. You need to use strategies for better understanding before, during and after you read. Some reading strategies that will help you gain full comprehension of a text are:

1. Access prior knowledge—what do you already know about this topic?
2. Look at the title and/or illustrations—what do you predict will happen?
3. Do a picture walk—have you skimmed the pages of the book to get an idea of what it will be about?
4. Connect—as you read, do you make connections to other stories, to your own experiences, or to the world around you?
5. Question—as you read, do you ask questions?
6. Reflect—after you have read, do you reflect on the information or relate it to a special character or to other information?
7. Extend and/or investigate—did you take your learning a step further by creating something new to showcase your learning or by checking other resources about the same topic?

All of these strategies will help you gain full understanding of your reading material. It's up to you whether you choose to use some or all of these strategies when reading.

When you are reading a textbook or studying for a test, one of the above strategies that is very useful is asking questions. You think up questions about your reading to help you look for the right information.

ASKING QUESTIONS

- As you read, break up the main sections into smaller sections.
- Ask yourself questions by using key words, headings and sub-headings, and topic sentences.

Example

Suppose in your science text you were reading about camouflage. As you read, look and see if you have phrases or words that you can turn into good questions, such as:

1. What is good camouflage?
2. How do animals/insects change their color?
3. In what other ways do animals/insects escape being noticed?
4. What are some of the quick changing creatures of the sea?
5. Which animals/insects use decoys?
6. Why would animals/insects use decoys?

4.RF.4b Read with sufficient accuracy and fluency to support comprehension. Read on-level prose and poetry orally with accuracy, appropriate rate, and expression on successive readings.

READ ALOUD FLUENTLY

Reading is a skill. When you become a master reader, you will be able to read with **fluency**, **accuracy** and **expression**. All three of these elements can affect each other.

In this lesson we are going to concentrate on reading with **fluency**.

Fluency in reading can be described as "reading with an effortless flow that is not choppy or broken." You should be aware of the punctuation within the text to help with your fluency, especially the periods and the commas.

• Periods in a text help you transition from one sentence or idea to the next. When you are reading aloud, the period will signal you that you must stop and take a breath.
• Commas in a text also help with transition **within** a sentence. When you are reading aloud, the comma will signal you to take a short breath, or at least a quick pause, and continue on.

A fluent reader does not take breaks within their reading to figure out an unfamiliar word. If you are a fluent reader, all or almost all of the words should be recognizable, allowing you to read them with ease.

Fluency is not about reading fast; it is about reading at a controlled, enjoyable and understandable pace.

WORK ON YOUR FLUENCY

Imagine that this symbol (*) is a breath or a pause in someone's reading. Read the following passage out loud, taking a breath each time you see the symbol (*).

Example

Mary and Joe were excited(*) for their first trip to the (*) mountains. (*) Joe had never seen so much snow in his life.(*) Mary(*) had not been (*)skiing in over 10 years (*)and could not wait to get onto the ski(*) hill. (*) They packed(*) up all of their clothes(*) and their (*)equipment(*) and set off for their (*) wintry (*)adventure.(*) The snow(*) seemed to(*) blow from every(*)direction and it became more and more(*) difficult to see the road as they (*)drove.(*) Suddenly, the car began to swerve.(*)

Mary (*)yelled, "Joe! (*)What is going on?"(*)

Joe (*) quickly(*) and (*)carefully pulled (*) over to the side of the road.(*) He got of the (*)vehicle and to his (*)horror, the front tire(*) was completely flat.(*)

How do you think that example sounded with all of those breaths? Very choppy, don't you think? Did it sound enjoyable to you? Do you think your audience might have a hard time understanding what you are reading? Probably so.

Let's look at the next example to see where you should take the appropriate breaths, for proper fluency while you read.

Example

Mary and Joe were excited for their first trip to the mountains.(*) Joe had never seen so much snow in his life.(*) Mary had not been skiing in over 10 years and could not wait to get onto the ski hill.(*) They packed up all of their clothes and their equipment and set off for their wintry adventure.(*) The snow seemed to blow from every direction and it became more and more difficult to see the road as they drove.(*) Suddenly, (*) the car began to swerve.(*)

Mary yelled,(*) "Joe!(*) What is going on?(*)"

Joe quickly and carefully pulled over to the side of the road.(*) He got of the vehicle and to his horror, (*) saw that the front tire was completely flat.(*)

How do you think that example sounded with the pauses only happening at the appropriate times (at the punctuation)? Do you hear the difference? The fluency is much better in the second example.

READ ALOUD ACCURATELY

Reading is a skill. When you become a master reader, you will be able to read with **fluency**, **accuracy** and **expression**. All three of these elements can effect each other.

In this lesson we are going to concentrate on reading with **accuracy**.

Accuracy in reading can be described as "reading without error." You must be aware of the words and the punctuation within the text to help with your accuracy while reading.

- Periods in a text help you transition from one sentence or idea to the next. The period will signal to you as the reader that you must stop and take a breath.
- Commas in a text also help you to make transitions **within** a sentence. The comma will signal you as the reader to take a short breath and continue on.
- An accurate reader does not take breaks within their reading to figure out an unfamiliar word. If you are an accurate reader, all or almost all of the words should be recognizable and read with ease.

WHAT AN ACCURATE READER DOES NOT DO

1. Omit words in the text
2. Add words into the text
3. Incorrectly read words in the text
4. Mispronounce words in the text
5. Repeat words in the text

YOUR TURN TO TRY

Let's look at the following passage with several errors included that were made by the reader:

Example

My sister and I were going on a horseback riding trip trip through the mountains. We could only take one one small back each. What would I need? I knew a first kit would be important. I also need plenty of water. After I finished packing I picked up my sister and set off on our adventure we arrived at the camp four hours later. It was freezing! I didn't antapate how much cold it would be in the mountains. I am wished I would have squeezed a sweater into my packed pack. I was immediately introduced to my horse Lucy who seemed by her kicking and panting.

How do you think that example sounded with all of those errors? Very choppy and confusing, don't you think? Did it sound enjoyable to you? Do you think your audience might have a hard time understanding what you are reading? Probably so.

The passage below is what the reader actually saw. Let's look at the correct version to see the difference when the errors in accuracy do not occur as the passage is read aloud.

My sister and I were going on a horseback riding trip through the mountains. We could only take one small backpack each. What would I need? I knew a first aid kit would be important. I also needed plenty of water. After I finished packing, I picked up my sister and set off on our adventure. We arrived at the camp four hours later. It was freezing! I didn't anticipate how much colder it would be in the mountains. I wished I would have squeezed a sweater into my tightly-packed backpack. I was immediately introduced to my horse, Lucy, who seemed, by her kicking and panting, to be quite anxious.

How do you think that example sounded, with no errors read? Do you hear the difference? The accuracy is much better in the second example, so therefore the fluency and comprehension of the text should be better as well.

4SL.4   Report on a topic or text, tell a story, or recount an experience in an organized manner, using appropriate facts and relevant, descriptive details to support main ideas or themes; speak clearly at an understandable pace.

READ ALOUD WITH APPROPRIATE PACING

Reading is a skill. When you become a master reader, you will be able to read with **fluency**, **accuracy** and **expression**. All three of these elements can affect each other.

Fluency is reading with an appropriate pace to increase understanding. When you are reading, your **pace** can affect your fluency. In this lesson we will be focusing on using the appropriate **pace** in your reading.

Pace is the speed at which you read a text. It can be measured by the amount of words read per minute.

Reading with the appropriate pace does not mean you must read fast or you must read slowly. The pace at which you read will depend on the different texts that you are reading.

- If you are reading for pleasure, your pace is fluent and steady.
- If you are searching through a lot of information, then your pace is more rapid.

PACE YOURSELF

Read the following passage. This passage should take you approximately a minimum of 2 minutes and 40 seconds to about 3 minutes to complete. If you are able to time yourself, you may find this helpful.

Example

An Invite from Uncle

Driving in Uncle's taxi was like entering another world, a crazy, mixed-up world where anything could and did happen. This world is my Uncle's home, not a taxi but a rolling chariot of dreams and tales and you as his special guest.

Just getting into Uncle's taxi, you knew this was something different. He would decorate the inside of his taxi with all kinds of frilly bits, a mix between kitsch and FOB, Christmas lights, pictures of Jesus, hanging tennis balls and even a disco ball.

Uncle also played a mix of Island and rock and roll music on his tape deck and you could be forgiven for thinking that you were riding in a rolling disco or even an evangelist tour bus. But this simply was Uncle, a part of him.

Uncle loved telling stories. He especially loved the one about the Elvis impersonator who jumped into his taxi and instead of paying for his fare plugged a microphone into Uncle's sound system and sang for the entire ride. Apparently, things got so carried away that when they stopped at the lights the impersonator jumped out and danced and sang on the street. Uncle turned up the sound and the whole street stopped to look and listen. It was a real traffic-stopper, Uncle would say.

Yep, Uncle had all the celebs in his taxi and it was funny how whoever was in the news at the time, Uncle just happened to have picked them up the night before: Mini-Me from *Austin Powers*, Mr. T from *The A-Team*, even Michael Jackson and his monkey. My Uncle had them all and with each there was a story, a fantastic story to be told.

Uncle's driving was a whole other experience too, a scary and nerve-racking one. He wouldn't drive as such but let his taxi drive while he sat and talked. Uncle would turn and look you straight in the eyes and have whole conversations, including hand gestures and self-applause, while the taxi swerved from side to side, over the median strip, towards parked and oncoming cars and back again. The whole time you would sit holding on for dear life, with a look of horror on your face as you screamed, "Look at the road!"

Then Uncle would drop you off, shaken and yet exhilarated. He would smile and say, "See you soon," and you would stand on the street dumbfounded at the very thought.

But you know what? Uncle never ever had an accident and driving with him was cheaper and more exciting than an amusement park or a show. So, if you're looking for an experience in the city, look for a taxi, the one with the flashing lights and a disco ball. There you'll find my Uncle. He'll invite you into his world, his home and an experience you won't soon forget.

—by Aaron Taouma

How did you do? How long did it take for you to read the above passage? If you completed the passage in less than 2 minutes and 40 seconds, you are probably reading at a very fast pace. This can affect your comprehension, fluency and accuracy in oral reading and you should try to slow down. If it took you longer than 3 minutes to read the above passage, then you may be taking too much time for pauses.

READ ALOUD WITH APPROPRIATE INTONATION

Reading is a skill. When you become a master reader, you will be able to read with **fluency**, **accuracy** and **expression**. All three of these elements can affect each other.

When you are reading aloud, it is important to focus on the **intonation** of your voice to add interest to your expression. Intonation is the way you adjust the volume of your voice to place more emphasis on certain words or phrases.

- The intonation can change a statement into a question or vice versa, depending on where you use intonation within the sentence.
- Intonation can affect the meaning of a sentence. The word that you stress can change the meaning of the sentence.

Read the following examples to see how intonation can affect the expression and meaning as you read:

Example

Mark moved yesterday?

Mark **moved** yesterday?

Mark moved **yesterday**?

_____

Intonation can also be affected by the situation the person is involved in. For example, the way that you would speak to your teacher may be very different from the way you would talk to a young child.

Your Turn

Try reading the following sentences in a variety of different ways.

Example

Read the following sentence as if you were talking to your friend.

I've missed you.

_____

Example

Read the following sentence as if you were talking to your favorite grandfather, who is very ill in the hospital.

I've missed you.

_____

Example

Read the following sentence as if you were talking to a small child or baby.

I've missed you.

Notice how your voice changes depending on your audience. This is the intonation changing in your reading or speaking.

READ ALOUD WITH APPROPRIATE EXPRESSION

Reading is a skill. When you become a master reader, you will be able to read with **fluency**, **accuracy** and **expression**. All three of these elements can affect each other.

In this lesson we are going to concentrate on reading with **expression**. Expression in reading can be described as "showing understanding of the text by using your voice as a way to produce emotions or interest." You must understand what you are reading to be able to use the appropriate expression. An expressive reader uses their voice in a variety of ways to make the text sound more interesting.

Exclamation marks: An exclamation mark will signal that you need to place more emphasis on what is being said. Your voice should go up in sound and in pitch.

Question marks: A question mark will signal that your voice should go up in pitch and volume towards the end of the sentence.

Quotation marks: Quotation marks signal that someone is speaking, so you must alter your voice to sound like the character.

AN EXPRESSIVE READER

1. Pays attention to the punctuation marks and changes their voice accordingly
2. Varies their pace where necessary
3. Emphasizes dialogue differently for each character

Expression is not about reading loud enough. It is about reading that uses a controlled, enjoyable and understandable pace, volume and tone.

TRY A MONOTONE

Look at the following passage. Read the paragraph out loud in a monotone voice. As you can see, there are no question marks, exclamation marks, or quotation marks to help signal you when to use more expression.

Example

Tracy was excited for her oldest and dearest friend to arrive from Newfoundland. She woke up Thursday morning and bounded out of her bed. The day had finally come. Her best friend would be arriving in only three short hours at the airport. There was so much to do before then.

Dad. We have to go to the mall right away. I forgot to pick up the last most important gift for Kayla's arrival.

Honey we just went yesterday. Do we really need to go again. The mall will be so busy and just finding parking will take up most of the time. We don't want to be late to pick Kayla up at the airport now do we. My dad said firmly.

I agreed sadly Ok. I guess it will have to wait.

How do you think that example sounded without any punctuation cues? Very bland, don't you think? Did it sound enjoyable to you? Do you think your audience might have a hard time understanding or being interested in what you are reading? Probably so.

TRY IT WITH EXPRESSION

Now look at the next example to see where the proper punctuation cues are used to signal the use of expression while you read. Use the cues to read the passage again, this time using appropriate expression.

Example

Tracy was excited for her oldest and dearest friend to arrive from Newfoundland. She woke up Thursday morning and bounded out of her bed. The day had finally come! Her best friend would be arriving in only three short hours at the airport. There was so much to do before then.

"Dad! We have to go to the mall right away! I forgot to pick up the last, most important gift for Kayla's arrival!"

"Honey, we just went yesterday. Do we really need to go again? The mall will be so busy and just finding parking will take up most of the time. We don't want to be late to pick Kayla up at the airport now, do we?" my dad said firmly.

I agreed sadly, "Ok. I guess it will have to wait."

How do you think that example sounded with the punctuation cues to help with your expression? Do you hear the difference? The expression should be much better in the second example.

USING THE RE-READ STRATEGY TO DETERMINE UNFAMILIAR WORDS

Sometimes when you are reading a text, you may come across a word that you do not understand. There are many different strategies you can try to figure out the unfamiliar word. One of those strategies is the re-read strategy.

When you come to the unfamiliar word, try going back and re-reading the sentence or even the paragraph, to review how the word is being used. This is called the **context**. Sometimes the context will trigger an idea that can help you determine the unknown word.

Re-reading has many benefits that help you with your comprehension of a text, and also help you determine those unfamiliar words.

BENEFITS OF RE-READING

1. It can help you determine the hard words in the text.
2. It can help you find things you may not have realized before.
3. It can help you make sense of what is happening in the text.
4. It can help you find mistakes in your reading, if you possibly missed a word or a sentence.

4W.1a   Write opinion pieces on topics or texts, supporting a point of view with reasons and information. Introduce a topic or text clearly, state an opinion, and create an organizational structure in which related ideas are grouped to support the...

4W.1b   Write opinion pieces on topics or texts, supporting a point of view with reasons and information. Provide reasons that are supported by facts and details.

CREATE A WRITTEN PIECE TO CONVINCE

There are at least three different ways to create a convincing or a persuading argument. We say that you need to appeal to an individual in order to convince them of an argument or a point of view. Three kinds of appeals are as follows:

1. Appeal to character
2. Appeal to reason
3. Appeal to emotion

Appeal to Character: The arguments involve people of high distinction in a particular field who provide their support.

Example

Doctors are always telling people to eat healthy and to stop smoking.

This statement is using appeal to character, because doctors are professionals that people trust when it comes to their health. Therefore, a person reading this sentence will be more willing to listen and incorporate the information into their life.

Appeal to Reason: This type of persuasion uses many different examples of factual information to help make a convincing argument.

Example

Going back to the example above about smoking, if you are trying to use appeal to reason, you would need to present factual arguments that are supporting your argument.

5.4 million people each year lose their lives due to smoking. According to the World Heath Organization, every 6.5 seconds, another smoker loses the battle with cigarettes. Smokers on average die 15 years sooner than non-smokers as recorded by the World Health Organization.

Appeal to Emotion: Using this type of persuasion, you will need to present arguments that evoke the readers' emotions. You want the readers to feel for your cause, making them want to support your point of view.

Example

Once again, using the example of smoking, you must think of the different ways to state your arguments so that people's emotions are supporting your cause.

Every year there are millions of children who will lose their parents to cigarette smoking. Smoking not only affects the smoker but the loved ones that are around them. Children are often addicted to smoking by the age of five, simply by inhaling second-hand smoke from their parents. People may get lung cancer from third-hand smoke; often this is from furniture where smokers may have sat, such as a movie theater chair.

The final thing that you will need to remember is that even though there are three different types of convincing arguments, the best argument that you can make will need to use all three. In other words, you will need to write a persuasive piece that uses appeal to character, reason, and emotion to create the best argument.

CREATE AN INTRODUCTORY PARAGRAPH

The purpose of the introductory paragraph is to tell your audience what they will be reading and learning about in the text.

The introductory paragraph should state the main idea of the writing piece and what main topics it will cover.

Your first sentence should introduce the main idea of the writing piece. The next sentences should state the main details that support the main idea, and about which the reader can expect to learn. The number of sentences usually varies depending on the length of the writing piece. The last sentence of the introductory paragraph will wrap up or summarize again the main idea or topic.

Example

Below is an example of an opening paragraph for a writing piece about how dogs are wonderful additions to our planet.

Dogs are wonderful animals and a great addition to our world. Dogs are known as very intelligent animals that can perform many different acts. Most dogs are great pets for humans. Dogs can also be helpful to people with disabilities or who have severe injuries. Dogs are amazing, helpful animals.

The above paragraph is an example of a beginning paragraph that supports the central idea of what the writing piece is about. It states the main idea - that dogs are extremely beneficial animals to have in our world. Then the paragraph gives some of the specific topics that you might learn about when reading the written passage about dogs. You will learn different acts that dogs can perform. You will learn about the different reasons why dogs make great pets. Then you will learn more about the ways that dogs help people with disabilities or injuries.

USE SIMILARITIES AND DIFFERENCES TO CONVEY INFORMATION

Using similarities and differences to convey information is sometimes known as comparing and contrasting.

To compare two or more things means to look for the **similarities** between them. To contrast two or more things means to look for the **differences** between them. For example, the following paragraph compares and contrasts millipedes and centipedes.

Millipedes and centipedes look similar but have different ecologies. Both look like worms with lots of legs. Millipedes are round in cross-section and have two pairs of legs on each body segment. Centipedes are flattened, and only have one pair of legs per segment. Millipedes are slow moving, often burrow, and eat dead leaves, detritus, and fungi. If threatened, they often curl up, and some exude bad-tasting chemicals. Centipedes are quick-moving predators, eating any small animals they can catch. They have a venomous bite, but no Michigan species are dangerous to people. Both centipedes and millipedes need a damp environment to survive and mostly stay on or under the ground.

To help you understand the differences and similarities between millipedes and centipedes, you can put all of the facts given in the paragraph into a Venn diagram. Draw two circles that overlap in the middle. Write the things that are true only about millipedes in one circle, and the things that are true only about centipedes in the other. In the area where the circles overlap, write the similarities that the two share.

Here is how it might look:

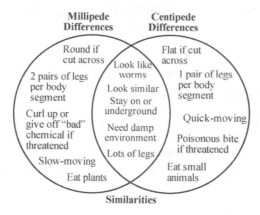

Try This!

What can you learn about the similarities and differences between plasma and LCD televisions, by looking at the Venn Diagram below?

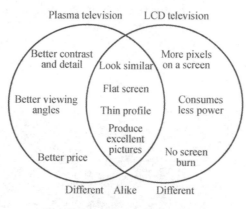

When you are conveying information by looking at similarities and differences, the information will be more clear and easy to understand if you put it on a comparison chart or a Venn Diagram like the above.

4W.2b   Write informative/explanatory texts to examine a topic and convey ideas and information clearly. Develop the topic with facts, definitions, concrete details, quotations, or other information and examples related to the topic.

CREATE SUPPORT PARAGRAPHS WITH FACTS, DETAILS, AND EXPLANATIONS

Once you have decided on your topic, you need to collect ideas and information about your topic. This is called shaping your ideas.

Here are some examples of what to have in your support paragraphs:

Facts and Statistics: Facts are objective pieces of information; statistics are collections of facts that are organized into numerical data. When using facts or statistics in your writing, remember to give the source from which you took them.

Contrast and Compare: The purpose of contrasting and comparing objects or ideas is not necessarily to show the superiority of one over the other; it may be to show their relationship to each other. By comparing a familiar object with one that is unfamiliar, a writer can introduce a reader to an unknown object within a known context or background.

Cause and Effect: The cause and effect writing strategy shows the relationship between events and their result. The paragraph does not need to begin with the first cause and work its way chronologically to the final effect. However, that is probably the easiest way for you to organize the paragraph.

4W.1c   Write opinion pieces on topics or texts, supporting a point of view with reasons and information. Link opinion and reasons using words and phrases.

USE CONNECTING WORDS TO LINK IDEAS IN SENTENCES

Connecting words help link ideas in sentences. Ideas are often linked by the words such as *and, or, but,* and *so.* Below are some examples of how you can take two short sentences and link them together, using a connecting word to make a longer sentence.

Example
1. I am going to dinner. Then we plan to see a movie.
   I am going to dinner **and** then we plan to see a movie.
2. You can send me a letter. You can write me an e-mail.
   You can send me a letter in the mail **or** just write me an e-mail.
3. I would love to join you for dinner. I have a guitar lesson.
   I would love to join you for dinner **but** I have a guitar lesson.
4. I returned the dress. It didn't fit.
   The dress didn't fit **so** I returned it.

IT'S YOUR TURN

There are many other words you can use to link your ideas together. Try linking the sentences below together with one or more of the following words: **however, but, although**

1. She broke her foot. She ran the race with crutches.
2. She never ate healthy. She lived to be 99 years old.
3. Hunter had a high fever. He still went to school.

The following are some possible solutions:

1. **Although** she broke her foot, she ran the race with crutches.
   She broke her foot; **however**, she ran the race with crutches.
   She broke her foot, **but** she ran the race with crutches.
2. **Although** she never ate healthy, she lived to be 99 years old.
   She never ate healthy; **however**, she lived to be 99 years old.
   She never ate healthy, **but** she lived to be 99 years old.
3. Hunter had a high fever; **however**, he still went to school.
   Hunter had a high fever, **but** he still went to school.
   Although Hunter had a high fever, he still went to school.

OTHER WORDS THAT LINK IDEAS

The following sentences illustrate some other words you could use to link ideas:

- She stayed out past her curfew; <u>therefore</u> she got grounded.
- He had to hurry <u>if</u> we were going to make the movie on time.
- Spread the sunblock on thick <u>because</u> you don't want to burn.
- I like to run <u>before</u> I eat breakfast.
- It was definitely at the park <u>that</u> I lost my purse.
- We swim <u>whenever</u> the weather is hot.

DEMONSTRATE KNOWLEDGE OF WORD ORIGINS

Hundreds and hundreds of years ago, in what is now known as Europe, there was a shared language called **Indo-European**. This common language was spoken by everyone living in Europe at that time. However, people moved around quite often, looking for food and grazing lands for their animals. After many years of this moving around, different groups of people became isolated from each other. Over time, the common language disappeared, as these isolated groups developed their own languages.

The three main branches of the Indo-European language that have most influenced the development of English are

- Germanic
- Italic
- Hellenic

The **Germanic** branch had the greatest influence on the English language, but Italian, Latin, French, Spanish, and Greek have all contributed words.

To this day, English is changing and growing. It is absorbing new words and phrases. Many of the words and phrases come from computer technology.

Prefixes are word parts added to the beginning of words. *Suffixes* are added at the end. Prefixes and suffixes change the meanings of words and often lead to new words being invented. Most prefixes and suffixes came to our language from Greek and Latin. Here are a few examples of prefixes derived from those languages.

Latin Prefix	Meaning	New Word
ante-	before	anterior, antemeridian (AM)
ben-, bon-	good, well	benefit, bonanza
bi-	two	bicycle, binary
mal-	bad, ill	malfunction, malnutrition
migr-	to move, travel	migrate, migration

Greek Prefix	Meaning	New Word
anti-	against	anticlockwise, anticlimax
auto-	self	automatic, automobile
hemi-	half	hemisphere, hemicycle
tele-	far off	telephone, telepathic
poly-	many	polygon, polygraph

Here are some examples of Latin and Greek suffixes, including their purposes (grammatical job in a sentence) and meanings.

Latin Suffix	Purpose	Meaning
-age	forms a noun	belongs to (storage)
-ance	forms a noun	state of being (appearance
-ible, -able	forms an adjective	capable of being (possible)
-ive	forms an adjective	belonging to or quality of (attractive)
-ly	forms an adverb	like, or to the extent of (happily)
-ate	forms a verb	to make (alienate)
-fy	forms a verb	to make (simplify)

Greek Suffix	Purpose	Meaning
-y	forms an abstract noun	state of (happy)
-ism	forms a noun	act or condition
-ic	forms an adjective	having the nature of (pathetic)

As you can see, there are many more Latin suffixes than there are Greek. This is probably because over the years many prefixes, suffixes and root words from both Latin and Greek were joined together and the English word is a combination of both.

Root words from Greek and Latin can sometimes appear to be prefixes and sometimes suffixes, but they are actually the roots or main parts of the words. For example:

Root	Origin	Meaning	Derivations
-bio-	Greek	life	biography, biology, microbiology
-lab-	Latin	to work	labor, laboratory, elaborate
-phone-	Greek	sound	phonograph, telephone, microphone
-port	Latin	to carry	portable, transport, transportation

The examples show that it is helpful to learn some Greek and Latin word parts and roots. This makes it easier to figure out the meanings of new words. Any word beginning with *micro*, for instance, is going to mean something small.

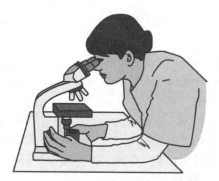

4W.1d   *Write opinion pieces on topics or texts, supporting a point of view with reasons and information. Provide a concluding statement or section related to the opinion presented.*

CREATE A CONCLUDING PARAGRAPH THAT SUMMARIZES MAIN POINTS

The concluding paragraph summarizes the points brought forward in the introduction, although you should *never restate* the introduction. The conclusion is your last chance to say something important to your reader; perhaps you want to motivate them to take action, to understand a topic differently, or to consider future inquiry or investigation of the topic.

In your concluding paragraph, you should always

- begin with a transition and let your reader know that you are summarizing the main points of your essay
- recall your major points
- explain the significance of your findings
- end with a strong sense of closure

Be sure to stay focused on your controlling or main idea right through to the concluding sentence of your essay.

Example

To sum it up, then, plastic packaging has allowed us to see what we are buying, which seemed like a benefit, at first. Now, however, the problems outweigh the benefits. Not only does plastic create a major trash overload for the world, but it is manufactured from two resources that are needed for other products: oil and petroleum. Plastic packaging is a luxury that the world must give up, or face the consequences.

Never introduce new ideas or material in your conclusion.

CREATE A WRITTEN PIECE TO INFORM

The main purposes an author has for writing are as follows:

- To inform
- To explain
- To entertain
- To impress
- To convince

As you review the different forms of writing, think about what a writer's purpose might be for using each of the forms. Always remember that the purpose comes first, and that the writer chooses the form that best suits that purpose.

The purpose of writing to inform is to give the reader specific information. School texts give information about specific subjects; newspapers inform the public about news events, and "how to" articles inform interested people how to make, draw, play, or do something. Dictionaries, encyclopedias, reference books, and Internet sites are all sources of information.

Example

The purpose of this paragraph is to inform you about how a microscope works.

A microscope is made up of a series of lenses (the eyepiece lens, the low power and the high power objective lenses) that magnify objects. Light is reflected by a mirror up through the hole on the stage and onto the object to be magnified, which lies directly over the hole. The objective lenses now magnify the object and send the image up to the eyepiece lens, which further magnifies the image before sending it to the eye.

As you can see from this example, *inform* can be very close to *explain* when it comes to purpose. The back of a medicine bottle is a better example of text that informs, because it provides information about the product and how to use it safely.

CREATE A WRITTEN PIECE TO EXPLAIN

The main purposes an author has for writing are as follows:

• To inform
• To explain
• To entertain
• To impress
• To convince

As you review the different forms of writing, think about what a writer's purpose might be for using each of the forms. Always remember that the purpose comes first, and that the writer chooses the form that best suits that purpose.

When the writer's purpose is to explain, he or she wants to give the reader the **why** or **how** of a situation. This is also known as explanatory writing because readers are given an explanation, not just told the facts of an event.

Example

Because he was afraid of the monster behind him, the dog ran as fast as he could through the neighbor's house. Unfortunately, he tracked mud all over the rug as he went.

When you are writing to explain, remember to use words like *how*, *why*, and *because*. Here are some topic ideas that would require you to explain something:

- How to make a creative pizza?
- Why you were late to your music lesson?
- How to take care of a pet?
- Why you want to take babysitter training?

CONSTRUCT MEANING USING HEADINGS

Headings support a book's title or a specific chapter in a book. They allow you to predict the information that follows, which helps to increase your understanding of what you read. Headings also help you find your way around a book. Heading should include key words that give the reader information about what's to come.

Example

The Life Cycle of a Butterfly (Heading)

Many changes occur in the lifespan of a butterfly. The story begins with…

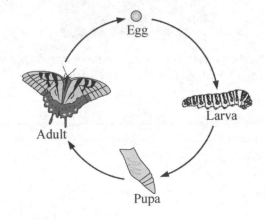

_____

YOUR TURN

Look at the headings in the passage below. How do they give you key information about the paragraphs that follow the headings?

Cat Talk

Anyone can learn cat "talk". It just takes lots of practice. Cats do use sounds—you hear them when they're fighting—but cats mainly use their own special signs. What follows is a kind of dictionary: a dictionary of *Cat*. Although this dictionary isn't complete, it'll get you started. Good luck!

Most people think that cats purr when they are happy. But sick and injured cats purr, too. Purring expresses friendship. Purring can also mean "dinner's served." Try it the next time you feed a cat.

Does your cat roll over when you come home and twitch the tip of its tail? Some people think that means "scratch my tummy." But most cats do not like their tummies touched. Rolling over is a sleepy way of saying hello.

Cats have a special way of saying "you are part of my family." They rub against us with the sides of their mouth, temple, and tail. Then they sit down and lick themselves. When your cat does this to you, it is marking you with its scent. Afterwards it licks its own fur to taste your scent. So if you do not want to belong to a cat, move away.

Making yourself as flat as possible, not looking at anyone directly, and keeping quiet is a way to submit in *Cat*. It's similar to how some people behave on their first day at a new school.

—*by* D.S. Long

Solutions

After you think about the headings, see if you agree with the answers below.

1. The first heading is the title of the article. It will be about how cats communicate with humans.
2. "Purring" tells the reader that the paragraph will explain the sound that cats like to make.
3. The "Saying hello" heading signals that the paragraph will explain what cats do to greet their owners.
4. "Scent sharing" says that the information will relate to how cats put their scent on people or objects.
5. The last heading suggests that cats have a way of showing submission to their owners.

Create Narratives that Use Concrete Sensory Details

You need to include more details about the facts that you give in your narrative compositions or stories. It is important that your details and examples fit the topic and are interesting. Your details also help to make your writing come alive for your reader.

When you picture a rainy day, for instance, what do you think of or see in your imagination?

- slick streets?
- umbrellas?
- rain streaming down windows?
- driving rain pounding on pavement?
- windshield wipers?
- dark, boiling clouds?

You need to create details for your reader that will help them to picture in their minds the kind of rainy day you are describing. Look at the chart below to see how ordinary writing comes alive when concrete details are added. Concrete means that the details are realistic or can be easily imagined through your senses.

Example

Without details	With details
It was raining.	The rain poured steadily down, drenching the fields and the children as they rushed home.
The food was good.	The fried chicken was well-browned and crisp, and the corn bread was so hot the butter melted straight off it.
The horse galloped by.	The steady, loud *clip-clop*, *clip-clop* of the horse's hooves drowned out all of the other night-time noises.

4W.2d   *Write informative/explanatory texts to examine a topic and convey ideas and information clearly. Use precise language and domain-specific vocabulary to inform about or explain the topic.*

USE CONTENT-SPECIFIC VOCABULARY IN YOUR WRITING

Diction is word choice. It is important that your ideas are expressed simply and accurately so that your reader can easily understand them. When you are speaking, your tone can be more readily attained from your body language, facial expressions, and intonation. However, when you are writing, your choice of words (your diction) indicates your tone or attitude.

Sometimes, identifying appropriate language is as simple as being sensitive to situations. For example, when you leave your locker and walk through the doorway of your English classroom, you will probably temporarily abandon the casual and slangy exchanges you were enjoying with your friends before class. You will instead adopt a more formal manner of expression for the duration of the class, particularly if the teacher calls upon you for a commentary on the Shakespeare play the class is studying, or you are asked to express your views on a topic by writing an essay.

Appropriate language refers to language that suits the expressive format being used or the situation. It ranges from formal to informal, from vernacular to precise, and covers many specialized categories, such as jargon and subject-specific terminology.

Some words in the English language are specific and some are general. Specific words give you more detail, while general words are more vague.

Let's look at the following sentence to show the different levels of specificity among the words in the sentence.

An animal bit the young boy's leg.

The word *animal* is a broad term. Let's change the sentence to tell what kind of animal.

A dog bit the young boy's leg.

The word *dog* is more specific but still leaves us wondering what kind of dog. Let's change it again to be more specific.

A German Shepherd bit the young boy's leg.

The word *animal* wasn't giving us much information but *German Shepherd* gives us a clear picture of what bit the young boy's leg.

There are many different levels of specificity among words. *Animal* is a general term but can be made more specific by changing it to *dog* and even more specific by changing it to *German Shepherd*.

Revision literally means "to look over again". Revision allows you as a writer to craft and shape your final product. You can make revisions to improve the content, clarity, and interest of your written work by using several types of strategies. These strategies might involve using a contrasting color of pen to underline or cross out text that you want to revise or using arrows or sticky notes to identify text that needs to be moved or inserted.

For example, if a classmate noted a lack of inclusive language (language that includes both genders) in your writing, you could go through your text changing all references to "policeman" to "police officer."

Try to use more exact and specific words. *Sun-drenched* is more exact than *sunny*. The overused verb *said* can be changed to more specific verbs like *announced, argued, wailed, screeched*, which are stronger verbs because they are more specific.

Add words that make your descriptions more vivid or clear. For instance *birch* or *maple* can be added to *trees* so that the reader can picture a certain type of tree. A color like *yellow* or *blue* can be added to *paper* to create a clearer picture for the reader. The adjective *chocolate* makes the word *milkshake* more specific.

Slang words are expressions used by a certain group of people, such as teenagers. Slang differs from *jargon* in the sense that slang is regarded as very casual or playful language, whereas jargon is usually used by professionals to discuss something specific. Slang expressions tend to come and go.
For example, in the 1950's, a "hot rod" referred to a powerful car, while today the term is used very rarely and may not be used to refer to a car.

Jargon refers to a specialized set of words and phrases commonly understood by a group, such as members of a profession, hobby, or field of study. For example, imagine going to the dentist. If, after examining your teeth and X-rays, the dentist tells you that you have a "cary on your 1-3," you would not know what she is talking about. She is using jargon that is specific to dentists, and she would have to explain to you that she has found a cavity in one of your teeth.

Jargon is common among different professions and can be confusing or meaningless to someone who does not belong to the special group for whom the jargon has meaning.

Most students today are, for the most part, computer literate. The Internet is still a new technology, and Internet jargon continues to grow and change. A good example is the blog. Words that have to do with blogs, such as *blogosphere*, *flaming*, and *vlogs* (video blogs), are all Internet-specific jargon words that not everyone will understand unless they use a computer in their daily lives.

In all forms of online writing you will find frequent use of shorthand. *Leetspeak* is often used to indicate emotions or actions that would take a long time to type out conventionally.

For example, rather than saying "I'm laughing out loud" or trying to indicate laughter by typing "ha ha ha," many people online just type "lol." This makes online conversation faster and more similar to real-time conversation. Leetspeak has quickly become incorporated into online communication. It is also easily adapted to text messaging on cellphones.

It is strongly discouraged, however, in any formal writing for school or work.

Subject-specific terminology refers to the terms that are central to an area or unit of study. These terms are generally introduced at the beginning of a new unit or chapter. For instance, before beginning a poetry unit, an English teacher will first review common poetry terms, such as *sonnet*, *lyric*, *metaphor*, *onomatopoeia*, and so on, because these terms are often used with respect to poetry.

Subject-specific words that are important are often

- bolded in math, social studies, and science textbooks
- defined at the beginning of a new chapter
- defined at the bottom of the page or at the back of the textbook
- used by the teacher on the board, overhead, or for assignments

When new words appear in content areas, you will better understand and remember information, ideas, and concepts by adopting the new words into your vocabulary. Ensure that you know the spelling and meanings of the word, and try to use the word, when appropriate, in conversation and writing.

- Before plunging into a new text, learn any terms that will help you to better understand the information. If the term is not defined in the text, use the glossary.
- List the terms beside their meanings in your notes for quick reference.
- Since most subject-specific terminology is not language that you use every day, learn it as you need it.
- Refresh your memory occasionally, and the words you need will be relatively easy to review later when you need them.

Most of the time, identifying appropriate language becomes almost an automatic skill. Identifying and using appropriate language tends to be a matter of courtesy, necessity, expediency, or straightforward common sense. It is wise to adapt as the situation requires.

4W.3a   Write narratives to develop real or imagined experiences or events using effective technique, descriptive details, and clear event sequences. Orient the reader by establishing a situation and introducing a narrator and/or characters; organize...

CREATE A STORY WITH A LOGICAL SEQUENCE

When writing a story, you want to make sure it follows a logical sequence so that it makes sense to your audience. One way to make sure that your story follows a logical sequence is to write the events of the story in chronological order.

LET'S TRY TOGETHER

Let's try writing a story together using a logical sequence. The easiest way to do this would be to list the events of the story in a timeline.

STEP ONE: STORY IDEA

The first step in writing any story is to come up with a good story idea. The best ideas come from the events in our own lives. How about writing a story about learning to ride a two-wheeled bike?

STEP TWO: DEVELOP YOUR CHARACTER

Next we need to create a character and a list of character traits. Sometimes it helps to think of a couple of people we know really well and create a character based on them.

STEP THREE: STORY PROBLEM

Your next step is to come up with a problem or struggle your character might have within your story idea. Our character's struggle is going to be learning how to ride a two-wheeled bike.

STEP FOUR: SETTING

Now we need to think about where our story should take place. Think about where you learned to ride a two-wheeled bike. Our story can take place on the quiet street where the main character lives.

STEP FIVE: TIMELINE

We can use a timeline to organize the events of our story. We want to place our events in chronological order. Each dot should include a character doing something somewhere.

- Dad and I are on the driveway taking the training wheels off my bike.
- I am nervous to ride with no training wheels and pretend my stomach hurts, but Dad doesn't believe me.
- I get on and Dad holds the back of my bike to steady my balance but I wobble and tell him not to let go.
- I begin to pedal and Dad holds on as I move forward. I lose my balance, tip over, and am mad at Dad.
- Dad helps me up. He tells me that I almost had it and tells me to try again.
- I climb back on, make Dad promise to hold on and I try again.
- I begin to pedal, to move faster down the sidewalk
- I begin to smile, then realize that Dad is no longer holding on. I am on my own.
- I stop my bike to turn and wave at Dad. He waves back with a big smile.

STEP SIX: WRITE THE STORY

Our next step now is to write our story. We begin with the first dot, which is our first event in our story and begin to write. We can think of each dot as a new paragraph, since each dot is a new event within the story. Writing your story in this order will create a story that follows a logical sequence.

Example

Losing the Wheels

"Dad, are you sure I am ready?" I questioned my Dad as I handed him the wrench.

"More than ready!" Dad responded as he turned the wrench loosening the bolt that attached my training wheels to my bike. I had been riding my bike all summer, up and down our quiet street, through the River Valley on Sundays with Dad and now at the end of summer we were finally taking off the training wheels that had supported my riding all summer.

My stomach began to fill with butterflies. I was so good a riding with those training wheels! I wondered if I would ever be able to ride the same way again without them. Dad finished removing that last training wheel and turned and looked at me and asked "Ready to give it a go, kiddo?"

A nervous smile came across my face as I said "Actually Dad, I am not feeling too great; my stomach is hurting again."

"Oh, kiddo you are just fine, you are just feeling a little nervous which is fair enough but you are ready, I know you are!"

In the above example, the first two dots of the timeline have been written into paragraphs. As you read, you can see how the story is following a logical sequence. The events of the story are being told in the order they would have actually happened.

YOUR TURN!

Now try writing the rest of this story using the above timeline.

CREATE A STORY WITH RELATIONSHIPS BETWEEN CHARACTERS AND PLOT

When you are writing a story, it is very important to know your characters well. When you know your characters well, your plot will develop from them. Writers spend a great deal of time getting to know their character so well that they would know what their character would do or say in any situation.

LET'S TRY

STEP ONE: DEVELOPING A CHARACTER

Your first step is to develop your main character, to think about what this person is really like on the inside (personality traits) and the outside (physical appearance). When you are developing your character, it is also very important to think about how a character's inside is reflected on their outside. If you say your character loves to play sports and is always ready to drop anything and join in a game, would it make sense that this character always wears high heels? No, you would imagine your character dressed more casually. Also, to help you get started in developing your character, it is sometimes helpful to think of one or two people you know really, really well. Basing your character lightly on a real person will make the character more realistic for your readers. As well, sometimes it is helpful to organize your thoughts in a chart to keep beside you as you write.

In the chart below, begin getting to know your character by listing details about them. Use the following questions to help you get started:

- Are they male or female?
- How old are they?
- What color is their hair, eyes?
- How tall are they?
- What do they like to do in their spare time?
- What is their family like (brothers, sisters, mom or dad)?
- Do they have any pets?
- Do they have any hobbies or play any sports?
- Who are their friends?
- What makes them happy, sad, nervous, excited, mad?
- What is their favorite thing to eat?
- What type of clothes do they like to wear?
- What are they like in new situations (friendly, nervous, outgoing, shy)?
- What are they like (kind, thoughtful, generous, funny, easy going, stubborn)?

Inside (personality traits)	Outside (physical appearance)

Step Two: What would your Character do?

After you have completed your chart and feel like you know your character very well, it is time to begin imagining your character in different situations.

In each of the following situations imagine what your character might do:

- First day at a brand new school
- At an amusement park and in line for the biggest roller coaster
- Leaving for summer camp
- Trying out for the school soccer team
- Auditioning for the school musical
- Watching young sister eat the last piece of birthday cake

When you know your character really well, it becomes easy to imagine what your character would do in any situation.

Step Three: Character and Plot

Now that you know your character well and can imagine them in any situation, you can see how your story plot can develop from your character. When writing a story after you have established your story idea, character and setting, your next step is to imagine how this story might unfold for your character.

Example

Imagine your character as a girl in fifth grade who is fun, friendly, outgoing, loves playing sports, is on the basketball team, lives with her mom, dad, older brother, and two younger sisters, has lots of friends but three best friends, always wears her hair in a pony tail, dresses casually and usually in her older cousin's hand me downs.

Now let's say the story idea is that she sprains her ankle right before the final basketball game. Her struggle is not being able to play the last game of the season. Based on what we already know about our character, we can easily imagine the plot of this story. Since she loves basketball so much, we know she is going to be upset. We also know she has three best friends, so we can also imagine what they might do to cheer her up because she can not play.

Character and plot go together. You cannot have a plot without character, because the plot develops from the character's actions in the story.

4W.3d   Write narratives to develop real or imagined experiences or events using effective technique, descriptive details, and clear event sequences. Use concrete words and phrases and sensory details to convey experiences and events precisely.

NARRATIVE-DESCRIPTIVE WRITING

Narrative writing tells a story. Usually, the story happens to characters that you imagine, but sometimes you are telling a personal story. You have had many experiences that could be turned into a great story. Whenever you write a story, you use narrative paragraphs. Organize these paragraphs in time-order, and add descriptive details to make your writing more interesting or exciting.

Here is an example of a narrative paragraph from the book *Jennie* by Paul Gallico, which is about a boy Peter, who takes care of a stray cat. In this narrative paragraph, Peter is giving the cat a bath.

Example

Peter found that after this recital he had need to wash himself energetically for a few moments, and then he went over to where Jennie was lying and washed her face too, giving her several caresses beneath her soft chin and along the side of her muzzle that conveyed more to her than words. She made a little soft, crooning sound in her throat, and her claws worked in and out, kneading the canvas hatch cover faster than ever.

Notice that the paragraph is also very descriptive:

• Telling how Peter washes himself "energetically"
• Describing "caresses" that show how much affection Peter already feels for the stray cat
• Using the moving claws of the cat to describe her contentment

IDENTIFYING THE SPEAKER OR NARRATOR IN A TEXT

An author writing a story is rather like a person using a camera taking to shoot a video. A person shooting a video decides where to stand and what to capture. What an author tells and how he or she decides to tell it are the author's point of view. There are three main points of view (or perspectives).

Sometimes as a reader it is very clear what the point of view in the story is and who is telling the story. Sometimes it is not so clear. Getting to know the different points of view and the clue words that are used to determine the point of view the author is using, is important and can directly affect your full understanding and comprehension of a text.

In **first person** point of view writing, the author decides to have one of the characters in the story tell about the events and what is said. The pronouns *I*, *me*, *my*, *mine*, *we*, and *us* are used. When a first person point of view is used, the reader usually knows only what the person who is telling the story thinks and feels.

Example

"I was scared because I thought I might fall when I climbed the tree to get the coconuts for our family's supper that night."

When an author uses a second person point of view, he or she talks directly to the reader. The pronouns *you* and *your* are used. This point of view is often used in choose-your-own-adventure stories and when an author wants to give directions, and sometimes in poetry.

Example

"When you are baking, you need to make sure you have all the ingredients ready before you start."

Stories written in **third person** point of view are told through the eyes of a narrator. The pronouns *he*, *she*, *his*, *her*, *they*, and *their* are used. When third person point of view is used, readers can sometimes know a great deal about the story because the narrator tells what is happening in many different places.

Example

"While John was playing with his friends at the park, Mary was having trouble trying to fix the car so that they could all go to visit their grandmother."

Try This!

Now it's your turn. Do you think you understand the different points of view an author or narrator can have in their texts? Try and determine which point of view is being used in each to the following questions. Once you think you have got them all correct, check your answers below.

1. Next, when you understand the first task, then you and your team will move onto task number two.
2. I enjoy all types of cakes.
3. Macy was clear on what she had to do. She knew her friends would not understand, but she had to do what was right for everyone.
4. I feel really sad when my friends don't say good-bye to me after school.

How do you think you did? Were you able to determine which point of view each sentence was written in? If you think you have got them all correct, check your answers below.

1. Next, when you understand the first task, then you and your team will move onto task number two.
   This is **second person point of view**. Notice how it uses the pronouns *you* and *your*.
2. I enjoy all types of cakes.
   This is **first person point of view**. Notice how it speaks with *I*.
3. Macy was clear on what she had to do. She knew her friends would not understand, but she had to do what was right for everyone.
   This is **third person point of view**. Notice how it speaks from a more general perspective, using the pronouns, *her* and *she*.
4. I feel really sad when my friends don't say good-bye to me after school.
   This is **first person point of view**. Notice how it speaks with *I* and *me*.

Write a Story Beginning that has Action

When you are writing a story you want to have an interesting and exciting beginning, one that catches the attention of your audience so that they want to continue reading to find out what is going to happen next.

One way to to begin a story is to use **action**, beginning your story with your **character doing something**.

Using Action

Example
Instead of "There was a black cat who wanted to catch a mouse."

Try "The black cat pounced quickly upon the little mouse that had just darted out from under the old sofa."

See and feel the difference? By using action in the second sentence, you make your audience want to know if the cat actually catches the mouse. Your audience will want to continue reading your story.

YOUR TURN!

Let's say your story was going to begin with your main character leaving for school in the morning. Try writing three story beginnings that use action to show your character leaving.

HOW DID YOU DO?

Below are three ways you could have begun your story with action:

- Mary ran down the stairs, quickly grabbed her coat and book bag from the front entrance, and rushed out the front door in an attempt to catch the school bus before it drove away.
- Mary chatted excitedly with her sisters as they walked out the front door of their home towards the bus stop.
- As Mary sat on the steps of her front porch, she looked at her watch again. Beth said she would be here by now. Mary thought to herself that if Beth didn't show up soon they would both be late for the first day of school.

The three above examples all have the main character Mary performing some type of action (doing something). These actions catch the attention of the audience and make them excited to hear more of the story.

CREATE A STORY BEGINNING USING DIALOGUE

When you are writing a story, it is important to have a strong beginning that catches the attention of your audience. One way to do this is to begin your story with dialogue, having your character say something that hooks the attention of your audience.

USING DIALOGUE

Example
Instead of:

The teacher asked the students to sit down on the bus.

"All of you need to sit down immediately. This bus isn't going anywhere until you are showing you are ready!"

The second beginning gets your attention! You can feel the teacher's frustration in the second beginning, while the first one just tells you what the teacher wants and shows no emotion. When writing, you want your audience to feel what your characters feel, so using dialogue is a good way to do this. Using dialogue at the beginning of a story will grab the attention of your audience.

LET'S TRY TOGETHER!

Let's say your story idea is about a surprise birthday party for you. First, close your eyes and imagine how this story might begin. Where are you? What are you doing? What might you be thinking? What might you say?

Story tell aloud a couple of different ways this might begin, using dialogue (having your character say something).

Example

- "Hey, Susan!" It was my best friend Meg, who lives just around the corner from me. "Do you think your mom might let you come to a sleepover Friday night? Just you and me!"
- "Susan, would you be able to babysit Tommy for a few hours Friday evening?"
  I was about to answer, "No, it's my bir..." when my mom popped her head around the kitchen door. "Is that Mrs. McNally? Does she want you to babysit? I think you should go, dear! We can have your birthday cake on Saturday."

YOUR TURN!

Choose one of your story ideas or the story idea of a surprise birthday party and try writing a couple of different beginnings that use dialogue to capture the audience's attention. Remember to appeal to emotion. You want your audience to feel what your character is feeling.

USE CHRONOLOGICAL ORDER FOR CONVEYING INFORMATION

Chronological order means that the information is organized according to the order in which it occurs. Some stories do not follow chronological order, but dates and times are provided for readers to understand the time frame. Chronological order provides a clear sequence of information for the reader, and is a good way to organize writing that describes a sequence of steps or events.

Example

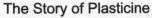

The Story of Plasticine

Have you ever wondered how Plasticine was invented? It was actually invented by an art teacher who didn't like clay. He found it to be heavy and difficult for his students to shape.

The teacher, William Harbutt, began mixing batches of clay-like dough in his basement. One day in 1887, the mix was perfect—it was soft, light, and easy to shape. He called the mix Plasticine.

Mr. Harbutt's students loved the fake clay, and so did his own six children. It was obvious that Mr. Harbutt needed to make more Plasticine to sell to others. After Mr. Harbutt began to advertise his invention, he was so swamped with orders that he hired an ex-soldier to mix and prepare huge batches of Plasticine. The final change that was made to Plasticine was the addition of color to the gray mix. You can still buy Plasticine like this in stores today.

Following is the chronological order of "The Story of Plasticine."

1. An art teacher mixed a substance to replace clay.
2. By 1887, the mixture was perfect.
3. Mr. Harbutt named his mixture Plasticine.
4. The students loved Plasticine.
5. Mr. Harbutt's children loved Plasticine.
6. Mr. Harbutt advertised his product.
7. Orders poured in.
8. Mr. Harbutt hired an old soldier to mix large batches of Plasticine.
9. Color was added to the gray Plasticine.

From reading this passage, you can see that there is a definite order in which the events occur, and that one event is related to or leads to the next.

Example

---

from Nim's Island

There were plants to prop up that had toppled over in the wind, weeds to pull, strawberries to nibble, and a huge bunch of bananas just green enough to pick.

Nim liked bananas, but what she liked even better was swinging Jack's machete. It was shiny and sharp and made her feel like a pirate.

"Aargh, me hearties!" she shouted, and chopped down the bunch.

She dragged them to the shed and hooked them to a rope looping over a beam in the roof.

"I'm swinging the bananas!" And she grabbed the rope just above her head. Fred jumped and clung to the end with his claws. Swinging hard and heavy, they hoisted the bananas up to the roof to ripen.

It would have been easier if Selkie had helped, but sea lions aren't much good at swinging on ropes.

Fred knew what she was thinking. He raced her up the path to the top of the waterfall.

Over thousands of years, the water trickling down the mountain had worn away the steep black rocks to make a curving slide. It was perfect for *whooshing* a girl and an iguana over bumps and dips and splashing them into the pool at the bottom.

Nim and Fred ran up and slid down until it was time for lunch. Then Nim picked up a tomato and an avocado that had fallen off in the wind and weeded quickly around the peas.

"They'll be ready tomorrow," she told Fred.

But Fred didn't like peas, and he was getting bored. He started chewing leaves and spitting them out.

"I won't bring you up to the garden again!" Nim said sternly. Fred spat out the last bit of pea leaf and crawled into the wagon for a wild ride down the hill.

—*by* Wendy Orr

Look below to see the chronological order of "Nim's Island".

- **First:** Nim chops down the bunch of bananas.
- **Then:** She drags them to the shed.
- **Then:** She hooks them to a rope looping over a beam.
- **Then:** She and Fred (the iguana) swing the rope to hoist the bananas to the roof to ripen.
- **Then:** Fred races Nim to the top of the waterfall.
- **Then:** Nim and Fred try the slide created by the trickling of water to the pool at the bottom.
- **Then:** Nim and Fred slide till lunchtime.
- **Then:** Nim picks a tomato and avocado from her garden and weeds the peas.
- **Last:** The two friends crawl into the wagon for a wild ride down the hill from the garden.

USE CAUSE AND EFFECT FOR CONVEYING INFORMATION

Authors often use a technique called cause and effect to develop a paragraph or story. This technique tells why events happened and why things are as they are. Cause-and-effect relationships are frequently used in writing that informs, explains, or persuades. The words *if* and *then* are used to show how one thing can lead to another. For example, if a person never practices writing, then that person will probably not become an author. Some other cause-and-effect words are *because*, *as a result*, *why*, *when*, *therefore*, *so*, and *for this reason*.

Example

The following passage by Farley Mowat, which is followed by a chart of cause-and-effect relationships.

There was a summerhouse in our back yard, and we kept about thirty gophers in it. We caught them out on the prairie, using snares made of heavy twine.

The way you do it is like this: You walk until you spot a gopher sitting up beside his hole. Gophers sit straight up, reaching their noses as high as they can, so they can see farther. When you begin to get too close, they flick their tails, give a little jump, and whisk down their holes. As soon as they do that, you take a piece of twine that has a noose tied in one end, and you spread the noose over the hole. Then you lie down in the grass holding the other end of the twine in your hand. You can hear the gopher all the while, whistling away to himself somewhere underground.

Cause	Effect
Gophers sit straight up	They can see farther
People try to get close to gophers	They flick their tails
	They give a jump
	They whisk down their holes

In science textbooks, you will often see cause/effect relationships, particularly with experiments. In social studies, cause/effect relationships are also evident, especially when you study the causes of a historical event, such as the Industrial Revolution or the California Gold Rush.

4W.4   *Produce clear and coherent writing in which the development and organization are appropriate to task, purpose, and audience.*

SET A PURPOSE FOR WRITING

Every author writes for a specific reason or purpose. The main purposes for writing are to inform, explain, entertain, impress, and convince. Decide what your purpose is going to be before you begin to write. Stick to your purpose. If you are trying to write out the directions to your house, stay focused on explaining. Don't sidetrack into a joke about the time you got lost on the way home. If you stay focused, your reader will see your purpose immediately.

Example

The given map shows the most direct way to my (Jim's) house from the school. If you pass a church on your right, you will have gone too far. If you miss the turn and that happens, just continue down the highway to the hospital at the edge of town. You can turn right into the hospital driveway and get turned around.

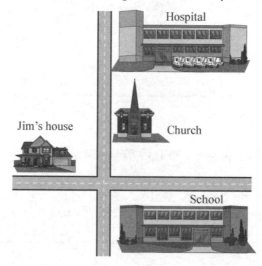

TO INFORM

When your purpose is to inform, you want the reader to understand the facts.

TO EXPLAIN

When your purpose is to explain, you want to give the reader the *why* or *how* of a situation. You are explaining something so that the reader will understand.

To Entertain

When your purpose is to entertain, you are trying to amuse your readers, make them laugh, or allow them to escape the real word for a while.

Example

The dog tore past us through the kitchen, yelping in fright. He collided with a small table, knocking over a fish bowl and finally coming to a screeching halt against the wall in a soggy jumble of dog, fish, table legs and flowers. He looked back with as much dignity as he could muster with a goldfish bowl stuck over his nose. To his great surprise, he saw that the monster chasing him was nothing but a tiny mouse, who now giggled happily from the doorway.

To Impress

When your purpose is to impress, you are trying to make readers feel strongly about something.

Example

Do you realize that here in our home country, where we make up 5% of the world's population, we create 30% of its garbage? Can we change that statistic? Of course we can, but everyone has to do their part.

To Convince

When you write to convince, you are trying to change the reader's mind about something. You try to get the reader to agree with you. This reason for writing is also called persuading.

Example

It is extremely important that you lock your doors to keep out that horrible black beast. You may think he is a harmless cuddly pup. However, he destroyed my rug and smashed my best vase. If you are not careful, he will do the same or worse to your home.

Mixed Purposes

It is always a good idea, most of the time, to stay focused on one purpose. That way, your readers don't get confused. Of course, you may experiment with writing for more than one purpose. For instance, you might write an entertaining story that also teaches the reader something while they are being amused.

Use Knowledge of a Rubric to Enhance Writing

It is important for you to understand how a rubric works so you may use it to help enhance your writing. This enhancement can happen once you see the areas that need improvement, after doing a writing project and observing your scores on a rubric.

Let's look at how a rubric works, in order to determine where you can use improvement in your writing projects.

A rubric is a way to grade or monitor your own or someone else's project or assignment. A rubric usually has different categories or skills which the project focuses on, or requires. The rubric has a low level of achievement, with a description of what that low level might look like for each category. It will also show you a high level of achievement, with a description of what that high level might look like for the same categories. Depending on the rubric, there may also be a couple of other medium or proficent levels of achievement in the center of the rubric, with descriptions of what those levels might look like, as well.

Level 1	Represents a writing project that is not adequate and needs improvement. It does not stay on topic. Purpose is unclear and/or unsuitable. Information often confusing, incorrect, or inadequate. Order is confusing, topic sentences unclear. Style inappropriate for audience and purpose. No variation in sentence lengths, and little or no description. Several errors in paragraph structure, many spelling, punctuation errors. Project is mostly unreadable.
Level 2	Represents a writing project that is adequate and needs some improvement. It is sometimes off topic, and the purpose is vague or not quite suitable. Information is sometimes confusing or inadequate. Order may be confusing. Some clear topic sentences, but no clear beginning, middle, and end. Style is not quite appropriate for audience and purpose. Some sentence lengths varied, description vague. Errors in paragraph structure, spelling, and punctuation. Somewhat readable.
Level 3	Represents a writing project that is proficient and needs minimal improvements. It is mostly on topic, with a generally clear purpose, and is suitable. Information is mostly clear and seldom inadequate for purpose. Order generally makes sense, with mostly clear topic sentences, and a generally clear beginning, middle, and end. Style is generally appropriate, with most sentence lengths varied. Description general. Minor errors in paragraph structure, spelling, and punctuation. Readable. The project will need slight improvement to get to a level of excellence.
Level 4	Represents a writing project that is at a level of excellence. It is always on topic, clear in purpose, and suitable for intended audience. Information is clear, correct, complete. The order makes sense, with clear topic sentences, and clear beginning, middle, and end. Style is appropriate, with varied sentence lengths. Description is vivid. Paragraph structure is correct, with no spelling or punctuation errors. Project is completely readable.

Below is an example of a score-based rubric.

Skill	Score Level (1 to 4)
Focus/Organization	4
Content	4
Style	4
Conventions	4
Total	16

If there were 4 categories or skills to be assessed, then you would be graded out of 1 to 4 on each skill. If you did exactly what was asked of you in each category with no room for improvement you might score top marks of 4 in all for categories. 4 plus 4 plus 4 plus 4 would equal a total of 16 points. 16 points would be the maximum amount you could score.

Another example of scoring a rubric may not look so perfect! Let's say that in two skills you scored a 2 out of 4, in another skill you scored 3 out of 4, and the last skill you scored 4 out of 4. What would your total score be?

Skill	Score Level (1 to 4)
Focus/Organization	2
Content	2
Style	3
Conventions	4
Total	11

If you guessed 11 out of 16, you would be correct. How did we come to the number 11? We added the **two** scores of 2, plus 3, plus 4.
2 + 2 + 3 + 4 = 11

If you had this type of scoring on a rubric, you might choose to look at what area you scored lowest on. In this case you would look at the two skills you scored a 2 in and work to improve those areas of your writing.

4W.5   *With guidance and support from peers and adults, develop and strengthen writing as needed by planning, revising, and editing.*

THINKING OF A STORY TOPIC

Your life is filled with so many small moments that you can write about! When you are thinking of a story topic, the best ideas come from your own life experiences! Three strategies you can use to help you think of a topic are to think of a person, place, or thing.

THINK OF A PERSON

Think of a person that matters to you and then begin writing a list of small memories you have with that person.

Example
My Sister:

- The moment she placed my new kitty in my hands
- The moment she told me she was going away for school
- The day we had the water balloon fight
- The time when we were eating ice cream and her scoops fell off her cone and to the ground

THINK OF A PLACE

Think of a place you have been that matters to you, and then begin writing a list of small memories you have had at that place.

Example
The Cottage:

- The day I learned to water ski
- The day the mouse ran into the bedroom and hid under my bed
- The time I ran through the screen door and broke it
- Playing kick the can with my cousins after dark
- Playing with my cousins on the raft and flipping it over in the water

THINK OF A THING

Think of a thing that matters to you and then begin writing a list of small memories you have about that thing.

Example
My Bike:

• Going to the bike store and picking my bike out
• Riding my bike for the first time up and down my street then falling off just in front of my house
• My friend Beth and I discovering we both had the same bike
• Riding my bike in a charity race for cancer

USING AN IDEA FOR WRITING

After you have created a list of story topics, choose one that matters the most to you and begin the story writing process.

USING A CHECKLIST TO EDIT YOUR STORY

An important step in the story writing process is editing your work. Some writers find it helpful to use a checklist as a guide. You can use the following checklist to help make your story an even stronger piece of writing.

A HELPFUL REMINDER

When using an editing checklist you will be reading your story many times. Each time you read your story, you will be looking for something different. Many writers find it helpful when editing their work to read their writing aloud, slowly pointing to each word as they read it. This will help you read what you **actually** wrote rather than what you **thought** you wrote.

Example
The first item on your checklist is to correct all misspelled words, so you are going to read your story just looking for misspelled words and correcting them. The next item on your checklist is correct verb tenses, so this time you are just going to read, checking for correct verb tenses. The next item on your checklist is variety of sentence types, so on your third reading you will just be looking for sentence types. You will continue on like this for each item on your checklist. As you can see, you will be reading your story LOTS! But you know that after all of this reading and editing you will have a fantastic story to share!

EDITING CHECKLIST

GENERAL:

- I have corrected all misspelled words.
- All my verb tenses are correct.
- I have used a variety of sentence types.
- I have organized my writing into paragraphs.

CAPITALIZATION:

- Each sentence begins with a capital letter.
- The names of people and places begin with a capital letter.
- The first letter of each word in the title begins with a capital letter.

PUNCTUATION:

- Each sentence ends with a period, question mark or exclamation mark.
- Commas are used where needed.
- Quotation marks are used to show where speech begins and ends.

DESCRIPTION:

- I have used descriptive language.
- I have shown my readers what is happening not told them.
- My readers can "see" the location of the story.

CHARACTER:

- My readers should be able to feel the emotions of the characters.
- The struggles of my character are clear.
- I have shown how my characters have grown and changed to overcome their struggles.

PLOT:

- My story follows a logical sequence of events.
- Each event has a character doing something somewhere.

REVISING YOUR WRITTEN WORK TO PROVIDE FOCUS

When you are writing, you should always be clear about your purpose for writing. Is it to entertain? To inform? To impress or persuade? When writing, you want to communicate the information to your audience in the most effective and direct way possible, always keeping in mind your purpose or focus for writing.

It is important to stay close to the topic you are writing about and the point or idea that you want to get across.

If you choose to write about the best ice cream flavor you've ever tasted, then it's probably not a good idea to start talking about different fast food restaurants, as that probably does not help add to the focus of your writing piece.

The best way to revise your writing to make sure it has the proper focus, is to read through each paragraph of your work to make sure that each paragraph is about your topic. You must make sure that it contributes to the entire piece as a whole. If you get to a paragraph or part of a paragraph that does not add to the topic, then it may be best to edit it out.

Make sure that each sentence and each paragraph stays consistent to the specific focus of your written piece. When you have parts that do not add to the main focus or topic, those parts become distractions instead of helping to add to the topic of your writing.

Let's look at a paragraph together about baseball being the greatest sport to watch.

Example
Baseball is one of the world's greatest sports to watch. Baseball is exciting, fun and engaging. When the stadiums are full, the crowds are excited and the players are focused, the games are best place to be. With a hot dog in one hand and a giant soda pop in the other watching the game, who could complain? I live 6 hours away from the nearest stadium. When the umpire yells, "He's safe!" or "You're outta here!" and the crowd erupts in either excited applauding or screaming disagreements, what could be more exciting than that? The energy in the stadium is the best and it's all because of the fans and the excitement for the game of baseball.

Something just doesn't belong here!

The line, "**I live 6 hours away from the nearest stadium.**" does not belong in the above paragraph, because it really has nothing to do with why baseball is the best sport to watch. It takes away from the focus of the written piece. Read the paragraph now, and see if you agree.

Example

Baseball is one of the world´s greatest sports to watch. Baseball is exciting, fun and engaging. When the stadiums are full, the crowds are excited and the players are focused, the games are best place to be. With a hot dog in one hand and a giant soda pop in the other watching the game, who could complain? When the umpire yells, "He's safe!" or "You're outta here!" and the crowd erupts in either excited applauding or screaming disagreements, what could be more exciting than that? The energy in the stadium is the best and it's all because of the fans and the excitement for the game of baseball.

Now It's Your Turn

Can you find any of the sentences that do not belong in the following paragraph about computers?

Computers are supposed to be something that helps our generation out. I tend to disagree. Whenever there is the slightest problem with my computer, I am hooped! I never have a clue how to fix the problem or what is going wrong. My only reasonable try at fixing a computer that is blinking "ERROR!" at me, is to press ESCAPE and if that doesn't work, the inevitable CTRL, ALT, DELETE! Sometimes I wish I could just press "CTRL, ALT, DELETE" on my Mom when she is complaining about me not getting my chores done. Computers are supposed to have great access to the internet where you can search for tons of information on any topic you want. But then our teachers tell us, "make sure it is a credible source" or, "make sure you don't just copy the website," how am I suppose to do that, with so much information out there? Then when I finally do get to a good website that I think is credible, BAM! I get a virus on my computer. Then it just sends me back to my trusted "CTRL, ALT, DELETE" strategy and it begins all over again. It's just so frustrating. In my opinion, computers are useless!

How Did You Do?

Were you able to identify which line does not belong within the paragraph? Check your answer below.

The highlighted sentence does not belong in this paragraph because it is irrelevant to why computers are unhelpful. As comical as it may be, it does not belong in this paragraph.

Computers are supposed to be something that helps our generation out. I tend to disagree. Whenever there is the slightest problem with my computer, I am hooped! I never have a clue how to fix the problem or what is going wrong. My only reasonable try at fixing a computer that is blinking "ERROR!" at me, is to press ESCAPE and if that doesn't work, the inevitable CTRL, ALT, DELETE! **Sometimes I wish I could just press "CTRL, ALT, DELETE" on my Mom when she is complaining about me not getting my chores done.** Computers are supposed to have great access to the internet where you can search for tons of information on any topic you want. But then our teachers tell us, "make sure it is a credible source" or, "make sure you don't just copy the website," how am I suppose to do that, with so much information out there? Then when I finally do get to a good website that I think is credible, BAM! I get a virus on my computer. Then it just sends me back to my trusted "CTRL, ALT, DELETE" strategy and it begins all over again. It's just so frustrating. In my opinion, computers are useless!

The paragraph should look like this:

Computers are supposed to be something that helps our generation out. I tend to disagree. Whenever there is the slightest problem with my computer, I am hooped! I never have a clue how to fix the problem or what is going wrong. My only reasonable try at fixing a computer that is blinking "ERROR!" at me, is to press ESCAPE and if that doesn't work, the inevitable CTRL, ALT, DELETE! Computers are supposed to have great access to the internet where you can search for tons of information on any topic you want. But then our teachers tell us, "make sure it is a credible source" or, "make sure you don't just copy the website," how am I suppose to do that, with so much information out there? Then when I finally do get to a good website that I think is credible, BAM! I get a virus on my computer. Then it just sends me back to my trusted "CTRL, ALT, DELETE" strategy and it begins all over again. It's just so frustrating. In my opinion, computers are useless!

REVISING YOUR WORK TO EXPAND RELEVANT IDEAS

As an author, you should always be clear about your purpose for writing. Is it to entertain? To inform? To impress or persuade? When writing, you want to communicate your purpose for writing to your audience in the most effective way possible.

While you want to stay close to the purpose of your writing, you also want to make sure that you are giving enough details to support your purpose for writing. Sometimes it may be important to elaborate on the topic being discussed within a paragraph. Elaborating on the important topics or details will make sure your reader is getting the most information, you, as the author, want them to, to support your purpose for writing.

Let's say you were writing a persuasive letter to your parents about having them raise your allowance. The letter might look like this:

Example

Dear Mom and Dad,

I believe you should give me a raise in my allowance because I am getting older, more mature and I am taking on more responsibilities around the house. My friends all have approximately the same chores as I do and their allowances are much larger than mine. I believe I should get a raise, because I deserve it and I think I have proven it over the last year.

Sincerely,
Your son, Ben

This paragraph sounds like it has some information about why Ben thinks he should get a raise, but as a reader, we are still left questioning many things. He did not give any specific details or ideas as to what he does around the house, or how much his friends actually make in comparison to him. He also did not state what amount he would like his raise to be. There are many areas where Ben could have provided more details to expand on the ideas inside his letter.

If we were to incorporate some more of these specific ideas into the persuasive letter, our readers (along with Ben's parents!) might be left with fewer questions as to why Ben deserves the raise in his allowance. It might be a lot less vague than the first paragraph. Let's give this a try again.

Example

Dear Mom and Dad,

I believe you should give me a raise in my allowance because I am getting older, more mature and I am taking on more responsibilities around the house. I am more and more willing to do the chores you want me to do, without you having to ask me to do them. I have begun mowing the lawn and raking the leaves during my free evenings to help out Dad. I have been helping Mom each evening to get supper ready for the past week, while she has been working late. I have even helped her clean the dishes after supper, with her only having to ask me a few times. I have taken care of our dog, Champ, regularly for the past year. I feed him, take him for walks, and bath him when he needs it without any help. My friends all have approximately the same amount of chores that I do, and their allowances are twice the amount of mine. I believe I should get a raise of at least 10 dollars more a month, because I feel like I have proven to both of you over the past year at least that I do truly deserve it.

Sincerely,

Your son, Ben

Did you notice?

Did you see how the second example of the same topic, elaborated a lot more on the specific reasons as to why he should get a raise in his allowance? Ben elaborated more on the specific chores that he has done to deserve the raise. He was also more specific on the amount he wanted for his raise.

Let's try another one together.

Example

Read the first paragraph and see how you might be able to add details to the description of the man standing in his office.

The man, wearing a suit and tie, entered his office and went directly to his book case and pulled a book down from it. He was not happy. He began flipping through the book and then stopped. "Could this be it?" he wondered.

Are there questions that come to you, as the reader, by reading that paragraph? What color was his suit? What about the color of his tie? How do we know he was not happy? Was the man frowning? How was he flipping through the book? Was it an old book or was it a new book? Was it big or small? As a reader, you may feel like many details have been left out. The writer could have definitely elaborated more on some of the details within the paragraph to help paint a more vivid picture for the reader. Let's try redoing this paragraph by including some of the answers to questions we were left wondering about.

Example

The middle aged, dark haired man, wearing a gray suit and a blue striped tie, entered his dingy office. He quickly went directly to his old, brown book case and pulled a torn, rustic looking book down from the shelf. He was frowning and the distinct anger in his dark brown eyes showed he was not happy. He looked like he was on a mission and frantically began flipping through the pages of the book. Suddenly he stopped, and his frown turned to a mischievous grin. "Could this be it?" he wondered.

Do you see how the second paragraph gave a few more details about what the scene and the man might look like? It also gave another feel to the story. If the author's purpose was to give the reader a dark, suspenseful feeling, then the second paragraph would probably come closer to doing that. It elaborated on more details and gave the reader a better chance to visualize the room, helping contribute to the author's possible intentions for writing.

This is what writers need to be conscientious of. They must be clear about their purpose for writing, yet, also paint a picture in their readers´ minds of what they are trying to portray. By giving more specific details or more examples, writers are more likely to make this happen for the reader.

Now it's your turn to try.

Example

The children play on the playground. They are having tons of fun playing with each other. There is a teacher watching them during the recess time. They are enjoying each area of the playground. The day is nice.

What does the playground look like? Why are the children having so much fun? What equipment are they playing on? How do we know the day is nice? What does the teacher look like? Is she young or old, mean or kind? What sounds or smells do you hear?

Can you take this paragraph and add some more details to it, so it helps the reader to truly visualize and have a solid understanding of the playground setting?

How do you think you did?

Were you able to add some details to the description of what the playground is like? Check below for a possible solution.

Example

There are hundreds of happy children playing on the playground on this beautifully warm and sunny Thursday afternoon. The energy on the playground is exciting. There is laughter ringing up to the heavens. There are screams and shrills of happiness bounding from the swing sets, leaping from the merry-go-round and jumping from the monkey bars. The joy of playing with their friends is enough to keep all the children smiling. Their young, kind teacher watches them with a giant smile across her face and the light breeze blowing through her soft brown hair. She is overjoyed at the happiness the students are displaying. The bell rings and the students run toward the red school doors. They are now ready to finish off the rest of their school day after their refreshing break on the playground.

GENERATING IDEAS FOR A NON-FICTION TOPIC USING A WORD WEB

When you are going to begin writing a non-fiction piece, it is always important to begin with generating ideas of what you may want to focus on in your written piece. One way that many people try to brainstorm and organize their ideas is by using a **word web.**

Many times a word web is a starting point for you to begin brainstorming ideas about what you know of the topic at hand. It is usually very general information, but helpful, none the less. Let's look at how this might look.

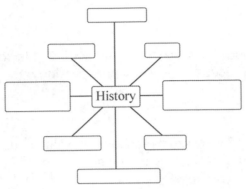

Let's say we were brainstorming about the word *history*.

What ideas might come to your mind, when you think of the word *history*?

When using a word web, you would place the word *history* in the center. Each word, idea, or topic that comes to your mind is then written down as an extension to the center word (in this case: History)

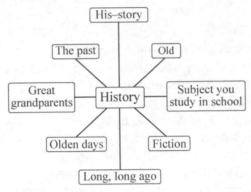

Some of the words that may come to your mind, may be: the past; old; great grandparents; olden days; his - story; fiction; long, long ago; subject you study in school.

These are all great starting points to get your mind thinking about the word history.

Depending on the area you are going to write about, by placing your ideas on the word web, you may be able to get an idea or a feel as to where you want your written piece to go.

A word web is just a great way to get your ideas flowing. Anything goes! So be brave and just start writing down anything that comes to your mind about your given topic.

Let's try this together.

If I said the word *baseball* what words might come to your mind?

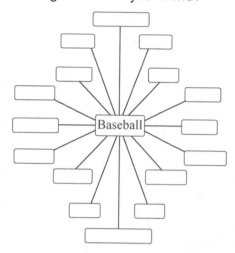

Brainstorm all the things that come to your mind. Write them down in a word web.

Baseball would be placed in the center of your word web.

Some of the extended pieces to your word web might be: innings, players, pitcher, hitter, back catcher, balls, bats, bases, home run, stadium, food, fans, crowds, boos, cheers, chants.

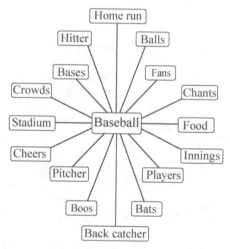

All of these words are ideas, or things you may think of when you think of baseball.

Generating ideas using a word web is an excellent idea when trying to figure out a non-fiction idea to write about because it helps you think about WHAT YOU KNOW. Writing about things that you know about and are interested in, is always a great start to your writing pieces.

Now it's your turn. Can you make a word web about the word *summer*? Once you think you have a great word web for the word *summer*, check out a possible word web example below.

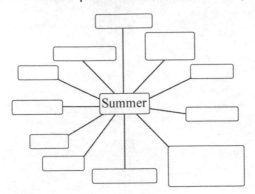

Remember to stick to what you know! What things, words, ideas, come to your mind when you think of summer? What do you do in the summer? What is the weather like in the summer? What do you wear in the summer? All these things are worth writing down for your word web about summer.

How do you think you did? If you have a word web about summer completed, look at the example below for more ideas or to compare your word web to.

Summer—vacations, hot, boating, waterskiing, kneeboarding, tubing, suntanning, sunscreen, music, towels, friends and family, hot weather.

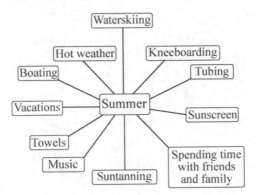

GENERATING IDEAS FOR A NON-FICTION TOPIC USING THE KWL CHART

When you are going to begin writing a non-fiction piece, it is always important to begin with generating ideas of what you may want to focus on in your written piece. One way that many people try to brainstorm and organize their ideas is by using a **KWL Chart.**

What is a KWL Chart?

A KWL Chart is a way to organize your ideas and or thoughts about a given topic. The letter **K** stands for WHAT DO YOU ALREADY **KNOW** about the given topic? The letter **W** stands for WHAT DO YOU **WANT** TO KNOW about the given topic? And the letter **L** stands for WHAT HAVE I **LEARNED** about the given topic.

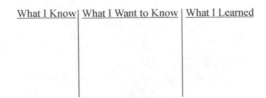

What I Know	What I Want to Know	What I Learned

As you can see, the chart is split into three columns. One heading is the **K**—where you ask yourself and jot down everything you already **KNOW** on the given topic. The next column is the **W**, where you jot down all the things you **WANT** to know about the given topic and the next section is the **L**. It is this section that you come back to after the research has been done, or even the whole written piece and reflect upon what you have **LEARNED** through out the research process.

Let's look at one KWL chart together.

Let's say we are brainstorming about the topic BOATS. Under the "K" section (What we KNOW) some of the things we might jot down are: Titanic, must float, they can be big and small boats, canoes, ships, fishing boats, or kayaks.

Under the "W" section (What we WANT to know about) we might write something appealing to our interests like: "What is the biggest boat ever made?" "How do heavy boats actually stay floating?" "What is the fastest boat ever made?"

Boats

What I Know	What I Want to Know	What I Learned
• Titanic • Must float • They can be big and small boats • Canoes • Ships • Fishing boats • Kayaks	• What is the biggest boat ever made? • How do heavy boats actually stay floating? • What is the fastest boat ever made?	

These are all questions you may choose to research into and possible create a non-fiction writing piece on.

Once you have finished researching about the topic BOATS, you then would go back and fill in the last section "L" (What we LEARNED)

GENERATING IDEAS FOR A NON-FICTION TOPIC USING MIND MAPPING

When you are going to begin writing a non-fiction piece, it is always important to begin with generating ideas of what you may want to focus on in your written piece. One way that many people try to brainstorm and organize their ideas is by using **mind mapping.**

Many times mind mapping can help as a starting point for you to begin brainstorming and organizing your ideas about the topic at hand. It can start off very general, and become more complex as you continue to brainstorm and add to the mind map. Let's look at how one might look.

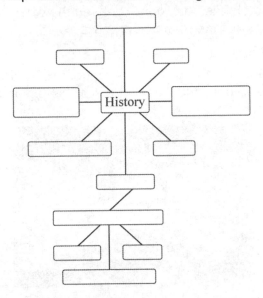

Let's say you were brainstorming about the word *history*.

What ideas might come to your mind, when you think of the word *history*?

When using a mind map, you would place the word *history* in the center. Each word, idea, or topic that comes to your mind is then written down as an extension to the center word (in this case: history).

Some of the words that may come to your mind may include: the past; old; great grandparents; olden days; his - story; fiction; long, long ago; subject you study in school.

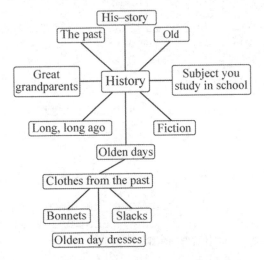

These are all great starting points to get your mind thinking about the word *history*.

Using mind maps is different from using a word web, as you can extend your ideas out even further into even smaller subsections and categories.

For example: from *History*, you may have written *olden days* and then attached to olden days you may have written *clothes from the past* and from there you may have an extended list of clothing like *bonnets, olden dresses, slacks,*etc.

A mind map is a great way to get your ideas organized into topics and subtopics.

LET'S TRY THIS TOGETHER

If I said the word *baseball* what words might come to your mind? You may begin to brainstorm ideas about baseball. "Baseball" would be placed in the center of your mind map.

Some of the ideas that come to your mind about baseball might include the following: innings, players, pitcher, hitter, back catcher, balls, bats, bases, home run, stadium, food, fans, crowds, boo's, cheers, chants,

All of these words are ideas, or things you may think of when you think of baseball. When you use mind mapping, it can help you to organize your thoughts into categories or sub topics. In the middle of your mind map you would put the word *baseball*, then an extension of that might be BASEBALL EQUIPMENT, then attached to that might be the words *balls*, *bats*, *bases*. Another section attached to the word *baseball*, may be *fans*, and then attached to that might be the words *crowds*, *boo's*, *chants*, *cheers*.

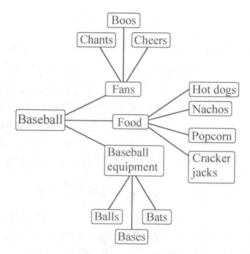

Maybe when you used the mind map to brainstorm things about baseball, you came up with the word *food*, and that sparked an idea to write about all the types of food you might eat if you were at a baseball game.

Do you see how the mind map can help you organize your thoughts?

Generating ideas using a mind map is an excellent idea when trying to figure out a non-fiction topic to write about, because it helps you think about WHAT YOU KNOW. Writing about things that you know about and are interested in, is always a great start to your writing pieces.

IT'S YOUR TURN

Below are some things a person might brainstorm about SUMMER. Can you organize these ideas into a mind map, breaking the words down into subsections?

Summer: vacations, boating, waterskiing, kneeboarding, tubing, suntanning, sunscreen, music, towels, time spent with friends and family, hot weather, tornado weather, sunshine, rain, barbecues, get-togethers.

How Did You Do?

Were you able to organize the brainstormed words into separate categories? Check a possible solution below.

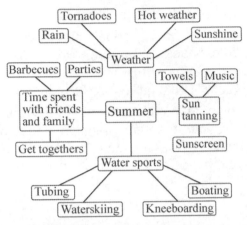

From the original list, you may have created a mind map that looks like this SUMMER

with a sub topic attached to it, WATER SPORTS, with the words *boating, waterskiing, knee boarding, tubing* attached to it. Then attached to SUMMER you may also have the sub topic SUN TANNING attached to it, with the words *sunscreen, music, towels* attached to it. Then another sub topic attached to SUMMER may be WEATHER, and attached to that may have the words *hot weather, sunshine, rain, tornadoes*. Another sub category attached to the word *summer* might be TIME SPENT WITH FRIENDS AND FAMILY and attached to that might be *barbecues, parties, get togethers*.

Using A Checklist to Edit your Non-Fiction Writing

The purpose of non-fiction writing is to communicate accurate and concrete information to an audience on a wide variety of different topics. The topics can range from different people, to different places, to different ideas, concepts, theories, events and even things.

When editing your non-fiction writing pieces, you must first begin by making sure your facts are accurate. A non-fiction piece must contain all true facts, or else it is considered fiction. Make sure that you have researched the information from a credible source before using it in your non-fiction writing piece.

Next, when evaluating your work, use an Editor's Checklist to make sure you have correctly edited all of your work and have it ready to continue on to the publishing stage.

A Checklist for Non-fiction Writing

1. Have I checked the beginning and end punctuation of my sentences to make sure they are all completed correctly?
2. Have I checked to make sure my sentences make sense and are clear to the reader?
3. Have I checked the spelling to make sure everything is spelt correctly?
4. Are all my paragraphs complete and only covering one important topic?
5. Is my beginning engaging and does it clearly introduce my topic?
6. Is my ending complete and does it wrap up my entire writing piece in a clear way?

Once you have read through your story, each time completing one of the above checklist points, you should be ready to publish your work, in whatever way you choose to do so.

Try This!

Let's edit the following non-fiction piece together. Remember that each time you read through your piece you should be checking for one of the checklist points. We will read through this non-fiction writing piece 6 times.

a tornado is a funnel of fast spinning air. Tornadoes usually start in thunderstorms and sometimes come with hale. Tornadoes can move at a rapid pace of 16 - 32 km per hour (10 - 20 miles). They usually only last traveling on the ground for up to 10 kilometers (6 miles). usually last at maximum 1 hour or so, and that is usually if it is classified as a violent tornado it is not very eesy to tell which direction a tornado's path may be, as its direction may change in a matter of minutes due to it's spinning nature.

1. Have I checked the beginning and end punctuation of my sentences to make sure they are all completely correct?

A tornado is a funnel of fast spinning air. Tornadoes usually start in thunderstorms and sometimes come with hale. Tornadoes can move at a rapid pace of 16 - 32 km per hour (10 - 20 miles). They usually only last traveling on the ground for up to 10 kilometers (6 miles). Usually last at maximum 1 hour or so, and that is usually if it is classified as a violent tornado it is not very eesy to tell which direction a tornado's path may be, as its direction may change in a matter of minutes due to it's spinning nature.

2. Have I checked to make sure my sentences make sense and are clear to the reader?

A tornado is a funnel of fast spinning air. Tornadoes usually start in thunderstorms and sometimes come with hale. Tornadoes can move at a rapid pace of 16 - 32 km per hour (10 - 20 miles). They usually only last traveling on the ground for up to 10 kilometers (6miles). **Tornadoes** usually last at maximum 1 hour or so, and that is usually if it is classified as a violent tornado. It is not very eesy to tell which direction a tornado's path may be, as its direction may change in a matter of minutes due to it's spinning nature.

3. Have I checked the spelling to make sure everything is spelled correctly?

A tornado is a funnel of fast spinning air. Tornadoes usually start in thunderstorms and sometimes come with **hail**. Tornadoes can move at a rapid pace of 16 - 32 km per hour (10 - 20 miles). They usually only last traveling on the ground for up to 10 kilometers (6 miles). Tornadoes usually last at maximum 1 hour or so, and that is usually if it is classified as a violent tornadoes. It is not very **easy** to tell which direction a tornado's path may be, as its direction may change in a matter of minutes due to **its** spinning nature.

4. Are all my paragraphs complete and only covering one important topic?

Because our example is only one paragraph long, it is best to just read over the paragraph to make sure it is all relevant to one topic. If not, then maybe a fact needs to be removed or in a larger text, moved to another paragraph where it fits. In this example, it is talking about tornadoes in general and the nature of them. Each sentence seems to fit this paragraph and no changes are necessary.

5. Is my beginning engaging and does it clearly introduce my topic?

Tornadoes are one of the world´s fascinating natural disasters. A tornado is a funnel of fast spinning air. Tornadoes usually start in thunderstorms and sometimes come with hail. Tornadoes can move at a rapid pace of 16 - 32 km per hour (10 - 20 miles). They usually only last traveling on the ground for up to 10 kilometers (6 miles). Tornadoes usually last at maximum 1 hour or so, and that is usually if it is classified as a violent tornado. It is not very easy to tell which direction a tornado's path may be, as its direction may change in a matter of minutes due to its spinning nature.

6. Is my ending complete and does it wrap up my entire writing piece in a clear way?

Tornadoes are one of the world´s fascinating natural disasters. A tornado is a funnel of fast spinning air. Tornadoes usually start in thunderstorms and sometimes come with hail. Tornadoes can move at a rapid pace of 16 - 32 km per hour (10 - 20 miles). They usually only last traveling on the ground for up to 10 kilometers (6 miles). Tornadoes usually last at maximum 1 hour or so, and that is usually if it is classified as a violent tornado. It is not very easy to tell which direction a tornado's path may be, as its direction may change in a matter of minutes due to its spinning nature. **Tornadoes can be dangerously unpredictable and destructive depending on its size and speed and how long it lasts for.**

Here is what the final paragraph might look like, once you have gone through each item to edit from the check list:

Tornadoes are one of the world´s fascinating natural disasters. A tornado is a funnel of fast spinning air. Tornadoes usually start in thunderstorms and sometimes come with **hail**. Tornadoes can move at a rapid pace of 16 - 32 km per hour (10 - 20 miles). They usually only last traveling on the ground for up to 10 kilometers (6 miles). **Tornadoes** usually last at maximum 1 hour or so, and that is usually if it is classified as a violent tornado. It is not very **easy** to tell which direction a tornado's path may be, as its direction may change in a matter of minutes due to its spinning nature. **Tornadoes can be dangerously unpredictable and destructive depending on its size and speed and how long it lasts for.**

REVISING YOUR NON-FICTION WRITING PIECE TO PROVIDE FOCUS

The purpose of non-fiction writing is to communicate and provide accurate and concrete information to an audience searching for information on a wide variety of different topics. The topics can range from different people, to different places, to different ideas, concepts, theories, events and even things. As long as the information is completely true, it is considered non-fiction.

It is important when you are writing a non-fiction piece, that you stay close to the topic you are writing about and the point or idea that you want to get across.

If you choose to write about sharks and where they live, you would not want to go off topic by talking about what they eat.

The best way to revise your writing is to read through each paragraph of your piece and make sure each paragraph is about the subtopic you are writing about. That subtopic should contribute to the entire piece. If you get to a paragraph or part of a paragraph that does not add to the topic, then it may be best to edit it out.

It is important to make sure each sentence and each paragraph stays focused on your topic. When you have pieces that do not add to the main focus, those pieces become distractions, instead of helping add to the topic.

Let's look at a paragraph together that is about turtles and the color of their shells. Is there any line in the paragraph below that does not fit in with this paragraph about the color of a turtle's shell?

Example

Turtles are amazing reptiles that have extraordinary shells. The shells can range in all types of colors, depending on the type of turtle it is. A turtle's shell is usually either a black, brown or olive green color. Some species of turtles may even have red, orange, yellow and gray colored spots and blotches on their shells. The tortoise, the turtle that lives on land has a very heavy shell. The eastern painted turtle is one of the most colorful turtles in the world, with its yellow and black or olive green shell and red markings around the outside of the shell.

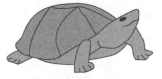

The line, "**The tortoise, the turtle that lives on land has a very heavy shell.**" does not belong in the above paragraph. Yes, even though it is talking about the turtle's shell, it is not talking about the **colors** of a turtle's shell, which is what the rest of the paragraph is talking about.

It's Your Turn

Can you find any of the sentences that do not belong in the following paragraph about honeybees and their appearances?

Honeybees are beautiful insects, with yellow and black stripes. Bees have three body parts. The thorax, which is the middle section of the bee, a head and an abdomen, which is the end section of a bee. The thorax has the bee's six legs and two wings attached to it. The honeybee has a stinger, or poison gland that sticks out of the abdomen. But don't worry, a bee will only sting you if you are mean to it. Honeybees are hairy.

There is **one** sentence that does not belong in the above paragraph.

How Did You Do?

Were you able to identify which line does not belong in the paragraph? Check your answer below.

Honeybees are beautiful insects, with yellow and black stripes. Bees have three body parts. The thorax, which is the middle section of the bee, a head and an abdomen, which is the end section of a bee. The thorax has the bee's six legs and two wings attached to it. The honeybee has a stinger, or poison gland that sticks out of the abdomen. **But don't worry, a bee will only sting you if you are mean to it.** Honeybees are hairy.

The highlighted sentence does not belong in this paragraph because it is only telling an outside idea about the bee's stinger, and it is not about the bee's appearance. It does not belong in this paragraph.

Revise Your Non-Fiction Writing to Expand on Relevant Ideas

The purpose of non-fiction writing is to communicate accurate and concrete information to an audience searching for information on many different topics. The topics can range from different people, to different places, to different ideas, concepts, theories, events and even things. As long as the information is completely true, it is considered non-fiction.

It is important when you are writing a non-fiction piece, that you stay close to the topic you are writing about and the point or idea that you want to get across.

While you want to stay close to your topic and be as direct as possible when writing about a non-fiction topic, you also want to make sure that you are giving **enough information** about the topic being discussed. Sometimes you may have to **elaborate or expand** on the subtopic being discussed within a paragraph. Elaborating on the important topics, or details, will make sure your reader is getting the most important information about the topic being discussed.

Example

Let's say you were writing a report on the African Elephant. The paragraph below might be an example of what African Elephants look like.

African elephants are gray. They are big and tall and they have really big ears. Elephants are heavy in weight. They have a long trunk and two tusks.

This paragraph sounds like it has quite a bit of information in it, but we are still left questioning many things. The elephant is gray? What kind of gray? It's big and tall and heavy too, but how heavy or how tall? What are its ears like? What does the trunk look like and what is it used for?

Example

If we were to answer these questions in a report, our readers might be left with a lot fewer questions, than they would be when reading the vague first paragraph. Let's give this a try again.

African elephants are one of the largest animals in the world. If you were to measure them up to their shoulders they might measure up to four meters high! They are extremely heavy in weight and can weigh more than 14,000 pounds! That's huge! African Elephants are well known for their large ears that droop down and look something like the continent of Africa. African Elephants have a very long trunk that is used for breathing, smelling, eating and drinking. The trunk has over 100,000 different muscles in it! On either side of the trunk, the elephant has something called tusks, and these tusks are made out of ivory. Elephants are huge, unbelievable mammals to see.

Did you see how the second example of the same topic elaborated a lot more of the African Elephant's appearance, and gave the reader a more vivid idea of what the elephant might look like? This is what writers need to be aware of. They want to be able to paint the picture of what they are talking about into their readers' minds. By giving more specific details, you can make this happen for your readers.

Now It's Your Turn to Try

Can you take this paragraph and add some more details to it, so it helps the reader to truly visualize what peacocks look like? Once you think you have a great paragraph, look at the solution below, as well.

Peacocks are colorful birds. There are typically the Blue Peacocks and the Green Peacocks. They both have lots of large feathers and lots of "eye" looking circles on their feathers.

Peacocks are very colorful birds. There are typically called Blue Peacocks or Green Peacocks. Depending on which peacock it is, the name gives away the color of body the peacock will have. Both peacocks have many large feathers that fan out from their body. Their feathers are 60% larger than the length of their bodies. On their feathers they have bright blue, gold, red as well as other hued circles, that many refer to as looking like a singular eye. These "eye" looking markings are found all over the feathers.

USE THE APPROPRIATE GRAPHIC ORGANIZER TO SORT INFORMATION

A graphic organizer is a great tool for students to visually sort and organize information.

When sorting information, a commonly used graphic organizer is the Venn Diagram. A Venn Diagram is best used to sort two or more items, separating their differences on each side with the center consisting of the item's similarities. It looks likes circles overlapping each other about half way.

Below are a list of facts that relate to either a shark, a dolphin or both. A Venn Diagram would be an example of a graphic organizer to sort the information into groups.

CHARACTERISTICS OF SHARKS

- Tough, elastic skin
- More teeth
- Great sense of smell
- A scary appearance
- Are a fish

CHARACTERISTICS OF DOLPHINS

- Smooth, rubbery skin
- Less teeth
- No sense of smell
- Friendly appearance
- Are mammals

Venn Diagram Organizer

There are many kinds of graphic organizers which can help you sort information. The type of graphic organizer you use depends on the needs of you as a student and the task.

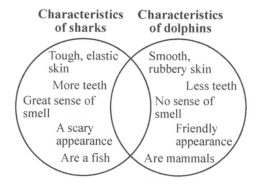

Other graphic organizers include the following:

- Plot diagrams
- Mind maps
- Thought webs
- Network trees
- Charts
- Tables

4W.6   With some guidance and support from adults, use technology, including the Internet, to produce and publish writing as well as to interact and collaborate with others; demonstrate sufficient command of keyboarding skills to type a minimum of...

Use Electronic Dictionaries and Thesauruses

The purpose of this lesson is to introduce you to a few online websites that have electronic word searches (dictionaries) and thesauruses. Please keep in mind that these are online sources, which means you need to treat them with caution. They might not always have the best information or the most accurate and up to date data.

Using an Online Word Search (Dictionary)

One of the most popular online dictionary and thesaurus websites is http://dictionary.reference.com/ but there are many more that you can use. Below you will find a list of online dictionaries along with a brief description for each one.

1. http://dictionary.cambridge.org/
    A great dictionary site that offers features like idioms, phrasal verbs and a learner's dictionary.
2. http://www.merriam-webster.com/dictionary/
    A great dictionary, a free translator, and even a medial dictionary that will read aloud most terms that you look up
3. http://www.thefreedictionary.com/
    A great site because even if you are not sure about the spelling of a word, you can type in the part that you know and it will figure out the rest. Another great feature of this site is that it can look up whole articles of information.
4. http://www.webster-dictionary.org/
    Webster dictionary is one of the most popular dictionaries out there. It is a reliable source of information. However, it is written at a higher level of complexity.
5. http://www.visuwords.com/
    This is an very helpful site that will look up the definition of a word. It is also both a thesaurus and a visual dictionary. Simply place your cursor over the word bubbles and the information will be shown.

USING AN ONLINE THESAURUS

If you would like to look up a word in a thesaurus, there are many great sites for that too. Below you will find a list of online thesauruses and a brief description for each one.

1. http://thesaurus.com/
    One of the most commonly used sites. It is fast and very easy to use.
2. http://www.visualthesaurus.com/
    A great site that will map out your word with others that have similar ideas, and will also read them aloud. Finally, it will look up the words it suggests.
3. http://freethesaurus.net/
    A nice site that suggests many words for anything you decide to search for. It is easy to use and uses simple language.
4. http://www.wordsmyth.net/
    A great feature of Wordsmyth is that you can select the level of language you would like it to use, anything from beginner, children, to advanced!

4W.7   Conduct short research projects that build knowledge through investigation of different aspects of a topic.

USE CRITERIA TO ASSESS THE RESEARCH PROCESS

Criteria are standards and expectations, usually set by the teacher. The criteria allow you to know exactly what is expected. A rubric is often used to lay out the pre-established criteria.

A rubric is a system used to evaluate the data and information that you find when you research a topic. It can also be used to evaluate the quality of your work. The chart form of a rubric makes it easier to assess an activity, a performance, or a product, because it lists all of the criteria necessary to make a complete evaluation.

A rubric uses levels of progress to assess the criteria. The levels of progress should show the rules and guidelines used to score your work. As the levels increase, the marks get higher. Depending on the rubric used, different levels may have different values. For instance, each level reached may be worth one mark, two marks, or even five marks. These marks are then added together to reach a kind of "score". The score lets you know how well you have done with your project.

Example

This example would not work for a research rubric, but shows how a rubric is set up like a chart. At each level on this rubric, you would be doing more cardio exercise, more strength training, eating more healthy food, and getting more sleep and vitamins, until you reached your healthiest peak at Level 4.

Criteria	Level 1	Level 2	Level 3	Level 4
Cardio	running 1 day a week	running 2 days a week	running 3 days a week	running 4 days a week
Strength	weight training 0 days a week	weight training 1 day a week	weight training 2 days a week	weight training 3 days a week
Nutrition	80% carbohydrates 10% unsaturated fats 10% proteins	70% carbohydrates 15% unsaturated fats 15% proteins	70% carbohydrates 25% unsaturated fats 5% proteins	65% carbohydrates 25% unsaturated fats 10% proteins
Sleep	< 3 hours	< 5 hours	< 7 hours	8 hours
Vitamins	took $\frac{0}{3}$	took $\frac{1}{3}$	took $\frac{2}{3}$	took $\frac{3}{3}$

CREATE A CRITERIA RUBRIC FOR YOUR PROJECT

Follow these steps to use a rubric to assess your research or project:

- Write down the tasks that are required or the criteria that have been set by the teacher.
- Make 3 or 4 levels like partly done, completed, completed and checked, etc.
- Match the completed work to the appropriate level on the rubric.
- Determine the mark for each category after each one has been evaluated individually.
- Add the marks assigned to each category to determine your final score.

Assessing the research process might look like you are creating a flowchart of your research. It helps to keep you on track, decide how much time you need to finish, plan the next stage of your work, and get help from an adult as needed. You can also write a paragraph summarizing what you learned about the research process.

4W.8   Recall relevant information from experiences or other relevant information from print and digital sources; take notes and categorize information, and provide a list of sources.

WHAT IS A BIBLIOGRAPHY?

When you look at the parts of the word, *bibliography*, it helps to know that "biblio" came from a Greek word meaning *book*, and "graph" came from a word meaning *write*. It means to write down your books. A bibliography is a list of books, magazines, films, and websites that you have used for your research.

It is important to list every source that you use. This shows respect for the authors and websites that have shared their information with you. A bibliography for someone's research on New Orleans might look something like the one below.

BIBLIOGRAPHY

Downs, Tom, Edge, John. "New Orleans." The Lonely Planet, 2006.

Faulkner, William. *New Orleans Sketches*. College Press of Mississippi: New Orleans, 2002.

Gotham, Kevin. *Authentic New Orleans: Tourism, Culture, and Race in the Big Easy*. College Press: New York, 2007.

"New Orleans Before and After Katrina", New Orleans Office of Tourism, www.bigeasy.org. 2010.

CREATE A BIBLIOGRAPHY

The creation of a bibliography starts as soon as you begin preparing a report, speech, or any researched writing project. You need to keep track of where you are getting your information. That way you are showing respect for the work or ideas belonging to someone else. This is done simply by writing the name of the author and title of the work that you are using.

Things that you need to keep in mind are:

- author's name
- title of work
- publishing company
- location of publishing company
- date

There are also websites that can help you manage all the information you need for your bibliography. **Noodletools.com** is a great site that asks you to fill in a few information boxes. Then, it will create the reference for you in the proper format that is needed.

Below you will find an example of how a bibliography is written. You must also remember that entries in your bibliography are written in alphabetical order according to the author's last name.

Example

Correct Order: Author's last name, author's first name. "Title of piece of work." Publishing company: publishing company's location, year of publication.

Bennet, Lerone. *What Manner of Man: A Biography of Martin Luther King Jr.* Chicago: Johnson, 1964.

King Martin Luther Jr. *Why We Can't Wait.* New York: Harper and Row, 1963.

Martin Luther King, Jr. Wikipedia, the free encyclopedia:Wikipedia.org/wiki/Martin_Luther_King_Jr.

Smith, John. "Importance of being Humble." College of Calgary Press: Calgary, 2010.

GATHER FACTS USING PRIMARY RESOURCES

Primary resources are valuable sources of information because they offer a believable inside view of a particular event. A primary source is an original source of information created at the time the event occurred.

Primary sources are valuable in gathering facts because they are not altered or changed. The facts that you gather are coming straight from someone who witnessed, first hand, the event in question.

Example

The Diary of Anne Frank and The Declaration of Independence are examples of primary resources.

Any original document, artifact, manuscript, diary or photograph is considered a primary resource.

Example

The following is a journal entry from an explorer of the Arctic circle on December 2, 1938:

"It was –38°C when our mission was aborted. Our ship hit an iceberg at 3:37 A.M.. No one witnessed it hit but we all felt it. The captain called the crew to the main deck to assess the damage. I stood at his side to support him as he broke the terrifying news. The ship has been punctured too many times and would soon capsize. We has less than 30 minutes to gather our things and evacuate the ship-the ship that had been my home for nearly 20 years. The life boats were almost prepared when the ship began sinking quickly. I witnessed two terrified men jump overboard into the icy water. Forty five men escaped the icy waters of the Arctic that early morning and only five men perished."

This journal entry is considered a primary resource because it was written by a man who not only witnessed the event at the time the event occurred, but also experienced it first hand.

If I were researching Arctic explorers and I came across this journal entry, it would provide me with valuable information about a tragic night that happened many years ago.

GATHER FACTS USING SECONDARY RESOURCES

A secondary resource is an interpretation of a primary resource. It's the next best thing if the primary (original) resource isn't available.

Secondary resources are valuable resources because they are summaries and interpretations of events that are created after the event has occurred. The facts included in a secondary resource can contain more details, because the writer many have included information from many sources before evaluating what important details should be included.

Example
An encyclopedia, a biography, and a newspaper article about a particular person or event are examples of secondary sources.

Figure 2: Europe – 1919

If you were gathering facts on World War II, it might be useful to look at newspaper articles and books written after the war so that you have post war facts. The secondary resources may be created from many other reviews of the War, and not by a person who fought in it.

ANALYZE DETAILS AND INFORMATION FROM REFERENCE MATERIAL

If you are asked to evaluate something you have read (a newspaper/magazine article or editorial cartoon), you need to describe the positive and negative qualities of the selection and then reach a conclusion about how good (or bad) the piece is.

As you evaluate the article, you will need to examine how well it is organized and whether the 5 W and 1 H questions are answered:

- Who is involved?
- What happened?
- When did it happen?
- Where did it happen?
- Why did it happen?
- How did it happen?

As you read the article, you will examine how well the information is supported by facts and opinions. The clearer the information is, the easier the article will be to read and understand.

BARKERVILLE GAZETTE

The lead, or first, paragraph of a newspaper article gives the main information.

DOG RESCUES OWNER

Local artist Warren McComb is grateful that his pooch, Coyote, hates the smell of burning oil paint. McComb had fallen asleep on the sofa in his studio, shortly after 9 P.M. last evening, when he awakened to the frantic barking of his small dog in the smoke-filled room. Fortunately, there was enough visibility for him to grab the dog and exit to the patio, where he called 911. Firemen arrived in moments and quickly extinguished flames coming from a wastebasket.

Fire officials are still investigating the cause of the fire. Fire Marshall Kennie reports that the culprit may well be the brave dog. A charred and partially chewed lamp cord was discovered, still plugged in, right next to an overflowing wastebasket.

Warren McComb needs to redecorate his studio, but will not punish Coyote for chewing on the cord. "I'll just buy him some real bones," he promised with a grin.

Analyze the Information

If you use the 5 W's and 1 H questions to guide your analysis of the information in the news article, you will discover the following details:

- Who - Local artist Warren McComb and his dog, Coyote
- What - a fire
- When - shortly after 9 P.M. last evening
- Where - Warren McComb's studio
- Why - dog was chewing on lamp cord
- How - wire was exposed by chewing, and ignited contents of wastebasket

MAKING INFERENCES WHILE READING
WHAT IS INFERENCING?

Inferencing is making a guess, inferring, or drawing conclusions about what is happening in a story.

Example
If I was holding a pencil in my hand then asked you for a pencil sharpener, why do you think I asked for a pencil sharpener?

You might guess that I need to sharpen my pencil. This is making a inference, I did not tell you what I needed the sharpener for you just guess that since I was holding a pencil I wanted to sharpen it.

___

Authors sometimes do this in their writing, they do not tell their readers everything but rather have their readers make inferences about what might be happening.

MAKING INFERENCES

Read the following scenarios and make an inference (guess) about what you think is happening or going to happen.

1. Before she left she put her raincoat on and grabbed her umbrella from the closet.
2. The children ran towards the pool with their swimsuits on.
3. Her bag was packed with her glove, bat and favorite ball.

What do you think was happening or going to happen next in the above scenarios?

Here are some possible answers:

1. Since she put on her raincoat and grabbed her umbrella before leaving we can infer that it was raining outside.

2. Since the children had on their swimsuits and were running towards the pool we can infer that they were going swimming.
3. Since her bag was packed with a glove, bat and ball we can infer that she was going to play baseball.

MAKING INFERENCES ABOUT CHARACTERS

The author of a story that you may be reading does not always provide you with all the details of how a character might be feeling or what they may do next. Sometimes the author just provides you with little hints and you are left to infer the character's actual feelings or motives. Making conclusions about a character's feelings or motives is called inferencing.

MAKING INFERENCES

Example

What can you infer about the characters in the following scenarios?

1. She reached for a tissue and took a deep breath as she wiped away her tears.

2. James' hands shook as he turned the nob and opened the door to the dark and deserted house.
3. The sun's rays were beating down as she wiped the sweat from her brow and panted across the finish line.

What inferences did you make about the above characters?

Here are some possible answers:

1. Reaching for a tissue, taking a deep breath and wiping tears away we can infer the character is sad.
2. Shaking hands opening a dark and deserted house we can infer that the character is nervous.
3. Sun's rays, wiping sweat, panting, and crossing the finish line we can infer that the character is hot and tired.

4W.10   Write routinely over extended time frames (time for research, reflection, and revision) and shorter time frames (a single sitting or a day or two) for a range of discipline-specific tasks, purposes, and audiences.

SELECT A PARAGRAPH FOCUS BASED ON PURPOSE

Reading without a purpose is like setting off on a road trip without a map. You find yourself wasting a lot of time because you do not know where you are going, what is important (e.g., road signs, last gas station for 100 miles), and the whole experience becomes very frustrating. At some point, you find yourself way off course because you went too far and did not think to stop and ask for directions. If you do not set a purpose for reading you may find yourself in the same situation.

What you do before you start to read can make or break the reading experience. First of all, you have to determine what your reason for reading is. Is it to research information for an essay, answer questions for an assignment, get instructions for assembling a new bike, find out the highlights of the basketball game, or to escape into the latest bestseller book. Once you decide what your reason is, you have also decided your purpose for reading…now you know where you are going.

Though your teacher may often set your reading purpose, you might want to clarify your purpose by asking yourself the "five W's" before you read: Who? What? Where? When? Why? How? Asking your own questions will help you read better and gain more meaning from the reading process.

Good readers know that when you have a purpose for reading you can keep a closer eye on your progress and know when to stop and turn around when something is not quite right. Sometimes you need to revisit your purpose, and sometimes your purpose changes—as in the case of state tests, when you often have to read the same story or article for different purposes.

PURPOSE-BASED PARAGRAPHS

Just as purpose is important to reading, it is important to writing. Look at the topic sentences below, to see how the purpose is set up in the first sentence of the paragraph.

1. If you follow three simple guidelines, it is possible to do well on a multiple-choice test. (Purpose of paragraph will be to explain)
2. My most embarrassing moment happened like this. (Purpose of paragraph will be to entertain)
3. If you read these instructions and examine the two diagrams, you will be able to tie a slip knot. (Purpose of paragraph will be to instruct)
4. Above all, never, never say, "I can't do that." (Purpose of paragraph will be to inspire or challenge)
5. Before us, spreading toward the horizon like a dream, lay the legendary Forgotten Valley. (Purpose of paragraph will be to describe)

SELECT A PARAGRAPH FOCUS BASED ON AUDIENCE

Your audience is the person who will read your writing. You must learn to write for a variety of audiences. Here are some examples of who you may be writing for:

- an adult, such as your parents, teacher, or principal
- classmates or other students
- younger children, for whom you are creating a folktale
- a friend, relative, or pen pal to whom you are writing a letter
- a guest speaker, such as the mayor of your town, political leaders, a sports star, a community helper like a fireman or policeman, or a famous person
- businesses in the community, such as the local newspaper, television, or radio station

Imagine you are going to share a story with your teacher. Would you use the same expressions and words with your teacher as you would with a friend? It is very likely that you would speak more formally with your teacher and use less formal words with your friends.

Example

Less Formal Words	More Formal Words
kids	children
thanks	thank you
see you	goodbye
cool	stylish

4SL.1a   Engage effectively in a range of collaborative discussions (one-on-one, in groups, and teacherled) with diverse partners on grade 4 topics and texts, building on others' ideas and expressing their own clearly. Come to discussions...

WORKING IN A GROUP: ADDING YOUR PART TO A DISCUSSION

Working with a group can be both fun and interesting. More people means more ideas and different points of view. On the other hand, more people might mean more confusion and more noise! This is why it is a good idea to have some rules about how your group will behave in a discussion. Helpful rules may include the following:

- Everyone gets a turn to speak.
- Speak in a strong, clear voice.
- Stay on topic.
- Only use respectful words.
- Raise your hand to ask a question.
- Ask questions if you do not understand.
- Pay attention to whoever is speaking.

4SL.1b   Engage effectively in a range of collaborative discussions (one-on-one, in groups, and teacherled) with diverse partners on grade 4 topics and texts, building on others' ideas and expressing their own clearly. Follow agreed-upon rules...

WORKING IN A GROUP: BEING A GOOD LISTENER

Listening is just as important in a group discussion as speaking. Being a good listener means doing the following things:

- Keeping your eyes and ears on whoever is speaking
- Smiling or encouraging the speakers, especially if you see they are feeling nervous about talking to the group
- Staying quiet and not speaking to others while someone is speaking
- Waiting until a speaker has finished before you ask questions or add your comments
- In a large group, putting up your hand if you want to add a question or comment
- Asking questions when you are not sure you understand what someone said
- Writing down notes if decisions are made or you are asked to do a job after the discussion

WORKING IN A GROUP: THE PRESENTER ROLE

Usually when you work in a group, it is a good idea to decide which job or role each group member will work on. One of the jobs that groups often use is that of presenter. Not every project ends with a presentation, but if there is one, the presenter's job will include:

- Introducing the project to the audience, including the topic or title and why the group chose it
- Introducing the group members to the audience
- Speaking in a clear, strong voice
- Describing the project, or reading it aloud, if it is a story or report
- Answering any questions from the audience

The presenter may also:

- Explain what the group learned from the project
- Describe any difficulties the group had and how they resolved them

4SL.1c   Engage effectively in a range of collaborative discussions (one-on-one, in groups, and teacherled) with diverse partners on grade 4 topics and texts, building on others' ideas and expressing their own clearly. Pose and respond to...

USE QUESTIONING FOR COMMUNICATING

We all ask questions many times a day. They are an important part of communicating with others and finding out about the world around us. Consider some of the following examples of types of questions.

Example

Type of Question	Examples
To find out a quick fact	"What time is it?" or "Where is Jacob today?"
To ask for permission	"May I have another cookie?"
To get an opinion	"Which do you like better, the red one or the blue one?" or "What do you think we should do to celebrate?"
To clarify meaning	"I'm not sure I understood that. Would you please explain a bit more?" or "Did you mean that you are the best artist in the class or that art is your best subject?"
To encourage other people to share their ideas	"What do you like about dragons?" or "Can you think of anything else we could add to this project?"
To show people we care about them	"How are you today?" or "Did you have a fun weekend?"
To learn new things	"Why do dogs sniff each other's pee?" or "Why do geese always fly in a V?"
To solve a problem	"If there are 12 cupcakes in a package, how many packages will I need to buy for a class with 24 students?" or "If it takes 1/2 an hour to get to Jonah's house, what time do I need to leave to get to his party at 3:00?"

When you work in a group, questions are important tools for getting work done. All the above types of questions can be used in group work. When you ask people questions, it shows that you care about them, their feelings and their thoughts. If you notice that someone in your group is very quiet or is not joining in discussions, questions may help them to participate more. Below, see how the same question types are used in a group discussion. The group is creating a display about how to create a school garden. Notice how the questions work better than the statements to make everyone in the group feel important.

Example

Type of Question	Useful Examples	Instead of These Statements
To find out a quick fact	"Amir, do you know who else is in our group?"	"I don't know who else is in my group."
To ask for permission	"Jake, may I please borrow a pencil?"	"Someone needs to lend me a pencil!"
To get an opinion	"What does everyone think - should we talk about just flower gardens or vegetable gardens too?"	"We should definitely talk about flower gardens and vegetable gardens."
To clarify meaning	"Did you mean that I should type one of the text boxes on my computer to test out which fonts and titles we want to use?"	"You've got to be kidding! I'm not going to type up all the words. You make me do all the boring work!"
To encourage others to share their ideas	"Mikkel, what do think we should add to the poster?"	"Mikkel, you never say anything or help us come up with ideas."
To show people we care about them	"How are you feeling today?"	"You don't have much to say today."
To learn new things	"Are there any other schools nearby that have started gardens? Who would like to find out?"	"You should find out if any other schools have started gardens."
To solve problems	"If we have to hand this in next Friday, how many days do we have left to work on this?"	"We have only 6 days to work on this, so you had better get busy!"

CLARIFYING MEANING IN A GROUP DISCUSSION

When you work in a group, it is very important to make sure you are communicating clearly, and also that you clearly understand other people in your group.

Sometimes when you tell people something, it seems really clear to you, but you look around and realize that perhaps other people did not quite understand you. Perhaps they completely misunderstood you, or perhaps they just look a bit unsure. If you go back and explain your meaning in a different way to make sure everyone understands, this is called clarifying.

Sometimes you need to help clarify what another person says. If you are not sure you understand his meaning or if you see that other people in your group look a bit unsure, clarification may be needed.

One way to do this is to say "I just want to make sure I understand what you just said," and say it again in your own words. Then say "Is this what you meant?" and give them a chance to explain further.

Example

Anna: "I think I should be the illustrator for our book because I am the best at that."

Grace: (notices that some kids look offended) "I just want to make sure I understand what you just said. You think you should be the illustrator because you think you are better at drawing than writing?"

Anna: "Yes, that's what I just said!"

In this example, Anna thought she was being very clear, but Grace noticed that some people thought Anna meant that she was better at drawing than the other group members. By stopping and clarifying Anna's meaning, Grace may have stopped an argument from breaking out and prevented feelings from being hurt.

Another way to get clarification is to say "I'm not sure if I understood you. Would you please explain that a little bit?"

What you **do not** want to do is say anything that might hurt another person's feelings. It is easy to get frustrated when people do not understand each other, but letting frustration show will probably not help to clarify things.

Example

Anna: "I think I should be the illustrator for our book because I am the best at that."

Orion: "You think you are the best artist? Thanks a lot! Maybe I wanted to be the illustrator!"

Anna: "That's not what I meant. I meant that I'm better at drawing than writing. I never know what to say! I guess you think I'm not good at anything!"

You see how, in this example, things got out of hand very quickly because Orion misunderstood Anna's meaning. He did not try to clarify it before he let his frustration show and they both ended up with hurt feelings.

MAKE AND SHARE CONNECTIONS WHEN INTERACTING WITH OTHERS

When we interact and have conversations with others, it allows us to share and compare ideas. We are then able to open our minds to opinions and ideas from other people. Discussing ideas can also allow us to look at something in a different way.

Sharing connections can help bring more understanding into a discussion.

Example
If we were discussing the impact that global warming is having on polar bears, and I did a research project on a similar topic a year ago, then I would bring some important ideas into the discussion. Perhaps my partner had watched a documentary on polar bears. This would enable us to have an in-depth discussion on the topic.

We share our connections with others to help us make more sense of things. We learn a lot about ourselves and our world by taking part in discussions with others.

ASKING AND ANSWERING QUESTIONS TO CONVEY INFORMATION

When you are reading a textbook or studying for a test, it is helpful to be able to use various reading strategies to help you remember what you have read. Asking yourself questions is one such strategy. To do this, think of questions about your reading to help you focus.

Take headings, key words, or topic sentences and turn them into questions. Suppose you were reading a book about Earth. Think of all of the questions you could ask, using what you already know, what you might like to know, and what you are learning through the information in the book. Asking questions and then using the text to answer them is a great way to study and remember the information you have read.

WRITE TO ANSWER A QUESTION

Posing a question is a smart way to begin your paragraph or writing project, especially if you are presenting information. Below are some sample questions that you could answer in a paragraph, report, or essay:

- What are the most seriously endangered animals on our planet?
- How can you design your own web page?
- How exactly would you go about creating a blog?
- How can we eat healthy now so that we won't suffer problems like obesity and diabetes later?
- What are the most important things for a babysitter to know?
- What should you do if you hear a tornado warning?
- Why are dolphins such amazing mammals?

4SL.1d   Engage effectively in a range of collaborative discussions (one-on-one, in groups, and teacherled) with diverse partners on grade 4 topics and texts, building on others' ideas and expressing their own clearly. Review the key ideas...

WORKING IN A GROUP: REFLECTING

When you talk with a group, people can share ideas, feelings, facts, questions, and plans. Sometimes it can be hard to remember all the things that were discussed by the time you have your next group meeting. As well, you may find it hard to understand everything that is happening during the meeting. Perhaps things went too quickly, or someone started talking about a new topic while you were stilling thinking about the first one. One thing that can help you to sort out your thoughts and remember important things is called reflecting. When your face is reflected in a mirror, your face looks back at you. This kind of reflecting is like the mirror except that it is your mind that looks or remembers back to what you talked about in the group discussion.

Reflecting is more than just remembering, however. It is more like remembering, sorting, learning, and planning all rolled up together. As you think back to your group discussion, you might ask yourself the following questions to help your reflecting:

- Was there anything you did not understand? If so, what could you do to understand better? (e.g. talk to another person in your group, ask another friend or grown-up, read a book, etc.)
- What surprised you? Why? (e.g. Were you surprised that someone really like your idea? Why did that surprise you? Were you surprised to find out that Olivia is really good at spelling? How could this help your group?)
- What did you think was interesting? Do you want to find out more about that? How could you find out more? (e.g. Maya said that elephants are actually quiet when they walk. So why do people say that noisy kids sound like a herd of elephants?)
- Did you add your thoughts or ideas to the discussion? If not, what stopped you? What could change that for next time?
- Who spoke clearly in the group? Do you think that you spoke clearly when it was your turn?

You might write down the answers to these questions, or you might just keep them in your head. Some people keep a journal or reflection book so that they can remember better.

4SL.2   Paraphrase portions of a text read aloud or information presented in diverse media and formats, including visually, quantitatively, and orally.

PARAPHRASE INFORMATION SOURCES

Paraphrasing is restating someone else's ideas in your own words. Paraphrasing can help you to understand a piece of writing. Paraphrasing is most helpful when the author uses complicated words and long sentences, or when a situation is hard to follow. To paraphrase, take your time and restate what you read in your own words. In this way, you can concentrate and understand the meaning of the writing before you move on. Sometimes a teacher will ask you to paraphrase a sentence or a paragraph you have read, to make sure you really understood it. Paraphrasing is a lot like summarizing.

When you paraphrase, you restate something in your own words. When you summarize a text, you give a shortened version of it in your own words. In general, summarizing is used for longer passages and paraphrasing is used for sentences or short passages. In a summary, you need to be sure that you have included the main idea and the important supporting details, organized in a way that makes it easy for a reader to quickly understand what the passage is about. Here are some of the many ways to organize the ideas from a text.

- Classification—grouping the same kinds of ideas together
- Sequencing—arranging ideas in order; e.g., first, second, third
- Illustrations—using pictures, graphs, diagrams, or lists to explain ideas

Whatever you find that helps you the most is the method that you should use.

Example

Read the following passage and think about what information is most important to include in a summary.

If Dolphins Are Mammals, Why Do They Live in the Water?

All life originally came from the sea. Some animals crawled out of the water and slowly adapted to life on land. Dinosaurs were the major life-form on earth for millions of years. When they began to die out, the plants and animals that made up the dinosaurs' food were available for other animals to eat. Mammals helped themselves. Some of these new foods were found both in marshy land areas and along the ocean's edge.

Gradually, some mammals, including dolphins' ancestors, began to explore farther out into the ocean. There they found a buffet of delicious fish. More and more, these mammals swam for their supper. After a long period of time, they adapted to full-time life in the water and became marine mammals. Around 66 million years ago, their populations started to grow. They eventually spread into oceans all over the world.

Dolphins, porpoises, and whales are all mammals called *cetaceans*, which comes from the Greek word meaning "sea monster." Dolphins are divided into two distinct family groups. The larger, more common group is the Delphinidae family, which are saltwater dolphins. The smaller Platanistidae family is made up of freshwater dolphins.

—from *Everything Dolphin: What Kids Really Want to Know About Dolphins* by Marty Crisp

Now read this *summary* and see if it matches what you would have included.

All life started in the sea, but some animals came onto the land to live. After a long time, the dolphins and some other mammals returned to the sea because they found better food. Eventually, these mammals adapted to life in the sea and spread into all the world's oceans. Today, these sea mammals include dolphins, porpoises, and whales.

Summaries are very close to paraphrasing, but a paraphrasing of the article would be a little bit longer, because you would try to put all of the ideas from the article into your own words. When you are using paraphrasing and summarizing to record ideas in your own words, it is probably best to:

* paraphrase short portions that have difficult vocabulary
* use summarizing to record the main ideas in longer passages

DETERMINE RELEVANCE AND ADEQUACY OF INFORMATION

While you read informative text, or any kind of text, for that matter, be sure that the questions you ask yourself are relevant to:

* **what is in the text**. For example, if your topic was "Climbing Mount Everest", the question "Who was Edmund Hillary?" is relevant because he is mentioned in the text about Mount Everest climbers. The question "What is the elevation of Mount St. Helens?" is not relevant because that is not what the topic is about.
* **the topic**. If your topic were "Heroes", then the question "Could Mallory be considered a hero, even though he failed to survive?" is relevant to the topic. "What climbing mistake did Mallory make?" might be relevant to another topic, but it is not very relevant to the topic of heroes.

THINK ABOUT YOUR PURPOSE

At this point, think back to the purpose of your piece of writing to determine whether:

* all your information relates to your topic
* you have enough information

You may need to gather new material and get back on track. Maybe review your work with a friend or teacher for their input. Use a concept map, checklist, or flowchart to help you see:

- what you have done
- what you still need to do

SKIM AND SCAN

When you skim or scan what you are reading, you are quickly looking over all parts of the text. Note the

- pictures
- heading
- subheadings
- bolded or underlined words

Skimming and scanning is a helpful strategy to use both before and after reading in detail. It is an especially good way to read newspaper articles, textbooks, and websites when you are looking for articles that relate to your topic. Skimming just part of a story or report to find information will save time.

HOW DOES IT WORK?

Imagine that you were asked to write a report on Mount St. Helens' most recent volcanic activity. To locate this information, you could:

- search library databases for newspaper articles written about the eruption
- read print interviews or listen to recorded interviews with eyewitnesses
- run an Internet search
- locate a library book on volcanoes and scan the bibliography for other relevant sources

Once you have gathered all your materials, you would decide which ones are appropriate for your purpose (to write a report) and audience (in this case, the teacher/students reading the report). Evaluating the purpose and audience every time you conduct research will help you to leave materials that do not fill your needs and keep those that do.

BASIC GUIDELINES

Following these guidelines will make your research complete, suitable, and accurate:

- Compare facts using various resources and watch for differences or contradictions.
- Consider the publishing date: is the information recent?
- Consider the expertise and reputation of the source.
- Watch for biases. Is the information objective or does it favor or criticize a particular group?
- Double-check Internet sources: Is there proof of the writer's expertise? Is the site reliable overall? How recent is the information on the website? Is the website educational or commercial in nature?

Double-checking accuracy is an important part of publishing your work. Make sure your information is valid before doing a final print of your assignment. "Adequacy" means that you have collected enough information, followed assignment directions, and met the classroom expectations provided by the teacher.

SET A PURPOSE FOR PRESENTING

There are all kinds of ways to communicate ideas. The way you choose the most appropriate form for sharing your ideas, depends on the purpose and audience.

WHAT IS YOUR PURPOSE?

Your purpose may be to:

- entertain
- impress
- explain
- persuade
- share
- inform

When you know your purpose, then the form you choose for communicating your ideas may be narrowed down.

AUDIENCE AND PURPOSE

Your purpose must connect with your intended audience. You may not choose the same form of communication if you are presenting your ideas to a kindergarten class, versus presenting to your peers or a teacher. Knowing your audience is an important starting point for choosing the form you will use to present your ideas.

The different forms can be in writing, like in a report, an essay, a letter, or a list. You also may try presenting your ideas in a non-written form, such as a play or skit, a movie, a poster, a drawing, or an interview.

AUDIENCE, PURPOSE, AND VOICE

To a certain extent, your purpose for presenting will determine the voice or style of your writing.

If you are sharing or relating a personal experience, your voice would probably be first person (using pronouns like *I, me*) and would include specific details along with personal thoughts, feelings, and reactions.

If your purpose is to inform, your voice would most likely be third person objective (using pronouns like *he, she, it, they*). You would want a more unemotional voice. Adding humor might sound out of place or might detract from the information you are presenting.

If your purpose is to entertain or inform, your voice might vary. If you were planning to present an imaginary interview with your favorite author, you would use the second person (*you, your*) in the interview questions, but the voice would be serious because you are interviewing an adult.

On the other hand, if you were presenting an interview with a school athlete who happens to be in your class, your presentation would be friendly and much more casual because the athlete is your peer.

4SL.5   *Add audio recordings and visual displays to presentations when appropriate to enhance the development of main ideas or themes.*

USE VISUALS TO ENGAGE AN AUDIENCE

People like to see things. Looking at objects helps us to understand what we are learning about and also helps keep us interested. We remember more information if we can look at an object or a picture while we hear someone speak about a subject.

When you are giving a presentation to an audience (a group of people) you can help them pay attention by using visuals. Visuals are any objects that stand for what you are talking about. Photographs, maps, charts, books, models, and drawings are all examples of visuals.

Let's imagine you are giving a presentation on eagles. There are a number of visuals you could use that would help keep your audience interested in what you are saying.

- An eagle's egg
- An eagle's nest
- A photograph of an eagle
- A map of North America showing where eagles live

Almost any presentation you do will have visuals that you could use. Use your imagination to come up with ideas. Try asking your parents, your teacher, and your friends for suggestions. Or imagine you are someone in the audience. Ask yourself what you would like to see!

USE VISUALS TO SUSTAIN AN AUDIENCE THROUGHOUT A PRESENTATION

People like to see things. Looking at objects helps us to understand what we are learning about and also helps keep us interested. We remember more information if we can look at an object while we hear someone speak about it.

When you are giving a presentation to an audience (a group of people) you can help them pay attention by using visuals. Visuals are any objects that stand for what you are talking about. Photographs, maps, charts, books, models, and drawings are all examples of visuals.

Let's imagine you are giving a presentation on robins. There are a number of visuals you could use that would help keep your audience interested in what you are saying.

- A robin's egg
- A robin's nest
- A photograph of a robin
- A map of the USA so that you could show where robins live throughout the year

You can also plan ahead for when you are going to use your visuals in your presentation. Rather than showing the audience all of your visuals at once, you may want to bring the objects out one at a time.

Let's think about the robin presentation. Perhaps you start the presentation with the photograph of the robin to be sure everyone knows what one looks like. Further on in your presentation, when you talk about the robin's habitat, you could bring out your map that shows where robins live. Finally, when you are talking about the robin's nesting habits, you could bring out the nest and the egg.

Spacing out when you show your visuals will help keep audience members interested for your whole presentation. They will be curious to know what you are going to show them next.

Use Visuals to Engage an Audience at the End of a Presentation

People like to see things. Looking at objects helps us to understand what we are learning about and also helps keep us interested. We remember more information if we can look at an object while we hear someone speak about it.

Often by the end of a presentation, audience members are getting tired and their attention wanders. What could you do to keep them focused on what you are saying? One of the best ways is to give them something to look at.

Imagine you are doing a presentation on volcanoes. It would be impossible to bring an actual volcano into the classroom, but there are several things you could do instead. At the end of your presentation you could do the following:

- Show a short Internet-based video clip of an active volcano.
- Bring out a model of a volcano that you built (maybe even one that erupts when you combine baking powder and vinegar).
- Present a short slide show with photos of volcanoes from around the world.

Giving your audience members something to see at the end of your presentation will help to keep their interest and also help them to remember what you told them.

Use Audio to Engage an Audience

What is audio? Audio is anything to do with sound. Just by speaking to an audience you are using audio, your voice! To make things more interesting for your audience and to keep their attention, you might consider adding other forms of audio. Here are some examples of how you could add audio to a presentation to keep your audience's interest:

SOUND

Does your topic have a sound that represents it? If your presentation is on an animal, you could play a clip of the sound that animal makes: the call of a loon, the trumpet of an elephant, the clicking of dolphins.

LANGUAGE

Perhaps you are presenting on a particular country or group of people. Do they speak a language other than English? Play a clip of someone speaking that language.

MUSIC

Music can be an excellent way to set the mood for a presentation.

If there is a piece of music that you feel represents your topic, you could play it for your audience. If your presentation is on a particular country or group of people, you could play music from that country or culture. If your presentation is on a composer or instrument, you could play music written by the composer or a piece featuring that instrument.

4L.1a   *Demonstrate command of the conventions of standard English grammar and usage when writing or speaking. Use relative pronouns (who, whose, whom, which, that) and relative adverbs (where, when, why).*

USING ADVERBS IN YOUR WRITING

An **adverb** is a word that describes a verb, an adjective, or another adverb. Most adverbs tell where, how, or when.

Example
- Melissa went **quickly** running through the mall.
  ("quickly" tells us how Melissa went running through the mall.)
- Jacob saw the policeman walking **outside**.
  ("outside" tells us where Jacob saw the policeman walking)
- Robert **rarely** shares his cookies.
  ("rarely" tells us when Robert will share his cookies.)

IT'S YOUR TURN!

Fill in the blanks below using an adverb to complete the sentences.

1. The little witch in the story _____ went flying through the forest at night.
2. Nicole _____ screamed at the bumble bee.
3. The children played _____.

How did you do? Were you able to fill in the blanks with adverbs that would make sense? Here are some helpful suggestions:

1. The little witch in the story **rarely** went flying through the forest at night.
   The little witch in the story **always** went flying through the forest at night.
2. Nicole **loudly** screamed at the bumble bee.
   Nicole **nervously** screamed at the bumble bee.
3. The children played **outside**.
   The children played **nearby**.

USING PRONOUNS CORRECTLY IN WRITING AND SPEAKING

A *pronoun* takes the place of a noun. A noun names a person, place or a thing. Pronouns can include: **he, she, it, they, their, him, her, who** and I, etc. Whenever you come across the pronoun "I", you need to capitalize it.

Example

Lily and Derek are a happily married couple. Lily and Derek went to pick up their new BMW today.

He and she (or They) are a happily married couple. They went to pick up their new BMW today.

Pronouns: He, she, they, their

Example

Look at the sentences below and replace the nouns with a pronoun.

Johnny went rock climbing in Banff's National Park. Johnny took his dog Pete and a couple of friends along with him. The boys were very competitive, always challenging one another. Johnny, Phil and George's goal was to have a race to see who could reach the top of the mountain first. Johnny was the fastest because Johnny took Pete with him. Pete loved to run, especially when he could chase the creatures of the forest. Johnny, Pete, Phil and George had the time of their lives!

Answer:

Johnny went rock climbing in Banff's National Park. **He** took his dog Pete and a couple of his friends along with him. **They** were very competitive, always challenging one another. **Their** goal was to have a race to see who could reach the top of the mountain first. Johnny was the fastest because **he** took Pete with him. Pete loved to run, especially when he could chase the creatures of the forest. **They** had the time of their lives!

Example

There were other pronouns in the paragraph that were not highlighted. Go back and reread the original paragraph and make a list of the other pronouns you came across.

Pronouns used:

Johnny went rock climbing in Banff's National Park. Johnny took **his** dog Pete and a couple of friends along with **him**. The boys were very competitive, always challenging one another. Johnny, Phil and George's goal was to have a race to see **who** could reach the top of the mountain first. Johnny was the fastest because Johnny took Pete with **him**. Pete loved to run, especially when **he** could chase the creatures of the forest. Johnny, Pete, Phil and George had the time of **their** lives!

4L.1b   *Demonstrate command of the conventions of standard English grammar and usage when writing or speaking. Form and use the progressive verb tenses.*

USING APPROPRIATE VERB TENSES IN YOUR WRITING

The tense of a verb will tell when an action takes place. The tense of a verb is usually shown by the ending letters (play**s**, play**ed**) and by helping verbs (**will** play, **has** played)

There are three main types of verb tenses: *present* tense, *past* tense and *future* tense.

Present tense means that the action is happening now or that it happens all the time.

Example

Misha **plays** on our soccer team.

Past tense means that the action happened before or in the past.

Example
Misha **played** on our soccer team.

Future tense means that the action will take place at a later time or in the future.

Example
Tomorrow, Misha **will play** on our soccer team.

It's Your Turn

Can you change the verb tense in the following sentences according to the instructions?

1. Here is the sentence in the present tense: **Beyonce sings in a band.**
   Can you change the verb tense so it is in the past tense?
2. Here is the sentence in the present tense: **Michelle is coloring at school.**
   Can you change the verb tense so it is in the future tense?
3. Here is the sentence in past tense: **Ruby walked her dog, Bingo, around the block.**
   Can you change the verb tense to present tense?

How Did You Do?

How do you think you did? Check your answers below for possible solutions.

1. Here is a suggestion for the sentence to be in past tense: Beyonce **sang** in a band.
2. Here is a suggestion for the sentence to be in the future tense: Michelle **will be coloring** at school tomorrow.
3. Here is a suggestion for the third sentence to be in the present tense: **Ruby is walking her dog, Bingo, around the block.**

4L.1d   Demonstrate command of the conventions of standard English grammar and usage when writing or speaking. Order adjectives within sentences according to conventional patterns.

WHAT IS AN ADJECTIVE?

An adjective is a describing word. It describes a noun or a pronoun.

Adjectives will describe something that appeals to one of your five senses. They may describe how something looks, feels, sounds, tastes, or smells.

An adjective can also tell how many or what kind something is.

Example

The **brown** dog jumped in the **big** puddle. The word "brown" is describing what color the dog (the noun) is. The word "big" is describing the size of the puddle (the noun).

Example

He was so **kind**. The word "kind" is describing "he"(the pronoun).

IT'S YOUR TURN!

Can you identify the adjectives in the following sentences?

1. My beautiful mother wore a bright yellow dress.
2. The leprechaun ran through the dark, green forest.
3. The crystal blue waves of the ocean splashed onto the shore.
4. She was the most thoughtful person I've ever met!

Do you think you found all of the describing words? Check your answers below. The highlighted words are adjectives.

1. My **beautiful** mother wore a **bright yellow** dress.
2. The leprechaun ran through the **dark, green** forest.
3. The **crystal blue** waves of the ocean splashed onto the shore.
4. She was the most **thoughtful** person I've ever met!

HOW TO USE ADJECTIVES IN YOUR WRITING

An adjective is a describing word. It gives further description of a noun or pronoun.

Adjectives will describe something that appeals to one of your five senses. It may describe how something looks, feels, sounds, tastes, or smells.

An adjective can also tell how many or what kind something is.

Example

In the example below the bear is the noun and the color **brown** is the **adjective**.

The **brown** bear growled at the fox.

Example

In the example below, the word "**friendly**" is describing "he" (the pronoun)

He was **friendly**.

Friendly is the **adjective**.

GIVE IT A TRY

Try to fill in the following blanks with an adjective that will describe the noun or pronoun.

1. The _____ ocean was very deep.
2. The _____ girl ran home from school.
3. The _____ dogs chased the ball.
4. It tasted _____.

Were you able to add adjectives to the above sentences? Would they appeal to a person's senses to help describe the noun or pronoun?

MORE HELPFUL IDEAS

Here are some helpful ideas if you need them.

1. The **blue** ocean was very deep. (**Blue** tells what color the ocean was, appealing to a person's sense of sight)

    The **salty** ocean was very deep. (**Salty** tells what the ocean might taste like, appealing to a person's sense of taste)

2. The **frightened** girl ran home from school. (**Frightened** tells how the girl felt, appealing to a person's sense of emotion.)

    The **little** girl ran home from school. (**Little** tells how the girl looks, appealing to a person's sense of sight)

3. The **Labrador** dogs chased the ball. (**Labrador** tell what kind of dogs they are, appealing to a person's sense of sight.)

    The **two** dogs chased the ball. (**Two** tells how many dogs there are, also appealing to a person's sense of sight.)

4. It tasted **sweet**. (**Sweet** tells how "it" (the pronoun) tastes, appealing to a person's sense of taste.)

    It tasted **delicious**. (**Delicious** tells how "it" (the pronoun) tastes, appealing to a person's sense of taste.)

4L.1e   Demonstrate command of the conventions of standard English grammar and usage when writing or speaking. Form and use prepositional phrases.

COMBINING SENTENCES WITH PREPOSITIONAL PHRASES

It is important as you grow as a writer to use varying lengths and types of sentences in your writing. Sometimes when you are writing, it is important to shorten and combine your sentences, so your writing does not sound so choppy.

One way to improve your sentences is to combine short choppy sentences into one by using **prepositional phrases**.

Prepositional phrases are short groups of words that begin with a preposition. They add detail, or modify nouns or verbs.

Example
- above the tower
- before the game
- beyond the lane

COMMONLY USED PREPOSITIONS

- about, above, across, after, against, along, among, around, at
- before, behind, below, beneath, beside, between, beyond, by
- despite, down, during
- except
- for, from
- in, inside, into
- near
- of, off, on, outside, over
- past
- through, to, toward
- under, until, up
- with, without

You may use some of the above prepositions in your writing to combine short, choppy sentences into longer, flowing sentences.

Let's look at some examples together.

Example
A story might sound something like this.

The dog was on the sofa. The dog jumped down. He hurt himself. He banged his head. He kept playing.

Below is another version of the above story that uses prepositional phrases to combine the sentences.

The dog was **on the sofa** and he jumped **to the hardwood floor**. **Despite hurting his head**, he kept playing.

Now let's try another example of combining some ideas by using prepositional phrases.

Example
A sentence could look something like this.

Tonya sat.

This is a very short, simple sentence. One might ask where is she sitting? Whom is she sitting with? By answering these questions and adding to your sentence, you may need to use some prepositional phrases. Let try adding to it together.

Tonya sat **with her friend Maryon a park bench**.

Which sentence helped paint a better picture? The second one of course! By using prepositional phrases, you can really improve your sentences in your writing.

Let's try this again. Can we try to combine the following sentences using some more prepositional phrases?

Example
The teacher spoke. She taught about bugs. The class listened. It was boring.

We could combine the above four choppy sentences into one flowing sentence by using prepositional phrases.

The teacher spoke **about bugs** and the class listened **despite their boredom**.

Now It's Your Turn

Can you combine the following sentences using one or more prepositional phrases? Give it a try and when you think you've got it, check your answers below.

1. A man fell off his bike. The students laughed.

2. My cousins visited. They live in California.
3. Tori hid her candy bar. She put it under the pillow.

How did you do? Do you think you were able to combine the sentences using some prepositional phrases? Below are some suggestions you may have used.

1. The students laughed **at the man** when he fell **off his bike**.
2. My cousins visited **from California**.
3. Tori hid the candy bar **under the pillow**.

Let's Try One More Activity

To help us learn about adding prepositional phrases to help combine or improve our sentence writing. First there will be a simple sentence. In brackets there is a question prompt. Try to add to the sentence by answering the questions using prepositional phrases.

1. I watched a movie. (Where did you watch the movie and what was it about?)
2. The man tripped. (Where did the man trip?)
3. Charlie sat. (Where did Charlie sit?)

How do you think you did? Make sure you used prepositional phrases to add to the sentences. If you think you've got it, check some of the possible solutions below.

1. I watched a movie **about a dying dog, at home, on my sofa**.
2. The man tripped **off the sidewalk**.
3. Charlie sat **against the wall**.

Using Prepositions In Your Writing

Using prepositions in your writing can be very beneficial. Prepositions begin phrases which can act as adjectives or adverbs that add to your writing to make things clearer for the reader.

For example: Mary sat.

Many questions can still arise from this simple sentence, such as where Mary is sitting or with whom she is sitting.

If we were to add to this sentence using a preposition, we might say: Mary is sitting **beside** her brother **on** the park bench.

The words **beside** and **on** are both prepositions and they both give us a better idea of where Mary is sitting. Therefore they help the reader visualize a picture much more easily.

COMMONLY USED PREPOSITIONS

- above, across, after, against, about, along, among, around, at
- before, behind, below, beneath, beside, between, beyond, by
- despite, down, during
- except
- for, from
- in, inside, into
- near
- of, off, on, outside, over
- past
- through, to
- under, until, up
- with, without

Example
Let's look at some more examples together.

1. Millie watched a video game. (Where did Millie watch the video game and what was it about?)Millie watched the video game **at** home, **on** her sofa, **about** catching falling objects.
2. Tonya ran. (Where did Tonya run?)Tonya ran **across** the yard **into** her home.

Now it's your turn. Can you add one or more prepositions to the following simple sentences in order to give them more details?

1. Molly cried.
2. Chris walked.
3. Nicole drove.

How do you think you did? Make sure you used a preposition to add to the sentence. If you think you've got it, check some of the possible solutions below.

1. Molly cried **about** her pet bird, Polly, because she was now going to have to live **without** her.
2. Chris walked **over** the bridge and **around** the parking lot.
3. Nicole drove **through** the Grand Canyon.

4L.1f   *Demonstrate command of the conventions of standard English grammar and usage when writing or speaking. Produce complete sentences, recognizing and correcting inappropriate fragments and run-ons.*

WHAT IS A COMPLETE SENTENCE?

A complete sentence must contain at least one independent clause. An independent clause is a group of words that can stand on their own as a complete sentence. An independent clause can be its own sentence, or it can be joined with another simple sentence. It contains a noun and a verb.

Example
Sam (noun) studied (verb) in the library for her math quiz.

That dog (noun) runs (verb) really fast.

Can you find the independent clause within the sentence?

1. Because she was older than her brother, she got to stay up later.
2. In the book, the illustrator used pastels to create his pictures.
3. I was excited because I never had a surprise party before.
4. The key broke off in the door knob.

Let's see how you did. See the answers underlined below.

1. Because she was older than her brother, <u>she got to stay up later.</u>
2. In the book, <u>the illustrator used pastels to create his pictures.</u>
3. <u>I was excited</u> because I never had a surprise party before.
4. <u>The key broke off in the door knob.</u>

Each of the underlined clauses in the first three sentences could be used as a complete sentence.

WHAT IS A SENTENCE FRAGMENT?

Sentence fragments are groups of words that are punctuated like a sentence, but are not complete sentences.

Problem	Example
Sentence without a subject	Fell off the ladder.
Sentence without a predicate	My naughty brother.
Sentence without an independent clause	If my brother wasn't naughty.

These fragments do not make sense because information is missing. Without all of the information, your reader will have to guess at what you are trying to write.

RUN-ON SENTENCES

Run-on sentences occur when too many ideas are put together in one sentence without the correct punctuation.

Example

The day started out wet and windy, by noon the sun had came out we were able to go to the beach what a nice surprise the weather had for us.

To fix this, you can change the sentence using different methods. You can break the sentence down into three short sentences.

Example

The day started out wet and windy ☐ . By noon, the sun had come out ☐ . We were able to go to the beach.

You can use linking words called *conjunctions* to join some of your ideas. Conjunctions include words such as *and*, *but*, *because*, and *so*.

Example

The day started out wet and windy ☐ but ☐ by noon the sun had come out, ☐ so ☐ we were able to go to the beach.

4L.1g   Demonstrate command of the conventions of standard English grammar and usage when writing or speaking. Correctly use frequently confused words.

SPELL CORRECTLY ONE-SYLLABLE WORDS THAT ARE COMMON HOMOPHONES

Homophones are words that sound the same but are not spelled the same. The words have different meanings.

Here are some examples of one-syllable words that are homophones:

Example
1. *to* - toward
   too - also, as well
   two - the number 2
2. *threw* - did throw
   through - go in one side and out the other
3. *way* - direction or method
   weigh - to measure how heavy
4. *our* - belongs to us
   hour - a unit of time sixty minutes long
5. *their* - belongs to them *there* - place or location
   they're - contraction of "they are"
6. *flu* - sickness
   flew - did fly

You must hear the word used in a sentence (context) to be able to spell it correctly.

CORRECTLY USE VERBS (LIE/LAY;SIT/SET)

The verbs **lie/lay** can be tricky and are often misused when spoken and written. Let's begin by looking at the definition of each word.

Lay means to physically put something down. **Note:** An object will always follow this word in a sentence.

Example

You should **lay** that glass vase down before it gets broken.

Lie means to take a rest. **Note:** An object won't follow this word in a sentence.

Example

If I **lie** down for an hour my headache might go away.

Try This!

Read the sentences below and choose the answer that you think fits the sentence correctly. Is it **lie** or **lay**?

1. Every night, I _____ in my bed with my dog.
2. I want you to _____ down and take a break because you've been working too hard.
3. Mrs. Flynn will _____ her coffee on her desk each morning.
4. I like to _____ down for an hour after I eat dinner to let my food settle.

How do you think you did? Check your answers below.

1. Every night, I**lie** in my bed with my dog.
2. I want you to **lie** down and take a break because you've been working too hard.
3. Mrs. Flynn will **lay** her coffee on her desk each morning.
4. I like to **lie** down for an hour after I eat dinner to let my food settle.

Let's take a look at the verbs, **sit** and **set**. They too can be tricky and are often misused.

Let's look at what exactly each of these words means.

Set means to place something down. **Note:** An object will always follow this word in a sentence.

Example
Could you **set** those flowers down on the table please?

Sit means to be seated. **Note:** An object will not directly follow this action.

Example
You can **sit** in the rocking chair with your baby.

Try This!

Read the sentences below and choose the answer that you think fits the sentence correctly. Is it **sit** or **set**?

1. Please _____ the dishes on the table for dinner.
2. Mom _____ the present down on my lap.
3. I want everyone to move into the dining room and find a chair to _____ in.
4. Everyone needs to _____ and listen to the story.

How do you think you did? Check your answers below.

1. Please **set** the dishes on the table for dinner.
2. Mom **set** the present down on my lap.
3. I want everyone to move into the dining room and find a chair to **sit** in.
4. Everyone needs to **sit** and listen to the story.

4L.2a   Demonstrate command of the conventions of standard English capitalization, punctuation, and spelling when writing. Use correct capitalization.

CAPITALIZING PROPER NOUNS

What is a proper noun?

A proper noun is a specific individual, place, or object. All proper nouns must be capitalized.

Example

Individual (a person's name): Erin, Brett, Mr. Smith, Roger Rabbit

Place: Edmonton (city), Canada (country), Africa (continent), Trochu Valley School (school), Ramsey Park (park), McDonald's (restaurant)

Object (a thing): Empire State Building, CN Tower, Harry Potter and the Goblet of Fire (book title), Titanic (boat's name/movie title)

IT'S YOUR TURN!

Read the paragraph below. Which words should have a capital?

Marcie and her cat, calvin, were excited to take their trip to toronto. Marcie seemed to be more nervous than calvin. It was marcie's first time flying with her precious pet. She knew he would be by her side the entire ride, but was hoping the flight was not too long. As they neared toronto, Marcie looked out the window and saw the giant cn tower. She couldn't wait to visit the well-known tourist attraction when she arrived.

There are **8** letters that need to be capitalized. Did you find them all?
If not, go back and see if you can find them all.
When you find all of them, check the paragraph below to see if you are right!

CHECK!

Marcie and her cat, Calvin, were excited to take their trip to Toronto. Marcie seemed to be more nervous than Calvin. It was Marcie's first time flying with her precious pet. She knew he would be by her side the entire ride, but was hoping the flight was not too long. As they neared Toronto, Marcie looked out the window and saw the giant **CN T**ower. She couldn't wait to visit the well-known tourist attraction when she arrived.

STARTING A SENTENCE WITH A CAPITAL

A sentence must **always** start with a capital letter.

Example
- It is going to be a wonderful day.
- Although it was cold outside, he forgot to wear his mittens to school.
- Mary saw a butterfly outside of her window.
- The cat saw a black ball of string sitting on the floor. He jumped towards it like a leaping cougar.
- "When I grow up I want to be a famous singer!" she told her mother.

IT'S YOUR TURN!

Read the paragraph below. Can you tell where a capital should be used?

mya was excited for her birthday party that would be happening right after school. she could hardly keep her excitement in as she packed up her things near the end of the school day. once the bell rang, she quickly rushed from the classroom, looking in every direction for her friends that would be coming to her party."over here Mya!" called her friend.

There are 4 words that need to be capitalized. Did you find them all?

If not, go back and see if you can find them all.

When you find them all, check the paragraph below to see if you are correct.

CHECK!

Mya was excited for her birthday party that would be happening right after school. She could hardly keep her excitement in as she packed up her things near the end of the school day. Once the bell rang, she quickly rushed from the classroom, looking in every direction for her friends that would be coming to her party. "Over here Mya!" called her friend.

USING CAPITALS IN TITLES

When capitalizing a title, remember to follow these rules:

1. The **first** and the **last** word must always be capitalized in a title.
2. Capitalize all **nouns**, **pronouns**, **adjectives**, **verbs**, and **adverbs**, as well as the words like *as*, *because*, and *although*.
3. Capitalize words that have five characters (letters) or more like *after*, *among*, and *between*.
4. Lowercase all words like *and*, *or*, *nor*, and *to* unless they are the first or last word in a title.

Try This!
Now you try. What words should be capitalized in the following titles?

1. captain's field day
2. first grade at last
3. chocolate chippo hippo
4. wild wonderful world
5. bobby and sue's great adventure
6. caught between a cliff and a terrible tiger

CHECK YOUR ANSWERS

1. Captain's Field Day
2. First Grade at Last
3. Chocolate Chippo Hippo
4. Wild Wonderful World
5. Bobby and Sue's Great Adventure
6. Caught Between a Cliff and aTerrible Tiger

APPLY APPROPRIATE CAPITALIZATION WITH HOLIDAYS

Always capitalize the first letter in each important word of a special day or holiday.

Example
Valentine's Day

IT'S YOUR TURN

Re-type the sentences below, making sure that all the holidays are properly capitalized.

1. I love seeing the houses covered in lights during Christmas.
2. I have the scariest costume for Halloween this year.
3. I am giving my friend a box of chocolates for valentine's day this year.
4. I bought my dad the coolest tie for father's day.

CHECK YOUR ANSWERS

See how you did by checking your answers with the correct answers below.

1. I love seeing the houses covered in lights during Christmas.
2. I have the scariest costume for Halloween this year.
3. I am giving my friend a box of chocolates for Valentine's Day this year.
4. I bought my dad the coolest tie for Father's Day.

APPLY APPROPRIATE CAPITALIZATION WITH SPECIAL EVENTS

Always capitalize each key word in the name of a special event.

Example
- Tango Tuesdays
- Megan's Sweet 16 Birthday
- The Olympics
- Festival of Trees

See if you can correctly re-type the following sentences using capital letters wherever you see a special event.

1. The county artist awards are in town this weekend.
2. It's feline fridays at the pet store tomorrow.
3. I can't wait to go to the winter wedding show downtown on Saturday.
4. Cody's going to the festival of hats this evening.

Check your answers with the correct answers below to see how you did.

1. The County Artist Awards are in town this weekend.
2. It's Feline Fridays at the pet store tomorrow.
3. I can't wait to go to the Winter Wedding show downtown on Saturday.
4. Cody's going to the Festival of Hats this evening.

CAPITALIZE THE NAMES OF NEWSPAPERS

Each word in the title of a newspaper should begin with a capital letter.

Example

"The Northern Times"

"The Roddickton Herald"

NOW IT'S YOUR TURN

Which of the following names of newspapers are capitalized correctly?

1. New Jersey News
2. the Calgary Press
3. The Eastern Daily Times
4. California county herald

If you chose 1 and 3, then you are correct. Each word in the title must begin with a capital letter.

CAPITALIZE THE NAMES OF MAGAZINES CORRECTLY

The first word and each important word in the title of a magazine should begin with a capital letter.

The word "magazine" should only be capitalized if it is part of the publication's title.

Example

"Fitness Illustrated"

"Pets for You"

IT'S YOUR TURN

See if you can correctly identify which of the magazine names below are correctly written.

1. Ultimate pets
2. Fashion for you
3. Dogs and Pups
4. Soccer Illustrated

If you chose 3 and 4, then you are correct. The word *and* does not need to be capitalized in "Dogs and Pups" because it is not an important word or the first word in the title.

4L.2b   *Demonstrate command of the conventions of standard English capitalization, punctuation, and spelling when writing. Use commas and quotation marks to mark direct speech and quotations from a text.*

USE QUOTATION MARKS FOR SPOKEN WORDS

Quotation marks are used before and after spoken words to show exactly what the person is saying. The words that fall within the beginning quotation marks and the end quotation marks are the spoken words.

Example

The highlighted section shows the quotation marks. Notice how it frames the entire quote from the coach.

The coach explained, "The team was tired today, and we didn't seem to have enough energy to pull out a win."

The words, **"The team was tired today, and we didn't seem to have enough energy to pull out a win."** was exactly what the coach had said.

Example

The children were all playing nicely together when one of them screamed, "Wait, I have an even better idea!"

In this direct quotation, it was one of the children who screamed the exact words, **"Wait, I have an even better idea!"**

Please note how each quotation is introduced with a word like **explained** or **said**, or **screamed**, which is then followed by a comma and then the quotation marks to begin the spoken words, with another double quotation mark to end the spoken words.

YOUR TURN

Do you think you understand how quotation marks work with spoken words? In the sentences below, try to place the beginning and end quotation marks in the proper spots to indicate the spoken words. When you think you have placed them in the proper spots, check your answers.

1. Emily said, Mom when is dinner going to be? I'm really hungry.
2. As they continued on their road trip, Natalie complained, It's so hot in this van and we've been on the road forever. I feel like we will never get there. Her mother took a deep breath and decided just to ignore her.
3. Mitchell was coming home and Caitlin was so excited for his arrival. He opened up the front door and instantly Caitlin screamed, Mitchell, I have missed you so much. I can't believe you are home! She lunged toward him and gave him a great big hug.

ANSWERS

Do you think you have placed the quotation marks in the proper places? Check out the answers below.

1. Emily said, "Mom when is dinner going to be? I'm really hungry."
2. As they continued on their road trip, Natalie complained, "It's so hot in this van and we've been on the road forever. I feel like we will never get there." Her mother took a deep breath and decided just to ignore her.
3. Mitchell was coming home and Caitlin was so excited for his arrival. He opened up the front door and instantly Caitlin screamed, "Mitchell, I have missed you so much. I can't believe you are home!" She lunged toward him and gave him a great big hug.

USING COMMAS IN DIRECT QUOTATIONS

When using direct quotations in your writing, it is important that you punctuate them properly. One of the main things you need to remember is to use the **comma** when quoting someone. The comma must always follow the word or phrase that names the speaker, and be placed before the quotation marks.

Example
Jill yelled, "Step away from the cookie jar!"

Notice where the highlighted comma is placed? It is right after the exclamatory word (yelled) and right before the beginning of the quotation, which is indicated by quotation marks.

___

Example
As Jonathan and Sarah looked up, they saw a kitten crossing out to the middle of the road where a car was coming. Sally turned to Jonathan and said, "If that cat doesn't get going, it's gonna get hit!"

Notice once again where the comma was placed: right after the word "said". It also falls right before the beginning of the quotation, before the quotation marks.

___

Example

When the speaker is named after the quotation, you still need a comma after the quotation.

"I sure hope that kitten has a home," remarked Sarah after the kitten made it safely across the road.

Notice that the comma goes **inside** the second set of quotation marks.

Example

If the naming of the speaker divides the sentence into two parts, you will need to use two commas.

Jonathan looked thoughtful. "Maybe," he suggested, "Mom will let us get a kitten from the animal shelter."

Now It's Your Turn

Can you find the appropriate spot to place the comma for the direct quotes in the sentences below?

1. The teacher responded "Tomorrow's test will be easy because you all know the material so well. You all can do it." The students all took a sigh of relief.
2. Marcus was stunned as he turned to his friend and said "How could that movie have ended so badly?"
3. Beth and Hillary were on their way to the fair. Beth squealed "I can't wait to ride the roller coaster. We are going to have so much fun!"
4. "Carlos can help us move the blocks" offered Sam.
5. "In a perfect world" Mother complained "my kids would do their homework without any nagging!"

How Did You Do?

Do you think you were able to place commas in the proper spots? If you think you've got it, check out your answers below.

1. The teacher responded, "Tomorrow's test will be easy because you all know the material so well. You all can do it." The students all took a sigh of relief.
2. Marcus was stunned as he turned to his friend and said, "How could that movie have ended so badly?"
3. Beth and Hillary were on their way to the fair. Beth squealed, "I can't wait to ride the roller coaster. We are going to have so much fun!"

4. "Carlos can help us move the blocks," offered Sam.
5. "In a perfect world," Mother complained, "my kids would do their homework without any nagging!"

4L.2c   Demonstrate command of the conventions of standard English capitalization, punctuation, and spelling when writing. Use a comma before a coordinating conjunction in a compound sentence.

Use Compound Sentences in Writing and Speaking

We use compound sentences all the time in our daily communication. Compound sentences allow us to take two or more closely related ideas and combine them into one sentence using a conjunction such as like *and*, *but*, and *or*.

Example
I tried to sing like Brittany, and my friend tried to sing like Cher.

Try This!

Create your own compound sentence by taking two of the related sentences and turning them into one compound sentence.

- I like to eat spinach salad.
- Jody likes to eat caesar salad.
- I ate at the salad buffet.

Let's see how you did. Below are some possible solutions.

1. I like to eat spinach salad, and Jody likes to eat caesar salad.
2. I like to eat spinach salad, but Jody likes to eat caesar salad.
3. I like to eat spinach salad, so I ate at the salad buffet.

WHAT IS AN INDEPENDENT CLAUSE?

What is a clause?

A clause is a group of words containing a subject and a predicate.

Example
- The <u>dog</u> *barked*.
- The <u>cowboy</u> *galloped across the prairie*.
- Because <u>he</u> *was hungry*.
- After <u>we</u> *ate lunch*.

In the examples above, one line has been drawn under the simple subject and the predicate is in italics.

There are two types of clauses: Independent and Dependent Clauses. This lesson will focus on **Independent Clauses.**

Independent clauses can form a complete sentence.

Example

<u>We</u> *enjoyed our pool.*

<u>Dad</u> *caught three fish.*

Independent clauses can be joined by "connecting" words called co-ordinating conjunctions. The most common co-ordinating conjunctions are *and, but, or,* and *so.*

Example
- The <u>children</u> *swam* **and** the <u>parents</u> *relaxed.*
- <u>I</u> *love asparagus,* **but** <u>I</u> *hate broccoli.*
- <u>We</u> *must win,* **or** the <u>coach</u> *will be disappointed.*
- <u>It</u> *was raining,* **so** <u>we</u> *finished the hike early.*

4L.2d   *Demonstrate command of the conventions of standard English capitalization, punctuation, and spelling when writing. Spell grade-appropriate words correctly, consulting references as needed.*

HOW TO USE A DICTIONARY

A **dictionary** is a tool that helps you find information about words. You can learn

- how to spell words
- their definitions
- their function or parts of speech
- where the word was first used
- how to pronounce words

A Dictionary Entry

When you look up a word, you will be reading a dictionary entry for the word that looks something like this illustration. This is where you will find the above information, and you can select the information you need. For example, you may only need to look at the pronunciation of the word.

> **rev•o•lu•tion** (rev'ə lōō'shən), n.
> 1. the overthrow and replacement of an established government or political system by the people governed.
> 2. a sudden, complete, or radical change.
> 3. rotation on or as if on an axis.
> 4. the orbiting of one heavenly body around another.
> 5. a single cycle in a rotation or orbit.
> —**rev'o•lu'•tion•ary,**
>
> *adj.*, **n.**, *pl*–ies. – rev'o•lu'•tion•ist,**n.**

How to Spell Words

Think of a word to look up. Open the dictionary, and look at the top corner of any page. You will see two words separated by a forward slash[/]. These words are the first and last words on the page. Next, you will need to decide whether you need to flip forwards or backwards to find the section your word is in. Don't forget that the words in a dictionary are found in alphabetical order.

Note: if you are unable to find the word that you are looking up, it might be because the word ends in "ed", "ing", or "s". You will need to find the root word. There, you will find its different endings.

Example

Think of a word: **fame**.

Open the dictionary: Suppose that you flipped to the page where it says **leap/leaves**.

As you can see these words start with the letter "L". We need to find the section that starts with the letter "F". That means we will have to flip back to the "F" section of the dictionary.

Keep on turning the pages until you get to the "F" section. Once you are in this section, look at the second letter of your word and repeat the first step. Since the second letter of **fame** is an "a" you will need to flip all the way back to the beginning of the "F" section since "a" is the first letter of the alphabet. You will need to repeat this process with each of the following letters of your word. Remember to check the bold words at the top of each page to see the range of words on the page.

DEFINITIONS

Once you find the word you are looking up, you will you will notice the part of speech it is. In this case, the letter "n." is representing the word "noun". Next, you will find one or more definitions of your word. You will have to read each definition to know which one best fits the way that your word is used in a sentence.

Example
fame. n

1. Great renown: a concert violinist of international fame.
2. Public estimation; reputation:a politician of ill fame.
3. Rumor. To make renowned or famous.
4. To report to be.

FUNCTION OR PART OF SPEECH

The first thing you need to know is that function is the same as part of speech. In the example that we have used (fame) you will notice that there is the letter "n." in front of the definition. This lets you know that "fame" is a noun. Other abbreviations you may find are: adj.- adjective, adv.- adverb, v.- verb, ANT.- antonym and SYN.- synonym.

FIRST USED

Along with definition you will also notice a country of origin. This is the country where the word was first used.

HOW PRONOUNCED

Before the definition of the word is given, you will notice brackets around how to say the word. The word will be spelled the way it sounds (phonetically), for example, fame (feym).

HOW TO USE A THESAURUS

Synonyms are words that have the same or similar meanings. Antonyms are words that have opposite meanings. A *thesaurus* lists words with their synonyms and, usually, their antonyms.

The words in a thesaurus are arranged in alphabetical order. Here is an example of an entry for the word "bright."

bright-adj	(adjectives/ synonyms)	1. fair, mild, balmy, brilliant, vivid, resplendent 2. brilliant, clever, gifted, talented, sharp, keen
	(antonyms)	1. flat, cloudy, dim, dingy, faded, leaden, pale, weak 2. bland, desensitized, dim, slow, thick-headed

How can a thesaurus help you? Here is a paragraph written by a student. Notice the emphasized words.

It was a *warm* spring day. Mother had asked me to *come* straight home because she had a *bright* idea. Out of the wood and chicken wire she had recently *bought*, we could *make* a *home* for our two bunnies, Springbank and Colchester. As a *good* carpenter, Mother would make a *great* assistant for the project.

Here is the same paragraph after the student used a thesaurus to find more interesting words to replace the emphasized ones.

It was a *balmy* spring day. Mother had asked me to *scurry* straight home because she had a *brilliant* idea. Out of the wood and chicken wire she had recently *purchased*, we could *construct* a *hutch* for our two bunnies, Springbank and Colchester. As a *gifted* carpenter, Mother would make a *superb* assistant for the project.

4L.3b   *Use knowledge of language and its conventions when writing, speaking, reading, or listening. Choose punctuation for effect.*

USE PERIODS

Periods belong at the end of a sentence.

Place periods in the paragraph below after each statement.

Last weekend, we went to our cabin at Sandy Lake We had so much fun I caught 2 fish with my new fishing rod Mom took a picture just as I was reeling it out of the water It was enormous It must have weighed 9 poundsDr. and Mrs. Miller came over to see what all the commotion was about I can't wait until next summer when I can spend every weekend at the cabin

See the corrections below:
Last weekend, we went to our cabin at Sandy Lake. We had so much fun. I caught 2 fish with my new fishing rod. Mom took a picture just as I was reeling it out of the water. It was enormous. It must have weighed 9 pounds. Dr. and Mrs. Miller came over to see what all the commotion was about. I can't wait until next summer when I can spend every weekend at the cabin.

USE QUESTION MARKS

Remember, a question mark (?) is used at the end of a sentence that asks a direct question.

Example
What is the name of Mike's dog?

It's Your Turn

Which of the following sentences below should have a question mark at the end?

1. We found a stray dog at the park
2. Can I sleep over at Julia's house tonight
3. Is there a rehearsal for the play today
4. I want to go swimming

If you chose 2 and 3, then you are correct!

Use Exclamation Marks

An exclamation mark (!) is a type of punctuation used at the end of a sentence to express strong feeling.

It's Your Turn

Which of the following sentences should have an exclamation mark at the end?

1. I went to the mall this morning
2. I've learned a new trick

3. Where were you born
4. It's a baby girl

If you answered 2 and 4, then you are correct.

4L.3c   *Use knowledge of language and its conventions when writing, speaking, reading, or listening. Differentiate between contexts that call for formal English and situations where informal discourse is appropriate.*

Demonstrate Voice Through Word Choice

What is a writer's voice? A writer's voice means how the writing sounds, or its effect on the writer's audience. The writer's voice includes careful word choices that express what the writer means, as well as the writer's attitude toward their topic. You might choose a serious voice to write a report, or a joking voice to write a story about your trials with a younger brother who steals your stuff without asking. Even punctuation plays a part. You will discover that you will use a changing writer's voice in different writing assignments. Try to make your voice fit the kind of assignment. Also make sure that it is right for your audience. Are you writing for classmates? Parents? A celebrity hero? The principal?

Whom Are You Writing For?

The word *diction* refers to word choice. You do not want to use big words just to impress your audience, if they will not be able to understand your ideas. Instead, try to choose accurate and precise words. Only turn to special terms when more commonly used words are not available. Diction is closely related to voice. The words you choose give readers an impression. If your writing contains many unusual or long words, some readers may feel annoyed and stop paying attention to what you have to say. Don't distract them with big words. Instead, impress them with clear ones that make sense to them.

Formal or Informal

Formal word choice is the way you would speak to an adult, especially a professional person like your teacher or family doctor. Informal word choice is the way you would talk to a friend or family member.

Example

A young girl peers into the microwave and sees that the pizza is overdone, burned, in fact. The examples below show how she might express her thoughts to a teacher, or, on the other hand, to a friend.

1. To her teacher: "Oh, Miss Allers! I am so sorry that I burned your pizza! I think I must have pushed the wrong numbers on this microwave. It looks like I hit 20 min instead of 2 min. I will get you a piece of mine right now!"
2. To her friend: "Alecia! Get over here! You burnt my pizza, you dummy! I'm takin' one of yours right now, dude!"

You should suit the level of formality in your writing to your audience. Your readers could be adults, peers, or children. If you have to use some technical language in a report, make sure you explain what it means. Do not expect your audience to be experts in your topic.

4L.4b   Determine or clarify the meaning of unknown and multiple-meaning words and phrases based on grade 4 reading and content, choosing flexibly from a range of strategies. Use common, grade-appropriate Greek and Latin affixes and roots as clues to...

WHAT ARE WORD ORIGINS?

Word origin refers to the original meaning of a word. **Etymology** is the study of the origins of words. Etymologists study how a word came to be.

Example

Let's take the word *telephone*:

- *tele* means long distance
- *phone* means speak

So you can see how the word *telephone* originated.

DEFINE UNFAMILIAR WORDS USING WORD ORIGINS

Knowing word origins can be helpful in spelling unfamiliar words. The chart below shows the main 'ancestors' of our English language. You can see, for instance, that Latin and Greek were both ancestors. That means that many of our English words once started out as Latin or Greek words.

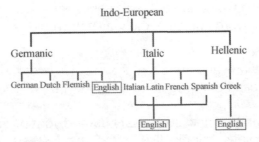

Example

In Latin, the word *ego* means "I." If you know this, then it will help you to define other words that contain the word *ego*, such as *egocentric* and *egotistical*.

The word *anti* has a Greek origin and means "against," so if you discover a word that contains *anti*, it will help you better understand the meaning of the word.

The same goes for the Latin word *sub*, which means "beneath" such as *submarine* (beneath or below water) and *subdue* (to bring down).

YOUR TURN

In Latin, *oper* means "to work." Read the sentences below, and try to figure out the meaning of the highlighted words.

1. Kelly's leg did not heal properly so she is scheduled to have an **operation** in the morning.
2. If we all **cooperate**, then we will get the job done quickly.

Let's see how you did.

Operation means "to work on, fix or improve a part of the body."

Cooperate means "to work together for a common goal."

4L.4c   *Determine or clarify the meaning of unknown and multiple-meaning words and phrases based on grade 4 reading and content, choosing flexibly from a range of strategies. Consult reference materials, both print and digital, to find the...*

USING A THESAURUS TO DETERMINE THE MEANING OF AN UNFAMILIAR WORD

Words can have different implied meanings, so when you come across a word you're not familiar with, you may want to use a thesaurus to compare your unknown word to those in the thesaurus to help you see a variety of other words that have a similar meaning.

Example
bright– ADJS (adjectives/synonyms) 1. sunny, fair, mild, balmy; brilliant, vivid, resplendent 2. smart, brainy, brilliant, clever, gifted, talented, sharp keen
– (antonyms) 1. dull, flat, dingy, cloudy, faded, leaden, dim, pale, weak, faint 2. slow-witted, dim, slow, thick-headed, bland, desensitized

A thesaurus is a list of synonyms (words that have similar meanings) and antonyms (words that have opposite meanings). It usually comes in one of two forms. One way is in a dictionary like form, where the words are in alphabetical order. If you are looking for a similar word for *happy*, you would look under the letter **H**.

The second way is in an index form. In an index type thesaurus, there is an index at the back, with the words listed in alphabetical order. If you were to look up the word "happy", in the index type thesaurus, you would look at the back index page under H and it might send you to several pages where "happy" would have synonyms. You might find "happy" listed under several other words within the thesaurus like "ecstatic" or "overjoyed" The index would guide you to the page or pages where "happy" appears.

A thesaurus is a valuable tool to help determine an unfamiliar word by locating words with similar meanings.

Example
Let's use the words "slender" and "skinny" for example. Both words are found under the heading **thin** in the thesaurus, but "slender" can have a more positive tone, while "skinny" may not.

"The slender man walked down the street." and "The skinny man walked down the street."

Both words may have two different images or create two different images, even though the words are similar.

It's Your Turn!

If you were reading a novel and read the following sentence, "He was aware of the **precarious** lifestyle of an undersea diver but he insisted that he still begin his training." **Precarious** might be an unfamilar word. You might want to look in the thesaurus alphabetically under the "P" words. Look in a thesaurus to locate the word PRECARIOUS. Some of the synonyms you could replace with the unknown word would be *hazardous, dangerous* or *tricky*.

Replacing the unknown word in context may help you understand the meaning of the word and help you to make sense of the text you are reading. Try out the different meanings for the word by substituting them below:

1. He was aware of the **hazardous** lifestyle of an undersea diver.
2. He was aware of the **dangerous** lifestyle of an undersea diver.
3. He was aware of the **tricky** lifestyle of an undersea diver.

What did you conclude? Because there are hazards, or dangers, the diver will need the training to be prepared. The meaning of **precarious** in this context probably doesn't mean tricky, because the diver is beginning his training. Precarious means that the diver could be in danger because of the risks of being underwater. That is why he needs to be well trained and prepared.

USING A DICTIONARY TO DETERMINE UNFAMILIAR WORDS

Sometimes when you are reading and you come across a word you are unsure of, the best solution to determine its meaning is to look in a **dictionary**. A **dictionary** is an alphabetical list of words and their meanings. Some words may have multiple meanings. Typically, dictionaries will list the most commonly used meanings first. If the dictionary does give multiple meanings for the unknown word, you will have to see what definition would make sense in the context of the text you are reading.

Each word that is explained in the dictionary is usually in bold type.

After the bold word, it may also show the word divided into syllables. (For example: cal-am-i-ty)

LET'S TRY THIS TOGETHER

Let's use the sentence below as our context to figure out what *sarcasm* means by using a dictionary.

Example

"How unselfish you are!" Mary said with **sarcasm**, as her brother took the biggest piece of cake from the plate.

When locating a word in a dictionary, you must look for it alphabetically. Using **sarcasm** as our example, and using the dictionary meanings below, let's determine which definition would be suitable for this context.

Sar*casm

- sharp or bitter irony
- sneering or cutting remark

Both definitions would make sense within this context, as we understand the girl is probably saying the opposite of what she is really thinking.

USING A PICTURE DICTIONARY TO DETERMINE AN UNFAMILIAR WORD

When reading, you may come across a word that you do not recognize or know the meaning of. If available, one resource you can use to help you is a **picture dictionary**. A picture dictionary is always listed in alphabetical order and will have a picture of the word along with the word being described. Usually the picture can give you hints about what the word means.

Example

island (i/lend), *n*. 1. a piece of land surrounded on all sides by water but too small for a continent. 2. something isolated and apart like an island.

If you were to look at the above example, after looking at the picture of the _____, you might assume _____ means _____.

Answer: After looking at the picture of the *island*, you might assume that *island* means a fairly small piece of land completely surrounded by water.

USING A GLOSSARY TO DETERMINE AN UNFAMILIAR WORD

If you are reading a textbook and come across a word that is **bolded**, you can usually find the definition of the word in a section in the back of the book, called the *glossary*.

A *glossary* is an alphabetical list of individual terms and their meanings that a reader may be unfamiliar with.

air pump a device for pumping air into or out of a vessel, a room, etc.

decompression a gradual lowering of pressure on a person who has been on an underwater dive

diving bell an open-bottomed box or bell, supplied with air, in which a person can be lowered into deep water

SCUBA Self Contained Underwater Breathing Apparatus

submarine a vessel able to operate under water

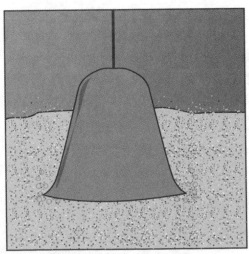

It is a great tool to use when you come across a word you are unfamiliar with in a text.

When you are reading, and the bold word does not make sense to you in the context, sometimes looking up the meaning of the word in the glossary can help it make more sense to you. Usually the bold words in a text are important words to know about, and that is why they are bolded.

4L.5a   Demonstrate understanding of figurative language, word relationships, and nuances in word meanings. Explain the meaning of simple similes and metaphors in context.

WHAT IS A METAPHOR?

A metaphor is a comparison of two objects or ideas. Unlike a simile, it does not use the words "like" or "as" to compare.

Example
After the argument, Blake was SMOLDERING for days.

The word SMOLDERING, is being compared to Blake's attitude after the argument.

Example
"Life is a zoo in a jungle."
(Peter De Vries)

Life is being compared to a "zoo in a jungle." Notice it is a comparison, but it is not using the words "like" or "as" like in a simile.

The next example shows how the author compares himself to a sword.

Example
I am a sword,
sharper than a tongue
nobody can defeat me,
because I am a sword,
I cannot be hurt by what people say about me,
I will not show my anger against someone else.

~By Alex ~

NOW IT'S YOUR TURN

Can you determine which sentences contain metaphors?

1. We all would have eaten more pizza if Tammy wasn't such a hog.
2. Mark was such a mule. We could not get him to change his mind.
3. The mouse didn't stand a chance as our cat, the lightning bolt, got him right away.
4. The baby was a feather to carry.
5. Misty was bouncing off the walls like a hyper child on sugar.

Think you have them figured out? Do you know which of the above sentences are metaphors? Check your answers below.

ANSWERS

The following sentences did contain metaphors:

1. **We all would have eaten more pizza if Tammy wasn't such a hog.** TAMMY is being compared to a HOG, because she ate like a hog.
2. **Mark was such a mule. We could not get him to change his mind.** MARK is being compared to a MULE, because he is being stubborn.
3. **The mouse didn't stand a chance as our cat, the lightning bolt, got him right away.** The CAT is being compared to a LIGHTNING BOLT, because of how fast it is.

4. **The baby was a feather to carry.** The BABY is being compared to a FEATHER, because it is so light.

The following example was not a proper metaphor:

5. Misty was bouncing off the walls like a hyper child on sugar.

The above sentence did not contain a proper metaphor. It contained what we call a simile, a comparison using "like" or "as". Metaphors do not use "like" or "as". **Metaphors will state something is something else.**

WHAT IS A SIMILE?

A **simile** is a figure of speech where you compare two unlike things using the words, "like" or "as". You can use a simile in a sentence to draw attention to certain characteristics of the subject being described.

Example
The woman was as **busy as a beaver** when she was getting ready for son's birthday party.

_____

Example
Our dog dived into the big wave and **swam like a fish** until we pulled him out.

_____

4L.5b   *Demonstrate understanding of figurative language, word relationships, and nuances in word meanings. Recognize and explain the meaning of common idioms, adages, and proverbs.*

WHAT ARE IDIOMS?

An idiom is a type of language that is used by a person or a group of people and is only used by them. When you are around your friends are there certain words that you only use around them? These words that you use around your friends are called idioms. If you use these words or phrases around other people, the words are often difficult for them to understand or may have a completely different meaning. Idioms can also be acronyms for a word or phrase. An acronym is a word that is formed from the beginning letters of several words. For example, "Bald eagles eat mice" would form the acronym BEEM.

Example

When people refer to the bathroom as a "loo," you will know that these people are originally from England and the word "loo" is unique to them.

Example

Another famous idiom is when someone says that "they are feeling under the weather." In this example, they do not actually mean they are under a cloud and the sun; what they mean is that they do not feel well or they feel sick.

Today, the meaning of the word *idiom* has changed to include acronyms that are often used in technology terminology by people who are referred to as the net generation. Some of the more famous acronyms are listed as follows:

Copyright Protected

Acronym	Meaning
LOL	Laughing Out Loud
BTW	By The Way
AKA	Also Known As
ETA	Estimated Time of Arrival
ROFL	Rolling On The Floor Laughing

4L.5c   Demonstrate understanding of figurative language, word relationships, and nuances in word meanings. Demonstrate understanding of words by relating them to their opposites (antonyms) and to words with similar but not identical meanings (synonyms).

WHAT ARE SYNONYM WORDS?

A *synonym* is word that has the same or almost the same meaning as another word. Synonyms are two words that can be interchanged (swapped) in a sentence, leaving the sentence with the same meaning.

Example

After the bears went **walking** in the trees, they made their way back to their **home**.

In the sentence above there are two words that are highlighted "walking" and "home". We will be replacing these words with synonyms that will add more meaning and flavor to our sentence. To do this, we have to think of other words that have the **same meaning** as "walking" and "home" but will add better expression to our sentence.

You need to be careful when you are replacing words, making sure not to change the meaning of the sentence!

Instead of the word "walking" what else can we use? We can use **strolling**, **pacing**, **toddling** or **sauntering**. After you have brainstormed for other words that mean the same as "walking", you will need to choose one that you think would fit best into your sentence. For this example, you could choose the word "strolling".

Now we will have to do the same steps again with the word "home". We will need to think of other words that mean "home" **and will add more descriptive expression to our sentence.**

Class Focus   254   Castle Rock Research

Instead of the word "home" what else can we use? We can use **residence**, **shelter**, **dwelling** or **habitat**. After you have brainstormed for other words that mean the same as home, you need to choose one that you think would **fit best into your sentence**. For this example, you might choose the word "shelter".

Rewriting the original sentence with our changes we get: "After the bears went **strolling** in the trees, they made their way back to their **shelter**."

Example

Some examples of synonyms are:

Original Word	Synonyms
home	shelter, residence, dwelling, habitat
see	watch, view, observe, witness, notice
fall	drop, collapse, plunge, plummet

DEMONSTRATE KNOWLEDGE OF SYNONYM WORDS

A *synonym* is word that has the same or almost the same meaning as another word. Synonyms are two words that can be interchanged (swapped) in a sentence, leaving the sentence with the same meaning.

Can you identity the appropriate synonym from the lists?

DEMONSTRATING YOUR KNOWLEDGE OF SYNONYMS #1

In the sentence below can you identify the appropriate synonym for the highlighted word?

The boys **ran** after the soccer ball hoping to get the first goal of the game.

1. scattered
2. strolled
3. crawled
4. lazily

Copyright Protected

DEMONSTRATING YOUR KNOWLEDGE OF SYNONYMS #2

In the sentence below can you identify the appropriate synonym for the highlighted word?

The girls were **mad** when they were told that there was no more ice-cream left!

1. sorry
2. content
3. blissful
4. irritated

DEMONSTRATING YOUR KNOWLEDGE OF SYNONYMS #3

In the sentence below can you identify the appropriate synonym for the highlighted word?

As the mouse looked at the **piece** of cheese its mouth began to plan its attack.

1. nil
2. morsel
3. naught
4. member

SOLUTIONS

In the examples above the best responses are: scattered, irritated, morsel.

WHAT ARE ANTONYM WORDS?

An *antonym* is a word that has the opposite meaning of another word. If a word in a sentence is replaced by its antonym, the sentence will have the opposite meaning.

USING ANTONYMS IN A SENTENCE

Example
In this example please pay attention to the highlighted word:

The boys went to the water park and had the **greatest** day of their lives. (Original sentence)

The boys went to the water park and had the **worst** day of their lives. (Antonym sentence)

Please notice that in the first sentence the word **greatest** is highlighted. By replacing this word with its antonym you have to think of a word that has the **opposite meaning**. The antonym word **should fit the flow of the sentence** while changing its meaning.

In the second example the word **greatest** was replaced with **worst** making the boys' day a very bad one.

TRY USING ANTONYM WORDS

Try This!

Now it's your turn. In the sentences below try replacing the highlighted words with appropriate antonyms.

One **sunny morning** a **small** group of friends got on their bikes and decided to go for a picnic at the park. When they got there, they decided to play a game of soccer. They had such a **wonderful** time kicking the ball around. After a few hours they started to get really hungry, so they sat down and started eating their **perfectly organized** lunch.

Reflection

Your thinking process should be something along these lines:

"What words can I use that have the opposite meaning for the words: **sunny morning**, **small**, **wonderful** and **perfectly organized**?"

Original words	Antonyms
sunny morning	depressing, cheerless, uncheerful, dreary
small	gigantic, colossal, massive, enormous
wonderful	ordinary, horrible, terrible, gross
perfectly organized	disorganized, messed up, destroyed, mangled

Now that you have a set of words to choose from you can start picking which words would fit best into the sentence, giving it the opposite meaning.

One **dreary afternoon** a **massive** group of friends got on their bikes and decided to go for a picnic at the park. When they got there, they decided to play a game of soccer. They had such a **horrible** time kicking the ball around. After a few hours they started to get really hungry, so they sat down and started eating their **mangled** lunch.

As you can see from the example above, the meaning of the first sentence has completely changed when you replaced the four highlighted words.

DEMONSTRATE KNOWLEDGE OF ANTONYM WORDS

An *antonym* is word that has the opposite meaning of another word. If antonyms are interchanged (swapped) in a sentence, the sentence takes on the opposite meaning.

DEMONSTRATE YOUR KNOWLEDGE OF ANTONYMS #1

Try This!

In the sentence below can you choose the best antonym for the highlighted word?

Students in Mr. Smith's science class are always **excited** to see what they are going to learn next.

A. enthralled
B. captivated
C. unenthusiastic
D. disrespectful

DEMONSTRATE YOUR KNOWLEDGE OF ANTONYMS #2

Try This!

Over the summer children **adore** playing sports, watching television and eating junk food all day.

In the sentence below can you choose the best antonym for the highlighted word?

A. detest
B. dread
C. enjoy
D. like

DEMONSTRATE YOUR KNOWLEDGE OF ANTONYMS #3

Try This!

In the sentence below can you choose the best antonym for the highlighted word?

Some people think that recycling is a **waste** of time and should not be done.

A. valuable use
B. misuse
C. stretching
D. misguided use

UNDERSTAND LANGUAGE APPROPRIATE FOR VARIETY OF CONTEXTS

When you are creating a project, whether it a written piece or an oral presentation, it is important to use the appropriate language for your intended audience. It is also important to understand the language that is appropriate for different situations, so that you feel comfortable and able to respond in a manner that fits the occasion.

Example

Here are a few situations when you would need to understand the kind of language that is appropriate:

- When you are riding a public bus with your friends, you are expected to watch your language and not use words that might be offensive to your fellow passengers, especially the adults.
- When you are picking up a few things for your mother at the grocery store, you would be expected to understand and use appropriate, courteous language.
- When you are presenting a research report to the class, you are expected to use correct English and fairly formal language.
- When you are babysitting your three year old brother, you are expected not to use "baby talk", but to use simple vocabulary that he will understand.

When writing a report for your peers, you will want to use words that are appropriate for your age or grade level. The following example would **not** be realistic wording for a Grade 5 class report on cougars:

Example

The puma concolor terrestrial mammal is a division of the Felidae family. Their primary provision sources are ungulates.

Instead, the following example is much more appropriate language to use for a Grade 5 class report on cougars:

Example

The cougar is a part of the feline, or cat family. The main foods cougars eat to survive are animals like deer, elk, and moose.

As you can see in the second example, the wording is much more child-friendly.

The same type of attention should be paid to the wording in an oral presentation. If you are presenting to your peers, you may want to include humor or relevant pop culture items that would be interesting and informative to your peers, but that still support your presentation.

If you are presenting to your teacher, you may want to be more professional and stick to the assigned guidelines. You can always talk to your teacher about what language would be appropriate to use within your presentation.

NOTES

NOTES

NOTES

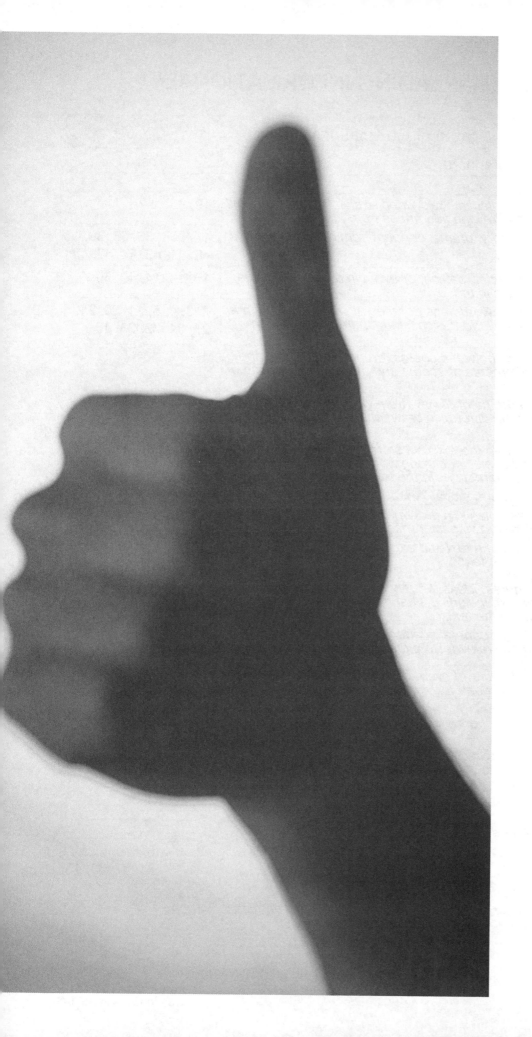

Practice Exercises

EXERCISE #1—READING INFORMATIONAL

Table of Correlations		
Standard		**Test #1**
4RL	Reading Standards for Literature	
4RL.1	Refer to details and examples in a text when explaining what the text says explicitly and when drawing inferences from the text.	19, 35
4RL.2	Determine a theme of a story, drama, or poem from details in the text; summarize the text.	1, 7, 26, 36, 38, 39, 40, 41, 43, 44, 47, 48
4RL.3	Describe in depth a character, setting, or event in a story or drama, drawing on specific details in the text.	10, 13, 14, 49, 50
4RL.4	Determine the meaning of words and phrases as they are used in a text, including those that allude to significant characters found in mythology.	2, 3, 4, 8, 11, 20, 21, 27, 31, 32, 33, 45
4RL.5	Explain major differences between poems, drama, and prose, and refer to the structural elements of poems and drama when writing or speaking about a text.	46
4RL.6	Compare and contrast the point of view from which different stories are narrated, including the difference between first- and third-person narrations.	12
4RL.7	Make connections between the text of a story or drama and a visual or oral presentation of the text, identifying where each version reflects specific descriptions and directions in the text.	28
4RI	Reading Standards for Informational Text	
4RI.1	Refer to details and examples in a text when explaining what the text says explicitly and when drawing inferences from the text.	19, 35
4RI.2	Determine the main idea of a text and explain how it is supported by key details; summarize the text.	1, 7, 26, 36, 38, 39, 40, 41, 43, 44, 47, 48
4RI.3	Explain events, procedures, ideas, or concepts in a historical, scientific, or technical text, including what happened and why, based on specific information in the text.	10, 13, 14, 49, 50
4RI.4	Determine the meaning of general academic and domain-specific words or phrases in a text relevant to a grade 4 topic or subject area.	2, 3, 4, 8, 11, 20, 21, 27, 31, 32, 33, 45
4RI.5	Describe the overall structure of events, ideas, concepts, or information in a text or part of a text.	46
4RI.6	Compare and contrast a firsthand and secondhand account of the same event or topic; describe the differences in focus and the information provided.	12
4RI.7	Interpret information presented visually, orally, or quantitatively and explain how the information contributes to an understanding of the text in which it appears.	28
4RI.8	Explain how an author uses reasons and evidence to support particular points in a text.	5, 22, 23, 30
4RF	Reading Standards: Foundational Skills	
4.RF.3a	Know and apply grade-level phonics and word analysis skills in decoding words. Use combined knowledge of all letter-sound correspondences, syllabication patterns, and morphology to read accurately unfamiliar multi-syllabic words in context...	2, 3, 4, 6, 8, 11, 20, 21, 27, 31, 32, 33, 45
4.RF.4a	Read with sufficient accuracy and fluency to support comprehension. Read on-level text with purpose and understanding.	18, 24

4.RF.4c	Read with sufficient accuracy and fluency to support comprehension. Use context to confirm or self-correct word recognition and understanding, rereading as necessary.	2, 3, 4, 8, 11, 20, 21, 27, 31, 32, 33, 45
4.W	**Writing Standards**	
4W.9a	Draw evidence from literary or informational texts to support analysis, reflection, and research. Apply grade 4 Reading standards to literature.	9, 17, 19, 34, 35
4W.9b	Draw evidence from literary or informational texts to support analysis, reflection, and research. Apply grade 4 Reading standards to informational texts.	5, 19, 22, 23, 30, 35
4SL	**Speaking and Listening Standards**	
4SL.3	Identify the reasons and evidence a speaker provides to support particular points.	5, 22, 23, 30
4L	**Language Standards**	
4L.1d	Demonstrate command of the conventions of standard English grammar and usage when writing or speaking. Order adjectives within sentences according to conventional patterns.	37
4L.1f	Demonstrate command of the conventions of standard English grammar and usage when writing or speaking. Produce complete sentences, recognizing and correcting inappropriate fragments and run-ons.	15
4L.2c	Demonstrate command of the conventions of standard English capitalization, punctuation, and spelling when writing. Use a comma before a coordinating conjunction in a compound sentence.	16
4L.4a	Determine or clarify the meaning of unknown and multiple-meaning words and phrases based on grade 4 reading and content, choosing flexibly from a range of strategies. Use context as a clue to the meaning of a word or phrase.	2, 3, 4, 8, 11, 20, 21, 27, 31, 32, 33, 45
4L.5c	Demonstrate understanding of figurative language, word relationships, and nuances in word meanings. Demonstrate understanding of words by relating them to their opposites (antonyms) and to words with similar but not identical meanings (synonyms).	25, 29, 42, 51, 52, 53

Read the following passage and answer questions 1 to 4

Monsters from the Deep and Other Imaginary Beings

Moving day. Groan. All that stuff. For most of us, moving day doesn't happen too often. For Michael Kusugak, growing up in the far north, moving was a way of life. For the first six years of his life, Michael lived in the age-old Inuit tradition of traveling. The family traveled by dog-team in search of whales, seals and cariboo. In winter they lived in

5 igloos. In summer they pitched a tent. The nomadic life is not a life for collecting possessions. The family had only the essentials—furs, weapons and tools. But they also had something that required no space and had no weight, but which was essential to their survival. They had stories.

Small Michael would fall asleep every night listening to the stories of his parents and
10 grandmother. Legends, family stories, funny stories, stories with something to teach. He heard tales of the animals he knew—the bear, the cariboo, the squirrel. And he heard stories of imaginary beings.

When Michael grew up, he remembered a story told in the spring. In the far north spring can be a dangerous time for children as the sea ice begins to break up. To keep their
15 children away from the hazardous shore, parents tell stories of the Qallupilluit, a witchy undersea creature who kidnaps children. In *A Promise Is a Promise* (written with Robert Munsch), Michael Kusugak invents his own version of the Qallupilluit and puts it into the world where he lives now—a world of jeans, TV and computers.

—from *The Young Writer's Companion* by Sarah Ellis

1. When Michael was a young child, he lived in
    A. igloos in summer and a tent in winter
    B. a tent in one place all summer and an igloo all winter
    C. a tent all year, but he and his family moved from place to place
    D. igloos in winter and a tent in summer, but he and his family moved from place to place

2. In the phrase "which was essential to their survival,"[line 7] the word "essential" means
    A. favorite
    B. additional
    C. necessary
    D. donated

3. The expression "age-old" means something that is
    A. new
    B. ancient
    C. done in old age
    D. done at a certain age

4. In the phrase "To keep their children away from the hazardous shore,"[line 14] the word "hazardous" means
    A. hazy
    B. haunted
    C. changing
    D. dangerous

Read the following passage and answer questions 5 to 8

Robots

Robots are machines. They can do some things that people do. And they can do some things that people can't. Robots don't have to eat. They don't have to drink. And they don't get lonely.

5 Robots can do the same things <u>over and over</u> exactly the same way. They don't get bored. They don't get tired. And best of all, robots can do things that are too dangerous for <u>us</u> to do.

That is why NASA uses robots. They send robots on long trips. They send them to places where there is no air to breathe. They send them where people can't go, or can't go yet.

10 The list below will tell you about a few NASA robots.

• <u>Robonaut</u> looks a lot like a human. It has a head, arms and upper body. Robonaut will go outside the *International Space Station*. It may work with astronauts on spacewalks. It may even go where it's not safe for humans.

• The space shuttle has a robot arm. It helps move things into and out of the shuttle. It
15 can also hold an astronaut who is working in space.

• Mars <u>rovers</u> are robots. They drive around on the land. Three NASA rovers are on Mars. Two of them are still working!

• *Stardust* was the first robot sent to a comet. It brought <u>bits</u> of the comet back to Earth in January 2006.

20 In the past, robots have helped NASA explore. Today, they are still important to NASA. In the future, we will use robots to help <u>return humans to the moon</u> and to travel to Mars and **beyond**.

—*from* NASA website

5. The information in the list section clearly highlights which of the following?
    A. Robots organized by the NASA missions they were used on
    B. Examples of NASA robots in no particular order
    C. NASA's uses for robots in order of importance
    D. NASA's use of robots from earliest to latest

6. The International Space Station belongs to
    A. many countries
    B. all the planets
    C. the moon
    D. NASA

7. This article says that robots are good for doing
   A. housecleaning
   B. unsafe tasks
   C. homework
   D. sports

8. When the writer says that robots will help "return humans to the moon,"[line 21] it means that humans
   A. belong to the moon
   B. have never been to the moon
   C. have already been to the moon
   D. got lost on the way to the moon

Read the following passage and answer questions 9 to 12

Joe's Junk

My name is Joe. All my life I have been a collector. I don't collect normal stuff like rocks or insects. I'm famous for my spectacular collection of junk.

"You trash it and I'll stash it!" That's my motto.

5   I am also a great inventor. My room is a workshop. I have a huge box of wire and some old bicycle parts. I have a ball of used string you wouldn't believe. I also have two enormous jars of nuts and bolts. And that's only the beginning.

Naturally, my room is my favorite place.

But Mother sighs when she walks by my room. My father says, "Unfit for human habitation," whatever that means.

10 I have made some really super inventions with my junk. I made a new kind of family pet. It did not shed or eat much. It just rolled around the room going, "Squeak, squeak!" My aunt was at the house when I wound it up. When she heard it, she suddenly said she had to run.

One day I needed my skateboard. All the kids were going to the park. I wanted to go too,
15 but the kids got tired of waiting for me. I searched for three hours before I finally found my skateboard. It was in a box of "S" things with a Superman cape, metal springs, and 23 shoelaces. When I got through digging around, my room was in worse shape than before. Even I was disgusted!

Another day I came home and found a line of kids at the front door. My own brother,
20 Alvie, was selling tickets to the World's Largest Indoor Dump. My room, of course.

My folks finally said, "Clear it up or clear out!"

It took me some time to get around to the clean-up. One day I could hardly open the door of my room. I couldn't find my homework, which upset my teacher. I couldn't find any clean clothes, which upset my parents. But worst of all, I couldn't find the parts I needed
25 for my inventions, which upset me!

My parents were right. My collection of junk had to go. But where? And how?

Then it hit me. A garage sale was the perfect solution to my problems. I would have the Sale of the Century!

So I began to work. There was a lot to do. But when the weekend came, I had the
30 greatest bunch of bargains that I had ever seen!

At first it was hard to see my treasures go. But when I took a good look at my customers,
I felt better. Many people were pulling broken wagons, just like mine. They looked like
collectors, too. My junk was going to good homes. I could tell!

Well, I sold most of my terrific junk. I left the rest for the garbage collector. This pleased
35 my folks. But I got a really creepy feeling when I went into my room. I mean, it was
EMPTY! So when I saw that broken typewriter in the trash, I knew just where to put it.
Likewise for the garden hose. And I have the best idea for a new invention.

—*by* Susan Russo

9. Which of the following words **best** describes how Joe felt after the sale?
   A. Sad
   B. Upset
   C. Angry
   D. Happy

10. Joe finally solved his junk problem by
    A. having a garage sale
    B. selling tickets to his show
    C. giving his junk away to friends
    D. leaving all his junk for the garbage collector

11. As it is used throughout the story, the word "junk" refers to a collection of
    A. tools
    B. rocks
    C. broken machines
    D. unusual odds and ends

12. The narrator of this passage is
    A. Joe's mom
    B. Joe's dad
    C. Alvie
    D. Joe

Islands in the Mind

Robert Louis Stevenson was a strange little boy. He was so skinny that people said he looked as if his bones would poke through his clothes. The damp climate of his Scottish home made his weak lungs worse, and he was sick more often than he was well. An only child, he never attended school regularly and, apart from his cousins, he had few friends.

5 If you had seen him sitting in an Edinburgh park—pale, weak and overprotected by his stern nanny—you might have felt sorry for him.

Yet inside his head, Louis had a rich, exciting life. He could make a whole world out of anything—toy soldiers, Bible stories, tales his nanny told him, his own terrifying nightmares. He could even make a world out of his breakfast.

10 When Louis and his cousin Bob had breakfast together, they made kingdoms in their porridge. Bob sprinkled sugar on his porridge and explained how his kingdom was a harsh northern land covered with snow. Louis poured milk on his porridge to make an island with bays and coves—an island in terrible danger of being swamped by the milky sea.

Years later Louis was doodling one day with some watercolor paints. On his paper
15 appeared an island. Something about the shape of his doodle delighted Louis, and he started to imagine the characters who lived on this island and the adventures they might have.

So began a furious fifteen-day writing frenzy in which Louis wrote the first fifteen chapters of *Treasure Island*, a pirate adventure story that has been enjoyed by readers for more than one hundred years.

20 —from *The Young Writer's Companion* by Sarah Ellis

13. Which of the following characters would **probably** be found in one of Louis's stories?
    A. A woodcutter
    B. A peasant
    C. A pirate
    D. A horse

14. Which character would be **most likely** to appear in Louis's story?
    A. a homeless wanderer
    B. a forgetful wizard
    C. a lonely princess
    D. a thieving pirate

15. The phrase "an island in terrible danger of being swamped by the milky sea"[line 13] is an example of a
    A. compound sentence
    B. sentence fragment
    C. simple sentence
    D. run-on sentence

16. The phrase "When Louis and his cousin Bob had breakfast together, they made kingdoms in their porridge"[line 10] is an example of a
    A. compound sentence
    B. sentence fragment
    C. simple sentence
    D. run-on sentence

Read the following passage and answer questions 17 to 21

from Crabs for Dinner

One summer, my grandmother came for a visit all the way from Africa.

"Ghana," she said. "That's where I come from."

She brought us funny-looking clothes, the kind they wear in Ghana. I had a smock made of a rough cotton fabric with stripes of bright colors woven into it.

5   It was long and loose, almost like a dress. Grandma said it was meant to be worn over a pair of trousers.

"I'm never going to wear those," I said to my mom.

But Emily wore hers, a colorful batik dress with embroidery around the neck.

She looked so pretty that I decided to wear my smock. When I did, I thought I looked
10 "cool." Especially when I wore the striped cotton cap that came with the smock.

Grandma had lots of stories to tell. Stories her grandmother told her when she was young. I liked the ones about a cunning "Spider man" who got in and out of all kinds of trouble.

She always ended in a funny way, saying: "This story of mine whether good or bad, may pass away, or come to stay. It is your turn to tell your story."

15 So we took our turn and told her stories. And she liked them just as much as we liked hers.

A week before she left for Ghana, she invited my aunts and uncle to dinner.

"She's going to make soup and yucky crab," Emily said. "I'll bet she makes a lot of it. But I won't even take a bite."

She did make the soup, only she put in okra too.

20 "That's going to make it slimy," I said.

"Double Yuk," said Emily.

But dinner got cooked and dinner was served and grace was said.

Emily and I were eating hot dogs and the grown-ups were eating slime.

Uncle Robert rolled his eyes upward. "Mmm," he said. "Exquisite!"

25 I had never heard him use that word for Mom's soup.

"My word," Aunt Pauline said, "I had almost forgotten the original taste."

My mom simply said, "Delicious."

Even Aunt Araba paused from the sucking and crunching to say one word, "Authentic!"

I noticed that Grandma's soup smelled really good, much better than Mom's soup.
30 Suddenly I wanted to taste just a little bit of the fufu with crab and soup.

"Can I have a little, please?" I heard Emily ask.

"Why, of course!" Grandma replied.

If Emily doesn't die, I'll have some, I thought.

Emily took a bite and didn't die. Instead she took another bite.

35 "And how about you?" said Grandma.

"Yes, please," I said.

It tasted different, not like the soups I knew. It was spicy and hot and really good. It was thick and smooth and I thought I could taste the flavor of ginger.

I broke off a tiny piece of crab and sucked it just like Mommy did. It was all soft inside.
40 Then I crunched on it, really hard, just as my Aunt Araba did.

Then I ate a whole bowl of fufu and soup and a huge piece of crab. When I was done I rolled my eyes up to the sky and said aloud, "Exquisite!"

I am not even sure what that means, but probably it is a way of saying that sometimes grandmothers cook better than mothers.

45 —by Adwoa Badoe

17. The reason the narrator did not want to wear the smock his grandmother had brought was **most likely** because it
   A. was covered with bright-colored stripes
   B. needed to be worn over trousers
   C. looked very strange to him
   D. came from Ghana

18. Which of the following quotations says what Grandma plans to do?
   A. "A week before she left for Ghana, she invited my aunts and uncle to dinner."[line 16]
   B. "'She's going to make soup and yucky crab,' Emily said."[line 17]
   C. "She did make the soup, only she put in okra too."[line 19]
   D. "Grandma had lots of stories to tell."[line 11]

19. Which of his senses made the narrator want to try the soup?
   A. Hearing
   B. Smell
   C. Taste
   D. Sight

20. When Aunt Araba calls Grandma's soup "Authentic," she means the soup is
   A. exquisite
   B. original
   C. bland
   D. fine

21. When Uncle Robert said the soup was "Exquisite," he meant that the soup was
    A. hearty
    B. delicious
    C. different
    D. slimy

Read the following passage and answer questions 22 to 25

"Understanding Your Rabbit"

Your rabbit makes soft grunts, but these won't tell you its mood. Your rabbit will squeal when it is frightened. It also warns other rabbits of danger by thumping its back legs. A rabbit finds out a lot by sniffing. It can even tell from another rabbit's smell whether it is a friend or enemy. Watch your rabbit, and you will soon understand much of what it is doing.

5 **Keeping a lookout**
When your rabbit hears a strange sound, it stands up on its hind legs to see what is happening.

Cuddling together
Rabbit kittens are very friendly. The brothers and sisters huddle together in a heap when they are sleeping. This helps keep them warm.

10 **Marking what's mine**
Your rabbit rubs a special scent, which is made in its skin, onto everything in its hutch, grazing ark, and enclosure. If your rabbit lives with another rabbit, it rubs its friend's chin to leave the scent.

Best of friends
15 Your rabbit will show you that you are its friend. It rubs its head against you to leave its special scent. It may even wash you with its tongue!

Signaling danger
When a mother rabbit thinks that her kittens are in danger, she will stand in front of them. If she is very worried, she will thump the ground with her back leg. This tells the
20 kittens, and other nearby rabbits, to run for cover.

Meeting the enemy
A rabbit may become angry with another rabbit. It will stare straight at its enemy to let the other know that it is annoyed.

Show of strength
25 If the timid rabbit doesn't run away, both rabbits will scratch the ground with their front paws. They may run at each other.

The fight

If neither rabbit is scared away, a fight begins. They charge forward and try to sink their teeth into each other's necks.

30 **The loser**

The weaker rabbit runs away when it is beaten. It will never forget the other rabbit's scent. Whenever it smells the other rabbit's scent, it will avoid it.

—from *Rabbits* by Mark Evans

22. A rabbit shows affection to its owner by
    A. scratching him or her with its claws
    B. rubbing its head against him or her
    C. squealing when it sees him or her
    D. nibbling him or her with its teeth

23. When a rabbit that has lost a fight smells the scent of the rabbit to which it lost, it will
    A. challenge it to another fight
    B. hide behind a bigger rabbit
    C. run away to avoid it
    D. offer it some food

24. Baby rabbits are often called
    A. cubs
    B. foals
    C. kittens
    D. puppies

25. Which of the following words is a synonym of the word "timid"[line 25]?
    A. Shy
    B. Quiet
    C. Sensible
    D. Confident

Read the following passage and answer questions 26 to 29

from "The Voyage of the Mayflower"

Pelted by rain under a black sky, the ninety-foot *Mayflower* rolled and pitched on mountainous waves. Its masts were bare because during a storm, a sailing ship must lower all its sails and drift with the wind to avoid capsizing or breaking apart.

5 Below the main deck, the passengers huddled in the dark. They could hear the wind howling and the waves thudding against the vessel's wooden sides and washing over the deck. Seawater dripped down on them through the canvas covering the deck gratings and seeped through the seams in the planking. The passengers were soaked and shivering; several were seasick besides. As frightened adults tried to comfort terrified children, they prayed for safety in the storm and an end to the long, terrible voyage.

10 Suddenly, above the din of the storm, they heard the noise of splitting timber. One of the beams supporting the deck had cracked! The ship was in danger of sinking. Then someone remembered a great iron screw brought from Holland. Carefully, the ship's carpenter positioned it beneath the beam and braced it. It would hold; the passengers and crew could reach land safely.

15 Crossing the Atlantic in 1620 was extremely risky. A wooden ship could leak or break apart in a storm. Since the sails could be raised only in fair weather, it was impossible to predict how long a voyage would last. To avoid the stormy autumn months, ships usually made the crossing in spring or summer. They almost never sailed alone.

Aware of these dangers, the Pilgrims had planned to cross the ocean in two ships in the 20 summer of 1620. The English Separatists from Holland (who called themselves Saints) borrowed money from London businessmen and purchased a small ship, the *Speedwell*. For the Separatists' safety, and to help them establish a profitable colony, the businessmen recruited additional volunteers in London. The businessmen rented the *Mayflower*, a ship three times the size of the *Speedwell*, for these recruits, whom the 25 Separatists called Strangers. The Saints and Strangers met for the first time in Southampton, England, a few days before the ships sailed on August 5.

The tiny *Speedwell* had been refitted with taller masts and larger sails so it could keep up with the *Mayflower*. These changes, however, caused the ship to leak badly at sea. On August 12, the ships put into Dartmouth. After the *Speedwell* was examined and 30 repaired, they set off again on August 23. Two days later, the *Speedwell* began to leak again, and the vessels headed for Plymouth, England. There the ships' masters, carpenters, and principal passengers agreed that the *Speedwell* could not make the crossing.

Over the next few days, the sixty-seven Strangers on the *Mayflower* made room for thirty-five of the Saints from the *Speedwell*, along with their belongings and provisions. 35 On September 6, the *Mayflower* set out from Plymouth alone. The one hundred two passengers, including thirty-four children, would not see land for sixty-six days.

The *Mayflower*, like all ships of the time, was built to carry cargo, not passengers. A few families crowded into the "great cabbin" in the stern. Most of the passengers, however, traveled in bunks or tiny "cabbins" below the main deck and above the hold, where cargo 40 was stored. In this "'tween decks" area, they had only five feet of head room. Each person's living space was smaller than the mattress of a modern twin bed.

The Pilgrims suffered other discomforts. Many were seasick, particularly at the beginning of the voyage. In storms, they were constantly wet and cold. They could not bathe or wash and dry their clothes and bedding. For toilet purposes, they used buckets.

45 In fair weather, the adults and children who had recovered from seasickness could leave their dim, foul-smelling quarters for the wind and spray of the main deck. The adults took deep breaths of the cold, tangy air and stretched cramped muscles. The younger children, forbidden to run around, played quiet games. Damaris Hopkins, age three, and Mary and Remember Allerton, ages four and six, "tended the baby" (played with dolls).

50 Six- and nine-year old brothers Wrestling and Love Brewster played "I Spy" and "Hunt the Slipper" with six- and seven-year-old Jasper and Richard More. Finger games such as cat's cradle and paper, scissors, stone were popular with eight-year-old Humility Cooper, Ellen More, John Cooke, John Billington, and Bartholomew Allerton. Elizabeth Tilley, age fourteen, and Mary Chilton and Constance Hopkins, both fifteen, helped

55 prepare the meals.

For cooking, the passengers built charcoal fires in metal braziers set in sandboxes. There was so little space, however, that only a few people could cook at once. When storms made lighting fires dangerous, everyone ate cold meals.

After morning prayers, they ate a simple breakfast of cheese and ship's biscuit (hard, dry

60 biscuit). If cooking was allowed, they might have porridge. Their midday meal might consist of ship's biscuit and cheese or, in fair weather, cooked "pease pottage," boiled salt fish, pork, or beef and any freshly caught bonito or porpoise. Before retiring, they had a light supper. Everyone, even the children, drank beer with their meals because it was preferred to water.

65 Not until December 11, more than a month after first sighting land, did the Pilgrims decide where they would build their colony. ...

—by Patricia M. Whalen

26. Who were the passengers on board the *Mayflower* in 1620?
    A. the crew
    B. the Pilgrims
    C. mainly convicts
    D. mainly refugees

27. As used in this passage, the word "Mayflower" refers to a
    A. flower
    B. sailing ship
    C. common noun
    D. person's name

28. The phrases "wind howling" and "waves thudding" appeal most to the sense of
    A. taste
    B. sight
    C. touch
    D. hearing

29. A synonym for the word "capsizing" is
    A. splitting up
    B. turning over
    C. cracking up
    D. breaking apart

Read the following passage and answer questions 30 to 33

Cheetahs

The cheetah is the fastest mammal on land and can reach speeds of over 100 km/h over short distances. It usually chases its prey at only about half that speed, however. After a chase, a cheetah needs half an hour to catch its breath before it can eat.

5　The cheetah's excellent eyesight helps it find prey during the day. Sometimes, a cheetah perches on a high place and watches for prey. Cheetahs eat small- to medium-sized animals, such as hares, impalas, and gazelles.

When it spots prey, a cheetah begins to stalk. It creeps as close as possible before the attack. The cheetah is hard to see because its spotted coat blends with the tall, dry grass of the plains.

10　Suddenly, the cheetah makes a lightning dash. With a paw, it knocks its prey to the ground and then bites its throat.

Once found throughout Asia and Africa, cheetahs today are racing toward extinction. Loss of habitat and declining numbers of their prey combine to threaten the future of these cats.

30. A cheetah would be **least likely** to eat a
    A. banana
    B. mouse
    C. rabbit
    D. deer

31. As it is used in the phrase "Once found throughout Asia and Africa,"[line 12] the word "throughout" means
    A. out the other side
    B. outside of
    C. inside out
    D. all over

32. When a cheetah stalks its prey, it
    A. crunches the bones of its dinner
    B. moves carefully and silently
    C. plays a trick on another animal
    D. roars very loudly

33. The word *prey* refers to
   A. an animal that is being hunted
   B. an animal that is hurt
   C. a small animal
   D. a hunter

Read the following passage and answer questions 34 to 37

from "The Court of King Arthur"

A long, long time ago, even before television was invented, there lived a knight called Sir Gadabout. This was in the days of the famous King Arthur and his Round Table. It was an exciting and mysterious time to live in, especially for a knight.

5   In a misty and remote corner of England stood the castle called Camelot, and there King Arthur gathered the best knights in the land to sit at the Round Table. These knights had to be prepared to go out at a moment's notice and fight villains, dragons, people who drop litter—and generally keep the peace.

If you could travel in time and visit Camelot, you would find the gallant King Arthur, tall and brave, much loved and respected. By his side would be the Queen—Guinivere,
10   beautiful, graceful, and a dab hand at woodwork. Around them you would find all the great knights, whose names might seem odd to us now: Sir Lancelot, Sir Gawain, Sir Dorothy (his name seemed odd even then) and Sir Gadabout.

Now, although Sir Gadabout sat at the Round Table with the best of them, he wasn't quite one of the best knights in the land. It has to be said that he was indubitably the
15   Worst Knight in the *World*. In fact, the March edition of the magazine *Knights Illustrated* voted him the "knight most likely to chop his own foot off in a fight." …

His armor was held together purely by rust—and anyway, he'd grown out of it by the time he was eleven. His spear was bent and only good for throwing round corners, and his sword was broken in five places and fixed with lots of sticky tape; it wobbled
20   alarmingly in a stiff breeze. His horse, Pegasus, was knockkneed and about ninety years-old.

King Arthur felt sorry for Sir Gadabout, who was hard-working and polite. That was probably why the King allowed him to join the otherwise glorious company of the Round Table.

To be honest Sir Gadabout had not performed as many heroic deeds as the other knights. He'd hardly performed any, unless you count the time when he accompanied the
25 fearsome Sir Bors de Ganis on a mission to rescue the fair maid Fiona from the Isles of Iona. Then he got lost in the eerie mists and ended up in Tipton, some three hundred miles from where Sir Bors was having to get on with the rescue all alone.

Sir Gadabout did once get a dear old lady's cat down from a tree. It wasn't stuck, as it happened (but *he* wasn't to know that) and it only took Sir Tristram three hours to get Sir
30 Gadabout back down again…

—from *Sir Gadabout* by Martyn Beardsley

34. Sir Gadabout was voted "knight most likely to chop his own foot off in a fight," which indicates that he is
   A. gallant
   B. clumsy
   C. fearsome
   D. respected

35. The days of the famous King Arthur are described as
   A. exciting and mysterious
   B. fearsome and villainous
   C. adventurous and heroic
   D. dull and boring

36. The writer suggests that the reason Gadabout was a member of the Round Table is that he was
   A. given an award by the magazine *Knights Illustrated*
   B. old and had performed many heroic deeds in his youth
   C. polite and hardworking and King Arthur felt sorry for him
   D. the only one who would accompany Sir Bors de Ganis on missions

37. The words mysterious, glorious, graceful, and beautiful are examples of
   A. verbs
   B. nouns
   C. adverbs
   D. adjectives

Read the following passage and answer questions 38 to 42

The St. Lawrence Beluga

Encountering a beluga whale is a real privilege. A somewhat ghostly animal, the beluga is a symbol of fragility and vulnerability. It knows the St. Lawrence like no other because it lives there year-round. The beluga herd in the St. Lawrence River is the only one in the world that does not live in the Arctic. The St. Lawrence provides habitat similar to the
5 Arctic: the salt water is nice and cold and there is lots of food.

There are many beluga herds in the Canadian North. The total beluga population is over 100,000. Other Arctic beluga herds live in northern Russia, Norway, Greenland, and Alaska.

A beluga has all the characteristics of a polar animal. Its white color acts as camouflage in the ice. It has a bumpy ridge extending along its back, instead of a dorsal fin, that
10 allows it to break through the ice to breathe without injuring itself. Belugas have a flexible neck, while all other whales have fused cervical vertebrae and cannot turn their head.

Belugas are highly social animals, which explains their extensive vocabulary. They have developed some of the most varied vocal repertoires in the animal kingdom. From its rounded forehead, a beluga sends out ultrasound waves to find its food.

15 The beluga herd in the St. Lawrence is not what it was a hundred years ago. At the turn of the last century, there were over 5,000 belugas in the River. Their numbers have dropped considerably since then. They were overhunted because it was thought that they were eating the salmon and cod that humans needed to survive. Authorities even offered a bonus of fifteen dollars for every beluga tail brought in, to encourage elimination
20 of the species as quickly as possible. The hunt was not brought to an end until the nineteen seventies. Now, there are between 700 and 1,200 in the St. Lawrence herd and the beluga is an endangered species.

Nowadays, because scientists have raised the alarm, the St. Lawrence beluga is protected. However, damage to its habitat and pollution continue to threaten its well-being.

25 The beluga is affected by various illnesses, but the link between disease and pollutants has yet to be found. Contaminants are not biodegradable, so the only way that belugas can get rid of them is through the female. A mother can reduce the level of pollutants in her body through her milk, but a newborn beluga starts life contaminated.

For all these reasons, the health of the St. Lawrence beluga is a concern. It will take
30 generations, many more studies, and a lot of determination to improve the situation. The beluga's health is definitely a reflection of the state of the St. Lawrence River.

—from *As Long As There Are Whales* by Evelyne Daigle, translated by Geneviève Wright

38. The St. Lawrence River habitat is similar to the Arctic because the water is
   A. cold with little food
   B. warm with little food
   C. cold with lots of food
   D. warm with lots of food

39. The people who warned about the need to protect the belugas were
    A. hunters
    B. scientists
    C. fishermen
    D. politicians

40. The beluga whale hunt ended in the
    A. 1950s
    B. 1960s
    C. 1970s
    D. 1980s

41. Which of the following countries is **not** identified as being part of the beluga's habitat?
    A. Russia
    B. Alaska
    C. Finland
    D. Norway

42. An antonym of the word "elimination," as it is used in the phrase "to encourage elimination of the species,"[line 19] is
    A. preservation
    B. eradication
    C. exclusion
    D. removal

Read the following passage and answer questions 43 to 46

How Stamps Are Printed: Part 1

What stamp is that?

Definitive stamps are expected to remain in circulation for a long time, so they have values that are acceptable and predictable for people who regularly buy stamps. The ordinary 50-cent stamp for a standard letter that remained the same price for a number of
5 years was a definitive stamp.

Commemorative stamps are special stamps created to honor special events or historical occasions that are significant to an entire nation. Such stamps of celebration generally mark anniversaries of at least 50 years, such as Confederation or Independence Day.

10 **Personalized stamps** permit the reproduction of an actual photograph on the tab of a legal postage stamp. In this way, individuals can have a tab beside the stamp on their letters displaying a photo of themselves, a friend, or even a beloved pet. Australia was the first country to introduce personalized stamps in 1999, but the practice has spread so that anyone can pay to have their own stamp, or at least their own tab attached to a
15 stamp, on the letters they mail.

Thematic stamps are collector stamps with a common theme such as flowers, cars, space travel, or endangered species. Some collectors prefer stamps that commemorate a special event such as the Olympic Games or a popular holiday season. Collectors of thematic stamps tend to discover their treasures among the stamps issued over a variety
20 of years and by a variety of countries around the world.

Instant stamps are just what they are called—instant! During the 2000 Olympic Games in Sydney, instant stamps were issued for every Australian gold medal athlete, not only printed but offered for sale the day after the medal win! Like personalized stamps, this was another world first for Australia.

25 **Living Legendsstamps** also originated in Australia. In 1987, the country which had once ruled that no living person (the exception being the Queen and her family members) could ever be shown on a stamp issued the first "Living Legends" stamp to recognize Sir Donald Bradman, Australia's most famous cricketer.

43. According to the text, Australia introduced the world's first
   A. commemorative stamp
   B. personalized stamp
   C. collector's stamp
   D. historical stamp

44. The **main** purpose of this article is to
   A. comment on famous Australian cricketer Donald Bradman
   B. list the various stamp themes that are available
   C. educate people about different types of stamps
   D. discuss the Sydney Olympics stamp collection

45. In the context of this passage, the word "commemorate"[line 17] means to
   A. honor an event or person
   B. remember what time it is
   C. declare a public holiday
   D. declare war

46. The type of writing used in this passage is **best** referred to as
   A. an interview
   B. a biography
   C. an article
   D. a story

Ancient Broom Games

Broom sports emerged almost as soon as broomsticks were sufficiently advanced to allow fliers to turn corners and vary their speed and height. Early wizarding writings and paintings give us some idea of the games our ancestors played. Some of these no longer exist; others have survived or evolved into the sports we know today.

5　The celebrated **annual broom race** of Sweden dates from the tenth century. Fliers race from Kopparberg to Arjeplog, a distance of slightly over three hundred miles. The course runs straight through a dragon reservation and the vast silver trophy is shaped like a Swedish Short-Snout. Nowadays this is an international event and wizards of all nationalities congregate at Kopparberg to cheer the starters, then Apparate to Arjeplog to
10　congratulate the survivors.

The famous painting *Günther der Gewaltig ist der Gewinner* ("Gunther the Violent is the Winner"), dated 1105, shows the ancient German game of **Stichstock**. A twenty-foot-high pole was topped with an inflated dragon bladder. One player on a broomstick had the job of protecting this bladder. The bladder-guardian was tied to the pole by a rope around his
15　or her waist, so that he or she could not fly further than ten feet away from it. The rest of the players would take it in turns to fly at the bladder and attempt to puncture it with the specially sharpened ends of their brooms. The bladder-guardian was allowed to use his or her wand to repel these attacks.The game ended when the bladder was successfully punctured, or the bladder-guardian had either succeeded in hexing all opponents out of
20　the running or collapsed from exhaustion. Stichstock died out in the fourteenth century.

In Ireland the game of **Aingingein** flourished, the subject of many an Irish ballad (the legendary wizard Fingal the Fearless is alleged to have been an Aingingein champion). One by one the players would take the Dom, or ball (actually the gallbladder of a goat), and speed through a series of burning barrels set high in the air on stilts. The Dom was
25　to be thrown through the final barrel. The player who succeeded in getting the Dom through the last barrel in the fastest time, without having caught fire on the way, was the winner.

Scotland was the birthplace of what is probably the most dangerous of all broom games—**Creaothceann**. The game features in a tragic Gaelic poem of the eleventh century, the first verse of which says, in translation:

30　*The players assembled, twelve fine, hearty men,*
They strapped on their cauldrons, stood poised to fly,
At the sound of the horn they were swiftly airborne
But ten of their number were fated to die.

Creaothceann players each wore a cauldron strapped to the head. At the sound of the
35　horn or drum, up to a hundred charmed rocks and boulders that had been hovering a hundred feet above the ground began to fall towards the earth. The Creaothceann players zoomed around trying to catch as many rocks as possible in their cauldrons. Considered by many Scottish wizards to be the supreme test of manliness and courage, Creaothceann enjoyed considerable popularity in the Middle Ages, despite the huge
40　number of fatalities that resulted from it. The game was made illegal in 1762, and though Magnus "Dent-Head" Macdonald spearheaded a campaign for its reintroduction in the 1960s, the Ministry of Magic refused to lift the ban.

Shuntbumps was popular in Devon, England. This was a crude form of jousting, the sole aim being to knock as many other players as possible off their brooms, the last person
45 remaining on their broom winning.

Swivenhodge began in Herefordshire. Like Stichstock, this involved an inflated bladder, usually a pig's. Players sat backwards on their brooms and batted the bladder backwards and forwards across a hedge with the brush ends of their brooms. The first person to miss gave their opponent a point. First to reach fifty points was the winner.

50 Swivenhodge is still played in England, though it has never achieved much widespread popularity; Shuntbumps survives only as a children's game. At Queerditch Marsh, however, a game had been created that would one day become the most popular in the wizarding world.

—from *Quidditch Through the Ages* by Kennilworthy Whisp (J. K. Rowling)

47. The object of Aingingein was to
   A. catch rocks in a cauldron
   B. puncture a dragon bladder
   C. knock people off their brooms
   D. throw a ball through a fiery barrel

48. Which of the following lists gives the countries where the ancient broom games originated?
   A. England, Sweden, Switzerland, Germany, and Austria
   B. Sweden, Germany, Ireland, Scotland, and England
   C. Sweden, Germany, France, and England
   D. England, Ireland, Scotland, and Wales

49. Scottish wizards valued Creaothceann as a supreme test of
   A. endurance and courage
   B. manliness and courage
   C. intelligence and agility
   D. wizardry and agility

50. The game in which the winner is **most likely** to be determined through speed and endurance is
   A. the annual broom race
   B. Swivenhodge
   C. Shuntbumps
   D. Aingingein

51. A synonym for the word "evolved," as it is used in the sentence "Some of these no longer exist; others have survived or evolved into the sports we know today,"[line 3] is
   A. died
   B. changed
   C. enlarged
   D. disappeared

52. As it is used in the sentence "The bladder-guardian was allowed to use his or her wand to repel these attacks,"[line 14] the word "repel" means
    A. fend off
    B. retaliate
    C. soak up
    D. remove

53. The word "flourished," which is used in the quotation "In Ireland the game of **Aingingein**[line 21] flourished, the subject of many an Irish ballad," is similar in meaning to the word
    A. thrived
    B. expired
    C. diminished
    D. disappeared

EXERCISE #2—READING INFORMATIONAL

Table of Correlations		
Standard		**Test #1**
4RL	Reading Standards for Literature	
4RL.1	Refer to details and examples in a text when explaining what the text says explicitly and when drawing inferences from the text.	54, 59, 60, 70
4RL.2	Determine a theme of a story, drama, or poem from details in the text; summarize the text.	55, 61, 71, 72, 74, 75, 76, 80, 81, 82, 83, 86, 87, 94
4RL.3	Describe in depth a character, setting, or event in a story or drama, drawing on specific details in the text.	62, 66, 88, 95, 96, 101
4RL.4	Determine the meaning of words and phrases as they are used in a text, including those that allude to significant characters found in mythology.	56, 57, 63, 64, 65, 67, 68, 77, 84, 92, 97, 104
4RL.7	Make connections between the text of a story or drama and a visual or oral presentation of the text, identifying where each version reflects specific descriptions and directions in the text.	85
4RL.9	Compare and contrast the treatment of similar themes and topics and patterns of events in stories, myths, and traditional literature from different cultures.	72, 81
4RL.10	By the end of the year, read and comprehend literature, including stories, dramas, and poetry, in the grades 4–5 text complexity band proficiently, with scaffolding as needed at the high end of the range.	69
4RI	Reading Standards for Informational Text	
4RI.1	Refer to details and examples in a text when explaining what the text says explicitly and when drawing inferences from the text.	54, 59, 60, 70
4RI.2	Determine the main idea of a text and explain how it is supported by key details; summarize the text.	55, 61, 71, 72, 74, 75, 76, 80, 81, 82, 83, 86, 87, 94
4RI.3	Explain events, procedures, ideas, or concepts in a historical, scientific, or technical text, including what happened and why, based on specific information in the text.	62, 66, 88, 95, 96, 101
4RI.4	Determine the meaning of general academic and domain-specific words or phrases in a text relevant to a grade 4 topic or subject area.	56, 57, 63, 64, 65, 67, 68, 77, 84, 92, 97, 104
4RI.7	Interpret information presented visually, orally, or quantitatively and explain how the information contributes to an understanding of the text in which it appears.	85
4RI.8	Explain how an author uses reasons and evidence to support particular points in a text.	58, 99, 100
4RI.9	Integrate information from two texts on the same topic in order to write or speak about the subject knowledgeably.	72, 81
4RF	Reading Standards: Foundational Skills	
4.RF.3a	Know and apply grade-level phonics and word analysis skills in decoding words. Use combined knowledge of all letter-sound correspondences, syllabication patterns, and morphology to read accurately unfamiliar multi-syllabic words in context...	56, 57, 63, 64, 65, 67, 68, 77, 84, 90, 91, 92, 97, 104
4.RF.4a	Read with sufficient accuracy and fluency to support comprehension. Read on-level text with purpose and understanding.	78, 79

4.RF.4c	Read with sufficient accuracy and fluency to support comprehension. Use context to confirm or self-correct word recognition and understanding, rereading as necessary.	56, 57, 63, 64, 65, 67, 68, 77, 84, 92, 97, 104
4.W	Writing Standards	
4W.9a	Draw evidence from literary or informational texts to support analysis, reflection, and research. Apply grade 4 Reading standards to literature.	54, 59, 60, 70, 103
4W.9b	Draw evidence from literary or informational texts to support analysis, reflection, and research. Apply grade 4 Reading standards to informational texts.	54, 58, 59, 60, 70, 99, 100
4SL	Speaking and Listening Standards	
4SL.3	Identify the reasons and evidence a speaker provides to support particular points.	58, 99, 100
4L	Language Standards	
4L.4a	Determine or clarify the meaning of unknown and multiple-meaning words and phrases based on grade 4 reading and content, choosing flexibly from a range of strategies. Use context as a clue to the meaning of a word or phrase.	56, 57, 63, 64, 65, 67, 68, 77, 84, 92, 97, 104
4L.4c	Determine or clarify the meaning of unknown and multiple-meaning words and phrases based on grade 4 reading and content, choosing flexibly from a range of strategies. Consult reference materials, both print and digital, to find the...	98
4L.5c	Demonstrate understanding of figurative language, word relationships, and nuances in word meanings. Demonstrate understanding of words by relating them to their opposites (antonyms) and to words with similar but not identical meanings (synonyms).	67, 73, 89, 93, 102, 105, 106

Read the following passage and answer questions 54 to 57

Beetles

Beetles, beetles, beetles! You are surrounded by beetles! That's right! It is a fact that beetles would outnumber every other kind of animal at a worldwide animal convention. That's because fully one-quarter of all animals are actually beetles. You can pretty much find beetles anywhere in the world, even under water! Scientists have spent many hours
5 trying to figure out what makes beetles champions at surviving in such huge numbers. The answer seems to lie in an impressive beetle adaptation called the elytra.

The elytra is like a special suit of protective armor for beetles. Gradually, a hard casing, or shell, develops above the soft front wings of the beetles, meeting in a straight line down their backs. This elytra not only protects the fragile wings, but also prevents attacks
10 from both parasites (creatures which burrow inside something living to eat it) and predators (creatures which chew on something living from the outside). Because the elytra is hard, it holds moisture and coolness inside for beetles. Beetles don't even mind desert heat because the elytra provides them with their own personal air conditioners. Some beetles are further protected by their shape. They can be very flat and able to hide
15 in tiny, safe locations deep inside cracks or under rocks.

Do you think that one million years is a long time? Try 350 million years! That's how long scientists believe that beetles have been adapting and reproducing. During that time, beetles have produced some weird and wonderful world beetle champions. Some of these champions are described here for you.

20 **WORLD BEETLE CHAMPIONS**

Largest

The largest beetle would be the South American beetle known as *Titanus giganteus*. The name means "huge giant". This tropical beetle can measure more than 17 centimeters (6 ½ inches) in length, and can chop a pencil in half with mighty jaws called mandibles.

25 ### Smallest

The smallest beetle would be the featherwing beetle. It is barely visible at a length of one quarter of a millimeter (1/100 inch).

Heaviest

The champion heavyweight would be the goliath beetle, which weighs in at up to 100
30 grams (3 ½ ounces). Picture a large apple for comparison!

Longest

The champion of length is the Brazilian longhorn beetle. It stretches to an impressive record length of 20 centimeters (8 inches).

Strongest

35 The mightiest beetle in the world is the African scarab or rhinoceros beetle. Because it is capable of lifting 850 times its own body weight, this beetle holds the record for being the world's strongest animal.

54. What is the name of the world's heaviest beetle?
   A. Rhinoceros beetle
   B. Feathering beetle
   C. Longhorn beetle
   D. Goliath beetle

55. According to scientists, beetles survive everywhere because they
   A. live in every temperature
   B. are well protected
   C. eat everything
   D. can kill others

56. According to the passage, a "parasite" is a creature that
   A. depends on others for food and shelter
   B. feeds on the bodies of others
   C. lives on the bodies of others
   D. dislikes others

57. The elytra are a beetle's
   A. wing covers
   B. soft wings
   C. antennae
   D. legs

Read the following passage and answer questions 58 to 65

Monsters from the Deep and Other Imaginary Beings

Moving day. Groan. All that stuff. For most of us, moving day doesn't happen too often. For Michael Kusugak, growing up in the far north, moving was a way of life. For the first six years of his life, Michael lived in the age-old Inuit tradition of traveling. The family traveled by dog-team in search of whales, seals and cariboo. In winter they lived in
5 igloos. In summer they pitched a tent. The nomadic life is not a life for collecting possessions. The family had only the essentials—furs, weapons and tools. But they also had something that required no space and had no weight, but which was essential to their survival. They had stories.

Small Michael would fall asleep every night listening to the stories of his parents and
10 grandmother. Legends, family stories, funny stories, stories with something to teach. He heard tales of the animals he knew—the bear, the cariboo, the squirrel. And he heard stories of imaginary beings.

When Michael grew up, he remembered a story told in the spring. In the far north spring can be a dangerous time for children as the sea ice begins to break up. To keep their
15 children away from the hazardous shore, parents tell stories of the Qallupilluit, a witchy undersea creature who kidnaps children. In *A Promise Is a Promise* (written with Robert Munsch), Michael Kusugak invents his own version of the Qallupilluit and puts it into the world where he lives now—a world of jeans, TV and computers.

—from *The Young Writer's Companion* by Sarah Ellis

58. In the passage, the Qallupilluit is described as a
A. whale spirit
B. sea serpent
C. sort of mermaid
D. witchy sea creature

59. Michael lived a nomadic life for how many years?
A. 3
B. 4
C. 5
D. 6

60. According to the passage, Michael Kusugak's family traveled by
A. horseback
B. camper
C. dog-team
D. snowmobile

61. Michael's family moved around in order to
    A. stay with the warmer weather
    B. tell their stories to other people
    C. hunt the caribou, whales, and seals
    D. follow the bear, caribou, and squirrels

62. Furs were **most likely** essential to Michael's family because they
    A. were fashionable
    B. could be sold for food
    C. could be used for camouflage while hunting
    D. were needed for warmth and protection from the cold weather

63. An age-old tradition is something that
    A. is done to celebrate birthdays
    B. people do when they reach a certain age
    C. people are unable to do before a certain age
    D. has been done the same way for a long time

64. An "imaginary being" is a creature that
    A. lives at the North Pole
    B. teaches life lessons
    C. is frightening
    D. is not real

65. Michael's nomadic life is described in the first paragraph. From this description, the word "nomadic" means
    A. poor
    B. northern
    C. living in igloos
    D. traveling around

Read the following passage and answer questions 66 to 69

Joe's Junk

My name is Joe. All my life I have been a collector. I don't collect normal stuff like rocks or insects. I'm famous for my spectacular collection of junk.

"You trash it and I'll stash it!" That's my motto.

5 I am also a great inventor. My room is a workshop. I have a huge box of wire and some old bicycle parts. I have a ball of used string you wouldn't believe. I also have two enormous jars of nuts and bolts. And that's only the beginning.

Naturally, my room is my favorite place.

But Mother sighs when she walks by my room. My father says, "Unfit for human habitation," whatever that means.

10 I have made some really super inventions with my junk. I made a new kind of family pet. It did not shed or eat much. It just rolled around the room going, "Squeak, squeak!" My aunt was at the house when I wound it up. When she heard it, she suddenly said she had to run.

One day I needed my skateboard. All the kids were going to the park. I wanted to go too,
15 but the kids got tired of waiting for me. I searched for three hours before I finally found my skateboard. It was in a box of "S" things with a Superman cape, metal springs, and 23 shoelaces. When I got through digging around, my room was in worse shape than before. Even I was disgusted!

Another day I came home and found a line of kids at the front door. My own brother,
20 Alvie, was selling tickets to the World's Largest Indoor Dump. My room, of course.

My folks finally said, "Clear it up or clear out!"

It took me some time to get around to the clean-up. One day I could hardly open the door of my room. I couldn't find my homework, which upset my teacher. I couldn't find any clean clothes, which upset my parents. But worst of all, I couldn't find the parts I needed
25 for my inventions, which upset me!

My parents were right. My collection of junk had to go. But where? And how?

Then it hit me. A garage sale was the perfect solution to my problems. I would have the Sale of the Century!

So I began to work. There was a lot to do. But when the weekend came, I had the
30 greatest bunch of bargains that I had ever seen!

At first it was hard to see my treasures go. But when I took a good look at my customers, I felt better. Many people were pulling broken wagons, just like mine. They looked like collectors, too. My junk was going to good homes. I could tell!

Well, I sold most of my terrific junk. I left the rest for the garbage collector. This pleased
35 my folks. But I got a really creepy feeling when I went into my room. I mean, it was
EMPTY! So when I saw that broken typewriter in the trash, I knew just where to put it.
Likewise for the garden hose. And I have the best idea for a new invention.

—*by* Susan Russo

66. Tickets to the "World's Largest Indoor Dump" were sold by Joe's
A. friends
B. parents
C. brother
D. aunt

67. The writer uses the word "enormous" in the phrase "two enormous jars of nuts and bolts"[line 5] to show that the jars are
A. long
B. wide
C. huge
D. tall

68. In the sentence "Even I was disgusted!"[line 18] the word "disgusted" is closest in meaning to
A. bitter
B. bored
C. fed up
D. worn out

69. The passage can be **best** described as
A. a personal narrative
B. an adventure
C. a short story
D. a mystery

Read the following passage and answer questions 70 to 73

Open Wide!
Regular dental care can help keep your pet healthy and happy

If you've noticed that your pet's breath smells less than kissably fresh lately, that could be indicative of a greater problem than his simply eating too many liver-flavored treats. Like humans, dogs and cats can develop a host of dental problems such as plaque and
5 tartar buildup, cavities and gingivitis. But unlike humans, pets can't brush their teeth every day, which can lead to an accumulation of bacteria that could be carried through the bloodstream to your pet's vital organs.

And since animals can't tell you when their teeth are sore, many pet owners don't even know when their pets are suffering. "There's a lot of pet dental problems that people
10 aren't aware of," says Dr. Michael Bratt, a veterinarian at Vancouver's Granville Island Veterinary Hospital. "The poor animals are in pain."

The most common signs of poor pet dental hygiene are bad breath, brown or discoloured teeth and bleeding gums. Other symptoms can include appetite changes and excessive drooling. Fortunately, most dental problems are preventable, with a little help from you.

15 The best way to ensure pets have healthy teeth and gums is to brush their teeth. Some veterinarians recommend you do this daily, but others say two or three times a week will do. Like many other aspects of training your pet, it's best to start brushing your cat or dog's teeth at a young age. But don't just slap some minty toothpaste on an old toothbrush and start brushing away.

20 "You want to work up to it," says Katie Naphtali, an animal health technician at Oak Animal Hospital in Vancouver. "A lot of animals are really sensitive about their mouths."

First, you want your dog or cat to get used to having your finger in their mouth. To do this, use a specially formulated pet toothpaste, available at pet stores or at your vet's office. (Toothpaste for humans can cause stomach problems in animals.) Start by putting
25 a bit of toothpaste on your finger, then lift your pet's upper lips and slowly massage the teeth. Keep sessions short and sweet at first and offer plenty of praise. Once your pet is comfortable with your finger, switch to a special pet toothbrush. Dr. Bratt recommends that you sit or stand behind your pet while you brush, as it's less confrontational than having you in their face.

30 Another way you can help keep your pet's mouth healthy is to use special dental toys that strengthen the teeth. But avoid ordinary chicken bones, as they can chip or break teeth and cause serious stomach damage should your pet swallow a piece of bone. And while tennis balls are great for playing catch, they can wear down the canines of larger dogs, so don't let your pet chew on them continually.

35 You can also purchase dental-friendly snacks, such as Whiskas and Pedigree oral care treats. "In essence, they gently scrape the teeth clean much like you do yourself when you use your toothbrush," explains Dr. Marie-Louise Baillon, a Pedigree and Whiskas dental expert. "When fed daily, certain treats—Pedigree Dentastix, for example—have been clinically proven to reduce plaque and tartar buildup by up to 60 per cent. It is never
40 too late to start a dental routine for your pet that includes regular checkups at the vet and feeding specially designed dental treats."

Regular checkups will also help ensure that all is well in your pet's mouth. And many vets recommend a professional teeth cleaning about once a year.

"There's a significant amount of dogs that, no matter what you do, they're going to need
45 scaling," says Dr. James Dodds from Vancouver's Kerrisdale Animal Hospital.

While dental care for animals is often overlooked, it's an important ingredient for a happy, healthy pet.

"Good dental hygiene means good health in general," says Dr. Dodds.

—by Sondi Bruner

70. The **best** source to find more information about pet hygiene is
   A. an encyclopedia
   B. a veterinarian
   C. a dictionary
   D. a pet store

71. The writer states that pets can get serious stomach damage from chewing on
    A. dog food
    B. sugary treats
    C. peanut butter
    D. chicken bones

72. Which of the following titles is also a good title for this text?
    A. "The Vet and Your Pet"
    B. "Your Pet—Tips for Teeth"
    C. "Get Mouthy With Your Pet"
    D. "Veterinarians Talk About Cavities"

73. In the sentence "Some veterinarians recommend you do this daily,"[line 15] the word "recommend" is **most similar** in meaning to which of the following words?
    A. Suggest
    B. Contest
    C. Oppose
    D. Differ

Read the following passage and answer questions 74 to 77

from "Soft-Stone Sculpture"

To create large stone sculptures like statues, artists cut into a huge block of rock with heavy tools until they have the shape they want. Here, you'll mix up a soft "stone" that's easy to carve.

Here's What You Need

5   Vermiculite (from a plant nursery or garden supply store)
Plaster of paris (from an art supply store)
Bowl
Water
Small waxed cardboard milk or juice container
10 Newspaper
Old blunt kitchen knife or grapefruit spoon
Nail

Here's What You Do

Mix equal parts of vermiculite and plaster in a bowl. Stir in water until the mixture is like a
15 thick gravy. Pour it into the container. Let dry for 24 hours. Peel off the container.

Working on newspaper, use the knife or spoon to gently carve into the soft stone. Why not make your favorite animal? Or, create an abstract sculpture in a design or shape that's pleasing to you. Use the nail to add details.

The Artist's Way: Michelangelo

20 You may have heard of Michelangelo, who lived in Italy in the 1500s. He is famous for his huge, detailed painting that covers the ceiling of the Sistine Chapel at the Vatican in Rome.

Michelangelo was also a talented sculptor. He used a sharp metal tool called a *chisel* (there may be one in your house you could take a look at) to carve statues out of huge blocks of marble. He had very strong ideas about an image or idea being locked inside 25 the stone, and once said that he was trying to release the form from its rocky prison. Isn't that an interesting way to view sculpting?

Michelangelo would often spend as long as eight months in the quarries (natural areas that stone is removed from) selecting a piece of stone for a statue. He carved one of his most famous sculptures, the 13' (4-m) *David*, from a block of stone that other sculptors 30 had rejected as being too tall and narrow.

—from *Kids' Art Works: Creating with Color, Design, Texture &More* by Sandi Henry

74. In this project, the nail is used to
   A. shape the soft stone
   B. hang the finished carving
   C. etch details into the carving
   D. poke a hole in the carving so that it can be hung

75. Which of the following gives the **most** accurate summary of the passage?
   A. Soft stone carving is an easy and fun way to make realistic and abstract designs. You can make this "stone" yourself using simple and inexpensive materials.
   B. Before you try to carve huge stone statues like Michelangelo, it is a good idea to start with carving with a soft "stone" that you make yourself.
   C. Michelangelo was a famous painter and sculptor who lived almost 500 years ago. He thought of sculpting as releasing a figure from its "prison."
   D. Stone sculptors cut into real stone with heavy metal tools to carve a design. One sculptor was the famous Italian Michelangelo. You can try out stone sculpting using a soft "stone" that is easy to make and carve yourself.

76. One of Michelangelo's most famous sculptures is called
   A. Michael
   B. Thomas
   C. David
   D. John

77. "Old blunt kitchen knife or grapefruit spoon"[line 11]

The word "*blunt*" as used in the materials list for making soft stone means

   A. old
   B. dull
   C. sharp
   D. smooth

Read the following passage and answer questions 78 to 81

from Crabs for Dinner

One summer, my grandmother came for a visit all the way from Africa.

"Ghana," she said. "That's where I come from."

She brought us funny-looking clothes, the kind they wear in Ghana. I had a smock made of a rough cotton fabric with stripes of bright colors woven into it.

5 It was long and loose, almost like a dress. Grandma said it was meant to be worn over a pair of trousers.

"I'm never going to wear those," I said to my mom.

But Emily wore hers, a colorful batik dress with embroidery around the neck.

She looked so pretty that I decided to wear my smock. When I did, I thought I looked
10 "cool." Especially when I wore the striped cotton cap that came with the smock.

Grandma had lots of stories to tell. Stories her grandmother told her when she was young. I liked the ones about a cunning "Spider man" who got in and out of all kinds of trouble.

She always ended in a funny way, saying: "This story of mine whether good or bad, may pass away, or come to stay. It is your turn to tell your story."

15 So we took our turn and told her stories. And she liked them just as much as we liked hers.

A week before she left for Ghana, she invited my aunts and uncle to dinner.

"She's going to make soup and yucky crab," Emily said. "I'll bet she makes a lot of it. But I won't even take a bite."

She did make the soup, only she put in okra too.

20 "That's going to make it slimy," I said.

"Double Yuk," said Emily.

But dinner got cooked and dinner was served and grace was said.

Emily and I were eating hot dogs and the grown-ups were eating slime.

Uncle Robert rolled his eyes upward. "Mmm," he said. "Exquisite!"

25 I had never heard him use that word for Mom's soup.

"My word," Aunt Pauline said, "I had almost forgotten the original taste."

My mom simply said, "Delicious."

Even Aunt Araba paused from the sucking and crunching to say one word, "Authentic!"

I noticed that Grandma's soup smelled really good, much better than Mom's soup.
30 Suddenly I wanted to taste just a little bit of the fufu with crab and soup.

"Can I have a little, please?" I heard Emily ask.

"Why, of course!" Grandma replied.

If Emily doesn't die, I'll have some, I thought.

Emily took a bite and didn't die. Instead she took another bite.

35 "And how about you?" said Grandma.

"Yes, please," I said.

It tasted different, not like the soups I knew. It was spicy and hot and really good. It was thick and smooth and I thought I could taste the flavor of ginger.

I broke off a tiny piece of crab and sucked it just like Mommy did. It was all soft inside.
40 Then I crunched on it, really hard, just as my Aunt Araba did.

Then I ate a whole bowl of fufu and soup and a huge piece of crab. When I was done I rolled my eyes up to the sky and said aloud, "Exquisite!"

I am not even sure what that means, but probably it is a way of saying that sometimes grandmothers cook better than mothers.

45 —by Adwoa Badoe

78. The cap that Grandma gives the narrator is
   A. a woolen garment
   B. a colorful batik
   C. striped cotton
   D. plain felt

79. What was the ingredient that the grandmother put into the soup that the narrator said would make it slimy?
   A. Hot dogs
   B. Ginger
   C. Okra
   D. Crab

80. Grandma always ended her stories
   A. in a funny way
   B. in a sad way
   C. with a laugh
   D. by cooking

81. The **main** idea or theme of this story is that it is
   A. fun to have large family gatherings
   B. important to keep cultural traditions alive
   C. a good idea to eat different types of food
   D. nice to have grandparents visit from other countries

Read the following passage and answer questions 82 to 85

Chocolate Chip Cookie

Next time you bite into a chocolate chip cookie, thank Ruth Wakefield for taking a shortcut.

Ruth Wakefield and her husband Ken owned the Toll House Inn, a restaurant near Boston, Massachusetts. One day in 1933 she decided to prepare a batch of cookies. The recipe called for chocolate. Wakefield wanted to save time, so instead of melting
5 semi-sweet chocolate she broke the bar into pieces and tossed the bits into the batter, thinking that the chocolate would blend into the cookie dough as it baked. To her surprise and delight, the chocolate chunks softened slightly, but stayed whole.

Wakefield's "chocolate crispies" became a customer favorite at the Toll House Inn. As word spread, she started giving out her cookie recipe to anyone who was interested.

10 Meanwhile Nestlé, the chocolate manufacturer, noticed something odd. All across the country, sales of their semi-sweet candy bar had dropped. Everywhere, that is, except around Boston. Nestlé sent sales representative to investigate. When Nestlé learned of the popular Toll House cookie, they decided to keep making the bars. They even tried to help out.

15 First they scored the bar so that it broke into pieces more easily. Then they invented a special chopper to break the chocolate into small bits. Finally, in 1939, they started marketing packages of chocolate chips just for cookie making. The company got permission to print Ruth Wakefield's Toll House Cookie Recipe on the package. In exchange, they supplied her with a lifetime's worth of free chocolate.

20 —from *Whose Bright Idea Was It?: True Stories of Invention* by Larry Verstraete

82. What trend did the Nestlé company notice everywhere in the country except in Boston?
   A. Nestlé cookies were very popular.
   B. Candy bar sales had increased.
   C. Sales of all candy bars had dropped.
   D. Sales of semi-sweet candy bars had dropped.

83. Before Nestlé found out about her new cookies, Ruth Wakefield's recipe was
   A. a closely guarded secret
   B. free to anyone who asked for it
   C. sold for a small fee to her customers
   D. free only to her restaurant customers

84. In the phrase "and tossed the bits into the batter,"[line 5] the word "tossed" does **not** mean
   A. added
   B. toasted
   C. put into
   D. included

85. What is the **most likely** reason that the words "chocolate crispies" are in quotation marks in the sentence "Wakefield's 'chocolate crispies' became a customer favorite at the Toll House Inn" [line 8]?
   A. They are part of a direct quote.
   B. They are words in a foreign language.
   C. They are from the title of this passage.
   D. They are what Ruth Wakefield called her cookies.

Read the following passage and answer questions 86 to 89

from "The Voyage of the Mayflower"

Pelted by rain under a black sky, the ninety-foot *Mayflower* rolled and pitched on mountainous waves. Its masts were bare because during a storm, a sailing ship must lower all its sails and drift with the wind to avoid capsizing or breaking apart.

Below the main deck, the passengers huddled in the dark. They could hear the wind
5   howling and the waves thudding against the vessel's wooden sides and washing over the deck. Seawater dripped down on them through the canvas covering the deck gratings and seeped through the seams in the planking. The passengers were soaked and shivering; several were seasick besides. As frightened adults tried to comfort terrified children, they prayed for safety in the storm and an end to the long, terrible voyage.

10   Suddenly, above the din of the storm, they heardthe noise of splitting timber. One of the beams supporting the deck had cracked! The ship was in danger of sinking. Then someone remembered a great iron screw brought from Holland. Carefully, the ship's carpenter positioned it beneath the beam and braced it. It would hold; the passengers and crew could reach land safely.

15   Crossing the Atlantic in 1620 was extremely risky. A wooden ship could leak or break apart in a storm. Since the sails could be raised only in fair weather, it was impossible to predict how long a voyage would last. To avoid the stormy autumn months, ships usually made the crossing in spring or summer. They almost never sailed alone.

Aware of these dangers, the Pilgrims had planned to cross the ocean in two ships in the
20   summer of 1620. The English Separatists from Holland (who called themselves Saints) borrowed money from London businessmen and purchased a small ship, the *Speedwell*. For the Separatists' safety, and to help them establish a profitable colony, the businessmen recruited additional volunteers in London. The businessmen rented the *Mayflower*, a ship three times the size of the *Speedwell*, for these recruits, whom the
25   Separatists called Strangers. The Saints and Strangers met for the first time in Southampton, England, a few days before the ships sailed on August 5.

The tiny *Speedwell* had been refitted with taller masts and larger sails so it could keep up with the *Mayflower*. These changes, however, caused the ship to leak badly at sea. On August 12, the ships put into Dartmouth. After the *Speedwell* was examined and
30   repaired, they set off again on August 23. Two days later, the *Speedwell* began to leak again, and the vessels headed for Plymouth, England. There the ships' masters, carpenters, and principal passengers agreed that the *Speedwell* could not make the crossing.

Over the next few days, the sixty-seven Strangers on the *Mayflower* made room for thirty-five of the Saints from the *Speedwell*, along with their belongings and provisions.
35   On September 6, the *Mayflower* set out from Plymouth alone. The one hundred two passengers, including thirty-four children, would not see land for sixty-six days.

The *Mayflower*, like all ships of the time, was built to carry cargo, not passengers. A few families crowded into the "great cabbin" in the stern. Most of the passengers, however, traveled in bunks or tiny "cabbins" below the main deck and above the hold, where cargo
40 was stored. In this "'tween decks" area, they had only five feet of head room. Each person's living space was smaller than the mattress of a modern twin bed.

The Pilgrims suffered other discomforts. Many were seasick, particularly at the beginning of the voyage. In storms, they were constantly wet and cold. They could not bathe or wash and dry their clothes and bedding. For toilet purposes, they used buckets.

45 In fair weather, the adults and children who had recovered from seasickness could leave their dim, foul-smelling quarters for the wind and spray of the main deck. The adults took deep breaths of the cold, tangy air and stretched cramped muscles. The younger children, forbidden to run around, played quiet games. Damaris Hopkins, age three, and Mary and Remember Allerton, ages four and six, "tended the baby" (played with dolls).
50 Six- and nine-year old brothers Wrestling and Love Brewster played "I Spy" and "Hunt the Slipper" with six- and seven-year-old Jasper and Richard More. Finger games such as cat's cradle and paper, scissors, stone were popular with eight-year-old Humility Cooper, Ellen More, John Cooke, John Billington, and Bartholomew Allerton. Elizabeth Tilley, age fourteen, and Mary Chilton and Constance Hopkins, both fifteen, helped
55 prepare the meals.

For cooking, the passengers built charcoal fires in metal braziers set in sandboxes. There was so little space, however, that only a few people could cook at once. When storms made lighting fires dangerous, everyone ate cold meals.

After morning prayers, they ate a simple breakfast of cheese and ship's biscuit (hard, dry
60 biscuit). If cooking was allowed, they might have porridge. Their midday meal might consist of ship's biscuit and cheese or, in fair weather, cooked "pease pottage," boiled salt fish, pork, or beef and any freshly caught bonito or porpoise. Before retiring, they had a light supper. Everyone, even the children, drank beer with their meals because it was preferred to water.

65 Not until December 11, more than a month after first sighting land, did the Pilgrims decide where they would build their colony. ...

—by Patricia M. Whalen

86. Why did the Pilgrims on board the *Mayflower* set sail for America?
    A. to visit a new land
    B. to establish business
    C. to build a new colony
    D. to gather valuable goods

87. Where did the Saints and Strangers meet for the very first time?
    A. London, England
    B. Southampton, England
    C. On board the *Speedwell*
    D. On board the *Mayflower*

88. The Pilgrims can **best** be described as
    A. brave and busy
    B. healthy and happy
    C. flexible and fearless
    D. adventurous and adaptable

89. What is another word used in the passage for *ship*?
    A. colony
    B. vessel
    C. cabin
    D. deck

Read the following passage and answer questions 90 to 93

Are All Giants All Bad?

GIANTS ARE THOUGHT BY MOST HUMANS—probably unfairly—to be as dangerous and cruel as they are large. Whatever the truth, they have a troublesome history.

Early Giants

5 The first giants were the Gigantes of ancient Greek mythology, born when the blood of Uranus (the Heavens) fell upon Gaea (Earth). The Gigantes fought the gods of Mount Olympus—Zeus, Hera, Apollo, and others. The Olympian gods needed the help of the hero Hercules to defeat them. The Gigantes were buried underneath mountains that then became volcanoes.

Another race of mythical Greek giants was known as the Cyclops. These monsters, who
10 had only one eye, created the thunderbolts of Zeus. In Homer's epic poem *The Odyssey*, the hero Odysseus and his men encounter a Cyclops and barely escape.

Both these races of giants, like those that followed, were said to be vicious cannibals.

British Giants

Among later giants, the legend of a pair named Gog and Magog spread throughout the
15 world, changing a bit from place to place. In Britain the story survives in the form of two large statues in Guildhall in London, first erected in the 1400s and said to portray the last of a race of giants destroyed by the legendary founder of London. (The statues, public favorites, have been replaced twice: first after the Great Fire of 1666, then after an air raid during the Second World War.)

20 A slightly different British legend combines those giants into a single monster named Gogmagog, who lived near Cornwall. In that version, a brave soldier threw the giant off a cliff, which is still called Giant's Leap.

Another British giant of legend, Gargantua, became famous in the 1500s as the main character in comical adventures written by a Frenchman, François Rabelais. Gargantua
25 was something like the gigantic American woodsman Paul Bunyan. He was so huge that a tennis court fit inside one of his teeth. It took the milk of 17,913 cows to quench his thirst. In some legends, he was employed by King Arthur, and was credited with defeating Gog and Magog.

Giants and Magic

30 According to the early historian Geoffrey of Monmouth, Stonehenge, the mysterious circle of huge stones in southern England, originated with the giants of Ireland. As he records, Merlin had been asked for advice on building a war memorial. The wizard replied:

"If you want to grace the burial place of these men with some lasting monument, send for the Giants' Ring which is on Mount Killaraus in Ireland. In that place there is a stone
35 construction which no man of this period could ever erect, unless he combined great skill and artistry. The stones are enormous and there is no one alive strong enough to move them. If they are placed in position round this site, in the way in which they are erected over there, they will stand for ever....

"These stones are connected with certain religious secret rites and they have various
40 properties which are medicinally important. Many years ago the Giants transported them from the remotest confines of Africa and set them up in Ireland at a time when they inhabited that country. Their plan was that, whenever they felt ill, baths should be prepared at the foot of the stones; for they used to pour water over them and to run this water into baths in which their sick were cured. What is more, they mixed the water with
45 herbal concoctions and so healed their wounds. There is not a single stone among them that hasn't some medicinal virtue."

As Geoffrey tells it, the king took Merlin's advice and had the stones transported to their present site.

A Secret Everyone Knows

50 In Harry's world, most wizards are prejudiced against giants. Hagrid never told anyone his mother was the giantess Fridwulfa because he was worried about what they would think. For the same reason, the headmistress of Beauxbatons, Madame Olympe Maxime, is reluctant to admit she is also half-giant. But anyone with common sense would guess that secret from her name. Olympe refers to the original giants of Olympus,
55 and *maxime* means "great" or "very large" in French.

—from *The Magical Worlds of Harry Potter: A Treasury of Myths, Legends, and Fascinating Facts* by David Colbert

90. As used in the word "giantess," the suffix *-ess* indicates that something is
    A. multiple
    B. female
    C. large
    D. male

91. Geoffrey of Monmouth was an early historian. A historian is someone who
    A. tells fairy tales
    B. illustrates wars
    C. writes records of events
    D. creates comical adventures

92. The quotation "the king took Merlin's advice and had the stones transported to their present site" [line 47] means that the
    A. stones were given as a gift
    B. king sent to Africa for new stones
    C. king destroyed the present site in southern England
    D. stones were moved from Ireland to southern England

93. In the phrase "there is a stone construction which no man of this period could ever erect,"[line 34] the word "period" is a synonym for
    A. end
    B. time
    C. chapter
    D. location

Read the following passage and answer questions 94 to 98

From Paper Bag To Paperback: How Children's Books Are Made

Making a picture book isn't as easy as it looks—especially not in 1980, when most publishers weren't yet using computers. Even with computers, there are many stages a storybook goes through before it gets to you. Here's how it usually works:

From Think to Ink:
5   First, a writer turns an idea into a story and writes that story down on paper. Most authors will rewrite a story several times before letting anyone read it. Each time, they make changes to make the story better. Bob makes these changes through telling, not writing. In fact, he never writes down a story until he's told it many, many times to groups of kids. "I'm a storyteller first and writer second," he says. "The stories change over time.
10   Children respond to different parts, get bored in some parts, and I change them based on their response." Only then does he write the story on paper. This paper copy of the story is called a manuscript and has no pictures.

Let it Get Edited:
    When happy with the story, the author gives the manuscript to a publisher to read. A
15   publisher is a person whose company decides which stories to make into books. The publisher and the author talk about how to make the story even better. The author rewrites the story again until it's just right. All this talking and rewriting is called editing.

Next Part's the Art:
    Once the story is at its best, the publisher finds an artist to make the pictures. This
20   illustrator then makes simple black and white drawings called sketches. The illustrator talks with the publisher and the author about which sketches work well, and then the illustrator turns them into color paintings.

A Fine Design:
    When the words are done, and when the pictures are ready, they both need to be put
25   together. The designer is the person who carefully arranges the words and pictures as they will look on the pages of the book and on the front and back covers. This work used to be done by cutting and pasting the words and pictures onto big pasteboards, which were then photographed. Today, it is usually done using scanners and computers.

Pressed for Time:

30 Almost done! All that's left is to turn those photos or computer files into real books. This is done by a printing company, which uses a large machine, called a printing press, that presses colored ink onto wide sheets of paper. Other machines then cut and fold and bind the paper into a book with a cover. A modern printing press can print as many as 176,000 color pages in an hour—that's almost 50 pages per second!

35 **Where the Wares Are:**

Once the books are printed, the printer puts them into boxes and sends them to the publisher's warehouse—a large building where all the books are stored. The publisher then ships boxes of books to bookstores and libraries all over the country.

A Storybook Ending:

40 At the bookstore or library, the staff unpacks the books and puts them on a shelf, where they wait to be picked up and read by someone like you.

—from *The Paper Bag Princess 25th Anniversary Edition: The Story behind the Story* by Robert Munsch

94. Which statement from the passage **best** supports the main idea that making a book is a long and complicated process?

A. Even with computers, there are many stages a storybook goes through before it gets to you.

B. A modern printing press can print as many as 176,000 color pages in an hour—that's almost 50 pages per second!

C. This work used to be done by cutting and pasting the words and pictures onto big pasteboards, which were then photographed.

D. At the bookstore or library, the staff unpacks the books and puts them on a shelf, where they wait to be picked up and read by someone like you.

95. Based on the information in the section "A Fine Design",[line 23] a pasteboard is **most likely** a

A. sticky cardboard fused to the book cover

B. wooden board on which to cut out the illustrations and text

C. big computer screen on which the book parts can be moved around

D. big stiff piece of cardboard made with layers of paper pasted together

96. A publisher is defined as a person who

A. draws the pictures in a book

B. writes stories that become books

C. decides which stories to make into books

D. arranges words and pictures into book format

97. Which of the following sentences uses the word "*cover*" in the same way as in the phrase "bind the paper into a book with a cover"[line 32]?

A. I stuck a photo of myself on the cover of my diary.

B. Many animals come out under the cover of darkness.

C. Cover the pot with a lid if you want it to boil more quickly.

D. Dan reminded Kevin to cover his head for protection from the sun.

98. Read the dictionary entry for the word "stage". Which meaning best fits the way the word is used in the first paragraph of this passage?

Stage

- *noun*
    1. a single step, level or period of time in a process
    2. a raised platform on which actors, dancers, musicians, speakers, etc. perform
    3. the stage – the theater as a profession: *He dedicated his life to the stage*
    4. stagecoach
- *verb*
    1. to present or exhibit, such as a play or show: *The school staged a production of Oliver! for their year-end show.*
    2. to plan, organize or carry out an event: *The students staged a protest against cruelty to animals.*

A. definition 1

B. definition 2

C. definition 3

D. definition 4

Read the following passage and answer questions 99 to 102

The St. Lawrence Beluga

Encountering a beluga whale is a real privilege. A somewhat ghostly animal, the beluga is a symbol of fragility and vulnerability. It knows the St. Lawrence like no other because it lives there year-round. The beluga herd in the St. Lawrence River is the only one in the world that does not live in the Arctic. The St. Lawrence provides habitat similar to the
5 Arctic: the salt water is nice and cold and there is lots of food.

There are many beluga herds in the Canadian North. The total beluga population is over 100,000. Other Arctic beluga herds live in northern Russia, Norway, Greenland, and Alaska.

A beluga has all the characteristics of a polar animal. Its white color acts as camouflage in the ice. It has a bumpy ridge extending along its back, instead of a dorsal fin, that
10 allows it to break through the ice to breathe without injuring itself. Belugas have a flexible neck, while all other whales have fused cervical vertebrae and cannot turn their head.

Belugas are highly social animals, which explains their extensive vocabulary. They have developed some of the most varied vocal repertoires in the animal kingdom. From its rounded forehead, a beluga sends out ultrasound waves to find its food.

15 The beluga herd in the St. Lawrence is not what it was a hundred years ago. At the turn of the last century, there were over 5,000 belugas in the River. Their numbers have dropped considerably since then. They were overhunted because it was thought that they were eating the salmon and cod that humans needed to survive. Authorities even offered a bonus of fifteen dollars for every beluga tail brought in, to encourage elimination
20 of the species as quickly as possible. The hunt was not brought to an end until the nineteen seventies. Now, there are between 700 and 1,200 in the St. Lawrence herd and the beluga is an endangered species.

Nowadays, because scientists have raised the alarm, the St. Lawrence beluga is protected. However, damage to its habitat and pollution continue to threaten its well-being.

25 The beluga is affected by various illnesses, but the link between disease and pollutants has yet to be found. Contaminants are not biodegradable, so the only way that belugas can get rid of them is through the female. A mother can reduce the level of pollutants in her body through her milk, but a newborn beluga starts life contaminated.

For all these reasons, the health of the St. Lawrence beluga is a concern. It will take 30 generations, many more studies, and a lot of determination to improve the situation. The beluga's health is definitely a reflection of the state of the St. Lawrence River.

—from *As Long As There Are Whales* by Evelyne Daigle, translated by Geneviève Wright

99. The **main** reason the number of belugas in the St. Lawrence has dropped is
   A. pollution
   B. over hunting
   C. they have moved to colder water
   D. they have been eaten by animal predators

100. The purpose of the beluga's rounded forehead is to
   A. help it attract a mate
   B. protect it from attack
   C. break through the ice pack
   D. send out signals to locate food

101. The beluga's well-being is dependent on the
   A. migration of the whales
   B. fishermen's hunting season
   C. progression of global warming
   D. health of the St. Lawrence River

102. A synonym for the word privilege as used in the phrase "Encountering a beluga whale is a real privilege",[line 1] is
   A. surprise
   B. danger
   C. honor
   D. rarity

Read the following passage and answer questions 103 to 106

Ancient Broom Games

Broom sports emerged almost as soon as broomsticks were sufficiently advanced to allow fliers to turn corners and vary their speed and height. Early wizarding writings and paintings give us some idea of the games our ancestors played. Some of these no longer exist; others have survived or evolved into the sports we know today.

5   The celebrated **annual broom race** of Sweden dates from the tenth century. Fliers race from Kopparberg to Arjeplog, a distance of slightly over three hundred miles. The course runs straight through a dragon reservation and the vast silver trophy is shaped like a Swedish Short-Snout. Nowadays this is an international event and wizards of all nationalities congregate at Kopparberg to cheer the starters, then Apparate to Arjeplog to
10 congratulate the survivors.

The famous painting *Günther der Gewaltig ist der Gewinner* ("Gunther the Violent is the Winner"), dated 1105, shows the ancient German game of **Stichstock**. A twenty-foot-high pole was topped with an inflated dragon bladder. One player on a broomstick had the job of protecting this bladder. The bladder-guardian was tied to the pole by a rope around his
15 or her waist, so that he or she could not fly further than ten feet away from it. The rest of the players would take it in turns to fly at the bladder and attempt to puncture it with the specially sharpened ends of their brooms. The bladder-guardian was allowed to use his or her wand to repel these attacks. The game ended when the bladder was successfully punctured, or the bladder-guardian had either succeeded in hexing all opponents out of
20 the running or collapsed from exhaustion. Stichstock died out in the fourteenth century.

In Ireland the game of **Aingingein** flourished, the subject of many an Irish ballad (the legendary wizard Fingal the Fearless is alleged to have been an Aingingein champion). One by one the players would take the Dom, or ball (actually the gallbladder of a goat), and speed through a series of burning barrels set high in the air on stilts. The Dom was
25 to be thrown through the final barrel. The player who succeeded in getting the Dom through the last barrel in the fastest time, without having caught fire on the way, was the winner.

Scotland was the birthplace of what is probably the most dangerous of all broom games—**Creaothceann**. The game features in a tragic Gaelic poem of the eleventh century, the first verse of which says, in translation:

30 *The players assembled, twelve fine, hearty men,*
They strapped on their cauldrons, stood poised to fly,
At the sound of the horn they were swiftly airborne
But ten of their number were fated to die.

Creaothceann players each wore a cauldron strapped to the head. At the sound of the
35 horn or drum, up to a hundred charmed rocks and boulders that had been hovering a hundred feet above the ground began to fall towards the earth. The Creaothceann players zoomed around trying to catch as many rocks as possible in their cauldrons. Considered by many Scottish wizards to be the supreme test of manliness and courage, Creaothceann enjoyed considerable popularity in the Middle Ages, despite the huge
40 number of fatalities that resulted from it. The game was made illegal in 1762, and though Magnus "Dent-Head" Macdonald spearheaded a campaign for its reintroduction in the 1960s, the Ministry of Magic refused to lift the ban.

Shuntbumps was popular in Devon, England. This was a crude form of jousting, the sole aim being to knock as many other players as possible off their brooms, the last person
45 remaining on their broom winning.

Swivenhodge began in Herefordshire. Like Stichstock, this involved an inflated bladder, usually a pig's. Players sat backwards on their brooms and batted the bladder backwards and forwards across a hedge with the brush ends of their brooms. The first person to miss gave their opponent a point. First to reach fifty points was the winner.

50 Swivenhodge is still played in England, though it has never achieved much widespread popularity; Shuntbumps survives only as a children's game. At Queerditch Marsh, however, a game had been created that would one day become the most popular in the wizarding world.

—from *Quidditch Through the Ages* by Kennilworthy Whisp (J. K. Rowling)

103. Magnus Macdonald **most likely** received the nickname "Dent-Head" because he
A. fell off his broom
B. was hit in the head with a spear
C. had been hit so often by falling rocks
D. had marks on his head from the cauldron straps

104. In the sentence "The course runs straight through a dragon reservation and the vast silver trophy is shaped like a Swedish Short-Snout,"[line 6] a Swedish Short-Snout is **most likely** a
A. pig
B. dog
C. parrot
D. dragon

105. A synonym of the word "fatalities," which is used in the phrase "despite the huge number of fatalities that resulted,"[line 39] is
A. fans
B. deaths
C. arguments
D. disqualifications

106. An antonym of the word "*reintroduction*" as it is used in the sentence
"The game was made illegal in 1762,[line 40] and though Magnus 'Dent-Head' Macdonald spearheaded a campaign for its reintroduction in the 1960s, the Ministry of Magic refused to lift the ban" is
A. discovery
B. obliteration
C. rehabilitation
D. discontinuation

EXERCISE #1—READING LITERATURE

Table of Correlations		
Standard		**Test #1**
4RL	Reading Standards for Literature	
4RL.1	Refer to details and examples in a text when explaining what the text says explicitly and when drawing inferences from the text.	118, 121, 131
4RL.2	Determine a theme of a story, drama, or poem from details in the text; summarize the text.	119, 134, 139, 140, 144, 145, 151, 152
4RL.3	Describe in depth a character, setting, or event in a story or drama, drawing on specific details in the text.	107, 108, 109, 120, 126, 127, 146, 147, 148, 149, 153, 157
4RL.4	Determine the meaning of words and phrases as they are used in a text, including those that allude to significant characters found in mythology.	110, 111, 128, 135, 150, 154, 158
4RL.5	Explain major differences between poems, drama, and prose, and refer to the structural elements of poems and drama when writing or speaking about a text.	113, 114, 122, 123, 124, 159
4RL.7	Make connections between the text of a story or drama and a visual or oral presentation of the text, identifying where each version reflects specific descriptions and directions in the text.	132
4RL.9	Compare and contrast the treatment of similar themes and topics and patterns of events in stories, myths, and traditional literature from different cultures.	144
4RL.10	By the end of the year, read and comprehend literature, including stories, dramas, and poetry, in the grades 4–5 text complexity band proficiently, with scaffolding as needed at the high end of the range.	136, 141
4RI	Reading Standards for Informational Text	
4RI.1	Refer to details and examples in a text when explaining what the text says explicitly and when drawing inferences from the text.	118, 121, 131
4RI.2	Determine the main idea of a text and explain how it is supported by key details; summarize the text.	119, 134, 139, 140, 144, 145, 151, 152
4RI.3	Explain events, procedures, ideas, or concepts in a historical, scientific, or technical text, including what happened and why, based on specific information in the text.	107, 108, 109, 120, 126, 127, 146, 147, 148, 149, 153, 157
4RI.4	Determine the meaning of general academic and domain-specific words or phrases in a text relevant to a grade 4 topic or subject area.	110, 111, 128, 135, 150, 154, 158
4RI.7	Interpret information presented visually, orally, or quantitatively and explain how the information contributes to an understanding of the text in which it appears.	132
4RI.9	Integrate information from two texts on the same topic in order to write or speak about the subject knowledgeably.	144

4RF	Reading Standards: Foundational Skills	
4.RF.3a	Know and apply grade-level phonics and word analysis skills in decoding words. Use combined knowledge of all letter-sound correspondences, syllabication patterns, and morphology to read accurately unfamiliar multi-syllabic words in context...	110, 111, 128, 135, 150, 154, 156, 158
4.RF.4a	Read with sufficient accuracy and fluency to support comprehension. Read on-level text with purpose and understanding.	125
4.RF.4c	Read with sufficient accuracy and fluency to support comprehension. Use context to confirm or self-correct word recognition and understanding, rereading as necessary.	110, 111, 128, 135, 150, 154, 158
4.W	Writing Standards	
4W.3a	Write narratives to develop real or imagined experiences or events using effective technique, descriptive details, and clear event sequences. Orient the reader by establishing a situation and introducing a narrator and/or characters; organize...	129
4W.3b	Write narratives to develop real or imagined experiences or events using effective technique, descriptive details, and clear event sequences. Use dialogue and description to develop experiences and events or show the responses of characters...	148, 149
4W.9a	Draw evidence from literary or informational texts to support analysis, reflection, and research. Apply grade 4 Reading standards to literature.	117, 118, 121, 130, 131, 143
4W.9b	Draw evidence from literary or informational texts to support analysis, reflection, and research. Apply grade 4 Reading standards to informational texts.	118, 121, 131
4L	Language Standards	
4L.1a	Demonstrate command of the conventions of standard English grammar and usage when writing or speaking. Use relative pronouns (who, whose, whom, which, that) and relative adverbs (where, when, why).	133
4L.1d	Demonstrate command of the conventions of standard English grammar and usage when writing or speaking. Order adjectives within sentences according to conventional patterns.	137
4L.1g	Demonstrate command of the conventions of standard English grammar and usage when writing or speaking. Correctly use frequently confused words.	115
4L.4a	Determine or clarify the meaning of unknown and multiple-meaning words and phrases based on grade 4 reading and content, choosing flexibly from a range of strategies. Use context as a clue to the meaning of a word or phrase.	110, 111, 128, 135, 150, 154, 158
4L.5a	Demonstrate understanding of figurative language, word relationships, and nuances in word meanings. Explain the meaning of simple similes and metaphors in context.	112
4L.5c	Demonstrate understanding of figurative language, word relationships, and nuances in word meanings. Demonstrate understanding of words by relating them to their opposites (antonyms) and to words with similar but not identical meanings (synonyms).	116, 138, 142, 155, 158
4L.6	Acquire and use accurately grade-appropriate general academic and domain-specific words and phrases, including those that signal precise actions, emotions, or states of being and that are basic to a particular topic.	115

Read the following passage and answer questions 107 to 112

How Brazilian Beetles Got Their Gorgeous Coats: A Story from Brazil

Long ago in Brazil, beetles had plain brown coats. But today their hard-shelled coats are gorgeous. They are so colorful that people often set them in pins and necklaces like precious stones. This is how it happened that Brazilian beetles got their new coats.

5   One day a little brown beetle was crawling along a wall. Suddenly a big gray rat darted out of a hole in the wall. When he saw the beetle, he began to make fun of her.

"Is that as fast as you can go?What a poke you are! You'll never get anywhere! Just watch how fast I can run!"

The rat dashed to the end of the wall, turned around, and ran back to the beetle. The beetle was still slowly crawling along. She had barely crawled past the spot where the rat
10   left her.

"I'll bet you wish you could run like that!" bragged the gray rat.

"You certainly are a fast runner," replied the beetle. Even though the rat went on and on about himself, the beetle never said a word about the things she could do. She just kept slowly crawling along the wall, wishing the rat would go away.

15   A green and gold parrot in the mango tree above had overheard their conversation. She said to the rat, "How would you like to race with the beetle? Just to make the race exciting, I'll offer a bright colored coat as a reward. The winner may choose any color coat and I'll have it made to order."

The parrot told them the finish line would be the palm tree at the top of the hill. She gave
20   the signal to start, and they were off.

The rat ran as fast as he could. When he reached the palm tree, he could hardly believe his eyes: there was the beetle sitting beside the parrot. The rat asked with suspicious tone, "How did you ever manage to run fast enough to get here so soon?"

"Nobody ever said anything about having to run to win the race," replied the beetle as
25   she drew out her tiny wings from her sides. "So I flew instead."

"I didn't know you could fly," said the rat with a grumpy look on his face.

The parrot said to the rat, "You have lost the contest. From now on you must never judge anyone by looks alone. You never can tell when or where you may find hidden wings."

Then the parrot turned to the brown beetle and asked, "What color would you like your
30   new coat to be?"

"I'd like it to be green and gold, just like yours," replied the beetle. And since that day, Brazilian beetles have had gorgeous coats of green and gold. But the rat still wears a plain, dull, gray one.

—from *How &Why Stories: World Tales Kids Can Read and Tell* by Martha Hamilton and
35   Mitch Weiss

107.At the end of the story, the beetle changes from being

A. plain brown to gorgeous green and gold

B. shiny black to gorgeous green and gold

C. green and gold to plain brown

D. green and gold to dull Gray

108. Which of the following words **best** describes the rat?
   A. Fast
   B. Mean
   C. Nosey
   D. Boastful

109. Which of the following words best describes the beetle?
   A. Humble
   B. Patient
   C. Snobby
   D. Competitive

110. In the sentence "One day a little brown beetle was crawling along a wall,"[line 4] the word "*crawling*" means
   A. stunting
   B. moving slowly
   C. scrambling across
   D. speeding movements

111. "Then the parrot turned to the brown beetle…"[line 29]

   In the sentence above, the word "*then*" means almost the same thing as which of these other transition words?

   A. Also
   B. Next
   C. However
   D. Although

112. The phrase "people often set them in pins and necklaces like precious stones"[line 2] is an example of
   A. onomatopoeia
   B. hyperbole
   C. metaphor
   D. simile

A Snake Named Rover

Mom wouldn't let me have a dog
"With all the mess they make!"
So, if I couldn't have a dog,
I said I'd like a snake.

5 My mother gasped quite audibly,
But Dad approved the plan.
"A snake," he gulped, "a real live snake…
Well, sure, I guess you can."

We went to Ralph's Repulsive Pets
10 And bought a yard of asp.
It coiled inside a paper bag
Held firmly in my grasp.

I put him in a big glass tank
And dubbed my new pet Rover,
15 But all the fun of owning it
Was very quickly over.

For all he did was flick his tongue
Once or twice each minute,
While nervous Mom rechecked the tank
20 To make sure he was in it.

Then one fine day, we don't know how,
My Rover disappeared.
My father told me not to fret,
But Mom was mighty scared.

25 We searched the house from front to back
And gave the yard a sweep.
By midnight we had given up
And tried to get some sleep.

At three AM my dad arose
30 To answer nature's call.
I heard him scream, I heard him swear,
And then I heard him fall.

For Dad had found the wayward pet
I'd given up for dead
35 Curled up inside his slipper,
Lying right beside his bed.

Now Rover's living back at Ralph's
With frogs, and newts, and guppies,
And now I have a dog named Spot—
40　She'll soon be having puppies.

　　—by Maxine Jeffris

113. What type of fiction is "A Snake Named Rover"?
　A. Poetry
　B. Mystery
　C. Fairy tale
　D. Short story

114. Which of the following types of poems describes this poem **best**?
　A. Haiku
　B. Limerick
　C. Rhyming poem
　D. Free verse poem

115. The statement "The snake is lying by the bed" can be rewritten in the simple past tense by using which of the following verbs?
　A. Lay
　B. Laid
　C. Lied
　D. Lain

116. In the quotation "I heard him scream, I heard him swear,"[line 31] the word "scream" means almost the same thing as which of the following words?
　A. Cry
　B. Laugh
　C. Shriek
　D. Whisper

Read the following passage and answer questions 117 to 120

from Judy Moody Predicts the Future

"Hey, look at this," said Judy. "This book can help us with our spelling test. For real."

"No way."

"Way! See this guy?"

5　"The bald guy with the bow tie?"

"Yep. It says that he lived right here in Virginia. They called him the Sleeping Prophet. When he was our age, like a hundred years ago, he got into trouble in school for being a bad speller. One night he fell asleep with his spelling book under his head. When he
10　woke up, he knew every word in the book. RARE!"

"I'm still going to study," said Frank.

"Not me!" said Judy, wiggling into her coat.

15 "What are you going to do?" asked Frank.

"I'm going to go home and sleep," said Judy.

◆◆◆

When Judy got home, Stink was at the door.

20 "I don't have to study for my spelling test," she said, and gave him a big fat hug.

"What's that for?" asked Stink.

"That's for just because."

"Just because why?"

"Just because tomorrow I am going to know tons and tons of words, like *woodbine*."

25 "Wood what?"

"It's a creepy vine. It wraps around trees."

"So go find a tree to hug," said Stink.

Instead, Judy went to find the dictionary. The fattest dictionary in the Moody house. She took it from her mom's office and lugged it up to her room. She did not open it up. She
30 did not look inside. She put the big red dictionary under her pillow. Then she got into her cozy bowling-ball pajamas. She pretended the bowling balls were crystal balls. When she brushed her teeth, she thought she saw a letter in her toothpaste spit. *D* for *Dictionary*.

Judy climbed under the covers and leaned back on her pillow. Youch! Too hard. She got two more pillows. At last, she was ready to dream.

35 Even before she fell asleep, she dreamed of being Queen of the Spelling Bee, just like Jessica Finch was one time for the whole state of Virginia. She dreamed of Mr. Todd's smiling face when he passed back the tests. Most of all, she dreamed of getting 110%—zero-wrong-plus-extra-credit—on her spelling test.

She could hardly wait for school tomorrow. For once, she, Judy Moody, not Jessica
40 (Flunk) Finch, would get a Thomas Jefferson tricorn-hat sticker for *Great Job, Good Thinking*.

ZZZZZZZZZZzzzzzz....

—by Megan McDonald

117. When Judy hugs Stink, he **most likely** feels
    A. content
    B. annoyed
    C. frustrated
    D. suspicious

118. When Stink tells Judy to "go find a tree to hug,"[line 27] he is comparing Judy to
    A. a plant
    B. a monster
    C. an environmentalist
    D. a plant-eating animal

119. After reading about the Sleeping Prophet, Judy decides to go home and
    A. study her spelling
    B. read a dictionary
    C. sleep on a book
    D. hug Stink

120. When Judy pretends that the bowling balls on her pajamas are crystal balls and she thinks she sees a letter in her toothpaste spit, she is **most likely** using her imagination to
    A. convince herself
    B. distract herself
    C. amuse herself
    D. amaze herself

Last One Into Bed

"Last one into bed has
to switch out the light."
It's just the same every night.
There's a race.
5　I'm ripping off my trousers and shirt—
he's kicking off his shoes and socks.

"My sleeve's stuck."
"This button's too big for its button-hole."
"Have you hidden my pajamas?"
10　"Keep your hands off mine."
If you win
you get where it's safe
before the darkness comes—
but if you lose
15　if you're last:
you know what you've got coming up is
the journey from the light switch
to your bed.
It's the Longest Journey in the World.

20　"You're last tonight," my brother says.
And he's right.
There is nowhere so dark
as that room in the moment
after I've switched out the light.

25　There is nowhere so full of dangerous things—
things that love dark places—
things that breathe only when you breathe
and hold their breath when I hold mine.
So I have to say:
30　"I'm not scared."
That face, grinning in the pattern on the wall
isn't a face—
"I'm not scared."
That prickle on the back of my neck
35　Is only the label on my pyjama jacket—
"I'm not scared."
That moaning-moaning is nothing
but water in a pipe—
"I'm not scared."

40 Everything's going to be just fine
    as soon as I get into that bed of mine.
    Such a terrible shame
    it's always the same
    it takes so long
45 it takes so long
    it takes so long
    to get there.

    From the light switch
    to my bed.
50 It's the Longest Journey in the World.

    —by Michael Rosen

121. Which of the following things is **not** seen, heard, or felt by the speaker on his way back to bed?
    A. Grinning in the pattern on the wall
    B. Prickle on the back of his neck
    C. Siren blaring from outside
    D. Water moaning in a pipe

122. What kind of poem is this?
    A. Haiku
    B. Cinquain
    C. Diamante
    D. Free verse

123. The reader can tell this passage is a poem because
    A. it contains many facts
    B. every second line rhymes
    C. it is broken up into verses
    D. the characters have a conversation

124. If this poem were a cinquain, it would have
    A. five lines in total
    B. a joke at the end
    C. many rhyming words
    D. a smooth, flowing rhythm

Read the following passage and answer questions 125 to 128

Not Owls Too!

The reason Dad said: "Oh NO! Not owls too" was because I already had some pets.

There was a summerhouse in our back yard and we kept about thirty gophers in it. They belonged to Bruce and me, and to another boy called Murray. We caught them out on the prairie, using snares made of heavy twine.

5   The way you do it is like this: You walk along until you spot a gopher sitting up beside his hole. Gophers sit straight up, reaching their noses as high as they can, so they can see farther. When you begin to get too close they flick their tails, give a little jump, and whisk down their holes. As soon as they do that, you take a piece of twine that has a noose tied in one end, and you spread the noose over the hole. Then you lie down in the grass
10 holding the other end of the twine in your hand. You can hear the gopher all the while, whistling away to himself somewhere underground. He can hear you, too, and he's wondering what you're up to.

After a while he gets so curious he can't stand it. Out pops his head, and you give a yank on the twine. You have to haul in fast, because if the twine gets loose he'll slip his head
15 out of the noose and zip back down his hole.

We had rats too. Murray's dad was a professor at the college and he got us some white rats from the medical school. We kept them in our garage, which made my Dad a little peeved, because he couldn't put the car in the garage for fear the rats would make nests inside the seats. Nobody ever knew how many rats we had because they have so
20 many babies, and they have them so fast. We gave white rats away to all the kids in Saskatoon, but we always seemed to end up with as many as we had at first.

There were the rats and gophers, and then there was a big cardboard box full of garter snakes that we kept under the back porch, because my mother wouldn't let me keep them in the house. Then there were the pigeons. I usually had about ten of them, but
25 they kept bringing their friends and relations for visits, so I never knew how many to expect when I went out to feed them in the mornings. There were some rabbits too, and then there was Mutt, my dog—but he wasn't a pet; he was one of the family.

Sunday morning my father said:

"Billy, I think you have enough pets. I don't think you'd better bring home any owls. In any
30 case, the owls might eat your rats and rabbits and gophers…"

He stopped talking and a queer look came into his face. Then he said:

"On second thought—maybe we *need* an owl around this place!"

So it was all right.

—from *Owls in the Family*, by Farley Mowat

125. The five paragraphs between the opening and closing paragraphs can **best** be described as
   A. supplementary information
   B. introductory information
   C. background information
   D. concluding information

126. Gophers usually live in
    A. high grasses
    B. a nest in a tree
    C. a hollow log
    D. underground burrows

127. In order to catch a gopher, a person must be
    A. gifted
    B. strong
    C. patient
    D. brave

128. A "snare" can be **best** described as a
    A. cage
    B. noose
    C. metal trap
    D. large rock

Read the following passage and answer questions 129 to 133

from "The Fishing Summer"

When I was a boy my three uncles lived in a big wooden house by the sea. Every summer they painted it white. They had white shirts, too. On Sundays they would do the laundry and hang their white shirts out on the line, where they would flap in the wind like big raggedy gulls.

5   My three uncles and my mother had been children in that white wooden house. Every summer my mother would take me there for a visit.

My uncles had a fishing boat. It was like a huge rowboat with a little cabin in the middle, hardly big enough to go inside. At the end of the little cabin was the engine.

That engine had started off in a big car. Uncle Thomas, who was the oldest and had a
10 long black beard, had taken the engine out of the car and put it in the boat. Even when it rained and stormed, Uncle Thomas could keep the motor going.

Uncle Rory was the middle uncle. His beard was black, but he kept it short by cutting it with the kitchen scissors. He could look at the sky and tell if it was safe to go out. And when the wind blew up the sea, and the clouds and fog fell over the boat like a thick
15 soupy blanket, Uncle Rory could find the way home.

Uncle Jim was the youngest uncle and my mother's twin. He had no beard at all. He was the fisherman. He had to know where the hungry fish would be, and what they would be hungry for.

At the end of each day I would stand at the dock, waiting. The boat would come in, and
20 my uncles would pick me up. Then we would go to the fish factory. There I would help my uncles load the fish into cardboard boxes to be weighed on the big scale. A giant with little eyes that looked like bright fox eyes would write down the numbers on a piece of paper. Then my uncles would take the paper to the cashier and get paid.

I wanted to go fishing.

25 "One day," Uncle Jim said, "when you get big."

"No way," my mother said. "You'll fall in and drown."

"I can swim," I said.

"You're only eight years old," my mother said.

"I started going when I was eight," said Uncle Thomas out of his big beard.

30 "Thomas," said my mother in a sharp voice that made the room go quiet. And I remembered another story. That my grandfather used to fish with his own brothers, and when one of the brothers got hurt, Thomas took his place. A few years later he dropped out of school and started fishing all year round. When my grandfather drowned, my other uncles started going out on the boat with Thomas.

35 —by Teddy Jam

129. The narrator of this passage is
A. a child
B. a mother
C. Uncle Rory
D. a grown man

130. The narrator's mother **most likely** did not want him to go fishing because he might
A. drown at sea like his grandfather
B. grow a beard like Uncle Thomas
C. enjoy fishing more than school
D. stay at the white house forever

131. Which of the following statements **best** describes the connection that the uncles had with the sea?
A. They watched the ocean's animals.
B. They made their living from the ocean.
C. They went swimming each day in the bay.
D. They made sailboats to sell to vacationers.

132. When the writer states that "fog fell over the boat like a thick soupy blanket,"[line 14] he **most likely** means the fog was a
A. warm cozy covering
B. wet dense haze
C. clear shiny rain
D. cool flat sheet

133. Which of the following adverbs **best** describes when the narrator wanted to go fishing?
A. Later
B. Tomorrow
C. Eventually
D. Immediately

The Crow and the Jug

IT WAS BONE-DRY IN THE COUNTRYSIDE. There had been no rain for weeks on end now. For all the animals and birds it had been a terrible time. To find even a drop of water to drink was almost impossible for them.

5 But the crow, being the cleverest of birds, always managed to find just enough water to keep himself alive.

One morning, as he flew over a cottage, he saw a jug standing nearby. The crow knew, of course, that jugs were for water, and as he flew down, he could smell the water inside. He landed and hopped closer to have a look. And sure enough, there was some water at 10 the bottom. Not much, maybe, but a little water was a lot better than no water at all.

The crow stuck his head into the jug to drink; but his beak, long though it was, would not reach far enough down, no matter how hard he pushed. He tried and he tried, but it was no good. However, he knew that one way or another he had to drink that water. He stood there by the jug, wondering what he was going to do. Then he saw pebbles lying on the 15 ground nearby, and that gave him a brilliant idea.

One by one he picked them up and dropped them into the jug. As each pebble fell to the bottom, the water in the jug rose higher, then higher and higher, until the crow had dropped so many pebbles in that the water was overflowing. Now he could drink and drink his fill. *What a clever crow*, he thought as he drank. *What a clever crow*.

20 WHERE THERE'S A WILL, THERE'S A WAY.
BUT IT HELPS IF YOU USE YOUR BRAIN.

—by Aesop

134. The crow was able to get more water than the other animals because he was
    A. more clever than the others
    B. greedy and stole from the others
    C. more determined than the others
    D. able to fly to things others could not reach

135. As it is used in the phrase "and that gave him a brilliant idea,"[line 15] the word *brilliant* means
    A. bold
    B. shiny
    C. brave
    D. smart

136. This story can best be described as
   A. an adventure
   B. a fairy tale
   C. a mystery
   D. a fable

137. The writer uses which of the following words to describe the dryness of the land?
   A. Terribly
   B. Desert
   C. Bone
   D. Very

138. A word that means almost the same as the word *jug* is
   A. mug
   B. glass
   C. bottle
   D. pitcher

Read the following passage and answer questions 139 to 142

Elephant and Hare

Hare and her friends had always lived peacefully among the tall grasses that grew on the shore of a clear blue lake. No one ever bothered them.

One day Elephant came crashing out of the jungle, followed by his herd. The elephants were thirsty and had been looking for water for a long time. When they saw the
5   shimmering blue lake, they were so excited, they stampeded through the grasses toward the water. They were in such a hurry, they didn't notice that they were trampling the burrows of Hare's friends beneath their huge feet.

After drinking and washing, Elephant led his herd back into the jungle to spend the night.
10   On their way, the elephants' enormous feet crushed many of the tender grasses that Hare and her friends used for food.

Hare was frantic with worry. She knew the elephants would return to the lake the next day, and the hares' homes and food would be destroyed completely. She thought very hard and finally came up with an idea.

15 "Don't worry," she told the other hares, "I have a plan."

A full moon was just peeking above the trees as Hare hopped to the jungle to talk to Elephant. She hopped right into the middle of the herd and started shouting as loud as she could, but no one paid any attention to her because her voice was tiny and hard for elephants to hear. When Hare was almost hoarse with shouting, Elephant flapped his
20 ears. He thought there was some kind of strange insect buzzing around his head. He flapped his ears again, but the noise wouldn't go away.

"What's that annoying sound?" he finally said.

"It's me!" shouted Hare.

Elephant looked down. He squinted at Hare and said, "Who are you?"

25 "I am a loyal subject of the all-powerful moon god," said Hare, bowing. "He has sent me to give you a message."

"Go on," said Elephant politely, although he didn't believe a word Hare was saying.

"When you and your herd went down to the lake today," said Hare, trying not to sound nervous, "you trampled the homes and food of the moon god's loyal subjects. This has
30 made the moon god extremely angry. He is so angry that he commands you to leave and never return."

"I don't believe in any moon god," scoffed Elephant. "Give me proof."

"Follow me to the lake then, and you will see the moon god for yourself," said Hare. "But watch where you're walking this time," she added.

35 When Elephant and Hare got to the edge of the lake, Hare pointed at the reflection of the full moon in the still water.

"There is the mighty moon god," she said. "Pay your respects by dipping your trunk in the lake.'

Elephant thought this was a silly thing to do, but he agreed. He stretched out his long trunk and touched the surface of the lake with it. Instantly, the water quivered and
40 rippled, making the moon's reflection burst into hundreds of shimmering pieces. Elephant threw back his trunk in fright.

"See how angry the moon god is?" shouted Hare.

"You're right," said Elephant, shaking with fear. "I promise I'll never annoy the moon god again!"

And with that, Elephant headed back to his herd in the jungle, being very careful indeed
45 not to step on any grasses or burrows on his way.

—retold by Jan Thornhill

139. The elephants trampled on the
   A. hares' burrows
   B. moonbeams
   C. tall grasses
   D. moon god

140. To the elephants, Hare's voice sounded like
   A. a lion roaring
   B. an insect buzzing
   C. a trumpet blasting
   D. a mouse squeaking

141. This passage can **best** be described as a
   A. play
   B. fable
   C. poem
   D. fairytale

142. Another word for *annoying* is
   A. bothersome
   B. soothing
   C. loud
   D. oily

Read the following passage and answer questions 143 to 146

My Friend Jacob

My best friend lives next door. His name is Jacob. He is my very, very best friend.

We do things together, Jacob and I. We love to play basketball together. Jacob always makes a basket on the first try.

He helps me to learn how to hold the ball so that I can make baskets, too.

5 My mother used to say, "Be careful with Jacob and that ball. He might hurt you." But now she doesn't. She knows that Jacob wouldn't hurt anybody, especially his very, very best friend.

I love to sit on the steps and watch the cars go by with Jacob. He knows the name of every kind of car. Even if he only sees it for just a minute, Jacob can tell you the kind of car.

He is helping me be able to tell cars, too. When I make a mistake, Jacob never ever
10 laughs. He just says, "No no, Sam, try again."

And I do. He is my best best friend.

When I have to go to the store, Jacob goes with me to help me. His mother used to say, "You don't have to have Jacob tagging along with you like that, Sammy." But now she doesn't. Jacob helps me to carry, and I help Jacob to remember.

15 "Red is for stop," I say if Jacob forgets. "Green is for go."

"Thank you, Sam," Jacob always says.

Jacob's birthday and my birthday are two days apart. Sometimes we celebrate together.

Last year he made me a surprise. He had been having a secret for weeks and weeks, and my mother knew, and his mother knew, but they wouldn't tell me.

20 Jacob would stay in the house in the afternoon for half an hour every day and not say anything to me when he came out. He would just smile and smile.

On my birthday, my mother made a cake for me with eight candles, and Jacob's mother made a cake for him with seventeen candles. We sat on the porch and sang and blew out our candles. Jacob blew out all of his in one breath because he's bigger.

25 Then my mother smiled, and Jacob's mother smiled and said, "Give it to him, Jacob dear." My friend Jacob smiled and handed me a card.

HAPPY BIRTHDAY SAM
JACOB

He had printed it all himself! All by himself, my name and everything! It was neat!

30 My very best friend Jacob does so much helping me, I wanted to help him, too. One day I decided to teach him how to knock.

Jacob will just walk into somebody's house if he knows them. If he doesn't know them, he will stand by the door until someone notices him and lets him in.

"I wish Jacob would knock on the door," I heard my mother say.

35 So I decided to help him learn. Every day I would tell Jacob, but he would always forget. He would just open the door and walk right in.

My mother said probably it was too hard for him and I shouldn't worry about it. But I felt bad because Jacob always helped me so much, and I wanted to be able to help him.

I kept telling him, and he kept forgetting. So one day I just said, "Never mind, Jacob,
40 maybe it is too hard."

"What's the matter, Sam?" Jacob asked me.

"Never mind, Jacob," was all I said.

Next day, at dinnertime, we were sitting in our dining room when I and my mother and my father heard this real loud knocking at the door. Then the door popped open and Jacob
45 stuck his head in.

"I'm knocking, Sam!" he yelled.

Boy, I jumped right up from the table and went grinning and hugged Jacob, and he grinned and hugged me, too. He is my very, very, very best friend in the whole wide world!

—by Lucille Clifton

143. Jacob has difficulty with
   A. writing
   B. basketball
   C. keeping a secret
   D. lifting heavy things

144. The **main** message of this story is that
   A. it is possible for people who are very different to be friends
   B. it is polite to knock before entering someone's home
   C. friends should help each other with important things
   D. a homemade birthday card is a nice surprise

145. The surprise that Jacob gave to Sam
    A. took a long time to make
    B. did not seem very special
    C. was something he bought
    D. was made at the last minute

146. The reason Sam's mother says, "You don't have to have Jacob tagging along with you like that, Sammy,"[line 13] is that she is **probably** worried that
    A. Sam will get hurt
    B. Jacob will get lost
    C. Sam will forget Jacob
    D. Jacob will bother Sam

Read the following passage and answer questions 147 to 150

A Horse That Wore Snow Shoes

Mr. Brown had to go to his camp at Pine Tree Valley, which is in the midst of the mountains in California.

His men were cutting down the giant trees, and piling them in readiness for the Spring
5 freshet, or floods of the river, when the snows melted. Then they would slide them down the mountain sides to the little villages below.

There was a great deal of snow on the mountains, and Mr. Brown knew it would be hard work climbing to the camp, but Lady Gray was strong, and used to it.

Lady Gray was Mr. Brown's pet horse, and carried him everywhere. She was always
10 happy when her master was in the saddle.

But to-day the snow was very deep and soon Mr. Brown had to get off, throw away the saddle, and lead her. They had to stop very often, and lean against the trees and rocks for support, while they rested and regained their breath.

In places the snow was so deep and soft, that they sank above their knees. Late in the
15 afternoon they reached the camp nearly exhausted, and it was several days before they were able to return.

The snow was still deep and Mr. Brown knew he must go back on snow-shoes, but he was afraid Lady Gray would have to be left behind.

Finally one of the men suggested making her some snow-shoes. They cut four round
20 pieces of board, twelve inches across, and fastened them on with rope. Lady Gray seemed to understand what they were for and tried very hard to walk in them.

She was very awkward at first and could hardly stand up, but by practicing a little every day she was soon able to manage nicely.

So Mr. Brown and Lady Gray both returned on snow-shoes, and how every one did laugh
25 when they saw them.

But Lady Gray never could have done it if she had not tried.

147. Which of the following words **best** describes Lady Gray?
   A. Sturdy
   B. Shaky
   C. Sassy
   D. Sorry

148. Which of the following statements **best** describes Lady Gray's reaction to the snowshoes?
   A. She knew how to use them right away.
   B. She made a big effort to use them.
   C. Lady Gray refused to use them.
   D. Lady Gray was not impressed.

149. When Mr. Brown reached the bottom of the mountain, people thought that Lady Gray was
   A. dangerous
   B. comical
   C. hungry
   D. brave

150. During a "freshet," the water in the river
   A. falls
   B. rises
   C. stops
   D. drains

Read the following passage and answer questions 151 to 155

The Snake on Second Avenue

It wasn't my idea to have a snake for a pet. I don't like animals much, and as far as wild animals go—well, cats are too wild for me. But my mother's batty about animals. She watches nature shows on TV and writes letters to the editor complaining about inhumane traps. I find it a little tiresome, but mostly Mum's all right. She never complains when she
5 has to pick me up after ball practice, even though she thinks I should be bird-watching instead.

We were in Saskatoon for a dentist appointment the day we found the snake. It was a little garter snake, the kind we have in the garden at home—green with yellow stripes. There was one thing unusual about this one, though. It was on Second Avenue right outside a shoe store. The snake looked really scared and I don't blame it. It was too
10 small to be made into shoes, but that wasn't its biggest worry. From the look of the crowd gathered around it on the sidewalk, the busy street would have been safer.

We noticed the crowd from the end of the block. As we got closer we could hear a kid scream over and over, "Kill it! Kill it!" I don't know why the kid didn't just leave.

15 As soon as Mum heard the kid yell she doubled her speed. I ran along with her because I was pretty curious about what all the people were staring at. A mouse? A Martian? A kid playing hooky?

Mum pushed her way through the crowd and I followed. The snake was coiled up on the sidewalk. Everyone seemed to be arguing about how to kill it.

20 "Oh, the poor thing!" exclaimed Mum. She went straight to the snake and picked it up. It was already so frightened that it didn't even try to get away. It just wrapped its tail around her wrist and poked its tongue in and out.

There was a horrified silence. Even the kill-it kid stopped yelling.

"It's just a garter snake," said Mum, quite loudly. "It's not poisonous and it's not a constrictor. The only things it can damage are insects." She paused, then said, "And I'm 25 going to take it home. Please excuse me." She didn't have to push her way out. The crowd just separated in front of her. She seemed to have forgotten me so I followed along behind, watching the snake move in her hands and wondering what it felt like.

We'd reached the car before I noticed where we were. "Hey, Mum!" I exclaimed. "I thought we were going to buy me some jeans."

30 "With a snake?" she asked. "We're going home now. You'll have to hold the snake."

I wish she'd waited till we were in the car. I don't want you to think I'm chicken, but the first time I hold a snake, I'd like advance warning.

Terrified that I might drop it, I just blinked and grabbed the thing around the neck. I was surprised at how it felt—not slimy at all, but hard and dry on the top and soft underneath. 35 Its head was amazingly small, but it still kept sticking its tongue out. I stuck mine out at it, then climbed into the car.

Mum started the engine and said, "I've heard that garter snakes make good pets."

I groaned, but I knew there was no point in arguing. And really, it wasn't so bad. I could probably write a science report on it and amaze all the teachers. After all, there are 40 worse things than living in the same house as a snake. At least it wasn't a cat.

—by Adele Dueck

151. This particular snake was unusual because it was
   A. big
   B. shy
   C. in a shoe store
   D. on Second Avenue

152. When Mum heard the kid yell, she
   A. sat down
   B. walked slowly
   C. called the police
   D. doubled her speed

153. The **most likely** reason that the crowd reacted aggressively toward the snake on the sidewalk is that they
    A. liked the snake
    B. did not know that the snake was young
    C. thought that the snake was dangerous
    D. thought that their yelling would scare the snake

154. In the statement "my mother's batty about animals",[line 2] the word "*batty*" means
    A. interested
    B. afraid
    C. nosey
    D. crazy

155. As it is used in the phrase "Terrified that I might drop it,"[line 33] the word "Terrified" means
    A. scared
    B. excited
    C. annoyed
    D. astonished

Read the following passage and answer questions 156 to 159

Matilda: Who told Lies, and was Burned to Death

Matilda told such Dreadful Lies,

It made one Gasp and Stretch one's Eyes;

Her Aunt, who, from her Earliest Youth,

Had kept a Strict Regard for Truth,

5 Attempted to Believe Matilda:

The effort very nearly killed her,

And would have done so, had not She

Discovered this Infirmity.

For once, towards the Close of Day,

10 Matilda, growing tired of play,

And finding she was left alone,

Went tiptoe to the Telephone,

And summoned the Immediate Aid

Of London's Noble Fire-Brigade.

15 Within an hour the Gallant Band

Were pouring in on every hand,

From Putney, Hackney Downs, and Bow,

With Courage high and Hearts a-glow

They galloped, roaring through the Town,

20 "Matilda's House is Burning Down!"

Inspired by British Cheers and Loud

Proceeding from the Frenzied Crowd,

They ran their ladders through a score

Of windows on the Ball Room Floor;

25 And took Peculiar Pains to Souse

The Pictures up and down the House,

Until Matilda's Aunt succeeded

In showing them they were not needed

And even then she had to pay

30 To get the Men to go away!

It happened that a few Weeks later

Her Aunt was off to the Theater

To see that Interesting Play

The Second Mrs. Tanqueray.

35 She had refused to take her Niece

To hear this Entertaining Piece:

A Deprivation Just and Wise

To punish her for Telling Lies.

That Night a Fire *did* break out—

40 You should have heard Matilda Shout!

You should have heard her Scream and Bawl,

And throw the window up and call

To People passing in the Street—

(The rapidly increasing Heat

45 Encouraging her to obtain

Their confidence)—but all in vain!

For every time She shouted "Fire!"

They only answered "Little Liar!"

And therefore when her Aunt returned,

50 Matilda, and the House, were Burned.

—by Hilaire Belloc

156. When Matilda tried to obtain the "*confidence*" of the people in the street, it means that she wanted their

A. trust

B. esteem

C. approval

D. calmness

157. The setting for this poem is

A. Asia

B. Europe

C. Australia

D. North America

158. In the line "A Deprivation Just and Wise,"[line 37] the word "*Deprivation*" is a synonym of

A. punishment

B. remorse

C. removal

D. gift

159. This poem can **most accurately** be called a

A. ballad

B. sonnet

C. lyric poem

D. narrative poem

EXERCISE #2—READING LITERATURE

Table of Correlations		
Standard		**Test #1**
4RL	Reading Standards for Literature	
4RL.1	Refer to details and examples in a text when explaining what the text says explicitly and when drawing inferences from the text.	169, 170, 184
4RL.2	Determine a theme of a story, drama, or poem from details in the text; summarize the text.	162, 165, 171, 172, 173, 178, 185, 186, 198, 199, 205
4RL.3	Describe in depth a character, setting, or event in a story or drama, drawing on specific details in the text.	163, 181, 182, 187, 188, 189, 190, 200, 206
4RL.4	Determine the meaning of words and phrases as they are used in a text, including those that allude to significant characters found in mythology.	166, 174, 183, 194, 195, 202, 207
4RL.5	Explain major differences between poems, drama, and prose, and refer to the structural elements of poems and drama when writing or speaking about a text.	167, 175, 179, 203, 208, 211
4RL.7	Make connections between the text of a story or drama and a visual or oral presentation of the text, identifying where each version reflects specific descriptions and directions in the text.	202
4RL.9	Compare and contrast the treatment of similar themes and topics and patterns of events in stories, myths, and traditional literature from different cultures.	162
4RL.10	By the end of the year, read and comprehend literature, including stories, dramas, and poetry, in the grades 4–5 text complexity band proficiently, with scaffolding as needed at the high end of the range.	167, 175, 208
4RI	Reading Standards for Informational Text	
4RI.1	Refer to details and examples in a text when explaining what the text says explicitly and when drawing inferences from the text.	169, 170, 184
4RI.2	Determine the main idea of a text and explain how it is supported by key details; summarize the text.	162, 165, 171, 172, 173, 178, 185, 186, 198, 199, 205
4RI.3	Explain events, procedures, ideas, or concepts in a historical, scientific, or technical text, including what happened and why, based on specific information in the text.	163, 181, 182, 187, 188, 189, 190, 200, 206
4RI.4	Determine the meaning of general academic and domain-specific words or phrases in a text relevant to a grade 4 topic or subject area.	166, 174, 183, 194, 195, 202, 207
4RI.7	Interpret information presented visually, orally, or quantitatively and explain how the information contributes to an understanding of the text in which it appears.	202
4RI.9	Integrate information from two texts on the same topic in order to write or speak about the subject knowledgeably.	162
4RF	Reading Standards: Foundational Skills	
4.RF.3a	Know and apply grade-level phonics and word analysis skills in decoding words. Use combined knowledge of all letter-sound correspondences, syllabication patterns, and morphology to read accurately unfamiliar multi-syllabic words in context...	166, 174, 176, 177, 183, 194, 195, 197, 202, 207

4.RF.4a	Read with sufficient accuracy and fluency to support comprehension. Read on-level text with purpose and understanding.	161
4.RF.4c	Read with sufficient accuracy and fluency to support comprehension. Use context to confirm or self-correct word recognition and understanding, rereading as necessary.	166, 174, 183, 194, 195, 202, 207
4.W	Writing Standards	
4W.3a	Write narratives to develop real or imagined experiences or events using effective technique, descriptive details, and clear event sequences. Orient the reader by establishing a situationand introducing a narrator and/or characters; organize...	201
4W.3b	Write narratives to develop real or imagined experiences or events using effective technique, descriptive details, and clear event sequences. Use dialogue and description to develop experiences and events or show the responses of characters...	163, 187, 188
4W.9a	Draw evidence from literary or informational texts to support analysis, reflection, and research. Apply grade 4 Reading standards to literature.	160, 164, 168, 169, 170, 180, 184, 193, 209, 210
4W.9b	Draw evidence from literary or informational texts to support analysis, reflection, and research. Apply grade 4 Reading standards to informational texts.	169, 170, 184
4L	Language Standards	
4L.1g	Demonstrate command of the conventions of standard English grammar and usage when writing or speaking. Correctly use frequently confused words.	191
4L.4a	Determine or clarify the meaning of unknown and multiple-meaning words and phrases based on grade 4 reading and content, choosing flexibly from a range of strategies. Use context as a clue to the meaning of a word or phrase.	166, 174, 183, 194, 195, 202, 207
4L.5a	Demonstrate understanding of figurative language, word relationships, and nuances in word meanings. Explain the meaning of simple similes and metaphors in context.	196
4L.5c	Demonstrate understanding of figurative language, word relationships, and nuances in word meanings. Demonstrate understanding of words by relating them to their opposites (antonyms) and to words with similar but not identical meanings (synonyms).	192, 194, 204, 207, 212
4L.6	Acquire and use accurately grade-appropriate general academic and domain-specific words and phrases, including those that signal precise actions, emotions, or states of being and that are basic to a particular topic.	194

Read the following passage and answer questions 160 to 163

Daniel's Duck

Jeff and Daniel were brothers. They lived in a cabin on a mountain in Tennessee. Jeff had a good knife, and he could carve things out of wood. He made a dish, a cup, and a spoon. "Some day," Jeff said, "I want to carve an animal like Henry Pettigrew's."

5   Henry Pettigrew lived in the valley, and although Jeff and Daniel had never met him, they had seen his work. Some said he was the best woodcarver in Tennessee. All his animals looked real; his birds looked as if they could fly, and his horses looked as if they could run.

"I want to carve an animal, too," said Daniel.

"You're not old enough," Jeff told him.

"Yes, I am," said Daniel. "I could carve one if I had a good knife and some wood."

10 "It takes more than a good knife and some wood," said Jeff. "Animals are hard to do, and you have to know how."

"I know how," answered Daniel.

"Let's see if you do," said his father, and he gave Daniel a knife like Jeff's and a block of wood.

It was winter, and the nights were long.

15 "This is a good time to sit by the fire and carve," said Jeff. "I'm going to make something for the spring fair."

Every spring there was a fair in the valley. It was a time for people to meet after the long winter and show what they had made. Sometimes they also sold or traded things.

On winter nights Father made moccasins to take to the fair, and Mother cut pieces of
20 cloth which she sewed together into a quilt.

"I'm going to make a box," said Jeff, "and carve little moons on the lid." He looked at his brother. "You haven't done anything with your block of wood. What are you going to make?"

"I have to think," said Daniel.

Days went by. Then he began to carve.

25 "What are you making?" asked Jeff.

"You'll see," said Daniel.

One night Jeff looked at what Daniel was carving. He saw a neck and a head and a wing. "Now I see," he said. "It's a bird."

"It's a duck," said Daniel.

30 "You're not doing it right," Jeff told him. "Its head is on backward."

"I want it that way," said Daniel. "My duck is looking back."

"That's no way to do it," said Jeff.

Father interrupted. "Let him do it his way."

Spring came, and it was time for the fair. Mother had finished her quilt, and Father had
35 made three pairs of moccasins.

Jeff's box was done. "It took a long time," he said.

"My duck took a long time, too," said Daniel.

"Are you sure you want to take it to the fair?" asked Jeff.

"Yes," said Daniel.

40   They went down the mountain in a wagon, and Father drove the horses into town. People were everywhere. Father took the quilt, the moccasins, Jeff's box, and Daniel's duck, and he left them at the hall, a long house in the middle of town. "This is where the show will be," said Father. "People are getting it ready now."

45   They walked down the street and saw the river and talked with friends. Then they went to the show. People had made pictures, quilts and rugs, baskets, dolls, and coonskin caps.

"Where are the woodcarvings?" asked Daniel.

"Over here," Jeff answered, and they went to the two tables at the end of the hall. On the small table was a carved deer, so beautiful that people were quiet when they looked at it. Everyone knew it had been done by Henry Pettigrew. On the big table were the carvings
50   that Jeff and Daniel and others had done.

Many people were looking at the carvings. Some were laughing.

"What are they laughing at?" asked Daniel, but Jeff didn't answer.

Someone said, "Look at the duck!"

More people came to look, and they were laughing, too. Someone else said, "That duck
55   is so funny!"

Now Daniel knew they were laughing at his duck. At first he wanted to hide, but then he was angry. He went to the table, picked up his duck, and ran out of the hall with it.

Someone was running after him, but Daniel ran faster, until he came to the river. He wanted to throw the duck as far as he could.

60   But before he could, a man grabbed his arm and asked, "What are you doing with that duck?"

"I'm going to throw it in the river!" said Daniel.

"You can't do that," said the man.

"I can if I want to," said Daniel. "It's mine."

"Did you make it?" asked the man, and he let go of Daniel's arm.

65   "Yes," said Daniel.

"Then why were you going to throw it away?"

"They all laughed at it," said Daniel.

"Listen to me," said the man. "There are different ways of laughing. The people *liked* your duck; they laughed because they liked it."

70   "No. It's ugly," said Daniel.

"It *isn't* ugly. It's a good duck, and it made me feel happy. That's why I laughed." But the man wasn't laughing now. "You're hot and tired," he said. "Come and rest in the shade."

They sat under a tree. "Would you sell your duck?" asked the man.

"Who would buy it?" asked Daniel.

75 "I might think of someone," answered the man.

A boy and girl came up to them. "How are you, Mr. Pettigrew?" they asked.

"I'm fine," he answered, and when the boy and girl walked on, Daniel looked at the man again.

"You're Henry Pettigrew!"

"Yes," he said. "I'm a woodcarver, too."

80 "I know," said Daniel, and he looked down at his duck. It wasn't ugly; it was a good duck. Henry Pettigrew had said so, and he was the best woodcarver in Tennessee!

—*by* Clyde Robert Bulla

160. The reason that Daniel feels good at the end of the passage is that
   A. Mr. Pettigrew talked to him and not the other children
   B. a respected carver admired his work
   C. a person wanted to buy his duck
   D. he went to the fair

161. A "coonskin cap" refers to a
   A. lid for a container
   B. hat made of fur
   C. covering for an animal
   D. picture drawn on leather

162. A teacher would **most likely** read this passage to her students to show the importance of
   A. listening to older brothers
   B. learning how to carve properly
   C. getting the opinion of well-known artists
   D. believing in yourself even when people laugh

163. After his conversation with Henry Pettigrew, Daniel will **most likely**
   A. give up carving
   B. try to do another carving
   C. throw his piece into the river
   D. try to make moccasins instead

Read the following passage and answer questions 164 to 167

from A Seal in the Family

"What shall we call this little seal?" he said. "How about Lucille?"

All the animals crowded around, admiring her silvery whiskers, her gray speckled coat and her soft brown eyes. And Teelo was pleased, because he was the one who'd found Lucille.

Suddenly, Lucille opened her mouth and gave an ear-splitting cry, for she was very, very hungry.

5 "Mah, mah, mah!" she cried, while Victor searched through his fridge and cupboards.

He found cheese and bread and peanut butter and ice cream and pickles, and dog food and cat food and chicken food and parrot food and snake food—but nothing that a baby seal could eat.

10 "Mah, mah, MAH!" she wailed, while Victor took his fishing rod off the wall, hurried down to his kayak and paddled out to sea.

"MAH MAH MAH!" she yelled, and she didn't stop until Victor rushed into the house with sculpins and shiners, which she gulped down in one big swallow.

At last, Lucille was quiet, and everyone fell asleep. As the moon rose over Cloud Island,
15 all that could be heard inside the snug little house were gentle snores and the ticking of the clock. Until …

"MAH! MAH! MAH! MAH!"

Lucille woke everyone with her cries that night, and the next night, and every night for weeks. She cried all day as well, and Victor had to dash home in his lunch hours to feed
20 her, catching fish along the way. He was always tired and grumpy, he was too busy to shave or change his clothes, and he couldn't take a bath because Lucille was in the tub. He looked a mess! The house was messy too, with dustballs and fish bones all over the kitchen floor. Teelo was miserable, and wished he'd never found Lucille!

—*by* Maria Coffey

164. The baby seal's fur is described as being
   A. soft gray
   B. soft brown
   C. shiny brown
   D. speckled gray

165. Some of the foods that Victor found in his fridge and cupboards were
   A. peanut butter, cat food, and cereal
   B. cheese, biscuits, and vegetables
   C. bread, ice cream, and pickles
   D. snake food, jam, and butter

166. In the phrase "admiring her silvery whiskers,"[line 2] the word "admiring" means
   A. looking at with wonder and delight
   B. showing jealousy and envy
   C. sharing willingly
   D. mocking

167. This passage is an example of
   A. a poem
   B. a report
   C. an essay
   D. a narrative

Read the following passage and answer questions 168 to 171

from Judy Moody Predicts the Future

"Hey, look at this," said Judy. "This book can help us with our spelling test. For real."

"No way."

"Way! See this guy?"

5   "The bald guy with the bow tie?"

"Yep. It says that he lived right here in Virginia. They called him the Sleeping Prophet. When he was our age, like a hundred years ago, he got into trouble in school for being a bad speller. One night he fell asleep with his spelling book under his head. When he
10 woke up, he knew every word in the book. RARE!"

"I'm still going to study," said Frank.

"Not me!" said Judy, wiggling into her coat.

15 "What are you going to do?" asked Frank.

"I'm going to go home and sleep," said Judy.

◆◆◆

When Judy got home, Stink was at the door.

20 "I don't have to study for my spelling test," she said, and gave him a big fat hug.

"What's that for?" asked Stink.

"That's for just because."

"Just because why?"

"Just because tomorrow I am going to know tons and tons of words, like *woodbine*."

25 "Wood what?"

"It's a creepy vine. It wraps around trees."

"So go find a tree to hug," said Stink.

Instead, Judy went to find the dictionary. The fattest dictionary in the Moody house. She took it from her mom's office and lugged it up to her room. She did not open it up. She
30 did not look inside. She put the big red dictionary under her pillow. Then she got into her cozy bowling-ball pajamas. She pretended the bowling balls were crystal balls. When she brushed her teeth, she thought she saw a letter in her toothpaste spit. *D* for *Dictionary*.

Judy climbed under the covers and leaned back on her pillow. Youch! Too hard. She got two more pillows. At last, she was ready to dream.

35 Even before she fell asleep, she dreamed of being Queen of the Spelling Bee, just like Jessica Finch was one time for the whole state of Virginia. She dreamed of Mr. Todd's smiling face when he passed back the tests. Most of all, she dreamed of getting 110%—zero-wrong-plus-extra-credit—on her spelling test.

She could hardly wait for school tomorrow. For once, she, Judy Moody, not Jessica
40 (Flunk) Finch, would get a Thomas Jefferson tricorn-hat sticker for *Great Job, Good Thinking*.

ZZZZZZZZZZzzzzzzz....

—by Megan McDonald

168. As Judy falls asleep, she feels
   A. frustrated
   B. distracted
   C. confident
   D. nervous

169. The faulty conclusion Judy has drawn from the story of the Sleeping Prophet is that the bigger the book, the
   A. more words the speller will be able to spell
   B. greater the possibilities as to what may happen
   C. more pillows will be required to get a good sleep
   D. longer the speller must sleep in order to learn all the words

170. As Judy drifts off to sleep, the outcome that she is hoping for the **most** is to
   A. make Mr. Todd happy
   B. get 100% on the spelling test
   C. become Queen of the Spelling Bee
   D. get a perfect score plus extra credit

171. Judy and Frank are worried about having to take a test in
   A. health
   B. spelling
   C. mathematics
   D. social studies

Very Last First Time

Eva Padlyat lived in a village on Ungava Bay in northern Canada. She was Inuit, and ever since she could remember she had walked with her mother on the bottom of the sea. It was something the people of her village did in winter when they wanted mussels to eat.

5 Today, something very special was going to happen. Today, for the very first time in her life, Eva would walk on the bottom of the sea alone.

Eva got ready. Standing in their small, warm kitchen, Eva looked at her mother and smiled.

"Shall we go now?"

"I think we'd better."

10 "We'll start out together, won't we?"

Eva's mother nodded. Pulling up their warm hoods, they went out.

Beside the house there were two sleds, each holding a shovel, a long ice-chisel and a mussel pan. Dragging the sleds behind them, they started off.

Eva and her mother walked through the village. Snow lay white as far as the eye could
15 see—snow, but not a single tree, for miles and miles on the vast northern tundra.
The village was off by itself. There were no highways, but snowmobile tracks led away and disappeared into the distance.

Down by the shore they met some friends and stopped for a quick greeting.

They had come at the right time. The tide was out, pulling the sea water away, so there
20 would be room for them to climb under the thick ice and wander about on the seabed.

Eva and her mother walked carefully over the bumps and ridges of the frozen sea.
Soon they found a spot where the ice was cracked and broken.

"This is the right place," Eva said.

After shoveling away a pile of snow, she reached for the ice-chisel. She worked it under
25 an ice hump and, heaving and pushing with her mother's help, made a hole.

Eva peered down into the hole and felt the dampness of the air below. She breathed deep to catch the salt sea smell.

"Good luck," Eva's mother said.

Eva grinned. "Good luck yourself."

30 Her eyes lit up with excitement and she threw her mussel pan into the hole. Then she lowered herself slowly into the darkness, feeling with her feet until they touched a rock and she could let go of the ice above.

In a minute, she was standing on the seabed.

Above her, in the ice hole, the wind whistled. Eva struck a match and lit a candle.

35 The gold-bright flame shone and glistened on the wet stones and pools at her feet.

She held her candle and saw strange shadow shapes around her. The shadows formed a wolf, a bear, a seal sea-monster. Eva watched them, then she remembered.

"I'd better get to work," she said.

40 Lighting three more candles, she carefully wedged them between stones so she could see to collect mussels. Using her knife as a lever, she tugged and pried and scraped to pull the mussels off the rocks. She was in luck. There were strings of blue-black mussel shells whichever way she turned.

Alone—for the first time.

45 Eva was so happy she started to sing. Her song echoed around, so she sang louder. She hummed far back in her throat to make the echoes rumble. She lifted up long strings of mussels and let them clatter into her pan.

Soon her mussel pan was full, so she had time to explore. She found a rock pool that was deep and clear. Small shrimps in the water darted and skittered in the light from her candle. She stopped to watch them. Reaching under a ledge, she touched a pinky-purple

50 crab. The fronds of the anemones on the ledge tickled her wrist.

Beyond the rock pool, seaweed was piled in thick, wet, shiny heaps and masses. Eva scrambled over the seaweed, up and onto a rock mound. Stretching her arms wide, tilting her head back, she laughed, imagining the shifting, waving, lifting swirl of seaweed when the tide comes in.

55 The tide!

Eva listened. The lap, lap of the waves sounded louder and nearer. Whoosh and roar and whoosh again.

Eva jumped off the rock, stumbled—and her candle dropped and sputtered out. She had gone too far. The candles she had set down between the stones had burned to nothing.

60 There was darkness—darkness all around.

"Help me!" she called, but her voice was swallowed. "Someone come quickly."

Eva closed her eyes. Her hands went to her face. She could not bear to look.

She felt in her pockets. She knew she had more candles there, but she could not seem to find them.

65 The tide was roaring louder and the ice shrieked and creaked with its movement.

Eva's hands groped deeper. She took a candle out at last and her box of matches, but her fingers were shaking and clumsy. For a long, forever moment, she could not strike the match to light the candle.

The flame seemed pale and weak.

70 Eva walked slowly, fearfully, peering through the shadows, looking for her mussel pan.

At last, she found it and ran stumbling to the ice-hole. Then, looking up, Eva saw the moon in the sky. It was high and round and big. Its light cast a circle through the hole onto the seabed at her feet.

Eva stood in the moonlight. Her parka glowed. Blowing out her candle, she slowly began

75 to smile.

By the time her mother came, she was dancing. She was skipping and leaping in and out of the moonglow circle, darkness and light, in and out.

"Eva," her mother called.

"I'm here," she called back. "Take my mussel pan." Eva scrambled onto a rock and held
80 the pan up high to her mother. Then her mother's hands reached down and pulled her
up, too, through the hole.

Squeezing her mother's hand, Eva saw the moon, shining on the snow and ice, and felt
the wind on her face once more.

"That was my last very first—my very last *first* time—for walking alone on the bottom of
85 the sea," Eva said.

—*by* Jan Andrews

172. Which of the following titles would also be good for this passage?
   A. "Sailing with the Tide"
   B. "A Mother and Daughter"
   C. "The Village in the North"
   D. "Alone at the Bottom of the Sea"

173. Which of the following lists presents the sea creatures in the order that Eva saw them at the rock pool?
   A. Anemones, a pinky-purple crab, small shrimps
   B. Small shrimps, a pinky-purple crab, anemones
   C. Small shrimps, anemones, a pinky-purple crab
   D. A pinky-purple crab, small shrimps, anemones

174. As it is used in the sentence "Eva and her mother walked carefully over the bumps and ridges of the frozen sea,"[line 21] the word "ridges" means
   A. ditches
   B. peaks
   C. holes
   D. gaps

175. This story can be **best** described as
   A. fiction
   B. a letter
   C. a poem
   D. non–fiction

Lines and Squares

Whenever I walk in a London street,
I'm ever so careful to watch my feet;

And I keep in the squares,
 And the masses of bears,

5   Who wait at the corners all ready to eat
The sillies who tread on the lines of the street,

Go back to their lairs,
 And I say to them, "Bears,
 Just look how I'm walking in all of the squares!"

10 And the little bears growl to each other,

"He's mine,

As soon as he's silly and steps on a line."
 And some of the bigger bears try to pretend
 That they came round the corner to look

15 for a friend;

And they try to pretend that nobody cares
 Whether you walk on the lines or squares.
 But only the sillies believe their talk;
 It's ever so portant how you walk.
20   And it's ever so jolly to call out, "Bears,
 Just watch me walking in all the squares!"

—by A. A. Milne

176. To the child speaking, "sillies" are people who forget about
    A. bears and step on the squares
    B. squares and step on the bears
    C. lines and step on the bears
    D. bears and step on the lines

177. Which of the following word is a word that the writer has shortened to make it sound like a young child is speaking?
    A. I'm
    B. He's
    C. Sillies
    D. Portant

178. The **main** idea of the poem is that
    A. if you walk on a line in a London street, a bear will eat you
    B. bears are dangerous and should be locked in a zoo
    C. shopping in London can be frightening
    D. it is better to drive than to walk

179. This passage can **best** be described as a
   A. fable
   B. poem
   C. fairy tale
   D. short story

Read the following passage and answer questions 180 to 183

The New Boy

The desks in our classroom are arranged in a sort of circle, so we all face each other. Mr. Donaldson had squeezed in an extra desk with the name *Jean-Pierre* printed on a card to match the others. I watched, steaming, while Alyssa guided the poor boy to his place as if he were blind.

5 "I speak English," I heard him say. "And I can see."

His voice was a bit husky, which made his accent sound like someone in a movie. He was even cuter close up, with hazely eyes and long lashes. Alyssa just kept standing there, staring at him. Her pal Megan leaned over and poked her to stop making a fool of herself.

"Take your seats, people. Settle down. Welcome back, everyone. I'd like to officially
10 welcome our newcomer, Jean-Pierre de LaTour."

Jean-Pierre saluted and smiled a crooked smile. His desk was directly opposite mine, so I caught the main shine. Hubert is next to me, and Alyssa is three over, well out of smile range.

"You'll have plenty of time during the day to show Jean-Pierre how friendly New Yorkers can be." Mr. Donaldson looked around. "Ah, Hubert? Would you be Jean-Pierre's buddy
15 for today?"

Hubert blushed and nodded at Jean-Pierre to introduce himself. In our class, it is well known that Hubert does not like to speak out loud. Especially not to strangers. Mr. D picked him on purpose—an exercise in torture disguised as social encouragement.

"Show him around, make sure he finds the cafeteria and other essential facilities...."
20 Mr. Donaldson always calls the bathroom "the facilities."

Jean-Pierre nodded back at Hubert and spun his yo-yo like a top across his desk.

"Toys are not allowed in the classroom," said Mr. Donaldson, with a laser-beam squint. "Since it's your first day, I'll let you off with a warning." He laughed to try to show he was a nice guy, but we all knew he was dying to add that yo-yo to the collection of our
25 treasures in his bottom drawer.

"All right then, listen up, people. We have a busy quarter ahead of us, with the first focus on your projects about medieval life. We have a couple of field trips coming up, starting this week—"

"Are we going on a school bus or the subway?" asked Josh

30 "—with an excursion, on a school bus, to the Cloisters. That's Friday, leaving first thing. We'll be seeing a marvelous reconstruction of medieval architecture as well as—yes Josh?"

"Do we have to bring a lunch?"

"You'll need to bring a bag lunch, no glass bottles, no candy—yes, Josh?"

"Can we have soda, sir?"

35 "Yes, you *may* have soda. Eyes on me, people. This trip will be very instructive for all who—"

I noticed Hubert was watching Jean-Pierre instead of the teacher. I guess we all were.

I wrote a note and passed it along with my elbow.

Don't worry. I'll help you with the new kid.

Hubert and I waited after class while Jean-Pierre collected a stack of textbooks from Mr.
40 D. and stuffed them into a plastic shopping bag. Alyssa hovered at the door, trying, as usual, to barge in where she's not wanted.

Jean-Pierre saw us looking at the plastic bag.

"I was waiting to see what the other kids use," he said shrugging. "I want to look like a New Yorker!"

45 "We all have backpacks." I turned around to show him.

"Billie would probably die without her backpack." Alyssa giggled, tugging on my strap.

I yanked away from her.

"See? Taking Billie's backpack would be like ripping a shell off a turtle."

Alyssa has been suspicious of my backpack ever since the day last fall when my puppy,
50 Harry, came to school inside it. Thanks to my secret weapon, he was invisible at the time, but he wiggled enough to nearly give himself away. Now Alyssa pokes my pack whenever she can, just in case it will move. She won't give up the hope that she might uncover something to get me in trouble.

What if she knew the truth? I have to keep it hidden from my ever-curious little sister, so I
55 carry it with me at all times. In my backpack is enough Vanishing Powder to make Alyssa disappear from my life.

—from *The Invisible Enemy* by Marthe Jocelyn

180. Billie **most likely** thinks of Alyssa as being
  A. clumsy
  B. annoying
  C. dishonest
  D. organized

181. Which of the following characters does the narrator like the **least**?
  A. Megan
  B. Hubert
  C. Alyssa
  D. Jean-Pierre

182. Which of the following statements about Jean-Pierre is **most likely** a true statement?
  A. Jean-Pierre has just moved to Billie's school from another school in New York.
  B. Jean-Pierre is from France and is just visiting Billie's school for a couple of weeks.
  C. Jean-Pierre has just arrived at Billie's school after having recently moved to New York.
  D. Jean-Pierre has just returned to Billie's school after having been away for a year in France.

183. In the phrase "with an excursion, on a school bus,"[line 30] the word "excursion" means
  A. a test
  B. an outing
  C. a vacation
  D. a museum

Read the following passage and answer questions 184 to 187

Not Owls Too!

The reason Dad said: "Oh NO! Not owls too" was because I already had some pets.

There was a summerhouse in our back yard and we kept about thirty gophers in it. They belonged to Bruce and me, and to another boy called Murray. We caught them out on the prairie, using snares made of heavy twine.

5 The way you do it is like this: You walk along until you spot a gopher sitting up beside his hole. Gophers sit straight up, reaching their noses as high as they can, so they can see farther. When you begin to get too close they flick their tails, give a little jump, and whisk down their holes. As soon as they do that, you take a piece of twine that has a noose tied in one end, and you spread the noose over the hole. Then you lie down in the grass
10 holding the other end of the twine in your hand. You can hear the gopher all the while, whistling away to himself somewhere underground. He can hear you, too, and he's wondering what you're up to.

After a while he gets so curious he can't stand it. Out pops his head, and you give a yank on the twine. You have to haul in fast, because if the twine gets loose he'll slip his head
15 out of the noose and zip back down his hole.

We had rats too. Murray's dad was a professor at the college and he got us some white rats from the medical school. We kept them in our garage, which made my Dad a little peeved, because he couldn't put the car in the garage for fear the rats would make nests inside the seats. Nobody ever knew how many rats we had because they have so
20 many babies, and they have them so fast. We gave white rats away to all the kids in Saskatoon, but we always seemed to end up with as many as we had at first.

There were the rats and gophers, and then there was a big cardboard box full of garter snakes that we kept under the back porch, because my mother wouldn't let me keep them in the house. Then there were the pigeons. I usually had about ten of them, but
25 they kept bringing their friends and relations for visits, so I never knew how many to expect when I went out to feed them in the mornings. There were some rabbits too, and then there was Mutt, my dog—but he wasn't a pet; he was one of the family.

Sunday morning my father said:

"Billy, I think you have enough pets. I don't think you'd better bring home any owls. In any
30 case, the owls might eat your rats and rabbits and gophers…"

He stopped talking and a queer look came into his face. Then he said:

"On second thought—maybe we *need* an owl around this place!"

So it was all right.

—from *Owls in the Family*, by Farley Mowat

184. Which animals does the narrator describe having the **most** of?
   A. Dogs
   B. Rabbits
   C. Pigeons
   D. Gophers

185. In this story, the gophers belong to
   A. Bruce's dad
   B. Billy's family
   C. Bruce, Billy, and Murray
   D. Murray's brother and sister

186. Billy and his friends acquired the white rats from
   A. the prairie
   B. Billy's garage
   C. the storehouse
   D. Murray's father

187. The **most likely** reason that Billy's mother would not let him keep the box of snakes in the house is that she
   A. was afraid of snakes
   B. thought they were poisonous
   C. thought they needed fresh air to survive
   D. was concerned that the snakes would eat the rats

from Ronia, The Robber's Daughter

AND THEN SPRING CAME LIKE A SHOUT OF JOY TO THE WOODS AROUND Matt's Fort. The snow melted, streaming down all the cliff faces and finding its way to the river. And the river roared and foamed in the frenzy of spring and sang with all its waterfalls a wild spring song that never died. Ronia heard it every waking hour and even in her
5 nightly dreams. The long, terrible winter was over. The Wolf's Neck had long been free of snow. There was a turbulent stream rushing down it now, and the water splashed around the horses' hooves when Matt and his robbers came riding early one morning through the narrow pass. They sang and whistled as they rode out. Oh, ho, at last their splendid robbers' life was beginning again!

10 And at last Ronia was going to her woods, which she had missed so much. The moment the snow melted and all the ice thawed away, she should have been there to see what was happening in her domain, but Matt had stubbornly kept her at home. The spring forests were full of dangers, he claimed, and he would not let her go until it was time for him to set out with his robbers.

15 "Off you go then," he said, "and don't drown yourself in some treacherous little pool."

"Oh, yes, I shall," Ronia said. "To give you something to make a fuss about at last."

Matt gazed gloomily at her. "My Ronia," he said with a sigh. Then he flung himself into the saddle, led his robbers down the slopes, and was gone.

As soon as Ronia saw the last horse's rump disappear through the Wolf's Neck, she
20 followed at a run. She, too, was singing and whistling as she waded in the cold water of the brook. Then she was running, running, until she reached the lake.

And there was Birk, as he had promised. He was stretched out on a flat rock in the sunshine. Ronia did not know if he was asleep or awake, so she picked up a stone and tossed it into the water to see if he heard the splash. He did, and he sprang up and came
25 toward her.

"I've been waiting a long time," he said, and once again she felt that little spurt of joy because she had a brother who waited and wanted her to come.

And here she was now, diving headfirst into spring. It was so magnificent everywhere around her, it filled her, big as she was, and she screeched like a bird, high and shrill.

30 "I have to scream a spring scream or I'll burst," she explained to Birk. "Listen! You can hear spring, can't you?"

They stood silently, listening to the twittering and rushing and buzzing and singing and murmuring in their woods. There was life in every tree and watercourse and every green thicket; the bright, wild song of spring rang out everywhere.

35 "I'm standing here feeling the winter run out of me," said Ronia. "Soon I'll be so light I can fly."

—by Astrid Lindgren

188. Which of the following sentences **best** indicates how Matt and the robbers feel about spring?
  A. "They sang and whistled as they rode out."
  B. "Matt and his robbers came riding early one morning"
  C. "And at last Ronia was going to her woods, which she had missed so much."
  D. "Then he flung himself into the saddle, led his robbers down the slopes, and was gone."

189. The reason that Ronia tosses a stone into the water is to
  A. scare Matt
  B. signal Birk
  C. see if it would skip
  D. test the depth of the water

190. When Ronia screeches "like a bird, high and shrill,"[line 29] it is a sign of her
  A. fear
  B. delight
  C. frustration
  D. astonishment

191. In the phrase "Then he flung himself into the saddle,"[line 17] the word "flung" is the past tense of
  A. fling
  B. flow
  C. flee
  D. fly

192. A synonym of the word "turbulent" as it is used in the sentence "there was a turbulent stream rushing down it now"[line 6] is
  A. wild
  B. quiet
  C. shallow
  D. trickling

Read the following passage and answer questions 193 to 196

from The Lives of Christopher Chant

Christopher was called to Mama's dressing-room that afternoon. There was a new governess sitting on the only hard chair, wearing the usual sort of ugly grayish clothes and a hat that was uglier than usual. Her drab cotton gloves were folded on her dull bag and her head hung down as if she were timid or put-upon, or both. Christopher found her
5 of no interest. All the interest in the room was centered on the man standing behind Mama's chair with his hand on Mama's shoulder.

"Christopher, this is my brother," Mama said happily. "Your Uncle Ralph."

Mama pronounced it Rafe. It was more than a year before Christopher discovered it was the name he read as Ralph.

10 Uncle Ralph took his fancy completely. To begin with, he was smoking a cigar. The scents of the dressing-room were changed and mixed with the rich incense-like smoke, and Mama was not protesting by even so much as sniffing. That alone was enough to show that Uncle Ralph was in a class by himself. Then he was wearing tweeds, strong and tangy and almost fox-colored, which were a little baggy here and there, but blended
15 beautifully with the darker foxiness of Uncle Ralph's hair and the redder foxiness of his mustache. Christopher had seldom seen a man in tweeds or without whiskers. This did even more to assure him that Uncle Ralph was someone special. As a final touch, Uncle Ralph smiled at him like sunlight on an autumn forest. It was such an engaging smile that Christopher's face broke into a return smile almost of its own accord.

20 "Hallo, old chap," said Uncle Ralph, rolling out blue smoke above Mama's glossy hair. "I know this is not the best way for an uncle to recommend himself to a nephew, but I've been sorting the family affairs out, and I'm afraid I've had to do one or two quite shocking things, like bringing you a new governess and arranging for you to start school in autumn. Governess over there. Miss Bell. I hope you like one another. Enough to forgive
25 me anyway."

He smiled at Christopher in a sunny, humorous way which had Christopher rapidly approaching adoration. All the same, Christopher glanced dubiously at Miss Bell. She looked back, and there was an instant when a sort of hidden prettiness in her almost came out into the open. Then she blinked pale eyelashes and murmured, "Pleased to
30 meet you," in a voice as uninteresting as her clothes.

"She'll be your last governess, I hope," said Mama. Because of that, Christopher ever after thought of Miss Bell as the Last Governess. "She's going to prepare you for school. I wasn't meaning to send you away yet, but your uncle says—Anyway, a good education is important for your career and, to be blunt with you, Christopher, your Papa has made a
35 most *vexatious* hash of the money—which is mine, not his, as you know—and lost practically all of it. Luckily I had your uncle to turn to and—"

"And once turned to, I don't let people down," Uncle Ralph said, with a quick flick of a glance at the governess. Maybe he meant she should not be hearing this. "Fortunately, there's plenty left to send you to school, and then your Mama is going to recoup a bit by
40 living abroad. She'll like that—eh, Miranda? And Miss Bell is going to be found another post with glowing references. Everyone's going to be fine."

His smile went to all of them one by one, full of warmth and confidence. Mama laughed and dabbed scent behind her ears. The Last Governess almost smiled, so that the hidden prettiness half-emerged again. Christopher tried to grin a strong manly grin at
45 Uncle Ralph, because that seemed to be the only way to express the huge, almost hopeless adoration that was growing in him. Uncle Ralph laughed, a golden brown laugh, and completed the conquest of Christopher by fishing in a tweed pocket and tipping his nephew a bright new sixpence.

—by Diana Wynne Jones

193. Christopher was further assured that his uncle was special by his
  A. clothes and grooming
  B. manner of speaking
  C. habit of smoking
  D. way of smiling

194. In the context of the quotation "I know this is not the best way for an uncle to recommend himself to a nephew,"[line 20] the verb "to recommend" means to
  A. grant praise
  B. give representation
  C. offer poor references
  D. create a favorable impression

195. As it is used in the quotation "Christopher, your Papa has made a most vexatious[line 34] hash of the money," the word "vexatious" means
  A. troublesome
  B. enormous
  C. scary
  D. mean

196. The description of Uncle Ralph's smile as being "like sunlight on an autumn forest"[line 18] is an example of
  A. simile
  B. metaphor
  C. hyperbole
  D. personification

The Snake on Second Avenue

It wasn't my idea to have a snake for a pet. I don't like animals much, and as far as wild animals go—well, cats are too wild for me. But my mother's batty about animals. She watches nature shows on TV and writes letters to the editor complaining about inhumane traps. I find it a little tiresome, but mostly Mum's all right. She never complains when she
5 has to pick me up after ball practice, even though she thinks I should be bird-watching instead.

We were in Saskatoon for a dentist appointment the day we found the snake. It was a little garter snake, the kind we have in the garden at home—green with yellow stripes. There was one thing unusual about this one, though. It was on Second Avenue right outside a shoe store. The snake looked really scared and I don't blame it. It was too
10 small to be made into shoes, but that wasn't its biggest worry. From the look of the crowd gathered around it on the sidewalk, the busy street would have been safer.

We noticed the crowd from the end of the block. As we got closer we could hear a kid scream over and over, "Kill it! Kill it!" I don't know why the kid didn't just leave.

As soon as Mum heard the kid yell she doubled her speed. I ran along with her because I
15 was pretty curious about what all the people were staring at. A mouse? A Martian? A kid playing hooky?

Mum pushed her way through the crowd and I followed. The snake was coiled up on the sidewalk. Everyone seemed to be arguing about how to kill it.

"Oh, the poor thing!" exclaimed Mum. She went straight to the snake and picked it up. It
20 was already so frightened that it didn't even try to get away. It just wrapped its tail around her wrist and poked its tongue in and out.

There was a horrified silence. Even the kill-it kid stopped yelling.

"It's just a garter snake," said Mum, quite loudly. "It's not poisonous and it's not a constrictor. The only things it can damage are insects." She paused, then said, "And I'm
25 going to take it home. Please excuse me." She didn't have to push her way out. The crowd just separated in front of her. She seemed to have forgotten me so I followed along behind, watching the snake move in her hands and wondering what it felt like.

We'd reached the car before I noticed where we were. "Hey, Mum!" I exclaimed. "I thought we were going to buy me some jeans."

30 "With a snake?" she asked. "We're going home now. You'll have to hold the snake."

I wish she'd waited till we were in the car. I don't want you to think I'm chicken, but the first time I hold a snake, I'd like advance warning.

Terrified that I might drop it, I just blinked and grabbed the thing around the neck. I was surprised at how it felt—not slimy at all, but hard and dry on the top and soft underneath.
35 Its head was amazingly small, but it still kept sticking its tongue out. I stuck mine out at it, then climbed into the car.

Mum started the engine and said, "I've heard that garter snakes make good pets."

I groaned, but I knew there was no point in arguing. And really, it wasn't so bad. I could probably write a science report on it and amaze all the teachers. After all, there are
40 worse things than living in the same house as a snake. At least it wasn't a cat.

—by Adele Dueck

197. Which of the following words was **not** made out of the word *amazingly*?
   A. Gala
   B. Lazy
   C. Game
   D. Lay

198. The mother writes letters to editors complaining about
   A. bad behavior
   B. inhumane traps
   C. how she loves animals
   D. the ill treatment of animals

199. Before being handed the snake, the narrator would have liked
   A. a chance to clean his or her hand
   B. advance warning
   C. to be given a choice
   D. some advice

200. When the mother picks up the snake and carries it away from the crowd, she can be **best** described as
   A. exhausted
   B. excited
   C. nervous
   D. calm

Read the following passage and answer questions 201 to 204

Lost and Found

This morning, Mom reminded me
to check the Lost and Found.
So just to make her happy,
I took a look around.

5   The box was like a stinky mouth,
whose grin was dark and wide.
I gulped and took a monster breath
then reached my arm inside.

I dug around without a sound
10   through swirls of clothes and dirt.
To my delight, the box spit out
my favorite soccer shirt.

I peered a little deeper down,
and there, to my surprise,
15   a little face gazed up at me
with wide and eager eyes.

I took a triple-double take
and saw it was my sister.
It's sad to think—for several weeks,
20   we hadn't even missed her.

    —by Ted Scheu

201. The narrator of this poem is **most likely** a
    A. mother
    B. girl's uncle
    C. boy's sister
    D. young child

202. When the poem states that the narrator "took a monster breath,"[line 7] it **most likely** means that the narrator took a
    A. small breath
    B. very big breath
    C. stinky breath like a monster
    D. breath away from a monster

203. What style of poem is "Lost and Found"?
    A. Haiku
    B. Limerick
    C. Rhyming poem
    D. Triangular poem

204. As it is used in the lines "To my delight, the box spit out / my favorite soccer shirt,"[line 11] an antonym of the word "delight" is
  A. disgust
  B. dismay
  C. disdain
  D. disarray

Read the following passage and answer questions 205 to 208

from Coram Boy

It was not just because he seemed a gentleman that made Alexander different. Although the boys joked about him, they never laid a finger on him, and Thomas soon realised they respected him after all, for no one doubted that Alexander had the finest voice of them all and, more than that, was the most musically gifted. Even the bishop treated him
5 with awe and called him "our little genius." Not only did Alexander have the voice of an angel, but he played the harpsichord and virginal precociously well and had composed obsessively from the age of six. His anthems and choral pieces were often sung at services and concerts.

At first, Thomas was disappointed to find himself ordered to sit next to this surly,
10 uncommunicative boy in the schoolroom. Strange that Alexander, who had advised Thomas to make the boys laugh, seemed impervious to jokes and wise-cracking. When Thomas tried to get even a smile out of his companion, his attempt was received with a blank uncomprehending stare. But Thomas was gifted at algebra, and when he saw Alexander drifting helplessly over a calculation, he offered to help him. Alexander
15 grudgingly accepted his assistance and, in due course, reciprocated by helping Thomas with Latin, Greek and French. Then, when Thomas took up the violin, he soon showed himself to be such a skillful performer, Alexander began writing pieces for him. Without realising it, they had become friends.

—by Jamila Gavin

205. Alexander's voice is described as the voice of
  A. an angel
  B. a genius
  C. a star
  D. a boy

206. Thomas' strongest musical skill was
  A. playing the harpsichord
  B. playing the violin
  C. composition
  D. singing

207. As it is used in the phrase "surly, uncommunicative boy,"[line 9] the word "*uncommunicative*" means
     A. outspoken
     B. outgoing
     C. nervous
     D. silent

208. The genre of writing used in this passage is called
     A. historical fiction
     B. science fiction
     C. mystery
     D. fantasy

Read the following passage and answer questions 209 to 212

Gramma's Apron

   Gramma's gone, but not forgotten,
    that's her apron hanging there.
   It still hangs in Grampa's kitchen.
    Sometimes he looks at it and stares.

5   When Gramma wore her apron
    it was magical to see.
   The pockets held such treasures
    for the grandkids just like me.

   Saw it shine up Grampa's fender once
10   just as pretty as you please,
    and it wiped my brother's cheek off
    one time when he sneezed.

   It took cookies from the oven,
    it rushed to wipe a tear,
15   got a grain of sand out of your eye,
    made a lap for the stories we'd hear.

   It wiped spills up from the countertop
    when she was baking pies,
    a symbol of her love and care
20   and it showed, too, in her eyes.

   Sometimes I'm sad to look at it
    when I see my Grampa stare.
   Gramma's gone, but not forgotten.
    That's her apron hanging there.

25   —by C. J. Heck

209. The first stanza infers that Gramma
     A. is on a holiday
     B. forgot her apron
     C. has passed away
     D. dislikes the apron

210. Grampa **most likely** leaves the apron hanging in the kitchen because
    A. he uses it frequently
    B. nobody else wants it
    C. it reminds him of Gramma
    D. that is where aprons are kept

211. The rhyme scheme of this poem is
    A. *aabb*
    B. *abab*
    C. *abca*
    D. *abcb*

212. Which of the following pairs of words are synonyms?
    A. Stories and treasures
    B. Gone and forgotten
    C. Apron and kitchen
    D. Look and stare

EXERCISE #1—LANGUAGE ARTS

Table of Correlations		
Standard		**Test #1**
4RL	Reading Standards for Literature	
4RL.10	By the end of the year, read and comprehend literature, including stories, dramas, and poetry, in the grades 4–5 text complexity band proficiently, with scaffolding as needed at the high end of the range.	222, 223, 224
4RF	Reading Standards: Foundational Skills	
4.RF.3a	Know and apply grade-level phonics and word analysis skills in decoding words. Use combined knowledge of all letter-sound correspondences, syllabication patterns, and morphology to read accurately unfamiliar multi-syllabic words in context...	217, 218, 219, 220, 221
4.W	Writing Standards	
4W.1c	Write opinion pieces on topics or texts, supporting a point of view with reasons and information. Link opinion and reasons using words and phrases.	213
4W.2a	Write informative/explanatory texts to examine a topic and convey ideas and information clearly. Introduce a topic clearly and group related information in paragraphs and sections; include formatting, illustrations, and multimedia when...	214, 215, 216
4W.9a	Draw evidence from literary or informational texts to support analysis, reflection, and research. Apply grade 4 Reading standards to literature.	224
4L	Language Standards	
4L.1a	Demonstrate command of the conventions of standard English grammar and usage when writing or speaking. Use relative pronouns (who, whose, whom, which, that) and relative adverbs (where, when, why).	225, 226, 227
4L.1b	Demonstrate command of the conventions of standard English grammar and usage when writing or speaking. Form and use the progressive verb tenses.	228, 229, 230, 231, 232
4L.1d	Demonstrate command of the conventions of standard English grammar and usage when writing or speaking. Order adjectives within sentences according to conventional patterns.	233, 234, 235, 236, 237
4L.1f	Demonstrate command of the conventions of standard English grammar and usage when writing or speaking. Produce complete sentences, recognizing and correcting inappropriate fragments and run-ons.	238, 239, 240, 241
4L.2a	Demonstrate command of the conventions of standard English capitalization, punctuation, and spelling when writing. Use correct capitalization.	242, 243, 244, 245, 246, 247, 248
4L.3b	Use knowledge of language and its conventions when writing, speaking, reading, or listening. Choose punctuation for effect.	249, 250, 251
4L.4c	Determine or clarify the meaning of unknown and multiple-meaning words and phrases based on grade 4 reading and content, choosing flexibly from a range of strategies. Consult reference materials, both print and digital, to find the...	252, 253, 254, 255, 256
4L.5a	Demonstrate understanding of figurative language, word relationships, and nuances in word meanings. Explain the meaning of simple similes and metaphors in context.	257, 258, 259
4L.5b	Demonstrate understanding of figurative language, word relationships, and nuances in word meanings. Recognize and explain the meaning of common idioms, adages, and proverbs.	260

4L.5c	Demonstrate understanding of figurative language, word relationships, and nuances in word meanings. Demonstrate understanding of words by relating them to their opposites (antonyms) and to words with similar but not identical meanings (synonyms).	261, 262, 263, 264, 265

213. Which branch of the Indo-European language has had the **greatest** influence on the English language?
  A. Latin
  B. French
  C. German
  D. Spanish

214. Which set of words is correctly grouped with a main heading?
  A. Carrot—potato, onion, vegetable
  B. Potato—carrot, vegetable, onion
  C. Onion—carrot, potato, vegetable
  D. Vegetable—carrot, potato, onion

215. Which of the following groups of words would be listed under the heading "Vegetables"?
  A. Hoe, shovel, rake
  B. Rabbit, mouse, rat
  C. Beef, pork, chicken
  D. Carrot, celery, onion

216. Which of the following words would be found under the main heading "Trees"?
  A. Water, park, shade
  B. Birch, oak, redwood
  C. Grass, lawn, garden
  D. Club, tree house, ladder

Use the following information to answer the next question.

Prewashed lettuce is lettuce that has been washed _____ you buy it.

217. The word that makes the given sentence correct is
  A. after
  B. once
  C. while
  D. before

218. Which of the following prefixes can be added to the beginning of the word *agree* to make a new word that means "do not agree"?
  A. In-
  B. Dis-
  C. Mis-
  D. Un-

219. Which of the following prefixes can be added to the beginning of the word *visible* to make a new word that means "not visible"?
    A. *in-*
    B. *un-*
    C. *dis-*
    D. *mis-*

220. Which of the following prefixes can be added to the front of the word *certain* to make a word that means "not sure"?
    A. In-
    B. Un-
    C. Dis-
    D. Mis-

221. Which of the following suffixes can be added to the end of the word *teach* to make a new word that means "someone who teaches"?
    A. -er
    B. -ed
    C. -ing
    D. -est

222. A story with the title "Clever Monkey Finds a Wife" is **most likely** an example of a
    A. myth
    B. legend
    C. folk tale
    D. fairy tale

223. Stories from around the world that teach a lesson are called
    A. myths
    B. legends
    C. folk tales
    D. fairy tales

224. In a fable, the characters are often
    A. toys
    B. robots
    C. ghosts
    D. animals

Use the following information to answer the next question.

My sister won first prize in the contest!

225. Which of the following pronouns could replace the underlined words in the given sentence?
    A. I
    B. Us
    C. Her
    D. She

Use the following information to answer the next question.

I was able to see much more _____ after I received my new glasses.

226. Which of the following adverbs would **best** complete the given sentence?
    A. clearly
    B. greatly
    C. fiercely
    D. awkwardly

Use the following information to answer the next question.

Drew went to the comic book store to buy a comic for Drew's (i) sister Ella because Drew (ii) knew that Ella (iii) loves them.

227. Which of the following tables matches the underlined words in the given sentence with the pronouns that could correctly replace them?

A.
i	ii	iii
he	his	her

B.
i	ii	iii
his	he	she

C.
i	ii	iii
his	he	her

D.
i	ii	iii
he	his	she

Use the following information to answer the next question.

In the future, I _____ harder.

228. What is the correct way to write the missing part of the given sentence?
    A. work
    B. do work
    C. will work
    D. did work

Use the following information to answer the next question.

Who knows what scientists _____ in the next century.

229. What is the correct way to complete the missing part of the given sentence?
   A. discovered
   B. did discover
   C. will discover
   D. had discovered

Use the following information to answer the next question.

Right now, Alice _____ the dishes out of the dishwasher.

230. What is the correct way to write the missing part of the given sentence?
   A. Took
   B. Did take
   C. Will take
   D. Is taking

Use the following information to answer the next question.

When my grandfather was a little boy, he _____ to school on a horse.

231. What is the correct way to complete the missing part of the given sentence?
   A. rode
   B. rides
   C. will ride
   D. was riding

Use the following information to answer the next question.

I am late because I did not hear the alarm and I _____ in.

232. What is the correct way to complete the missing part of the given sentence?
   A. slept
   B. do sleep
   C. will sleep
   D. am sleeping

233. In the sentence "Emily looked excitedly at the brightly wrapped parcels on the old table," a word that is an adjective is
   A. excitedly
   B. brightly
   C. looked
   D. old

Use the following information to answer the next question.

I blew a huge bubble with my gum.

234. The adjective in the given sentence is
    A. gum
    B. blew
    C. huge
    D. bubble

Use the following information to answer the next question.

The room was decorated with colorful ribbons for her party.

235. In the given sentence, the adjective is
    A. room
    B. party
    C. colorful
    D. decorated

Use the following information to answer the next question.

I had to carry my heavy sled all the way home because it was broken.

236. In the given sentence, the adjective is
    A. I
    B. sled
    C. carry
    D. heavy

Use the following information to answer the next question.

Andrew was excited to open his birthday present and find the fast remote-control truck he had wanted for so long.

237. The adjectives in the given sentence are
    A. *truck* and *present*
    B. *open* and *wanted*
    C. *birthday* and *fast*
    D. *Andrew* and *he*

238. Which of the following sentences is a complete sentence?
    A. Flew out of the sky and into the yard.
    B. The cola machine by the door.
    C. Gwen lost her shoes.
    D. Don's tired old cat.

239. Read this sentence.

Can you reach the top shelf of the closet?

In this sentence, the **subject** is

A. top
B. you
C. shelf
D. closet

Use the following information to answer the next question.

The hard rubber ball bounced all the way down the stairs.

240. In the given sentence, the subject is
A. ball
B. stairs
C. down
D. way

Use the following information to answer the next question.

The princess saw the little bird in the grass under the tree.

241. In the given sentence, the subject is
A. princess
B. grass
C. bird
D. tree

242. Read the sentence below. There may be a mistake in capitalization, punctuation, or usage. Which of the alternatives is written most clearly and correctly? If there is no mistake, choose *Correct as is*.

yes i have even seen the red road's

A. Yes I have even seen the red roads,
B. Yes, I have even seen the red roads.
C. Yes, I has even seen the red roads.
D. Correct as is.

243. Read the sentence below. There may be a mistake in capitalization, punctuation, or usage. Which of the alternatives is written most clearly and correctly? If there is no mistake, choose *Correct as is*.

Tasha and her grandmother make Oatmeal cookies?

A. Tasha and her Grandmother makes Oatmeal Cookies.
B. Tasha and her grandmother make oatmeal cookies.
C. Tasha and her Grandmother makes oatmeal cookie's!
D. Correct as is.

244. Which of the following sentences correctly uses capitalization?
    A. My mom searched the neighborhood for Trevor and me.
    B. My Mom searched the neighborhood for Trevor and me.
    C. My Mom searched the neighborhood for Trevor and Me.
    D. My mom searched the neighborhood for Trevor and Me.

245. Which of the following sentences is written correctly?
    A. My whole family is planning to take part in the red shirt walk-A-Thon in sycamore valley park this sunday.
    B. My whole Family is planning to take part in the red Shirt walk-a-Thon in Sycamore valley park this Sunday.
    C. My whole family is planning to take part in the Red Shirt Walk-A-Thon in Sycamore Valley Park this Sunday.
    D. My whole Family is planning to take part in the Red Shirt Walk-a-thon in Sycamore Valley Park this Sunday.

246. Which of the following sentences is written correctly?
    A. We have made plans to go to chicago this year to see the St. Patrick's day parade.
    B. We have made plans to go to chicago this year to see the st. patrick's day parade.
    C. We have made plans to go to Chicago this year to see the St. Patrick's day parade.
    D. We have made plans to go to Chicago this year to see the St. Patrick's Day Parade.

247. Which of the following sentences is written correctly?
    A. Chloe learned how to knit a scarf after she Read *Owlkids*.
    B. Chloe learned how to knit a scarf after she read *Owlkids*.
    C. Chloe learned how to knit a scarf after she read *owlkids*.
    D. Chloe learned how to knit a scarf after she Read *owlkids*.

248. Which of the following sentences is written correctly?
    A. Every morning when my parents wake up, they read the *Star City Journal* at the kitchen table.
    B. Every morning when my parents wake up, they read the *Star City journal* at the kitchen table.
    C. Every morning when my parents wake up, they read the *star city Journal* at the kitchen table.
    D. Every morning when my parents wake up, they read the *star city journal* at the kitchen table.

249. Read this sentence and decide which punctuation is needed.

    Are the cookies ready yet

    What is the correct punctuation mark for this sentence?

    A. a period
    B. a comma
    C. a question mark
    D. an exclamation mark

Use the following information to answer the next question.

After28 days, the eggs hatch

250.Which punctuation is needed to complete the given sentence?
  A. A period
  B. A semicolon
  C. A question mark
  D. An exclamation mark

Use the following information to answer the next question.

Why are there so many stars in the sky

251.Which type of punctuation needs to be added to the given sentence to make it complete?
  A. A period
  B. A comma
  C. A question mark
  D. An exclamation mark

Use the following information to answer the next question.

float /floht/ v. 1. to rest on water or another liquid without sinking. 2. to hang or drift suspended in a gas. n. 1. an object that floats on water, usually to mark an object's location in the water, or to hold up another object in the water. 2. a platform on wheels carrying a display in a parade.

252.In the sentence "They tied the boat up to the bright orange float," the word "float" means
  A. to hang or drift suspended in a gas
  B. to rest on water or another liquid without sinking
  C. a platform on wheels carrying a display in a parade
  D. an object that usually marks another object's location in the water

snap • *verb* (snapped, snap•ping)
1 to break suddenly with a cracking noise.
2 to grab or try to grab something suddenly with the teeth. 3 to speak in a short, sharp, or annoyed way.

• *noun* 1 a device that closes or opens something and often makes a sharp noise
2 a short period of cold weather 3 a sharp or cracking sound

253.Which of the following sentences uses *snap* in the same way as the first verb definition?
  A. The slender branch snapped under his weight and he fell.
  B. The hungry dog snapped the sandwich out of my hand.
  C. "That is a silly question," she snapped at her sister.
  D. "I'm sorry I snapped at you," she apologized.

254. Which of the following sentences uses *snap* in the same way as the third noun definition?
   A. Can you help your little sister do up the snaps on her jacket?
   B. Tent doors usually have snaps or zippers to open and close them.
   C. The weather has been warm except for one short cold snap last week.
   D. When I heard the snap, I knew that the mouse had been caught in the trap.

Use the following information to answer the next question.

> The word *train* can have the following meanings:
>
> - As a verb
>   - to make (someone) physically fit
>   - to give skills through discipline or instruction
> - As a noun
>   - a connected series of railroad cars
>   - the long part of a gown or robe that trails behind the person wearing it
>   - an orderly sequence of things or ideas

255. Which of the following statements uses the word *train* to mean an orderly sequence of things or ideas?
   A. The bride wore a beautiful gown with a long train.
   B. You can take the train, but a plane is much faster.
   C. Stop interrupting—you made me lose my train of thought!
   D. Do you have to train a long time to be able to swim so fast?

256. Which of these words would you find on a dictionary page with the guide words *blink* and *blood*?
   A. Brother
   B. Bottle
   C. Blend
   D. Bliss

257. A figure of speech that uses the words *like* or *as* to compare two unlike things is known as
   A. onomatopoeia
   B. alliteration
   C. a metaphor
   D. a simile

258. Which of the following sentences contains an example of a simile?
   A. My friends think my grandma is as sweet as honey.
   B. The five fish swam around in their fifty-foot fish tank.
   C. I was on a roller coaster of emotion while my grandpa was ill.
   D. I had to tell my little brother a million times to stay out of my room.

259. Which of the following sentences contains a metaphor?
    A. The little lost puppy looked very sad.
    B. The bee buzzed as he flew from flower to flower.
    C. My sister Chloe has always been a bright star in her class.
    D. When I was giving my speech, it felt like a million people were looking at me.

260. The phrase "Put a sock in it!" is a commonly used idiom that means to
    A. put a sock on your foot
    B. tell your friend to speak louder
    C. take a sock and put it in a noisy person's mouth
    D. tell a noisy person or group of people to be quiet

261. An antonym for the word *cluttered* is
    A. lost
    B. closed
    C. hidden
    D. organized

262. Which of the following pairs of words are synonyms?
    A. kind, mean
    B. made, maid
    C. weary, tired
    D. tall, short

263. Which of the following pairs of words are synonyms?
    A. banned, band
    B. loud, quiet
    C. fix, mend
    D. far, near

264. Which of the following pairs of words are antonyms?
    A. broad, wide
    B. beat, defeat
    C. threw, through
    D. strength, weakness

265. The words *loud* and *noisy* are
    A. antonyms
    B. synonyms
    C. homographs
    D. homophones

ANSWERS AND SOLUTIONS — EXERCISE #1—READING INFORMATIONAL

1. D	15. B	29. B	43. B
2. C	16. A	30. A	44. C
3. B	17. C	31. D	45. A
4. D	18. B	32. B	46. C
5. B	19. B	33. A	47. D
6. A	20. B	34. B	48. B
7. B	21. B	35. A	49. B
8. C	22. B	36. C	50. A
9. D	23. C	37. D	51. B
10. A	24. C	38. C	52. A
11. D	25. A	39. B	53. A
12. D	26. B	40. C	
13. C	27. B	41. C	
14. D	28. D	42. A	

1. D

The family is described as living in igloos all winter and a tent all summer and constantly moving to follow the animals.

2. C

The word "essential" means necessary or required.

3. B

The expression "age-old" means very old or ancient.

4. D

The word "hazardous" means dangerous. In this case, it refers to the melting ice on the shoreline, which would be very dangerous, especially for children.

5. B

The list gives examples of specific NASA robots organized in no particular order.
The introduction to the list tells you that what follows will be a list of examples.

6. A

If something is "international," it means that many countries share in it.

7. B

The passage says that robots do tasks that are too dangerous for people to do. "Dangerous" means the same as unsafe.

8. C

If you "return" to a place, it means that you go back to it again. This means you have to have been there once already.

9. D

At first, Joe was unhappy to be selling his junk. However, once he realized that his junk was going to the homes of other junk collectors, he was happy.

10. A

Joe decided that the perfect solution to his problem was to have a garage sale.

11. D

Joe's "junk" is a collection of unusual odds and ends that he has taken from other people's trash. He considers these things useful treasures.

12. D

Joe tells the story from his own perspective and experience. This is called first person point of view.

13. C

Louis's novel, *Treasure Island*, is a story about pirates and lost treasure.

14. D

Louis's novel, *Treasure Island*, is a pirate adventure story. Of the characters listed, the one who would be most likely to appear in Louis's story would be a thieving pirate.

15. B

A sentence fragment is an incomplete sentence.

16. A

A compound sentence is a sentence made up of two or more independent clauses.

17. C

The narrator says, "She brought us funny-looking clothing." This means that the narrator thought the clothing was very strange. This is probably the reason he did not want to wear it.

18. B

"'She's going to make soup and yucky crab,' Emily said" is the only response that says what Grandma plans to do. That she is planning to do something is the meaning of the phrase "She's going to make."

19. B

The narrator tells the reader that "I noticed Grandma's soup smelled really good, much better than Mom's soup. Suddenly I wanted to taste just a little bit."

20. B

When Aunt Araba says that Grandma's soup is authentic, she means that the soup tastes like the original African soup she probably remembers from Ghana.

21. B

The word *exquisite* usually refers to things that are beautiful or delicate. From the passage it is possible to guess that Uncle Robert is referring to the taste of the soup, not how it looks. In this context, Uncle Robert says "Exquisite" to mean delicious.

22. B

A rabbit will rub its head against its owner to leave its scent on him or her to demonstrate affection.

23. C

A rabbit never forgets the scent of another rabbit that has beaten it in a fight. Whenever it smells the stronger rabbit's scent, the weaker rabbit will avoid it.

24. C

The writer refers to baby rabbits as kittens.

25. A

A synonym of "timid" is *shy*. "Timid" means "shy or lacking in courage."

26. B

The Pilgrims were a group of English Separatists from Holland who called themselves "Saints."

27. B

In this context, the *Mayflower* is a sailing ship.

28. D

The words "howling" and "thudding" are sounds and therefore appeal most to the sense of hearing.

29. B

A synonym is a word with a similar meaning. The term "capsizing," as used in the story, "The Voyage of the Mayflower" means turning over.

30. A

The passage mentions that cheetahs eat animals. Since a banana is a fruit, it is unlikely that a cheetah would eat a banana

31. D

The word "throughout" means all through or all over. When the passage states that cheetahs were "Once found throughout Asia and Africa," it means that cheetahs once lived all over Asia and Africa.

32. B

The word *stalk* means to follow or track. To catch its prey, a cheetah must not be seen. This way, it can surprise the other animal. The cheetah must blend in with the grass and be very quiet and cautious.

33. A

The word *prey* refers to an animal that is caught for food. The cheetah is a hunter that must hunt and kill its prey to survive.

34. B

A clumsy person moves or handles things in a careless or awkward way. The fact that many people believe Sir Gadabout would be likely to chop off his own foot indicates that he tends to be clumsy.

35. A

According to the passage, the days of the famous King Arthur were "an exciting and mysterious time to live in."

36. C

The writer describes Gadabout as polite and hard–working and says that King Arthur felt sorry for Gadabout.

37. D

An adjective is a word that describes a noun. The words mysterious, glorious, graceful, and beautiful are words that describe nouns, therefore they are adjectives.

38. C

The passage reveals that the St. Lawrence River and the Arctic have a similar habitat: "the salt water is nice and cold and there is lots of food."

39. B

It is stated in the passage that scientists "raised the alarm" to protect the belugas.

40. C

The passage states that the whale hunt ended in the nineteen seventies.

41. C

Russia, Alaska, and Norway are listed as being part of the beluga's habitat; Finland is not.

42. A

An antonym is a word with the opposite meaning. The word *preservation* means to maintain something or keep something alive, which is the opposite of the word "elimination."

43. B

The text states, "Australia was the first country to introduce personalized stamps in 1999."

44. C

This article provides various pieces of information about the many types of stamps that have been introduced and are available for use and collecting.

45. A

To commemorate something means to remember and honor it in a special way. Some stamps commemorate important events or people in history.

46. C

This text provides factual information on a topic in the form of an article.

47. D

The object of Aingingein was for participants to speed quickly "through a series of burning barrels set high in the air on stilts" while carrying the Dom, which was a ball made from a goat's gall bladder. The Dom was thrown into the last fiery barrel.

48. B

The passage says that Sweden founded an annual broom race, Stitchstock originated in Germany, Aingingein began in Ireland, Scotland was the birthplace of Creaothceann, and England is home to Shuntbumps and Swivenhodge.

49. B

Creaothceann was valued as a test of manliness and courage because many people died proving these attributes.

50. A

The Swedish annual broom race is a test of speed and endurance, where players must navigate a grueling course and cross the finish line.

51. B

In the context of the sentence, a synonym for the word "evolved" is *changed*. The writer is saying that some of the ancient broom games have changed into sports that are familiar in the present day.

52. A

In this case, the word "repel" means fend off. The task of the bladder guardian was to keep the other players away from the bladder.

53. A

The word "flourished" is synonymous with the word *thrived*. Both words suggest that the game was quite successful.

ANSWERS AND SOLUTIONS — EXERCISE #2—READING INFORMATIONAL

54. D	68. C	82. D	96. C
55. B	69. A	83. B	97. A
56. A	70. B	84. B	98. A
57. A	71. D	85. D	99. B
58. D	72. B	86. C	100. D
59. D	73. A	87. B	101. D
60. C	74. C	88. D	102. C
61. C	75. D	89. B	103. C
62. D	76. C	90. B	104. D
63. D	77. B	91. C	105. B
64. D	78. C	92. D	106. D
65. D	79. C	93. B	
66. C	80. A	94. A	
67. C	81. B	95. D	

54. D

The world's heaviest beetle is the goliath beetle.

55. B

Scientists believe that beetles survive everywhere because they are well protected.

56. A

In this passage, "parasites" are defined as creatures that eat beetles from the inside out. This means the creature lives inside a beetle's body while it is feeding, and it receives both food and shelter from its host. The passage describes parasites as living inside the bodies of others rather than on them.

57. A

The elytra are the hard casings of a beetle's forewings that cover and protect a beetle's hind wings, which are used for flying.

58. D

The Qallupilluit is described as a "witchy undersea creature who kidnaps children."

59. D

According to the passage, Michael lived in the age-old Inuit tradition of nomadic living for the first 6 years of his life.

60. C

The passage states that the family "traveled by dog-team in search of whales, seals, and cariboo." The reader can infer that dog teams would most likely be used only in the winter, and that the family would travel by foot or some other means in the other seasons.

61. C

The family followed the caribou, whales, and seals. They followed these animals in order to hunt them for skins, oil, and food.

62. D

According to the passage, furs were an essential item for Michael's family. This is most likely because furs provided warmth and protection against the extremely cold temperatures of the far north.

63. D

An age-old tradition is a custom that has been handed down or done in the same way for a very long time.

64. D

An "imaginary being" is a creature that does not exist in real life.

65. D

The word "nomadic" describes a lifestyle in which people are constantly moving or traveling from place to place.

66. C

Joe's brother, Alvie, sold tickets to this event.

67. C

The word "enormous" means extremely large. The jars are huge.

68. C

When Joe is through digging around in his room, it is in worse shape than before. At this point in the story, Joe says, "Even I was disgusted!" He is fed up with the mess in his room.

69. A

The narrative is a recollection of events or experiences that Joe has lived personally. He is telling his story from his perspective.

70. B

Consulting your local veterinarian is the best source for more information about pet hygiene.

71. D

This is a very important point to recall for the safety of a pet. Chicken bones can cause serious stomach damage if your pet swallows a piece of bone.

72. B

Another good title for this text would be Your "Pet—Tips for Teeth," because it provides direction for the theme of the text. The text is about pet dental hygiene.

73. A

The word *suggest* is closest in meaning to "recommend." These two words are synonyms.

74. C

According to the instructions, the nail can be used to add details to the carving.

75. D

The passage is divided into two sections. An accurate summary should address both these sections. The first section explains how to create and carve soft stone as an easy way to try stone sculpting. The second section provides an example of a famous sculptor and explains the process of creating a real stone sculpture. With this in mind the best response is: "Stone sculptors cut into real stone with heavy metal tools to carve a design. One sculptor was the famous Italian Michelangelo. You can try out stone sculpting using a soft "stone" that is easy to make and carve yourself."

76. C

Under the heading "The Artist's Way," the writer refers to the statue David as one of Michelangelo's most famous sculptures.

77. B

When a knife is blunt, it is no longer sharp. It is dull.

78. C

Grandma brings the narrator a smock with a striped cotton cap.

79. C

The narrator says that the grandmother "did make the soup, only she put in okra too." Then, the narrator says to his sister, "That's going to make it slimy."

80. A

The narrator says that Grandma ended her stories in a funny way.

81. B

Grandmother brought the children traditional clothes ("the kind they wear in Ghana"); she told "stories her grandmother told her when she was young," including "Spider man" stories; and she cooked Ghanaian food, proclaimed by one aunt to be "authentic." It is inferred throughout the story that Grandmother wanted to keep the family's customs and traditions alive among her extended family who had emigrated to America.

82. D

Nestlé observed that sales of semi-sweet candy bars had dropped everywhere, except around Boston.

83. B

The author describes Mrs. Wakefield "giving out her cookie recipe to anyone who was interested." This suggests that there was no cost to anyone who wanted the recipe and that she did not try to keep it a secret.

84. B

The word "tossed" does not mean toasted.

85. D

The words "chocolate crispies" are in quotation marks to indicate that this is what Ruth Wakefield called her cookies.

86. C

The Pilgrims on board the *Mayflower* set sail for America to build a new colony.

87. B

They met for the first time in Southampton, England, a few days before the two ships sailed on August 5.

88. D

The Pilgrims would have had to have been adventurous in order to set out on a voyage such as they did and they showed their adaptability when "sixty-seven Strangers… made room for thirty-five Saints". They would have needed to be able to adapt readily to their new surroundings once they arrived on land. The Pilgrims were undoubtedly brave, but the passage does not portray them as particularly busy even though they would have been once they landed. There is nothing to support the idea that the Pilgrims were fearless; in fact, at times on the journey, they probably would have been terrified.

89. B

Another word used in the passage for "ship" is "vessel."

90. B

A suffix is added to the end of a word to make a new word. The suffix -*ess* changes the word *giant* to mean a female giant.

91. C

A historian is someone who writes or compiles records of events that have taken place.

92. D

The word "transported" means to have carried something from one place to another.
The "present site" is the place where the large stones currently sit, which is in southern England.

93. B

A synonym is a word that means the same thing as another word. *Time* is a synonym for the word "period," meaning an age.

94. A

The reference to there being many stages in the making of a book best supports the idea that the process is long and complicated.

95. D

Based on the context clues in the paragraph, it can be determined that a pasteboard is a big piece of cardboard on which to glue the various pieces of the book into the right layout. While the passage does not directly define it as being made of cardboard, the other definitions can all be eliminated based on the context.

96. C

The publisher decides which stories should be made into books. The person who draws the pictures is the illustrator, the person who writes the story is the writer, and the person who arranges the words and pictures is the designer.

97. A

In this context, the word "cover" is used as a noun meaning a binding or case for a book. This is an example of a homograph.

98. A

The word "stages" is used in the passage as a noun meaning the steps involved in creating a book.

99. B

The passage states that belugas were over hunted because it was thought they were eating the fish that humans needed to survive.

100. D

Ultrasound waves come from the beluga's rounded forehead, and assist it in locating food.

101. D

The last two paragraphs show the connection between the beluga's well being and the river being free of pollutants, in other words the health of the river.

102. C

A synonym is a word that means the same thing as another word. In this context, a privilege is an honor or advantage.

103. C

The most likely explanation for the nickname "Dent-Head" is that, as a Creaothceann player, Magnus Macdonald was hit by a number of falling rocks, and these permanently damaged his head.

104. D

Since the sentence describes how the course runs through the middle of a dragon reservation, this suggests that a Swedish Short-Snout is probably a dragon.

105. B

The word "fatalities" is a synonym of the word *deaths*. The game Creaothceann was very dangerous for players, and many players died from injuries suffered during the game.

106. D

The correct response is "discontinuation". The word "*reintroduction*" means to restart something that had been discontinued.

ANSWERS AND SOLUTIONS — EXERCISE #1—READING LITERATURE

107. A	121. C	135. D	149. B
108. D	122. D	136. D	150. B
109. A	123. C	137. C	151. D
110. B	124. A	138. D	152. D
111. B	125. C	139. A	153. C
112. D	126. D	140. B	154. D
113. A	127. C	141. B	155. A
114. D	128. B	142. A	156. A
115. A	129. D	143. A	157. B
116. C	130. A	144. A	158. A
117. D	131. B	145. A	159. D
118. A	132. B	146. D	
119. C	133. D	147. A	
120. A	134. A	148. B	

107. A

At the beginning of the story, the beetle has a plain brown coat. After he wins the race, the parrot awards him a gorgeous coat of green and gold.

108. D

The rat's character as self-important is evident in the manor that he conducts himself to the beetle. He is outright rude and boldly boasts to the beetle that she is a poke and that he can run much faster, revealing his self-centered motives.

109. A

The beetle complimented the rat and proceeded to carry on her way, never saying a word about the things that she could do. This is evidence to her appearance as a humble character.

110. B

The word "*crawling*" means moving slowly and making slow progress.

111. B

"*Then*" is closest in meaning to the word "next." It shows timing of events.

112. D

A simile is a comparison between two objects using the words *like* or *as*. The phrase "people often set them in pins and necklaces like precious stones" compares beetle shells to precious stones using the word "like."

113. A

Poetry refers to poems, which often have rhythm and rhyme. This passage is a poem. If you read this passage out loud, you can hear a rhythmic pattern of strong and weak "beats." Also, in each verse, you can see that the last words in the second and final lines rhyme: "make" rhymes with "snake," "plan" with "can," "asp" with "grasp," and so on. Poems often use colorful and expressive language. You can see examples of this in phrases like "coiled inside a paper bag" and the line "I heard him scream, I heard him swear."

114. D

The poem does not follow the specific structures of a haiku or a limerick. It does have a rhyming scheme, thus it cannot be described as free verse. It is a rhyming poem.

115. A

When the verb "to lie" means "to rest in a horizontal position," its past tense is "lay." The statement rewritten in the simple past tense is "The snake lay by the bed."

116. C

The word *shriek* means almost the same thing as the word "scream."

117. D

Stink's reaction, "What's that for?" suggests that he is suspicious. He does not appear to be particularly happy nor does he appear to be frustrated. He may be somewhat annoyed, but more than that he wants to know why she is acting so nice.

118. A

When Stink tells Judy to hug a tree, he is comparing her to woodbine, the "creepy plant" that Judy says "wraps around trees."

119. C

Judy tells Frank that she is going home to sleep. She does hug Stink, but she does not do this because she made a conscious decision to hug Stink after she read about the Sleeping Prophet. By deciding not to do any more studying that night, Judy is putting all of her trust in sleeping on a book.

120. A

Judy probably uses her imagination to convince herself that she, too, is a Sleeping Prophet. She is imagining what kind of mystical signs a Sleeping Prophet might see and is finding them in her surroundings. This shows how badly she wants to believe that her strategy will work.

121. C

On his way back to bed, the speaker sees a grinning face in a pattern on the wall, feels a prickle on the back of his neck, and hears the moaning of water in a pipe. He does not hear a siren blaring from outside.

122. D

This poem is a free verse poem. The poem does not follow any particular rhyme, line, or verse pattern.

123. C

A characteristic of most poetry is that it is divided into sections called verses.

124. A

A cinquain is a poem with five lines that follows a specific pattern.

125. C

The information given in the five paragraphs between the opening and closing paragraphs is background information to help the reader clearly understand Billy's father's concerns about the owls.

126. D

Gophers dig underground homes, or burrows, in the prairies. Gophers connect these burrows with tunnels.

127. C

Billy explains that to catch a gopher, one must lie down in the grass and wait for the gopher to stick his head up out of his hole. To do this, a person must have a lot of patience.

128. B

A snare is a noose, usually formed with heavy twine. Snares are used for capturing small game.

129. D

The narrator is a grown man who is looking back on his childhood. The passage begins "When I was a boy," which means that the child in the memory has grown into a man.

130. A

The most likely reason the narrator's mother did not want him to go fishing was that her father had drowned at sea, and she was scared that the same thing could happen to her son.

131. B

Evidence can be found throughout the passage that the uncles made their living by fishing. The passage describes in detail how the uncles brought their catch of fish to the factory for payment every day.

132. B

By comparing the clouds and fog to a "thick soupy blanket," the writer is describing how thoroughly everything is surrounded in a wet dense haze.

133. D

The narrator wanted to go fishing right then (immediately) with his uncles. He did not want to wait until he got older. The narrator remembers trying to convince his mother and his uncles that he should go fishing right then, even though he was only eight years old. The narrator's uncle Jim and his mother suggested that he was too young.

134. A

The crow is described as "the cleverest of birds," and he is able to get water when the other animals could not.

135. D

In this context, the word "brilliant" means smart or clever.

136. D

A fable is a short story (usually with animals as the main characters) that teaches a lesson and gives a moral at the end. The moral is often written in capital letters at the end of the story.

137. C

The introductory statement of the story "IT WAS BONE-DRY IN THE COUNTRYSIDE" informs the reader that the land was as dry as a bone.

138. D

A word that means almost the same as the word "jug" is water pitcher.

139. A

The elephants were thirsty and rushed toward the lake. They were in such a hurry that they did not notice that they were trampling on the hares' burrows.

140. B

The elephants could barely hear Hare because Hare was so small and they were so large. To their ears, Hare's voice sounded like an insect buzzing.

141. B

This passage is a fable, which is a story that teaches a lesson.

142. A

Another word for "annoying" is "bothersome".

143. A

Sam explains that Jacob stayed in the house for half an hour every day before the boys' birthdays, working on Sam's birthday card. It took him a very long time to write the birthday message, which indicates that writing is difficult for him.

144. A

Sam and Jacob are best friends in spite of their differences. Sam is only eight, and Jacob is seventeen. They have different strengths and weaknesses, but they can help each other become better at the things they need to work on. For example, Jacob helps Sam with basketball and learning to recognize different types of cars, and Sam helps Jacob remember the meanings of traffic lights and reminds him to knock when he visits people's homes. Their differences complement each other, and they are very good friends.

145. A

The surprise Jacob gave to Sam took a long time to make. Jacob stayed in the house every day for half an hour working on it.

146. D

At first, it was hard for Sam's mother to understand that an eight-year-old boy could enjoy the company of a much older boy with special needs. She worried that Jacob was bothering Sam by tagging along with him.

147. A

The word *sturdy* can mean strong or muscular. The story says "There was a great deal of snow on the mountains, and Mr. Brown knew it would be hard work climbing to the camp, but Lady Gray was strong, and used to it."

148. B

Lady Gray must have found it very unusual to have snowshoes on her feet. The story says that she was "very awkward at first" when the snowshoes were fastened on. However, she "tried very hard to walk in them," and she was "practicing a little every day." That means she made a big effort to use the snowshoes.

149. B

The word *comical* means funny. In the story, everyone laughed when they saw Lady Gray with her snowshoes on. They thought she looked funny.

150. B

The passage explains that a "freshet" is a flood. During a flood, there is a lot of water, and the river level rises.

151. D

It was unusual to find the snake on Second Avenue because these snakes are generally found in gardens and not on the road.

152. D

According to the passage, "As soon as Mum heard the kid yell she doubled her speed."

153. C

The crowd's aggressive behavior was most likely because they thought that the snake was dangerous. They were unaware that the snake was harmless.

154. D

In this statement, the word "batty" means crazy. The narrator's Mum is crazy about animals: she loves them.

155. A

A person who is terrified is scared of something. In this passage, the narrator was scared of dropping the snake before getting into the car.

156. A

Matilda tried to gain the people's trust so that they would listen to her pleas. Unfortunately, they were too tired of her deceptions to take her seriously.

157. B

The poem is set in the city of London, England, which is located in the European continent. This can be seen in the line "Of London's Noble Fire-Brigade" where it is revealed that Matilda has called the local firefighters in London, England.

158. A

A synonym of the word "*Deprivation*" is punishment. Not being able to attend the play was a punishment for Matilda since she had been telling lies. Her aunt tried to discipline her by having her lose out on something fun.

159. D

This poem can be best described as a narrative poem. A narrative poem tells a story with a beginning, a middle, and an end.

ANSWERS AND SOLUTIONS — EXERCISE #2—READING LITERATURE

160. B	174. B	188. A	202. B
161. B	175. A	189. B	203. C
162. D	176. D	190. B	204. B
163. B	177. D	191. A	205. A
164. D	178. A	192. A	206. B
165. C	179. B	193. A	207. D
166. A	180. B	194. D	208. A
167. D	181. C	195. A	209. C
168. C	182. C	196. A	210. C
169. A	183. B	197. C	211. D
170. D	184. D	198. B	212. D
171. B	185. C	199. B	
172. D	186. D	200. D	
173. B	187. A	201. D	

160. B

Daniel looks up to Mr. Pettigrew as an artist. Mr. Pettigrew says that Daniel's duck is good, and this means a lot to Daniel because he respects Mr. Pettigrew.

161. B

The word "coonskin" refers to the pelt of a raccoon. In the past, people made warm hats from raccoon pelts. The raccoon pelts covered people's heads, and the tails hung down people's backs to keep their necks warm and free from flies and mosquitoes.

162. D

The most important thing that Daniel learns is that sometime people laugh for good reasons and it is important not to let laughter hurt your feelings.

163. B

Although Daniel is discouraged when people appear to be laughing at his carving, the words of a person he respects give him confidence. Daniel was confident enough to try an animal for his first carving. He will surely try again.

164. D

Lucille's coat is described as "gray speckled." When referring to animals, the word *coat* means the same thing as the word *fur*.

165. C

The foods that Victor found in his fridge and cupboards were "cheese and bread and peanut butter and ice cream and pickles, and dog food and cat food and chicken food and parrot food and snake food."

166. A

To admire means to regard with wonder, delight, or approval. To admire is to be full of admiration.

167. D

A narrative is a fictional story that is told in an entertaining way.

168. C

Judy is feeling confident and sure of herself because she believes that she will wake up in the morning knowing all the spelling words.

169. A

Judy decides that if the Sleeping Prophet learned all the words in his spelling book by sleeping on the book, she can maximize the number of new words that she is able to spell by sleeping on the biggest book she can find. She fails to realize that the Sleeping Prophet's experience was not only rare but most likely took place because he had been studying the book on which he fell asleep. If he had slept on a book he had not been studying, he would not have woken up to find that he knew how to spell the words he was studying. Thus, her assumption—that the bigger the book, the more words the speller will be able to spell—is faulty, even by the standards of the Sleeping Prophet.

170. D

When Judy is drifting off to sleep and eagerly awaiting the next day, the outcome she is most hoping for is to get 110%, or "zero-wrong-plus-extra-credit" on her spelling test. For her, this would be even better than being Queen of the Spelling Bee, making Mr. Todd happy, or getting 100%.

171. B

Judy and Frank are worried about a spelling test that will take place the next day. As the passage begins, Judy thinks she has found a book to help with spelling.

172. D

This story is about a child who goes under the ice to the seabed where she collects mussels on her own. Thus, another good title would be "Alone at the Bottom of the Sea".

173. B

Eva first saw small shrimps, then a pinky-purple crab, and then the anemones.

174. B

In the context of the passage, a ridge is a peak or a raised feature on the ice. Ditches, holes, and gaps do not rise up out of the landscape.

175. A

Fiction is imaginative writing that is not necessarily based on facts. Someone who has collected mussels from the bottom of the sea might have inspired this story, but the story itself is still made up.

176. D

The child insists that if one steps on the lines, bears will come. Those who ignore this and step on the lines are "sillies."

177. D

The writer has shortened the word "important" to "portant", in a way that a young child might say it.

178. A

The poem revolves around a little boy's desire to walk inside the squares, as the bears eat the "sillies" who walk on the lines on the sidewalk.

179. B

The passage is best described as a poem because of the way its lines look on the page and because the last word of each line rhymes. For example, the words "street" and "feet" rhyme and so do the words "squares" and "bears."

180. B

Billie talks about Alyssa "trying, as usual, to barge in where she's not wanted." Billie also mentions wanting to make Alyssa disappear from her life. This indicates that Billie probably finds Alyssa annoying.

181. C

The narrator appears to have very little patience or respect for Alyssa. She talks about Alyssa "making a fool of herself" and waiting to "barge in where she's not wanted." At the end of the passage, the narrator mentions wanting to make Alyssa disappear from her life.

182. C

Mr. Donaldson asks the children to give Jean-Pierre a "New Yorker welcome." This indicates that Jean-Pierre has probably never been to New York before. He is introduced as a new student. This means that he is probably there to stay rather than just visiting. He has an accent, presumably French, which means that he is unlikely to be someone who has just been away for a year. These clues suggest that Jean-Pierre has recently moved to New York to live from a French-speaking country, and that he has just arrived at Billie's school.

183. B

An excursion is a short trip or outing to a special place.

184. D

The author describes having a dog and about 30 gophers and 10 pigeons. He says he also has "some" rabbits, but he does not say exactly how many. He probably does not have anywhere near 30 rabbits, because they are mentioned as if they were not very important or significant. Moreover, 30 rabbits would require a lot of space and feeding.

185. C

The speaker in this story is Billy. He says the gophers "belonged to Bruce and me, and to another boy called Murray." The three boys own the gophers.

186. D

Billy and his friends got the rats from Murray's father, who was a professor at the college and got the rats from the medical school.

187. A

Billy's mother probably would not let him keep the snakes in the house because she was afraid of them.

188. A

The singing and whistling indicates that Matt and his robbers are happy that spring has arrived. This behavior suggests that the robbers are pleased to be out in the forest.

189. B

Ronia tosses the stone to make sure that Birk knows she is there. Although she could have called out, this is Ronia's playful way to let Birk know that she has arrived.

190. B

Ronia's screech is a sign of her delight at being outside in the forest enjoying the first signs of spring after being stuck indoors all winter.

191. A

Flung is the past tense of the word *fling*, which means to throw or to toss.

192. A

The sentence says that the stream is rushing, which is a clue about the meaning of the word "turbulent." The whole paragraph describes the spring arriving in a noisy and exciting way; this is another clue. A synonym of turbulent as it is used in this sentence is wild.

193. A

Christopher was further assured that his uncle was special because he "had seldom seen a man in tweeds or without whiskers."

194. D

Uncle Ralph was concerned that he would not be received in a good light. In this context, "to recommend" is used in the sense of creating a favorable impression.

195. A

As it is used in the quotation, the word "vexatious" means annoying or troublesome. Christopher's father had made a troublesome mess of the money, and Mama needed Uncle Ralph's help to sort out the mess.

196. A

A comparison using *like* or *as* is known as a simile. In this case, Uncle Ralph's smile is compared to sunlight shining on an autumn forest.

197. C

The word game cannot be spelled out of the letters in the word amazingly because there is no *e* in amazingly.

198. B

The narrator says that mum "watches nature shows on TV and writes letters to the editor complaining about inhumane traps."

199. B

The narrator would have liked to receive advance warning from his or her mother before being handed the snake.

200. D

The mother is calm and confident as she picks up the snake and removes it from the crowded street. She knows that the snake is harmless, and she is not afraid to pick it up.

201. D

In the poem, the narrator has been reminded by his or her mother to check the lost-and-found box at school, suggesting that the narrator is a young child.

202. B

Monsters are typically large. A "monster breath" means the narrator took a very large breath before reaching inside the box.

203. C

"Lost and Found" is a rhyming poem. A rhyming poem is a verse with a regular return of similar sounds. A limerick is a humorous verse that consists of five lines. A haiku is a Japanese verse form consisting of three lines of five, seven, and five syllables, respectively. A triangular poem is a short poem written in the form of a triangle.

204. B

An antonym is a word that means the opposite of another word. The word *dismay* is an antonym of "delight."

205. A

The "voice of an angel" is a metaphor for a beautiful singing voice.

206. B

The correct response is "playing the violin". According to the passage, "When Thomas took up the violin, he soon showed himself to be such a skillful performer, Alexander began writing pieces for him."

207. D

Silent is a synonym for the word "*uncommunicative.*"

208. A

In historical fiction the story is set among historical events. The instruments that the boys play and the subjects they study in school point to this story being historical fiction.

209. C

The first stanza infers that Gramma has passed away. Gramma is "gone but not forgotten." The speaker thinks of her whenever he sees her apron hanging in Grampa's kitchen.

210. C

The last stanza of the poem infers that Grampa probably leaves the apron hanging in the kitchen because it reminds him of Gramma and keeps her memory alive.

211. D

This poem has a simple, four-line rhyme scheme, *abcb*. The second and fourth lines of each stanza rhyme.

212. D

The words *look* and *stare* are synonyms.

ANSWERS AND SOLUTIONS — EXERCISE #1—LANGUAGE ARTS

213. C	227. B	241. A	255. C
214. D	228. C	242. B	256. D
215. D	229. C	243. B	257. D
216. B	230. D	244. A	258. A
217. D	231. A	245. C	259. C
218. B	232. A	246. D	260. D
219. A	233. D	247. B	261. D
220. B	234. C	248. A	262. C
221. A	235. C	249. C	263. C
222. C	236. D	250. A	264. D
223. C	237. C	251. C	265. B
224. D	238. C	252. D	
225. D	239. B	253. A	
226. A	240. A	254. D	

213. C

The German branch of the Indo-European language has had the greatest influence on the English language.

214. D

Carrot, potato, and onion are all examples of vegetables.

215. D

Carrot, celery, and onion are all types of vegetables.

216. B

Birch, oak, and redwood are all types of trees.

217. D

The prefix *pre-* means "before," so it changes the meaning of the word "washed."

218. B

The prefix *dis-* means "not." If you add the prefix *dis-* to the word *agree*, it changes the meaning of the word to "do not agree."

219. A

The prefix *in-* means "not." If you add the prefix *in-* to the word *visible*, it changes the meaning to "not visible."

220. B

The prefix *un-* means "not." If you add the prefix *un-* to the word *certain*, it changes the meaning of the word to "not certain" or "not sure."

221. A

If you add the suffix *-er* to a verb, it changes the meaning of the verb to refer to someone who does the verb. For example, if you add *-er* to *teach*, you get the word *teacher*—someone who teaches.

222. C

This is probably a folk tale from a different part of the world.

223. C

Stories from around the world that teach a moral or lesson are called folk tales.

224. D

The characters in a fable are often animals.

225. D

The pronoun *She* could replace "my sister."

226. A

The adverb that would best describe how the subject could see is *clearly*. The remaining choices do not appropriately describe how someone would see after receiving new glasses.

227. B

Using the correct pronouns, the sentence becomes "Drew went to the comic book store to to buy a comic for his sister Ella because he knew that she loves them." The pronoun *his* refers to "Drew's" (i), *he* refers to "Drew" (ii), and *she* refers to "Ella" (iii).

The following table correctly matches the underlined words with the pronouns that could replace them.

i	ii	iii
his	he	she

228. C

This sentence is referring to an action that will happen in the future. The alternative *will work* is the future tense of *work*.

229. C

The sentence is referring to something that will happen in the future. *Will discover* is the future tense of the word *discover*.

230. D

The sentence is referring to something that is happening in the present. The alternative *is taking* is the present tense of *take*.

231. A

The sentence is referring to something that happened in the past. The word *rode* is the past tense of *ride*.

232. A

The sentence is referring to something that happened in the past. The word *slept* is the past tense of *sleep*.

233. D

The words "excitedly" and "brightly" are adverbs describing, respectively, the verbs "looked" and "wrapped." "Old" is the only adjective in the sentence describing the table.

234. C

The word "huge" is an adjective that describes the word "bubble."

235. C

An adjective is a word that describes a noun. In this sentence, the word "colorful" is used as an adjective to describe the noun "ribbons."

236. D

An adjective is a word that describes a noun. In this sentence, the word "heavy" is used as an adjective.

237. C

The words *birthday* and *fast* are used as adjectives in this sentence. The word *birthday* describes the kind of present Andrew was opening, and the word *fast* describes the kind of truck Andrew finds inside. The words *truck* and *present* are used as nouns in this sentence. The words *open* and *wanted* are used as verbs in this sentence. The word *Andrew* is used as a proper noun and the word *he* is used as a pronoun in this sentence.

238. C

The only complete sentence is: "Gwen lost her shoes." A complete sentence must contain a subject (Gwen) and a verb (lost).

239. B

"You" is the subject of the sentence.

240. A

"Ball" is the subject of the sentence.

241. A

The word "princess" is the subject of the given sentence.

242. B

The correct response is: "Yes, I have even seen the red roads." The first word and the word "*I*" are capitalized in this sentence. This sentence is not in the form of a question; therefore, a period is used as the end punctuation. There is a comma after the word "*yes*" before leading into the rest of the sentence. There are no apostrophes in this sentence because there are no contractions or words showing possession. The verb must match the subject (first person singular: "I have").

243. B

The correct response is: "Tasha and her grandmother make oatmeal cookies." Only the first word in this sentence is capitalized. This sentence is not in the form of a question; therefore, a period is used as the end punctuation. There are no apostrophes in this sentence because there are no contractions or words showing possession. The verb must match the subject (third person plural: "they make").

244. A

Only two words require capitalization—the word beginning the sentence (My) and the proper noun (Trevor).

245. C

Proper nouns (specific people, places, and things) and special events must be capitalized. Therefore, this sentence is written correctly: My whole family is planning to take part in the Red Shirt Walk-A-Thon in Sycamore Valley Park this Sunday.

246. D

The sentence that uses correct capitalization is "We have made plans to go to Chicago this year to see the St. Patrick's Day Parade." Capitalize proper nouns (specific people, places, and things) and holidays.

247. B

Names of magazines should be capitalized. Therefore, the following sentence is correct: Chloe learned how to knit a scarf after she read *Owlkids*.

248. A

Names of newspapers need to be capitalized. Therefore, the following sentence is correct: Every morning when my parents wake up, they read the *Star City Journal* at the kitchen table.

249. C

This sentence asks a question so it should end in *a question mark*.

250. A

This sentence needs a period at the end. It is a declarative sentence.

251. C

A question mark (?) is used at the end of a sentence that asks a direct question.
The sentence "Why are there so many stars in the sky" needs to be completed with a question mark because it asks a direct question.

252. D

The word "float" is used in the sentence as a noun meaning an object that sits on the water to mark a location. In this case, it might be the location of an anchor.

253. A

The sentence "The slender branch snapped under his weight and he fell." uses *snap* in the same way as the first verb definition.

254. D

The sentence "When I heard the snap, I knew that the mouse had been caught in the trap." uses *snap* in the same way as the third noun definition.

255. C

In the statement "Stop interrupting—you made me lose my train of thought," the word "train" means an orderly sequence of ideas.

256. D

The dictionary uses guide words to help you find the word you are looking for. In alphabetical order, the word *bliss* would fall between *blink* and *blood*.

257. D

A figure of speech that uses the words *like* or *as* to compare two unlike things is known as a simile.

258. A

A simile is a figure of speech that uses the words *like* or *as* to compare two unlike things. The sentence "My friends think that my grandma is as sweet as honey" contains the simile "grandma is as sweet as honey."

259. C

A metaphor is a comparison of two or more things without using the words *like* or *as*. The sentence "My sister Chloe has always been a bright star in her class" contains the metaphor "bright star."

260. D

The phrase "Put a sock in it!" is used to tell a noisy person or group of people to be quiet.

261. D

An antonym is a word that means the opposite of another word. An antonym for the "cluttered" is organized.

262. C

The words that are similar in meaning (synonyms) are *weary* and *tired*.

263. C

The words *fix* and *mend* are similar in meaning (synonyms).

264. D

The opposite (or antonym) of *strength* is *weakness*.

265. B

These two words are similar in meaning; therefore, they are synonyms.

Writing

EXERCISE #1—WRITING

EXTENDED (LONGER) WRITING PIECE (55 MINUTES)

Look at the picture carefully. What do you think is about to happen? Write an exciting story about what happens.

The activity will take about 55 minutes to complete.

Overview

Time

2 minutes	Overview and directions for the student
3 minutes	Writing topic
2 minutes	Criteria
8 minutes	Planning
35 minutes	Written work
5 minutes	Look back on your writing

Directions to the Student

1. You do not need to use all of the pages provided.

2. Remember to write double-spaced (on every other line) so you have room to go back to your writing and make changes and corrections.

3. You may use a dictionary or thesaurus.

4. You will be marked on the "Written Work" pages only (not the planning).

Writing Topic

Your writing should be about **two** to **four** pages long.

Criteria (Story/Narrative)

Check your work for the following things:	
Did I write an exciting story about the picture?	☐
Is my story complete and easy to follow?	☐
Does my story include details to make it interesting to the reader?	☐
Did I choose words and ideas to make my reader feel something (happy, sad, surprised, excited) and are the words appropriate?	☐
Does my story have a beginning, middle, and end?	☐
Does my story have interesting characters (e.g., dialogue, description)?	☐
Have I made corrections in spelling, punctuation, and use of words?	☐

Planning

My purpose

To write an interesting story about the picture.

My audience

The teachers who will mark my writing.

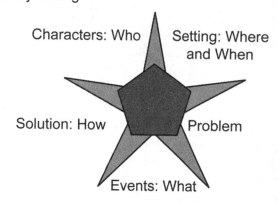

Written Work

Take 35 minutes to write your story. Use the criteria and your planning page as a guide when you write. Be careful to include words and actions that are appropriate for all readers.

Look Back on Your Writing

Take 5 minutes to look back on your writing.

Carefully go through your writing and make any changes or corrections. Use the criteria at the top of this page to guide you.

SAMPLE RESPONSES—EXERCISE #1

EXAMPLE OF WRITING RESPONSE PROFICIENT

One day me and my brothers went camping. When my mom and dad had gone for a walk we stayed by the camp fire, we did'nt see the alians coming out of there space ship to us. Then we saw them and I said WOW look at those creters and Tyler said they are alians from out of space. They walked across the river and came to us and said we want to be your friend because we have just landed on earth and we are hungary. Tyler went into the tent and came out with some hot dogs and we poked them with sticks and put them in the fire and cooked them and then we gave them to the alians to eat. They really liked them! And they eat 4 each. Then the alians told us about there plannet and it was awsome because everything on it is green. It is called the green plannet. Then the alians said they had to go and thanked us and walked back to there space ship and it just vanished. When mom and dad came back we told them about the alians and they said how exiting and we all went to bed.

RATIONALE FOR RESPONSE SATISFACTORY

Content

The majority of the events, actions, and ideas are appropriate for the context established by the writer (three children are camping when they see aliens approach them from their spaceship).

Details are general, but are appropriate for the story (e.g., "They walked across the river and came to us," "we have just landed on earth and we are hungry," and "alians told us about their planet").

The writing generally holds the reader's interest and provides some support for a main idea, as it tells about the children meeting and communicating with the aliens.

Organization

The beginning directly presents information about events (e.g., "One day me and my brothers went camping"), characters (e.g., "me and my brothers"), and setting (e.g., "we stayed by the camp fire").

Connections and/or relationships between events, actions, details, and/or characters are generally maintained (e.g., "said we want to be your friend because we have just landed on earth" and "the alians said they had to go and thanked us").

The ending ("When mom and dad came back we told them about the alians and they said how exiting and we all went to bed") is predictable and contrived but is connected to events and actions.

Sentence Structure

Sentence structure is generally controlled, but run-on sentences are present (e.g., "we stayed by the camp fire, we di'dnt see the alians coming" and "they said how exiting and we all went to bed").

Sentences may vary in type and length (e.g., "Then the alians told us about there planet and it was awsome because everything on it is green" and "It is called the green planet").

Some variety of sentence beginnings (e.g., "One day…," "When my mom…," and "Tyler went…") is evident.

Vocabulary

Words chosen (e.g., "mom and dad had gone for a walk" and "Then we saw them") tend to be common or ordinary.

Expressions (e.g., "they are alians from out of space" and "we poked them with sticks and put them in the fire and cooked them") are usually more general than specific.

Words and expressions (e.g., "WOW" and "it was awsome") generally enhance the writing.

Conventions

Conventional end punctuation and capitalization are usually correct.

Many familiar words (e.g., "camping," "friend," and "vanished") are spelled correctly; errors (e.g., "did'nt," "creters," "hungary," and "there") suggest uneven control of spelling rules; unfamiliar words (e.g., "alians" and "plannet") are generally spelled phonetically.

Errors (e.g., "how exiting") are sometimes intrusive and may affect the clarity of communication.

EXAMPLE OF WRITING RESPONSE PROFICIENT

The Aliens

I felt very excited because we were going camping for the first time this summer. We all got ready and packed the tents and things and then we drove to our very favorite place. It was in the woods and a rushing river was near by and we could catch fish and swim in the river. After setting up the tent and putting our sleeping bags inside and having a apple mom and dad lighted the fire and then went to find more wood so we could cook hot dogs and roast marshmellows for supper. Tracy and me were just sitting there by the fire when we saw a bright shiny light across the river. The light turned into a space ship and it landed and out of it came three little green aliens with big round heads and antenas sticking out of the top of their heads. "Look at that!" I yelled at Tracy. "WOW!!" she said. "What do they want? I wondered. They walked across the river and did'nt seem to notice that it was very cold and they came towards us. We were very frightend but they were nice and one of them beamed us a message that said we just landed on this planet and we are lost and hungry. Do you know where we are? I said "You are on earth and we can give you some apples and hot dogs if you like." They said "Yes please and if we are on earth we know how to get back to our planet by flying though the milky way." After they had eaten their food they thanked us and went back to their space ship and we watched them take off with a WOOSH and then they dissappeared into the darkness.

RATIONALE FOR RESPONSE PROFICIENT

Content

Events, actions, and ideas are appropriate for the context established by the writer (children are camping when they see a space ship and aliens land on the other side of the river).

Details (e.g., "we could catch fish and swim in the river," "we saw a bright shiny light," and "The light turned into a space ship") are specific and generally effective.

The writing engages the reader's interest and presents a supported main idea (e.g., "We just landed on this planet").

Organization

The beginning ("I felt very excited because we were going camping for the first time this summer. We all got ready and packed the tents and things and then we drove to our very favorite place. It was in the woods and a rushing river was near by and we could catch fish and swim in the river.") clearly establishes events, characters, and setting, and provides direction for the writing.

Connections and/or relationships between events, actions, details, and characters are maintained (e.g., "mom and dad lighted the fire and then went to find more wood," "out of it came three little green aliens," and "We were very frightend").

The ending ("After they had eaten their food they thanked us and went back to their space ship and we watched them take off with a WOOSH and then they dissappeared into the darkness") provides an appropriate finish for event and actions.

Sentence Structure

Sentence structure is controlled (e.g., "Tracy and me were just sitting there by the fire when we saw a bright shiny light across the river").

Sentence type and sentence length (e.g., "What do they want?" and "We were very frightend but they were nice and one of them beamed us a message that said we just landed on this planet and we are lost and hungry") are usually varied and effective.

Sentence beginnings (e.g., "After setting up…," "The light turned…," and "Do you know") are often varied.

Vocabulary

Well-chosen words (e.g., "rushing river" and "a bright shiny light") are often used.

Expressions (e.g., "three little green aliens with big round heads and antenas sticking out of the top of their heads" and "beamed us a message") are usually specific and effective.

Words and expressions (e.g., "WOW!!," "get back to our planet by flying though the milky way," and "WOOSH") are descriptive and often enhance the writing.

Conventions

End punctuation and capitalization are essentially correct.

Familiar words are spelled correctly; spelling errors (e.g., "frightend" and "dissappeared") are "slips"; unfamiliar words (e.g., "marshmellows" and "antenas") may be spelled phonetically.

Errors that are present (e.g., "Tracy and me," "did'nt seem," and "the milky way") rarely affect the clarity of communication.

EXAMPLE OF WRITING RESPONSE EXCELLENT

What a Camping Trip!

"Now remember to stay close to the camp sight and don't let the fire go out" said Dad when he and Mom set off for their usual night time walk. My brothers and me were used to this, every night after supper Mom and Dad went for a walk and left us to look after our things. Tonight was different. There was a bright full moon in the sky and the stars were extra bright and sparkling. Suddenly what looked like a falling star came crashing down to earth just across the river. "Wow! Awesome!" we cried out in amazement. We realized it was not a falling star because it was shaped like a space ship and climbing slowly down a ladder came three crimson red aliens. They had large heads with one big bulgeing eye, two legs that were so long they looked like spiders and two arms that had eight fingers on each hand. They skipped towards the bubbling river and noisily splashed across the cold water. When they reached our camp sight they beamed a message to us through their big eye and said "We are friendly aliens and we wonder if you would like to come for a ride in our space ship." "YES! YES!" we shouted together. "This is so exciting and amazing." "But...but...but what about Mom and Dad?" asked my little brother. "Don't worry." said one of the aliens. "We will have you back before your parents return."

We rushed as fast as a speeding bullet to get our shoes and jackets and then we went with the aliens across the river to their space ship. I had to help Bobby up the ladder because he couldn't reach the steps but we made it and once the door was shut we blasted off. We felt like we were on a speed boat but suddenly everything became smooth and we glided over the earth. We looked out the window and saw the rocky mountains and lakes and then we were over the ocean and could see dolphins and hump back whales swimming in the sea. We climbed higher and higher until the earth was a big round blue globe below us. It was truly miraculous and just like the pictures that I had seen in books. All too quickly we were back on earth beside the gurgling river and across from our camp sight. We thanked the aliens for an awesome adventure and said we would never forget them and we would tell everyone that aliens are really friendly and nice. They said "See you next year and we will take you for another ride into space!" We got back to the camp before Mom and Dad and decided to keep our visit with the aliens a secret.

Content

Events, actions, and ideas are consistently appropriate for the context established by the writer (three children see a space ship with aliens descend to Earth, and they travel with the aliens for a visit to outer space)

Details (e.g., "came crashing down to earth just across the river" and "they beamed a message to us through their big eye") are specific and consistently effective, and the reader experiences the excitement felt by the writer of the arrival of the aliens.

The writing captivates the reader's interest and presents a well-supported main idea ("We are friendly aliens and we wonder if you would like to come for a ride in our space ship").

Organization

The beginning captures the reader's attention ("'Now remember to stay close to the camp sight and don't let the fire go out' said Dad when he and Mom set off for their usual night time walk. My brothers and me were used to this, every night after supper Mom and Dad went for a walk and left us to look after our things.") clearly establishes events, characters, and setting, and provides direction for the writing.

Connections and/or relationships between events, actions, details, and characters are consistently maintained (e.g., "it was shaped like a space ship and climbing slowly down a ladder came three crimson red aliens," "we were over the ocean and could see dolphins and hump back whales swimming," and "We climbed higher and higher until the earth was a big round blue globe below us").

The ending ("We thanked the aliens for an awesome adventure and said we would never forget them and we would tell everyone that aliens are really friendly and nice. They said "See you next year and we will take you for another ride into space!" We got back to the camp before Mom and Dad and decided to keep our visit with the aliens a secret.") ties events and actions together.

Sentence Structure

Sentence structure is consistently controlled (e.g., "'But...but...but what about Mom and Dad?'").

Sentence type and sentence length (e.g., "Tonight was different" and "I had to help Bobby up the ladder because he couldn't reach the steps but we made it and once the door was shut we blasted off") are varied and effective.

Sentence beginnings (e.g., "Now remember...," "Suddenly what looked...," "We rushed...," and "All too quickly...") are consistently varied.

Vocabulary

Well-chosen words (e.g., "bright full moon in the sky and the stars were extra bright and sparkling" and "skipped towards the bubbling river and noisily splashed across") are used effectively.

Expressions (e.g., "came crashing down," "Wow! Awesome!," "YES! YES!," and "was truly miraculous") are consistently precise and effective.

Words and expressions (e.g., "three crimson red aliens," "large heads with one big bulgeing eye, two legs that were so long they looked like spiders and two arms that had eight fingers on each hand," "as fast as a speeding bullet," and "the gurgling river") are used to create vivid images and enhance the writing.

Conventions

End punctuation and capitalization are correct.

Most words, familiar and unfamiliar, are spelled correctly; spelling errors (e.g., "camp sight" and "bulgeing") are understandable "slips."

Errors that are present (e.g., "My brothers and me" and "rocky mountains") do not affect the clarity or effectiveness of communication.

EXERCISE #2—WRITING

Extended (Longer) Writing Piece (55 minutes)

In this activity, you will write a story after looking carefully at the picture. Imagine you see a fairground on an island. You cannot imagine how to reach the fairground. Write an interesting story about what happens.

Overview

Time

2 minutes	Overview and directions for the student
3 minutes	Writing topic
2 minutes	Criteria
8 minutes	Planning
35 minutes	Written work
5 minutes	Look back on your writing

Directions to the Student

5. You do not need to use all of the pages provided.

6. Remember to write double-spaced (on every other line) so you have room to go back to your writing and make changes and corrections.

7. You may use a dictionary or thesaurus.

8. You will be marked on the "Written Work" pages only (not the planning).

Writing Topic

Your writing should be about **two** to **four** pages long.

Criteria (Story/Narrative)

Check your work for the following things:

Did I write an exciting story about the picture? □

Is my story complete and easy to follow? □

Does my story include details to make it interesting to the reader? □

Did I choose words and ideas to make my reader feel something (happy, sad, surprised, excited) and are the words appropriate? □

Does my story have a beginning, middle, and end? □

Does my story have interesting characters (e.g., dialogue, description)? □

Have I made corrections in spelling, punctuation, and use of words? □

Planning

My purpose

To write an interesting story about the picture.

My audience

The teachers who will mark my writing.

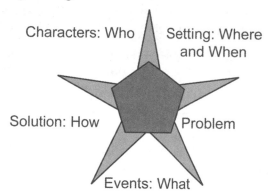

Written Work

Take 35 minutes to write your story. Use the criteria and your planning page as a guide when you write. Be careful to include words and actions that are appropriate for all readers.

Look Back on Your Writing

Take 5 minutes to look back on your writing.

Carefully go through your writing and make any changes or corrections. Use the criteria at the top of this page to guide you.

SAMPLE RESPONSES—EXERCISE #2

SAMPLE OF WRITING RESPONSE: SATISFACTORY

The Islands fair

"Aaaaahhhh" I heard in a scream as the faris wheal suddenly came to a pause. All the fair workers were running to get the kids of the faris wheal. When all the kids had returned to the ground all the fair workers called a meeting to find out what coused the faris wheal to stop. At the end of the meeting they finally suspected that the faris wheal was sabatoshed by one of the fair workers that was on deyty yesterday at the faris wheal. So it is eather Bob or Jarramy that was at the faris wheal yesterday but what could they have done to make it break down like that and just pause and not start again there has to be an explanaition for it, it cannot just have broken down on it's own and just without anyone taking a part of a machine from it causing it to break down and go into a pause. I'm going to go find the Janator and see if he can fix the faris wheel said one of the workers. When he found the Janator the Janator took a look at it and sadly said "I'm sorry but there is no way I can fix it there is too many damages so more than one thing happen to it, it is also very old and has been used a lot, so it's probably worn out, I think its time for a new faris wheel."

About a year later they got the money to buy a turbo speed one and it never broke down and all the kids loved it.

RATIONALE FOR RESPONSE SATISFACTORY

Content

The majority of the events, actions, and ideas are appropriate for the context established by the writer (a fairground has a Ferris wheel for children to ride).

Details are general, but are appropriate for the story (e.g., "find out what coused the faris wheal to stop" and "so it's probably worn out").

The writing generally holds the reader's interest and provides some support for a main idea (it refers to the Ferris wheel that has broken down, but the idea of sabotage is not followed through).

Organization

The beginning directly presents information about events, characters, and setting (e.g., "'Aaaaahhhh' I heard in a scream as the faris wheal suddenly came to a pause. All the fair workers were running to get the kids of the faris wheal").

Connections and/or relationships between events, actions, details, and/or characters are generally maintained (e.g., "fair workers called a meeting to find out what coused the faris wheal to stop" and "there is no way I can fix it there is too many damages").

The ending ("About a year later they got the money to buy a turbo speed one and it never broke down and all the kids loved it") is predictable and contrived but is connected to events and actions.

Sentence Structure

Sentence structure is generally controlled but sentence run-ons are present (e.g., "So it is eather Bob or Jarramy that was at the faris wheal yesterday but what could they have done to make it break down like that and just pause and not start again there has to be an explanaition for it, it cannot just have broken down on it's own and just without anyone taking a part of a machine from it causing it to break down and go into a pause").

Sentences may vary in type and length (e.g., "I heard in a scream as the faris wheal suddenly came to a pause" and "I'm going to go find the Janator and see if he can fix the faris wheel said one of the workers").

Some variety of sentence beginnings (e.g., "All the fair…," "At the end…," and "I'm going…") is evident.

Vocabulary

Words chosen (e.g., "were running" and "no way I can fix it") tend to be common or ordinary.

Expressions (e.g., "what could they have done to make it break down" and "the Janator took a look at it and sadly said") are usually more general than specific.

Words and expressions (e.g., "'Aaaaahhhh'," "sabatoshed," and "has to be an explanaition") generally enhance the writing.

Conventions

Conventional end punctuation and capitalization are usually correct.

Many familiar words (e.g., "suddenly," "finally suspected," "machine," and "damages") are spelled correctly; errors (e.g., "faris wheal," "coused," "deity," "eather," and "explanaition") suggest uneven control of spelling rules; unfamiliar words (e.g., "sabatoshed" and "Janator") are generally spelled phonetically.

Errors (e.g., "anyone taking a part of a machine from it causing it to break down and go into a pause," "there is too many damages so more than one thing happen to it," and "I think its time") are sometimes intrusive and may affect the clarity of communication.

SAMPLE WRITING RESPONSE: PROFICIENT

The Island

"Mom are we there yet?" Britt asked.

"10 minutes until we are at the beach honey" Mom said. We were going to mexico beach and it was 10 hours drive from our house. My mom finally stopped the car and said "We are here!" We unpacked all our things and put them into the hotel room. Everything was real close which was good so we headed off to the beach. I wasn't really a good swimmer so I could only go as deep as my belly button. I had a little swim splashing around in the shallow water and when I dried off I noticed another island. It had a ferris wheel, carousel, a big top tent and one big roller coaster. There were some kids on the island and they were going down a very big water slide. It looked so much fun and I wanted to go on the island but I knew my mom wouldn't let me because I couldn't swim. After some time Mom went back to the hotel so I quickly went into the water up to my neck. Then I just started sinking. I was down at the bottom of the ocean when BOOM a big dark thing went over me and a boy picked me up. I shut my eyes tight and the boy bought me to a chair and sure enough I was on that island. My eyes shot open. This island was paradise. 2000 hours on this island is like 5 seconds in my world so no way would my mom get all worried. I met other kids and made three friends, Taka, Lana and Louis who rescued me. We had so much fun going on the rides and my favourite was the water slide because it was the longest and fastest I have ever seen and we got soaking wet every time we went on it.

After some time I began to get homesick. It hadn't even been 1 second in my world but I just wanted to go home because I had had my fun. I wanted Louis Lana and Taka to come and see my world. Their parents said it was ok with them. Louis taught me how to swim. Lana taught me different things you can do in the water like handstands and playing tag and Taka showed me how to do all kinds of dives. I showed them the outer world and things like cars and airplanes and Mcdonalds and the hotel we were staying in and they thought it was so amazing. I told them I'm so happy to have you for my friends because I never had true friends before. My life was complete and my mom didn't even know I went in the waters and about my new friends. My water friends went back to there home (island). Me and my mom went to the beach more often.

RATIONALE FOR RESPONSE PROFICIENT

Content

Events, actions, and ideas are appropriate for the context established by the writer (a young girl discovers a fantasy island where she meets friends and has many experiences).

Details (e.g., "2000 hours on this island is like 5 seconds in my world" and "we got soaking wet every time we went on it") are specific and generally effective, and the reader is caught up in the island's fantasy world where time stands still.

The writing engages the reader's interest and presents a supported main idea (stating that "This island was paradise" because time as we know it does not exist).

Organization

The beginning ("'Mom are we there yet?' Britt asked. '10 minutes until we are at the beach honey' Mom said. We were going to mexico beach and it was 10 hours drive from our house. My mom finally stopped the car and said 'We are here!' We unpacked all our things and put them into the hotel room. Everything was real close which was good so we headed off to the beach. I wasn't really a good swimmer so I could only go as deep as my belly button. I had a little swim splashing around in the shallow water and when I dried off I noticed another island") clearly establishes events, characters, and setting, and provides direction for the writing.

Connections and/or relationships between events, actions, details, and characters are maintained (e.g., "It had a ferris wheel, carousel, a big top tent and one big roller coaster," "We had so much fun going on the rides," and "It hadn't even been 1 second in my world but I just wanted to go home because I had had my fun").

The ending ("My life was complete and my mom didn't even know I went in the waters and about my new friends. My water friends went back to there home (island). Me and my mom went to the beach more often") provides an appropriate finish for events and actions.

Sentence Structure

Sentence structure is controlled (e.g., "My mom finally stopped the car and said 'We are here!'").

Sentence type and sentence length (e.g., "'Mom are we there yet?'" and "I had a little swim splashing around in the shallow water and when I dried off I noticed another island") are usually varied and effective.

Sentence beginnings (e.g., "My mom finally…," "After some time…," "This island was…," and "Louis taught me…") are often varied.

Vocabulary

Well-chosen words (e.g., "paradise," "we got soaking wet," and "I began to get homesick") are often used.

Expressions (e.g., "as deep as my belly button," "down at the bottom of the ocean," "BOOM a big dark thing," and "My life was complete") are usually specific and effective.

Words and expressions (e.g., "splashing around in the shallow water," "My eyes shot open," and "no way would my mom get all worried") are descriptive and often enhance the writing.

Conventions

End punctuation and capitalization are essentially correct.

Familiar words are spelled correctly; spelling errors (e.g., "the boy bought me" and "to there home") are "slips."

Errors that are present (e.g., "mexico," "real close," and "Me and my mom") rarely affect the clarity of communication.

The length and complexity of the response has been considered.

SAMPLE WRITING RESPONSE: EXCELLENT

Thrillville

John and Linda were at the beach with their parents for their summer vacation when their mom and dad were called home because their grandma was sick. Linda was 17 so she said she could look after John. After their parents said goodbye and be good John and Linda headed for the beach. It was a beautiful hot sunny day and they played in the water and lay in the sun. John was watching some sail boats flying across the lake as the wind caught their sails when suddenly he noticed a small island in the middle of the lake that he hadn't seen before. "Hey look Linda" he yelled. "What is it?" asked Linda. "There is an island on the lake and there is a fair on the island. Can we go?" John said. "Sure" said Linda it sounds like fun. "But how will we get there?" "Let's rent a canoe and we can paddle there." said Linda. It did'nt take them long to find the canoes for rent and to head for the island. They both were good paddlers because they always went canoeing with their mom and dad. When they arrived at the island they paid $5 to go into the fair and John ran straight towards the ferris wheel. "Wait up John!" called Linda. They both got in line and when they got on the ferris wheel started up and hummed quietly as it went around and around. When they reached the top they had amazing views of the whole area. They could see the hotel and on the other side of the lake there was a gigantic forest and green hills and lots of smaller lakes and they could see the road they drove on to get to the beach. After the ferris wheel they decided to go to the big tent where the circus was because they wanted to see what animals they had. The circus was SUPER because of the acrobats who climbed to the top of the tent and swung on bars and leaped from one swing to another catching each other in mid air. The trapeeze acts looked dangerous and risky but no one fell and the clowns were hillarius. After that Linda demanded that they go on the biggest roller coaster ever built. Once they were locked in the roller coaster started the slow steep climb to the very top. John hated the roller coaster because he thought that they would break but Linda loved them. At the top John closed his eyes and held on tight to Linda's hand. He could feel them going through the loop-d-loop when suddenly …he opened his eyes and they were back on the straight track. All of a sudden it stopped. Everyone started yelling and screaming and then the guy who runs the ride said "The generator has shut down. It should be back in a few minutes. Stay in your seats please. "I knew it would break!" said John. Finally the generator started up again and they returned to earth. Now it was nearly dark so Linda and John got their canoe and went back to the hotel and had supper. The next morning they went to the beach and they couldn't believe their eyes because the island and the fair had dissapeared. They wondered if it had been a dream.

RATIONALE FOR RESPONSE EXCELLENT

Content

Events, actions, and ideas are consistently appropriate for the context established by the writer (a boy and a girl see a fair on an island in the middle of the lake and paddle across in order to go to the fair).

Details (e.g., "they payed $5 to go into the fair and John ran straight towards the ferris wheel" and "swung on bars and leaped from one swing to another catching each other in mid air") are specific and consistently effective, and the reader is caught up in fair activities that the children find on the island.

The writing captivates the reader's interest and presents a well-supported main idea (stating that "'There is an island on the lake and there is a fair on the island. Can we go?'" John said. 'Sure' said Linda it sounds like fun").

Organization

The beginning captures the reader's attention, clearly establishes events, characters, and setting ("John and Linda were at the beach with their parents for their summer vacation when their mom and dad were called home because their grandma was sick. Linda was 17 so she said she could look after John") and provides direction for the writing (e.g., "There is an island on the lake and there is a fair on the island").

Connections and/or relationships between events, actions, details, and characters are consistently maintained (e.g., "They both were good paddlers because they always went canoeing with their mom and dad," "When they reached the top they had amazing views of the whole area," and "At the top John closed his eyes and held on tight to Linda's hand").

The ending ("Now it was nearly dark so Linda and John got their canoe and went back to the hotel and had supper. The next morning they went to the beach and they couldn't believe their eyes because the island and the fair had dissapeared. They wondered if it had been a dream") ties events and actions together.

Sentence Structure

Sentence structure is consistently controlled (e.g., "It was a beautiful hot sunny day and they played in the water and lay in the sun").

Sentence type and sentence length (e.g., "But how will we get there?" and "They could see the hotel and on the other side of the lake there was a gigantic forest and green hills and lots of smaller lakes and they could see the road they drove on to get to the beach") are varied and effective.

Sentence beginnings (e.g., "John and Linda were...," "When they reached...," "Finally the generator...," and "Now it was...") are consistently varied.

Vocabulary

Well-chosen words (e.g., "circus was SUPER," "looked dangerous and risky," and "clowns were hillarius") are used effectively.

Expressions (e.g., "sail boats flying across the lake as the wind caught their sails," "ferris wheel started up and hummed quietly," "amazing views," and "catching each other in mid air") are consistently precise and effective.

Words and expressions (e.g., "a gigantic forest and green hills and lots of smaller lakes" and "going through the loop-d-loop") are used to create vivid images and enhance the writing.

Conventions

End punctuation and capitalization are correct.

Most words, familiar and unfamiliar, are spelled correctly; spelling errors (e.g., "did'nt" and "dissapeared") are understandable "slips." The words "trapeeze" and "hillarius" are spelled phonetically.

Errors that are present (e.g., "'Sure' said Linda it sounds like fun" and "John hated the roller coaster because he thought that they would break") do not affect the clarity or effectiveness of communication.

GRADE 4 PASSAGE CREDITS

Robot Storybook—Public Domain

The Fox—Public Domain

Pygmalion, Act I—by George Bernard Shaw, Public Domain

Chocolate Chip Cookie—by Larry Verstraete, found in *Whose Bright Idea Was It? True Stories of Invention*, published by Scholastic Canada, 1997

The Voyage of the Mayflower—by Patricia Whalen, found in *SRA Open Court Reading Level 4*, published by SRA (McGraw-Hill), 2004

How Brazilian Beetles Got Their Gorgeous Coats: A Story From Brazil—by Martha Hamilton and Mitch Weiss, found in *How & Why Stories: World Tales Kids Can Read and Tell*, August House Inc., 1999

The Dinner Party—by Mona Gardner, found in *The Saturday Review of Literature*, published by Holt, Rinehart, and Winston of Canada Ltd., 1941

Cheetahs—National Geographic for Kids website

The Fishing Summer—by Teddy Jam, Groundwood Books, 1997

Weather Lore—by Terence Dickinson, found in *Sky by Day*, Firefly Books Ltd., 1988

Lines and Squares—by A.A. Milne, found in *When We Were Very Young*, Dutton Children's Books, 1952

A Seal in the Family—by Maria Coffey, Annick Press Ltd., 1999

The Crow and the Jug—by Michael Morpurgo, found in *McElderry Book of Aesop's Fables*, published by Margaret K. McElderry, rights Simon & Schuster Children's Publishing Division, 2005

Soft-Stone Sculpture—by Sandi Henry, found in *Kids' Art Works! Creativity with Color, Design, Texture & More*, Williamson Publishing Co., 1999

Snakes Eat Frogs—by Skid Crease, found in In the Great Meadow, Annick Press Ltd., 1994

Joe's Junk—by Susan Russo, Henry Holt and Co., 1986

The Watcher—by Brenda Silsbe, Annick Press Ltd., 1995

Last One Into Bed—by Michael Rosen, found in *Poetry Plus*, Copp Clark Pitman Ltd, 1988

A Horse that wore Snow Shoes—Public Domain, apples4the teacher.com

Elephant and Hare—by Jan Thornhill,found in *Crow and Fox and Other Animal Legends*, Greey de Pencier Books, 1993

Gramma's Apron—by C.J.Heck, found on *Barking Spiders and Other Such Stuff*, SterlingHouse Publisher Inc., 2006

From Paper Bag To Paperback: How Children's Books Are Made—by Robert Munsch, found in *The Paper Bag Princess 25th Anniversary Edition: the Story behind the Story*, Annick Press Ltd., 2005

The St. Lawrence Beluga—by Evelyne Daigle, found in *As Long As There Are Whales*, Tundra Books, 2004

Judy Moody Predicts the Future—by Megan McDonald, Candlewick Press, 2005

Hoot—by Carl Hiaason, Random House Inc., 2002

Owls in the Family—by Farley Mowat, The Canadian Publishers, 1961

My Friend Jacob—by Lucille Clifton, Dutton Juvenile, 1980

Very Last First Time—by Jan Andrews, found in *The Meadow Mouse Treasury*, Groundwood Books/Douglas & McIntyre, 1995

Open Wide!—by Sondi Bruner, Appeal Magazine, 2006

A Snake Named Rover—by Maxine Jeffris, Meadowbrook press, 1991

Nim's Island—by Wendy Orr, Scholastic Inc., 1999

How are stamps printed?—found in *Bugs and Butterflies*—http://www.auspost.com.au/philatelic/stamps/bugs/collect/printed.htm, published by Australia Post, 2003

Cat Talk—by D.S. Long, found in the School Journal, Part 3 Number 1, 1990

A Secret Lost in the Water—by Roch Carrier, found in *The Hockey Sweater and other Stories*, House of Anansi, 2012

Lost and Found—by Eileen Delehanty Pearkes, found in *Facts and Arguments: Selected Essays from The Globe And Mail*, Penguin Group, 2012

Understanding Your Rabbit—by Mark Evans, found in *Rabbit: A Practical Guide to Caring for your Rabbit*, Stoddart Publishing Co. Ltd., 1992

Monsters from the Deep and Other Imaginary Beings—by Sarah Ellis, found in *The Young Writer's Companion*, Groundwood Books, 1999

If Dolphins Are Mammals, Why Do They Live in the Water?—by Marty Crisp, found in *Everything Dolphin: What Kids Really Want to Know About Dolphins*, Northward Book for young readers, 2004

The Night Troll and Her Boat at Mývatn—from *A Traveller's Guide to Icelandic Folk Tales*, © Jón R Hjálomarsson, 2000, English translation © Anna Yates, 2002

Daniel's Duck—by Clyde Robert Bulla, Perfection Learning Corporation, 1982

The Clever Turtle—by A.K. Roche, found in *The A.K. Roche Collection*, Prentice Hall, 1969

The Snake on Second Avenue—by Adele Dueck, found in *Swinging below a Star*, Nelson Canada, 1991

The New Boy—by Marthe Jo, found in *The Invisible Enemy*, Dutton Children's Books, 2002

An Invite from Uncle—by Aaron Taouma, found in *Home: New Short Stories from New Zealand Writers*, Random House

Ancient Broom Games—by J.K Rowling, found in *Quidditch Through the Ages*, Raincoast Books, 2001

Ronia, the Robber's Daughter— by Astrid Lindgren, published by Penguin Group, 1981.

Are All Giants All Bad?—by David Colbert, found in *The Magical Worlds of Harry Potter*, Lumina Press, 2001

Crabs for Dinner—by Adwoa Badoe, Sister Vision Press, 1995

A Secret for Two—by Quentin Reynolds, found in Experiences, Wiley Publishers, 1975

The Court of King Arthur—by Martyn Beardsley, found in *Sir Gadabout*, Dolphin paperbacks, 1992

The Outlaw Who Wouldn't Give Up—by Brenda Z Guiberson, found in *Mummy Mysteries: Tales from North America*, Henry Holt and Company, 1998

Islands in the Mind—by Sarah Ellis, found in *The Young Writer's Companion*, Groundwood Books/Douglas & McIntyre, 1999

The Legend of the Panda—by Linda Granfield, Tundra Books, 1998

The Lives of Christopher Chant—by Diana Wynne Jones, Harpercollins, 1988

Matilda: Who Told Lies, and was Burned to Death—by Hilaire Belloc, found in *Poems for Boys and Girls Book 3*, The Copp Clark Publishing Co. Limited, 1956

Coram Boy—by Jamila Gavin, Nick Hern Books, 2000

NOTES

NOTES

NOTES

SOLARO Study Guides
Ordering Information

Every SOLARO Study Guide unpacks the curriculum standards and provides an overview of all curriculum concepts, practice questions with full solutions, and assignment questions for students to fully test their knowledge.

Visit www.solaro.com/orders to buy books and learn how SOLARO can offer you an even more complete studying solution.

SOLARO
Study Guides

SOLARO Study Guide—$29.95 each plus applicable sales tax

SOLARO Common Core State Standard Titles	
Mathematics 3	Algebra I
Mathematics 4	Algebra II
Mathematics 5	Geometry
Mathematics 6	English Language Arts 3
Mathematics 7	English Language Arts 4
Accelerated Mathematics 7 (Int.)	English Language Arts 5
Accelerated Mathematics 7 (Trad.)	English Language Arts 6
Mathematics 8	English Language Arts 7
Accelerated Mathematics I	English Language Arts 8
Mathematics I	English Language Arts 9
Mathematics II	English Language Arts 10
Mathematics III	English Language Arts 11
Accelerated Algebra I	English Language Arts 12

To order books, please visit
www.solaro.com/orders

Volume pricing is available. Contact us at
orderbooks@solaro.com